PRECIOUS APOTHECARY

PUBLISHED BY AVALONIA

BM AVALONIA
LONDON
WC1N 3XX
ENGLAND, UK
WWW.AVALONIABOOKS.COM

PRECIOUS APOTHECARY: A CATHOLIC GRIMOIRE

ISBN: 978-1-910191-19-4
FIRST PAPERBACK EDITION, DECEMBER 2020
DESIGN BY SATORI

BRITISH LIBRARY CATALOGUING IN PUBLICATION DATA. A CATALOGUE RECORD FOR THIS BOOK IS AVAILABLE FROM THE BRITISH LIBRARY.

Precious Apothecary
A Catholic Grimoire

Compiled from the writings of Ângelo Sequeira,

for

the acquisition and sustenance of Grace, the Blessing of the Virgin, the Succour of her Divine Son our Lord, and the patronage of one hundred and twenty Saints

Teaches the blessings of Holy Water, Oils, Flowers, Vestments and many other such saintly things

José Leitão

Published by Avalonia
www.avaloniabooks.com

Senhor dos perdoẽs das Recolhidas da Lapa
de Lisboa. G. Boulenx. f. 1755.

Penitente Arrependido

Table of Contents

Frei Gaspar da Encarnação [between 1752 and 1800?],
Biblioteca Nacional de Portugal, Cota: inv. 13474, Colecção de Pintura da BNP.

Introduction

In this work, which I put to print, I expose to all the faithful a collection of spiritual goods, an apothecary filled with remedies, which all may achieve with no more cost or expense than that of devotion.

- Ângelo Sequeira, 'Prologue', in *Botica Preciosa.*

ON THE MULTIPLICITY OF UNITY

The claim of universality by the Catholic Church at times obfuscates the specificities of its particular expressions. While such has been long admitted and known regarding folk aspects of religious practice, such observations often seem to border on implicit paternalism and a certain intellectual disregard of such peoples and their practices as 'inferior' or 'ignorant' in light of true and pure religious observance (this being the actual meaning of the word 'syncretism'). However, this same variability of Catholic practice needs to be equally realized of the upper echelons of the Catholic intellectual establishment.

The Council of Vatican II has, in part, contributed to this general ignorance of Church specificity by offering a new and renovated self-constructed vision of this institution as an ecumenical trans-cultural body. This is not a criticism in itself, and a great deal of praise can be made regarding the new humanistic ideals of the contemporary Church, but the enforcement of this novel vision has led the theologically observant faithful to become oblivious of the Catholic traditions of their forefathers. Again, this is beyond the folk aspects of Catholicism; the forefathers we speak of are the men of the cloth who sustained the Church in all corners of the world as it assumed various particular and unique expressions of a single ideal and cosmological vision. The capacity for centralization and the mechanisms for quick communication which the past century has offered is leading many to gradually forget the local Church as an expression of personal and unique religious sensitivity and experience.

The results of this are numerous and nuanced, but among them is the noted lack of focus on the local Saint as a 'living' participant in religious practice and observance. Saints were often the focal point of local Catholicism; their bones were quite literally what the Altar was built upon. Saints were the centre and protector of the community, the example to be followed, and the theological weapon for church, convent, monastery and sanctuary power struggles which allowed for the establishment of local authority, constellations of pilgrimage sites, miracle narratives or the flow of devotion. By the control of relics, publication of hagiographies, miracle and cure propaganda, the specificity of the local grew from the fall of the classical world onwards, across medieval, modern and contemporary times, creating the only human way any church could hope to be Universal: by becoming infinitely local.

Still, specificity within the Church hasn't been lost, and novel groups, lay associations and orders do in fact exist, and increasingly so, each with its own rites and patrons. But such, given birth from within the current Church, seem to borrow more from Reformation ideals than ancestry and locality acknowledgement. Once again, this is likely to be an unfair criticism (if it is indeed criticism), since the Church as a living body existent in the present, and led by one single Shepherd (the Pope) as an actuation and representative of Peter, is meant for change. Consequently, such flavourless and colourless changes still need to be acknowledged as legitimate and spiritually valid… even if boring.

Importantly, traditionalists seem to miss the point that the Pope has authority to go against tradition, and if you don't accept the legitimacy of papal innovation then you are not really Catholic, but rather a heretic whose heresy has not been made manifest for lack of opportunity. The search for ideal 'traditionalism' is equally destructive since traditionalism is not constructed on a base of living organic creation, but rather erosion. Traditionalism encysts practice on a strict adherence to a particular circumstantial orthodoxy, and personal and particular expression become a danger to be combated. Speaking Latin does not make you more interesting, just a different shade of bore.

Between progressives and conservatives, modernists and traditionalists, rightfully or not the Church that once was is indeed being forgotten, because that Church of bones and dirt is problematic to both sides of the trench. If we start turning back the clock on that which is today called the Catholic Church, even if we are not wanting to fall outside its orthodoxy, we will thus be able to find shades of unusual colour. By focusing on any one environment, and tracking its visible literary outputs, lines of unique tradition thus become visible. Based on cornerstones of long-standing local practices, often put in place by the necessities of Christianization or missionary work, unique lines of ideas, expositions and religious work and conceptualization take body and form. Such is valid for any environment, creating numerous forms of Catholic expression organized along regional, national and cultural lines, each distinct and somehow, mysteriously, part of the same cosmological universe.

The current trends of contemporary Occultism should take these musings into serious consideration. Contrarily to the fraudulent claims of Theosophists and Golden Dawn enthusiasts, 'Occultism' is not a universal ancient secret tradition; it is a specific product of very concrete Anglo-American mentalities of the 19th century. Peeling back the skin, the sources from which such a movement grew, and its very mental building blocks, derive considerably from church ranks; from the men and women who were seeking such personal and local experiences from within their circumstantial location in the Church.

The break which is claimed to exist between such Occultist movements and Christian practical and theological concepts has, first of all, placed an artificial aura of shiny novelty around Occultism, and, secondly, forced all those who join in to have to reinvent the wheel over and over again. The current trend of re-appreciation of folk magic and sensitivities, the push for non-literary and non-initiatory spiritual legitimacy, can in fact build itself into a true tradition of centennial continuity if such misinformed divisions are finally seen as artificial and as having been established to serve local political dynamics.

Anyone wanting to establish a relationship with their ancestors would find their job easier if, perhaps, together with the grimoire or magic book of their choice, they carried a devotionary to the Souls in Purgatory with them into the woods or circle. By doing so they would be claiming a living, traditional base for this practice and be either using the system their ancestors actually practised or that which their ancestors' practice helped give birth to. To do this act, to pick up a Catholic devotional or a prayer book, is not an act of submission in any way. When someone picks such a book up, they are not subjecting themselves to any earthly person or institution, rather, they are taking possession of the Church for themselves, to use in an individual and local way as their ancestors also did.

On a personal level, as a Portuguese man, having spent the better part of my adult life trying to map out what could, objectively, be called a 'genuine' form of local magic, independently of my personal ambitions or fantasies, the Church revealed itself to be unavoidable. The thing which might be called 'Portuguese Magic' seemed most often to be nothing but the application of local Catholicism to concrete and, often, mundane preoccupations. Such a realization is a two-way prism: if this 'object' in front of me is magic, and this magic is indistinguishable from the local understanding of Catholicism, where is the distinction between magic and religion to be found?

I do not personally believe this question has an answer, because I believe it is a false question. Such a distinction, in the environments where such 'magic' and 'religion' existed, was never made. At its core the distinction between 'magic' and 'religion' (and 'science') is a fallacy; such categories are western academic constructions emerging from the post-Reformation and the Enlightenment and have no real universal significance or impact. To impose such a distinction into an environment where no such distinction is made is a form of pure intellectual and cultural colonialism. The full understanding of what this implies means that one can thus look into the vast literary traditions of any local Church and begin to regard such hundreds of titles not merely as inconsequential texts of religious orthodoxy which repeat themselves throughout the centuries, but doors into the local spiritual and mundane preoccupations which are the *urgrund* of local magical ontology. Saints' devotionaries, instructions on sacramental reception, step by step manuals on spiritual exercises and retreats, handbooks and shorthand prescriptions for all ailments of the body and soul written by priests and theologians are an arsenal of practices which is criminally underexplored.

The particularities of the Portuguese (and Spanish) case do add their specific articulations on top of this. The impact of the local aspects of the Church in these regions is almost impossible to overestimate. The specific historical circumstances of these regions have, at times, created a microcosm of self-referencing ideas, dangerously excitable before foreign influence, be it by expressions of excessive violence or acceptance.

In the understanding of Giuseppe Marcocci and José Pedro Paiva, Portugal was left relatively untouched by the Reformation due to quick, heavy and efficient Inquisitorial action.[1] Yet such a claim is only true on the macroscopic scale. Revising Inquisition records and the muffled manifestations of Iberian heterodoxies reveals a different perspective. While no major ideological influxes from Protestantism reached the mainstream of Portuguese and Spanish theology, such ideas were impossible to hold back, and several late manifestations of heresy can be found in numerous aspects of Iberian mysticism. From within Church colleges, monasteries and sanctuaries, the constant articulation, the fitting and refashioning of local ideas, mutually permeable from the folk to the theological, with Erasmus, Hendrik Herp, Johannes Tauler, Francisco de Osuna, Bernardino de Laredo and many others, produced a maelstrom of ghosts and bright shadows. Aligned with the forms of Spanish Alumbradismo, Quietism, Molinism and all the heterodoxies to which 19th-century Occultism is indebted and doesn't even know it, such local heterodoxies were not only fit for cloistered priests but rather for all layers of society. The literary production of this Antonio de period, from the 16th to the 18th centuries, is one of the most interesting, fertile and chaotic I am aware of. Geronimo Cortez's encyclopedic works on cosmic functioning,[2] Vasconcellos' *Treatise of the Guardian Angel*,[3] D. Francisco Manuel de Mello's book on Catholic Cabala,[4] Friar Manuel de Azevedo's treatise on the evil eye[5] and Bernardo Pereyra's medical books against sorcery[6] are all expressions of particular local environments, which are often only missing the title of 'grimoire' to be rightfully placed in the canon of western magic.

In this same line of literary eccentricity, yet another case is that of Ângelo de Sequeira Ribeiro do Prado (1707-1776). Arguably one of the greatest Brazilian missionaries in history, inspired speaker, devotee of Our Lady of the Rock, miracle worker and writer of devotional and religiously

1 Marcocci & Paiva, *História da Inquisição Portuguesa*, 85.
2 See Leitão, *Bibliotheca Valenciana*.
3 Vasconcellos, *Tratado do Anjo da Guarda*.
4 Mello, *Tratado da Sciencia Cabala*.
5 Azevedo, *Correçam de Abusos, Introdusidos Contra o Verdadeyro Methodo da Medicina*.
6 Pereyra, *Anacephaleosis Medico-Theologica, Magica, Juridica, Moral, e Politica*.

pragmatic books. His work is an unexpected treasure trove of magico-religious techniques which is to be explored at this point.

ON ÂNGELO SEQUEIRA

To explore the life and works of Sequeira is to delve deep into the potential heterogeneity of 18th-century Ibero-American religious experience. As his biography shows, he was born in São Paulo to an influential local New-Christian noble family[7] of priestly and musical tradition, eventually studying arts (philosophy) at the local Jesuit College.[8] Being a noted kapellmeister, as were his father and brother,[9] in 1726 Sequeira received minor orders, subsequently studying moral and speculative theology in order to receive major orders, becoming a secular priest of St. Peter in Rio.[10] Besides ecclesiastic and musical teaching duties, his name can also be found around 1736 in numerous legal documents, as he became a respected and successful self-taught lawyer in his home town. Following what appears to be a textbook conversion narrative, while enjoying a life of wealth and success, oral tradition has it that one day he crossed paths with a man he had once defended against in court, being attacked and slapped across the face. Taking this as a divine awakening, Sequeira sold all of his possessions, gave the proceeds to the poor, to local churches and to his underage family members, and took the habit of a missionary.[11]

In this guise, with the support of the Bishop of Rio, D. Joaõ da Cruz,[12] he tracked the Sertões of the Goiazes and Cuiabás, founding churches and chapels dedicated to his devoted deity, the Lady of the Rock, also performing miraculous cures under the guidance of this Marian representation. Eventually heading to Rio, with the agreement of Bishop D. Antonio do Desterro,[13] he founded the Seminary of the Rock, as well as numerous other churches and oratories.[14] Of a heavy Marian devotion, in his teaching and prescribed practices, Sequeira would place an immense amount of emphasis on the sacrament of confession, establishing many temples which functioned as twenty-four-hour confession stands.

His work would lead him to the Capital of the Empire in 1753, to continue his missionary work and publish his books.[15] In Portugal he would continue founding new churches, one of them still very much existent and thriving in Porto, the Church of the Rock (Igreja da Lapa), originally called the Church of Our Lady of the Rock of the Confessions, located on the old road to Vila Nova de Famalicão and where roadside robbers would be allowed to confess their crimes and offer their ill-gotten

7 Rubert, 'O Missionário do Brasil,' 137.
8 Rubert, 'O Missionário do Brasil,' 138.
9 Neto, 'O "Atalaia da Fé" Contra as Máculas do Século,' 64.
10 Rubert, 'O Missionário do Brasil,' 138.
11 Rubert, 'O Missionário do Brasil,' 140.
12 Rubert, 'O Missionário do Brasil,' 141.
13 Rubert, 'O Missionário do Brasil,' 144.
14 Lamego, A Terra Goytacá, vol. 3, 36-37.
15 Rubert, 'O Missionário do Brasil,' 146-147.

gains to the brotherhood established there.[16] Even if only fulfilled after his death, a seminary was also established here in 1792, which would eventually become a relevant local school where notable Portuguese writers and intellectuals such as Eça de Queiroz and Ramalho Ortigão received their education.[17]

Sequeira travelled the country, with references to him being found in Lisbon, Cacilhas and Setúbal, and to the North in Vila Nova de Gaia, Porto Lordelo, Vila Viçosa, Ponte de Lima, Vila do Conde, Arcos de Val-de-Vez, Fão, Valadres, Melgaço, Chaves and others,[18] having established 23 churches dedicated to the Lady of the Rock and having consecrated 153 statues. He further travelled to Tuy (Galicia) where his miraculous cures using blessed oil became famous.[19]

Enjoying great esteem throughout the entire Empire, in 1765 Sequeira moved back to Brazil. His later years are somewhat of a mystery, but two years before his death his name is still associated with missions around the Bishopric of Rio. Eventually, housed in the Seminary of the Rock, he died on the 7th of September of 1776.[20]

While Sequeira's life does not suggest anything particularly notable outside of the general missionary environment of the 18th century, his textual production reveals a nuanced and complex religious ideology, a rare eclecticism of folk and theological preoccupations, making up a multidisciplinary opus of ambition and vision. His books were published in quick succession, and they often contain repeated sections and spiritual exercises, suggesting how all of these were to fit a single worldview and apostolic ambition. The first among these, and also probably the most notable, is the *Botica Preciosa*, or the *Precious Apothecary*, from 1754. This is his flagship of both intellectual and pragmatic religious practice; a collection of prayers, devotions and exercises to the Lady of the Rock and about one hundred and twenty other saints. Suffusing this with a missionary purpose, this book also contains detailed instructions for the consecration and blessings of oils, flowers, statues and food, together with several exorcisms and prayers for numerous ailments, many of which seem to be intended for situations where there was likely to be a notorious lack of able priests. Addressing largely the preoccupations of folk devotion, the book acquired a significant appreciation and usage among the populace in both Portugal and Brazil, and several versions of it are known to exist, containing different arrangements of Saintly illustrations, which suggests that these would be commonly added to or taken from its pages for personal use and devotion.[21]

In the following year, 1755, Sequeira published the *Pedra Iman da Novena da Milagrossissima Senhora da Lapa*, the *Magnet Stone of the Most*

---

16 Rubert, 'O Missionário do Brasil,' 148.
17 Coelho, *Venerável Irmandade de Nossa Senhora da Lapa*, 20.
18 Ferreira-Alves, 'Nótulas Setecentistas,' 88.
19 Rubert, 'O Missionário do Brasil,' 149.
20 Rubert, 'O Missionário do Brasil,' 156.
21 Moraes, *Bibliografia Brasileira do Período Colonial*, 338-339.

Miraculous Novena of the Lady of the Rock, a slim book consisting of selected republished material from the heavy *Botica Preciosa*, and in 1758 he published the *Livro do Vinde e Vede*, or *Book of the Come and See*, his only printed sermon, published by request of the local clergy,[22] in which he discourses on the end of times. This last one is a significant work for scholarly appreciation, due to it being the only one of his books not dealing with direct religious application, and it was reprinted in 1763.[23]

His fourth book, published in 1759, titled *Exercicios Devotos*, *Devotional Exercises*, is largely a reprint of his *Pedra Iman.*[24] Although frequently overlooked by biographers, it is presented as general spiritual instructions to be used by the priests of the Church of the Rock in Porto, founded by Sequeira.[25] In line with his missionary work, his next book is the *Penitente Arrependido*, the *Regretful Penitent*, an instruction book on repentance and confession. Finally, what is likely to be his rarest work is the 1761 *Fructuoso Desvelo*, the *Fruitful Revelation*, another book of popular devotions to saints, in particular to the severed head of Saint Fructuosus of Braga.[26]

Other than these, one can also find mentions of a manuscript book of sermons by him which never got published. This was probably meant to be Sequeira's magnum opus, a work exposing his missionary and apostolic thinking. Contradictory information exists about his sermons, with them at times being mentioned as referring to the 1755 Lisbon earthquake[27] and of there having been a five-volume work of all his mission sermons, which was under preparation in 1753.[28] Still, although his published works were of immense local influence, with prayers from them still used today for talismanic purposes in Brazil,[29] contemporarily all these are considered to be extraordinarily rare. Even with the conveniences of modern technology, I have never been able to find a copy of his last printed work, which cannot be located in either the Portuguese or the Brazilian National Libraries.

In terms of theological and moralistic content, Sequeira's books seem to derive from the Portuguese reformist and rigorist mentalities of his time, but with a surprising common thread in all of them of a very human conscience and preoccupation with the concerns and needs of the poor and underprivileged classes. While he constantly and insistently prescribes the strict adherence to the Sacraments, mental prayer, asceticism and meditation exercises typical of learned 18th century Iberian Catholicism, the largest part of his books are devoted to the most mundane preoccupations, the same where one would think magic could just as easily fit. Sequeira seems to ultimately be extraordinarily sensitive to the idiosyncrasies, cultural manifestations and human necessities of the

22 Rubert, 'O Missionário do Brasil,' 152.
23 Moraes, *Bibliografia Brasileira do Período Colonial*, 340.
24 Moraes, *Bibliografia Brasileira do Período Colonial*, 340.
25 Moraes, *Bibliografia Brasileira do Período Colonial*, 342.
26 Moraes, *Bibliografia Brasileira do Período Colonial*, 343.
27 Silva, *Diccionario Bibliographico Portuguez*, vol. 8, 90.
28 Rubert, 'O Missionário do Brasil,' 153.
29 Rubert, 'O Missionário do Brasil,' 155.

regions and social classes he worked with, opening various religious shortcuts for regretful thieves and murderers, and incorporating and expanding on folk and rural devotions in his books, systematizing them and offering new and rectified theological context for saintly work; a kind of inter-Catholic syncretism between the 'learned' and the 'folk'.[30]

This interesting duality, which ultimately places Sequeira's writings in their own category, can be most evidently identified by what seems to be the two main influences in his religious sensitivities. There is an undeniable appeal to the religious rigorist ideas popular in his day, and one may even argue that he was an active member of such reformist groups. On the opposite side of the scale, his utter devotion to the Lady of the Rock, an old Portuguese Marian representation of a profound folk character, casts a different light on all his actions and religious aesthetics, sweetening his underlying theological harshness.

ON THE JACOBEIA

Regarding Sequeira's theological rigorism, if one cross-references his life, and his moralistic and discursive works, with his time frame, one very specific religious movement does pop up. In the early 18th century, Portuguese (and consequently Brazilian) Catholicism would be rattled by a new fervour rising up from the fertile ground of peninsular mysticism and the echoes of Quietism and reformist ideas: the once-powerful and tragic Jacobeia.

This name of Jacobeia is first and foremost open to debate, and its very proponents often do not seem to agree as to where it originated from. Overall, the majority of them (as well as contemporary historians) believe it referred to the Biblical Jacob's ladder, indicating a doctrine of 'narrow path'.[31] In historical terms, the Jacobeia needs to firstly be understood as a movement and ideology constructed at various stages. As mentioned by Friar António Pereira da Silva, there is a strict and a broad Jacobeia[32] to be understood. The strict Jacobeia refers to a particular reformation movement directed towards the excessively relaxed Santa Cruz Monastery of Coimbra. The basic ideas behind this came from the writing of an Augustinian friar by the name of Francisco da Anunciação, the son of noble parents, doctor of Coimbra (and eventually Dean of the University between 1745 and 1757) and professor of philosophy and theology in the College of Graça in the same city,[33] where the core group of the Jacobeus would form after 1707.[34] These originally isolated ideas would later be taken up by Friar Gaspar da Encarnação, from the Franciscan convent of the Varatojo in Torres Vedras, and a noted doctor of Canon law from Coimbra, at one time Dean of the University (1710-15) and a minister of

30 Neto, 'O "Atalaia da Fé" Contra as Máculas do Século,' 92.
31 Moncada, *Mística e Racionalismo em Portugal no Século XVIII*, 9.
32 Silva, *A Questão do Sigilismo em Portugal no Século XVIII*, 122-123.
33 Moncada, *Mística e Racionalismo em Portugal no Século XVIII*, 38.
34 Costa, 'A Jacobeia,' 34.

King John V,[35] who was transferred to the College of Graça in order to reform the afore-mentioned Varatojo convent in 1723. Through him the initial ideology for the reformation of the Santa Cruz Monastery gained a sudden and widespread appeal via the Varatojo Franciscans[36] and began to not only spread into other religious institutions but to secular society,[37] initiating the broad Jacobeia.

In this way, there was a true novelty to the Jacobeia as compared with other similar movements of its time, in that it had clear universalistic ambitions and aimed at a complete reformation not only of the Church but of society at large,[38] although it never really reached the lower classes and was, overall, a movement of elites. For the Jacobeus, in this social struggle, men were divided into two categories: the spiritual, virtuous, pious, devout or perfect and the mundane, material, tepid, relaxed or lukewarm. Such divisions weren't particularly new, being also common to many Christian sects frequently placed under the category of Gnosticism. However, for the Jacobeus such categories were meant to be fluid, and mundane men could be easily called to sanctity by preaching and example.[39]

Besides the two already-mentioned friars, other relevant names in this movement were those of Miguel da Anunciação, once again a doctor of Canon Law from Coimbra, and eventually Bishop of the city,[40] and D. Miguel da Távora, archbishop of Évora, student in the College of Graça (where he became Francisco da Encarnação's favourite pupil),[41] and member of the powerful Távora family.

As a whole, the Jacobeia drew heavily from the writings of St. John Chrysostom as spiritual readings. Their practices were based on daily mental prayer, constant examination of conscience and participation in the Sacraments, with particular emphasis on Confession, which should be made to specially selected confessors who would become strict spiritual directors of the confessant.[42] The importance given to this aspect of the Jacobeia cannot be overstated. A spiritual director in the Jacobeia way would, as a matter of fact, be the very vehicle of perfection for an adherent and the mechanism for spiritual attainment, for it was by his action and direction that personal will could be abdicated and a completely clear conscience acquired. This system was particularly justified by the reading of the lives of the Saints, where it could be observed that Divine Providence leading to Sainthood would frequently manifest through secondary causes and creatures. Thus, a carefully prepared spiritual director could place himself as the designer and narrator of a personal

---

35 Moncada, *Mística e Racionalismo em Portugal no Século XVIII*, 39.
36 Costa, 'A Jacobeia,' 32.
37 Silva, *A Questão do Sigilismo em Portugal no Século XVIII*, 122-123.
38 Moncada, *Mística e Racionalismo em Portugal no Século XVIII*, 9.
39 Moncada, *Mística e Racionalismo em Portugal no Século XVIII*, 19-20.
40 Moncada, *Mística e Racionalismo em Portugal no Século XVIII*, 40.
41 Castro, 'Jacobeia,' 5.
42 Costa, 'A Jacobeia,' 32.

path of Sainthood on behalf of God.[43] For the Jacobeia, the spiritual director, through his instructions and guidance, would become the hagiographer of a new Saint in training.

In more general terms the Jacobeia advocated a return to primitive Christianity, being particularly interested in the study of moral theology, music, liturgy and Church history, with their preachings having a strong eschatological tendency.[44] Ideologically, they were anti-sophistic, opposing themselves to speculative theology, preferring the ways of asceticism, mysticism and personal experience of God. In the Augustinian tradition, these claimed the superiority of mysticism over speculation, love over understanding, and beatific vision over theoretical discourse,[45] being guided by the thirty rules of personal government created by Francisco da Anunciação (see Annex).[46] These constructed a 'wall of protection', where one would fit exercises for the vision of God, prayer, mortification, abdication of personal will (a Quietist staple and a dangerous heresy), fasting, merciful works, zeal in the salvation of souls, self-knowledge, disregard for the material world, modesty, poverty and austerity; many of these with the specific purpose of being publically visible, so as to further its apostolic and missionary ideals.[47]

As their most marked characteristic, one should also note their rigorous anti-eroticism. While certainly not a novelty, in the Jacobeia this took on severe and deep preoccupations. The strict repression of carnal desire was itself accompanied by a repression of spiritual desire, what Cabral da Moncada refers to as a negative pan-sexualism which needed to be manifest at all moments and actions.[48] This meant a strict and conscious observation of Divine love and union, where the danger of mystical sensual degeneracy was a constant. External delights were not the only path to Hell, for also were the moments of disorderly 'delightful and lascivious' love for the Divine, present in prayer, communion and union with God.[49] Such was the power of the Devil, as seen by the Alumbrado Quietists,[50] that he was capable of entering even the most sacred of moments and completely inverting these into sin. As such, a great deal of attention was to be placed on the 'violences' or 'vexations' of the Devil, which, following the Varatojo Franciscan ideology, should be fought with exorcisms and divine precepts, constant examination of conscience, and abdication of will.[51]

On a social scale, Jacobeia ideals gained quick adherence among the clergy and the Portuguese aristocracy, and in 1745 such reformation ideas were already manifest in the Portuguese Benedictines, Cistercians,

---

43 Silva, *A Questão do Sigilismo em Portugal no Século XVIII*, 132-133.

44 Costa, 'A Jacobeia,' 32.

45 Moncada, *Mística e Racionalismo em Portugal no Século XVIII*, 10.

46 Costa, 'A Jacobeia,' 32.

47 Silva, *A Questão do Sigilismo em Portugal no Século XVIII*, 125.

48 Moncada, *Mística e Racionalismo em Portugal no Século XVIII*, 12.

49 Moncada, *Mística e Racionalismo em Portugal no Século XVIII*, 14.

50 Queirós, 'Jacobeia e redes clientelares,' 91.

51 Silva, *A Questão do Sigilismo em Portugal no Século XVIII*, 142.

Carmelites, Paulists and Tomarists.[52] However, what would cement their influence and power all over the Empire would be the support of King John V. This would come into play via a significant and observable change in the general procedure for the nomination of new Bishops for the kingdom. Traditionally, Portuguese Bishops originated from the 'first nobility', coming from powerful noble families and being skilled in politics and state affairs. However, from the 20s of the 18th century there was a sudden rise in Bishops drawn from noted religious characters,[53] mainly destined for the newly created dioceses in the Portuguese Empire.[54] This meant that an increasing number of new Bishops from this time on were consistently selected from among the Jacobeus or their sympathizers, and this became a relevant and powerful movement, capable of reaching the furthest reaches of the Empire, for instance in places such as Goa, Macau and Brazil.

This quick expansion, and their noted unreasonableness, quickly initiated the very mechanisms that caused the eventual downfall of the Jacobeia. Truth be said, from its inception, the Jacobeus had managed to collect a great number of enemies among the Jesuits, the Oratorians, the anonymous bourgeois, and the scholars and theologians, but most of all among the powerful *freiraticos*.[55] This last and curious group consisted mainly of well-to-do men who nurtured an inappropriate but more or less platonic love for nuns, and, as such, hounded convents and monasteries hoping to communicate with their nun of choice. This practice was mostly made possible by the general lack of persons of genuine religious vocation in large sections of both the male and female cloistered religious population, and it was theologically justified among its practitioners as the highest expression of amorous sensitivity. The types of relationships formed in this way would, at times, be compared by its *aficionados* to the non-sensual love one feels while 'holding a small puppy', while, actually, most were clearly erotic in character.[56]

This practice, while strange, had great acceptance among the Portuguese upper classes, with even King John V being a noted *freiratico*, and the Jacobeia was not shy in attacking the activity in all its expressions.

Still, having amassed a considerable number of powerful enemies, the smoking gun which eventually triggered the decline of the Jacobeia was their confessional zeal. Whatever the truth of the matter, on top of the animosity of powerful classes, during the 40s of the 18th century, the Jacobeus started to be accused by legal and unsympathetic ecclesiastic authorities of breaking the seal of Confession, the accusation known as Sigilism.

---

52 Costa, 'A Jacobeia,' 35.

53 Queirós, 'Jacobeia e redes clientelares,' 86.

54 Paiva, *Os Bispos de Portugal e do Império*, 492.

55 Castro, 'Jacobeia,' 5.

56 Moncada, *Mística e Racionalismo em Portugal no Século XVIII*, 29-30.

As applied to the Jacobeia, under long preparation by the Inquisition,[57] this accusation consisted in confessors associated with the movement frequently asking their confessants for the names and identities of all those who had participated in the narrated sins, at times refusing absolution if the information wasn't divulged. Besides being a clear breach of Canon law, this practice created a quarrel with the Portuguese Inquisition, since Sigilism could result in Confession being used for the investigation of heresy, something which belonged exclusively to the Inquisition's jurisdiction. While probably only a fraction of the Jacobeus were Sigilists,[58] the practice did exist, and, quite apart from the numbers involved, it was a serious enough accusation for its enemies to use as a concrete weapon and official condemnation of the movement as a whole.

Such an accusation did eventually happen in 1745, with an attack by the Inquisitor General Nuno da Cunha who, with papal support, demanded that accusations against all Sigilists be brought forward for persecution. Although this was not a direct attack on the Jacobeia, relevant Jacobeu Bishops such as Miguel da Távora and Miguel da Anunciançāo did step forward to deny the accusation and claim that the dealing of such a crime was an issue for the Bishops, and not part of the Inquisition jurisdiction, requesting further papal assistance on the matter. This move by the Bishops was, in fact, a defensive manoeuvre: since the accusation of Sigilism was constructed for specific use against all Jacobeus, by diverting the jurisdiction of this same crime from the Inquisition into their own courts they would be saving themselves from inevitable persecution at the hands of an Inquisition eager to stamp them out. They were not successful, however, and even if the movement was never explicitly condemned by the Pope, the Inquisition did win the jurisdiction battle, and was now free to persecute all Jacobeus as Sigilists (even if only one was ever condemned as such).[59]

However, the greatest blow to the Jacobeia only came in 1768, during the regime of the Enlightened Despot Sebastião José de Carvalho e Melo, the Marquis of Pombal.

With the death of King John V, the rise of King Joseph I meant that the protection offered to the Jacobeia was removed, and it became one of the main targets for attack by the new Enlightenment-sympathizing elites. Consequently, in just a short time the Jacobeia was dragged into a never-ending stream of anti-enlightenment accusations of mysticism, with potential Quietist, Molinist and Jansenist influences, all supported by the intellectual and theological clerical elites. In the midst of such an environment, unsatisfied with the path the country was taking, Miguel da Anunciançāo, a long time Jacobeu and by this time Bishop of Coimbra, issued a pastoral condemning the reading of Humanist, Enlightenment and regalist books.[60] This action was a direct attack on the power of the

57 Paiva, *Baluartes da Fé e da Disciplina*, 400.
58 Paiva, *Baluartes da Fé e da Disciplina*, 400.
59 Paiva, *Baluartes da Fé e da Disciplina*, 400.
60 Paiva, *Os Bispos de Portugal e do Império*, 169.

newly formed *Real Mesa Censória* (Royal Censorship Office)[61] and the bloodthirsty Marquis Pombal himself, who gladly took this as another opportunity to cement his regalist agenda and cripple the most powerful national institutions outside the crown.

The result of this conflict was quick and decisive: the Jacobeus became the target of an efficient slur campaign, being placed alongside the Jesuits (banned from Portugal by Pombal in 1759) as dangerous fanatics, to which the subscription of Miguel da Távora to the movement made easier, as the Távoras had already been brutally executed as traitors and conspirators in 1759. But most importantly, Bishop Miguel da Anunciação was immediately arrested and imprisoned, without being allowed a defence, the Jacobeia was outlawed, and its participants persecuted. A publication[62] by the *Mesa Censória* regarding the spiritual exercises and rules of the Jacobeia created by Francisco da Anunciação is a particularly revealing document in this point, being in essence an extensive exercise in rhetoric where the Jacobeia is continuously compared with Pharisees, Muslims, Donatists, Waldensians, Wiclefists, Puritans, Methodists, Cathars, Montanists, Jesuits, Nestorians, Molinists, Quietists and a few other heretical movements.

Finally, after being all but destroyed, Miguel da Anunciação was eventually released in 1777 by order of Queen Mary I, a declared enemy of Pombal and his brutal social reforms. From this point on, and apart from literature and a footnote in history, with the gradual death of its old supporters - too broken and fearful to ever express themselves publically again - the Jacobeia finally vanished from public sight, seventy years after its inception.[63]

Such is history as we know it, but no idea ever disappears into a vacuum, and looking back at Ângelo Sequeira, one can easily identify many significant parallels between the ideas he expresses in his writings and those of the Jacobeia. First and foremost, among his personal acquaintances one can at least mark two known Jacobeu Bishops active in Rio, the already-mentioned D. João da Cruz and D. António do Desterro.[64] Beyond this, his musical and missionary career, his asceticism and rigorist reformation ideas and noted obsession for Confession and examination of conscience, all indicate a clear continuity with Jacobeia ideas, as do his offering of exorcisms against the vexations of the Devil. While no concrete evidence or document has been found to unequivocally tie Sequeira to the Jacobeia, he clearly moved in its environment and was sympathetic to its ambitions and purpose, thus placing him within the orbit of complex theological conceptions of society, religion and mystical experience.

---

61 Paiva, 'A Igreja e o Poder,' 173.

62 N.a., *Juizo Decisivo que a Real Meza Censoria.*

63 Costa, 'A Jacobeia,' 44.

64 Paiva, *Baluartes da Fé e da Disciplina*, 401.

ON THE LADY OF THE ROCK

On the other side of Sequeira's sensitivities, one has a personal devotion with a marked folk root, which seems to soften his Jacobeu sympathies. While easily comparable to 'yet another' representation of the Virgin Mary, the Lady of the Rock, as many other older devotions, has its own complex implications. This representation is typically shown as a crowned Virgin Mary standing on top of a cloud, her hands together in a position of prayer; the model from which the current Lady of Fátima was constructed. Yet, this representation can vary, as can the origins of the several Lady of the Rock statues cultuated in Portugal and Brazil.

Historically, the main sanctuary of the Lady of the Rock is in Quintela, Sernancelhe, a county of Viseu. The current sanctuary, based on a 15th-century chapel, is a 17th-century Jesuit construction. Yet, in the interior of this, one can still find the primitive altar and 'chapel', actually made up of a large boulder with a cave under it, where the original statue of the Lady of the Rock was found. Following the collection by the Jesuit Antonio Leite, the whole story of this statue tells how in the 9th century, during the troubled times of Muslim rulership of Iberia, the Benedictine nuns of the Convent of Sismiro, fearing the approach of King Almansor and his troops, hid their miraculous statue of the Virgin in a cave, many of them being killed or enslaved.[65] There the 'Queen of Angels' remained until 1498, when a mute shepherd girl named Joana found it by chance. Becoming enamoured by the figure she took it as a doll, and from that moment on would spend her days adorning the statue with fine dresses and making her as beautiful as she could.[66]

Constantly occupied by these affairs, her home chores and work soon began to suffer, to the great irritation of her mother. This to such a point that, one day, in a fit of anger, she took the statue from Joana's hands and threw it into the fire, so that her daughter could be free from such useless distractions. Yet, miracle struck, as little mute Joana suddenly cried out: 'O Mother, what hast thou done!'. Not only did the mute girl suddenly find her voice, but the fire was not able to touch the statue, and it remained intact, while Joana's mother's arms were struck by paralysis as punishment, only being cured once the statue was removed from the fireplace.[67]

Recognizing that this was a holy image of the Virgin, the populace was quick to place it in their church, but, during the night, the image miraculously returned to her cave. They once again transported it back to a proper Catholic temple, but once again it fled, and did so three times. Faced with this, a new temple was built behind her rock, but the statue did not wish to be in any other place but the stone which had guarded it for centuries.[68] Facing the facts, the populace's only option became to

---

65 Leite, *Historia da Appariçam e Milages da Virgem da Lapa*, f.15v-f.15r.
66 Leite, *Historia da Appariçam e Milages da Virgem da Lapa*, f.32r-f.33v.
67 Leite, *Historia da Appariçam e Milages da Virgem da Lapa*, f.33r-f.34v.
68 Leite, *Historia da Appariçam e Milages da Virgem da Lapa*, f.35v-f.35r.

build her a church around her precious cave, where she has joyfully stayed until this very day.

While this is the most widespread story, and the Quintela sanctuary the most relevant one of this Marian devotion, the Lady of the Rock does possess a number of other churches and images which predate modern construction, such as those founded by Ângelo Sequeira during his missionary work. It is important to underline that this particular Marian devotion, taken in its several manifestations, is one which has considerable overlaps with other-than-learned-Christian practices and iconography. Particular among these is the potential call-backs the Lady of the Rock has with the *Mouras Encantadas*, the fairy-like spirits of Iberian folklore, frequently associated with large boulders, caves, water basins, snakes and other reptiles and buried treasure.

Overall, in a pure folk environment, visions and apparitions of the Virgin Mary aren't phenomenologically distinct from *Moura* visions and apparitions, being almost always tied to local topology or geographical landmarks.[69] Consultation of Inquisition reports and other documents where such descriptions can be found, shows that such visions are frequently described as being 'of a Lady', the identification of one of these 'Ladies' with the Virgin Mary or any other figure being usually a much later revelation for the seer or even the result of social or cultural pressure. These mark a useful contrast with upper-class literate mystical visions of the Virgin or other Saints, such as those by the already mentioned Quietists or Alumbrados, which are always described as purely 'spiritual visions' and unambiguously identified from their inception with concrete Catholic characters.[70]

In this way, the Lady of the Rock always stands at an ambiguous crossroad of elements and iconography. This is a Virgin of wild and hard to access places, surrounded by serpents and cave-dwelling shadows and reptiles. Still, she is taken as unfailing, the most miraculous Virgin of them all, and Lady of the Rock narratives can be expected to reflect this:[71]

> *There once was a married man who left his house in order to go to work. On the road, he leaned against a tree to rest. Near this tree there was a rock where the Lady of the Rock was in.*
>
> *In the meantime, the man fell asleep, and a snake entered his mouth. In dreams, the first thing he thought about was the Lady of the Rock, so as she would help get the snake out of his mouth.*
>
> *Then, as soon as he thought about her, the snake came out of his mouth very fast. The man woke up and continued on his way to work as if nothing had happened.*[72]

---

69 Ribeiro, *O Auto dos Místicos*, 316-319.

70 Ribeiro, *O Auto dos Místicos*, 326.

71 The following were collected from the website *Lendarium*, or 'The Archive of Portuguese Legends,' a project of the Centro de Estudos Ataíde Oliveira belonging to the University of the Algarve: www.lendarium.org and www.ceao.info

72 V.a., *Literatura Portuguesa de Tradição Oral*, L4.

Returning to the Quintela sanctuary, as part of a complex religious ceremony, the climax of the pilgrimage to this place consists of a particular rite of powerful symbolism. Devotees of the Lady of the Rock enter into the dark cave corridor, passing by the miraculous statue of the Lady, until they reach a narrow passage, the 'crack of Our Lady', through which they must squeeze until they come out the other side.[73] There, pilgrims rub their hands on the cave walls, gathering humidity on their palms, which they then rub over their skin. Continuing the path, one reaches the house of the weight, where, traditionally, pilgrims would weigh themselves and offer this value in wheat to the sanctuary. Today, however, this houses the 'lizard'.[74]

The 'lizard' is actually a stuffed alligator, and there are mentions of it at least as early as the 17th century. Usually this is taken as having been an offering of a devotee who travelled to India and killed the beast with the aid of the Lady, but it has itself attracted its own folk narratives which feed off and feed into the typical narratives of the Lady of the Rock:

> *It is told that a woman was coming from a village called Forca on the way to Quintela with a bag of linen skeins to weave. In the middle of the mountain, in a place known as Cova (burrow), she was attacked by a great lizard. This, with a huge mouth, tried to bite the woman who, in fear, asked for the aid of the Lady of the Rock. It was then that she had the idea of throwing the skeins at the monster, while keeping their ends in her hand.*
>
> *The creature kept swallowing the skeins that the woman threw at it. When she had a great number of threads from the skeins in her hand, the woman gave them a great pull by which the creature was choked.*
>
> *As a sign of gratitude, the woman offered the body of the lizard to the Lady of the Rock.*[75]

As noted by Moisés Espírito Santo, the Quintela sanctuary of the Rock possesses some of the most 'spontaneous' religious expressions known in Portugal, treading the border between accepted orthodox Catholic religious practice and the heterodoxy of folk lived religion.[76] Overall, the particular ritual of rebirth one performs in it is not at all dissimilar from a few others connected to other such Ladies, such as the Lady of the Star near Coimbra, mostly cultuated by pregnant women.[77]

Although not as relevant or complex as the Quintela sanctuary, following Agostinho de Santa Maria's monumental *Santuario Mariano*, a number of other churches, chapels and statues of this Lady can be found, which seem to suggest an overarching thematic in origin and folk conception. The first of these is the Lady of the Rock of Casais Novos, Tomar. This is described as a tiny statue made from an unknown material, at times referred to as having been made of ivory or, alternatively, as

73 Espírito Santo, *Origens Orientais da Religião Popular Portuguesa*, 5-6.
74 Espírito Santo, *Origens Orientais da Religião Popular Portuguesa*, 6.
75 V.a., *Literatura Portuguesa de Tradição Oral*, L3.
76 Espírito Santo, *Origens Orientais da Religião Popular Portuguesa*, 7.
77 Espírito Santo, *Origens Orientais da Religião Popular Portuguesa*, 7.

having an angelic origin.[78] This is mentioned as being quite similar to the Lady of Covões (also a possible synonym to 'Rock' or 'Cave') from Coimbra, and Agostinho de Santa Maria assumes this was also found by a shepherd girl.[79]

Another Lady of the Rock is located in Souto, near Lamego, technically referred to as Lady of the little Rock or Lady of the new Rock. This statue was made by a local woman skilled in sculpting and painting, a tertian Franciscan who had recurrent dreams about this image and the place where its chapel should be built.[80] Like other Ladies of the Rock this is located inside a small cave and is particularly known for healing illness and disease.[81]

The Lady of the Rock of Condeixa, near Coimbra has an origin closer to the Quintela one, but is, overall, stranger. Narratives around this tell that a poor woman once entered into the cave where this sanctuary is currently located to wash some clothes in the clear waters gathered there. In this labour she suddenly saw a woman, but looking closer, could find nothing, for which reason she took no note of it. Going there a second time, she once again saw the lady, this time much clearer, and this time thought this was a very beautiful woman. She then spread the news that there was a beautiful hidden woman living in the cave, carrying some beads in her hands and dressed in rich clothing. Hearing this, some people gathered to investigate, by which they entered into the cave and eventually found, in one of its chambers, a stone chair with a small image of the Our Lady on it.[82]

Once this was found, the local priest was called, who determined that the statue be moved to where it could be properly worshipped. Like the Quintela case, the statue miraculously abandoned the church and returned to its cave twice. On a third attempt, the statue was instead taken to the chapel of the Holy Spirit, where she indeed rested until a new and proper house was built for it.[83]

The Lady of Sardoal, a place whose name literally means 'land of lizards', once again tells a similar story, although the origin of the statue itself is not exactly known. This is another 'fleeing' statue, but this one, once a new chapel and sanctuary was built, accepted it after being begged to do so by the local populace. An image of Mary Magdalene was afterwards placed in its original cave.[84] A legend can also be offered concerning this one:

> *There exists in the parish of Sardoal, near the River Arcês, the chapel of Our Lady of the Rock.*

78 Santa Maria, *Santuario Mariano*, vol. 3, 476.
79 Santa Maria, *Santuario Mariano*, vol. 3, 477.
80 Santa Maria, *Santuario Maraiano*, vol. 3, 258.
81 Santa Maria, *Santuario Mariano*, vol. 3, 259-260.
82 Santa Maria, *Santuario Mariano*, vol. 4, 571-572.
83 Santa Maria, *Santuario Mariano*, vol. 4, 572-573.
84 Santa Maria, *Santuario Mariano*, vol. 7, 340.

> *Legend has it that, a long time ago for reasons we do not know, a bishop was deported to this place. This was a desert and because of this the bishop, when he heard of his punishment, was afraid. It was then that, when he was leaving to go there, he heard a voice which told him: 'Do not be afraid'.*
>
> *And the bishop went on his way and helped to build, with stones from the river, an altar, and there he began to offer Mass. This Mass was frequented by the shepherds who roamed around that place.*
>
> *Later the bishop had a chapel built there, and it is said that then an image of Our Lady appeared in a cave on the other side of the river. They took this statue to the little chapel, but she would always return to the cave.*
>
> *In memory of that voice who spoke to the bishop, that river was given the name of Ârces*[85] *and the chapel was given the name of Our Lady of the Rock, perpetuating in this way the memory of that image who insisted on returning to the cave.*[86]

Finally, the Lady of the Rock of Travasso, also known as the Lady of Succour, is particularly called upon against floodings by the river Vouga and Águeda. Although no information is given regarding the origin of this statue or its title, Antonio de Santa Maria once again suggests a hidden statue being found by an innocent shepherd.[87]

Besides these, Santa Maria also offers the location of other sanctuaries and chapels to the Lady of the Rock with a modern origin, such as those of São João do Foz,[88] Chaves[89] or various ones in Brazil. These are most often mentioned as having been constructed either by immigrants who were themselves devotees of the Lady of the Rock, or by locals interested in attracting the miraculous eye of this particular Marian representation.

In its manifestation and sanctuaries, the Lady of the Rock can be considered as a symbol of 'folk' religiosity in the face of clerical imposition. This Lady comes from the wild lands of shepherds and farmers and does not accept any other sanctuary but her own, made from rocks and water. The construction of churches around these same rocks is then a powerful symbol of local religious demand: the Lady and her people will not go to the Church, the Church must come to them and somehow find space within it for this unique religious practice.

Between Jacobs's ladder and the Lady's rock, one could expect a striking contradiction, but Ângelo Sequeira rather manages to create a surprising synthesis of opposites. As mentioned, throughout all of his books, there is a constant call for strict religious observance and Sacramental participation – particularly Confession –, subjection to a spiritual director and a draconian denial of Christianly conceived sin in all its forms, be it in body or mind. Yet, all such rigorous exercise is framed

85 A play on words with the original voice heard by the bishop which said: 'Vai não recês!'
86 Jana, *Histórias à Lareira*, 70.
87 Santa Maria, *Santuario Mariano*, vol. 7, 488.
88 Santa Maria, *Santuario Mariano*, vol. 5, 75.
89 Santa Maria, *Santuario Mariano*, vol. 7, 427.

on a base of spiritual devotion, mostly towards the Virgin Mary in her Lady of the Rock representation.

TO CONCEPTUALIZE A CATHOLIC GRIMOIRE

In terms of structure and content, should one gather all of Sequeira's writings under one single title, the patterns that emerge do begin to appear recognizable to someone familiar with magical literature. All in all, even if not claiming such a title by any means, there is a certain 'grimoiric' feel to Sequeira's works.

Although for someone from his background, the projection of the category of 'magic' would be completely unacceptable, from a contemporary magical perspective that is what his books mimic, but they simply do so from a Christian Catholic position, the position from which Magic has been historically defined as an antithesis of Religion. To now take the leap from argumentation and into concrete definition is thus problematic. To call this a book of Catholic magic is historically fallacious, for, objectively, this is simply a book of local Catholic practice applied to local preoccupations. 'Magic', as a category, might be applicable to it, but such application is itself the result of specific contemporary circumstances and bears no meaning besides that which the applicant wishes to convey for his own comfort.

To apply this category is not inherently wrong, as long as one does not become a tyrant about it. The categorization of Magic is only given here on the basis of pattern recognition and similarity. On his own terms, Sequeira was not a magician, he was a priest, and his books are not grimoires, they are Catholic devotionaries. Yet, the respect one has to afford his own self-definition does waver when one remembers that, objectively speaking, in this locality, magic and religion aren't actually distinguishable.

Throughout western history, the definition of 'Religion' is typically given from 'within' or as contrast to something else which 'Religion' wishes to separate from itself. Religious discourse, in regards to definitions, can be observed to be constructed on the base of the discussion between the existence of true and false religion, in which false religion may never be taken as religion in itself, but rather as the propagation of theological errors frequently gathered under the categories of heresy, superstition or blasphemy. As such, to speak of 'Religion', or anything else which is presented as inherently distinct from it, is to implicitly assume a theological or ethnocentric view; a position of groundless authority which allows one to determine what truth and falsehood are.

Returning to the Catholic/Christian sphere, 'Magic', together with 'Superstition', 'Witchcraft' and 'Sorcery', are categories of exclusion into which practices deemed unacceptable or erroneous can be cast for forgetfulness and theological condemnation, even if these practices did not claim such a title for themselves and were practised by their proponents as being valid forms of 'Religion'. 'Magician', 'Necromancer', 'Sorcerer' or 'Witch', historically, are also not definitions, but accusations, and to look back into history and project such titles onto individuals who never claimed them is a form of violent historical colonialism and says more about our current tyrannical tendencies than it ever does about our imagined traditions. Those who might want to argue against this point should first do themselves the favour of reading a few firsthand Inquisition processes and stop relying on what others, with their own agendas, have written about them.

To call Sequeira's books 'Magic' is assuredly a historical and potentially academic fallacy, but I am not, in any way, claiming Sequeira was a Magician. The attribution of the category of 'Magic' to his works, and the title of 'Grimoire' to his books, is simply the shorthand definition given contemporarily to such patterns of religious practice; in a period in history where such categories have been taken hold of by self-defining magicians as having implicit, concrete and positive significance.

The issue of contemporaneity is, in my opinion, unavoidable when bringing forth a new book of Magic for the present day. We may search and publish old grimoires as complete systems of bygone times, but the characteristics of today do not, in any way, respect the 'completeness' or self-contained character of such works, and it is often forgotten that ancient, medieval, early modern and modern magical systems weren't pure to begin with nor were they meant to be used exclusively. At the same time as the discussion on the border between 'Magic' and 'Religion', we, as author and readers, should all confront the fact that we live in a post-modern, post-chaos magic and post-New Age world, where the irreducibly contemporary value of 'individuality' has a definite impact on the meaning of 'authenticity'.

This book, as any other book, is only authentic on its own terms, and on the terms of those who accept it as such. It describes techniques which might be called Magic if one accepts them as Magic according to a system of categories which is entirely contemporary and does not touch on their origin as Catholic devotionaries in any way. This needs to be understood, otherwise we are tyrants.

MEDITATION ON CONTENT

Grace and Indulgences

Having walked past the dangerous maze of academic classifications, to project a vision of Magic onto Sequeira's writings requires the effort of understanding the logic behind his complex vision of Catholic syncretism. As its base, what Sequeira mostly proposes is a system of petition through intermediary spirits for the mitigation of earthly pains and necessities and the forgiveness of punishment over human weakness. This is usually requested of the Virgin, in her Rock representation, or a Saint of particular specialization.

The Virgin Mary standing as protection from the arrows (of plague) sent by God. 'The Virgin of Mercy responding to the intercessions of saints by protecting people from arrows symbolising disease; the Devil rules below, where plague attacks the land. Lithograph by L. Dittorini (?) after Benedetto Bonfigli, 1464 (?).' by Benedetto Bonfigli. Credit: Wellcome Collection. CC BY

Overall, his books do advise a strict adherence to values such as those of the Jacobeia, but the mechanics to do so are partially given over to the Saints and the Virgin, spirits who carry with them an irreducible humanity and compassion, and are accessible through 'folkish' devotions. Coupled with this, Sequeira also offers all the necessary tools to follow this line of religious work in less-than-ideal circumstances. This means that he supplies methods for the indefinite postponement of Confession, the tecniques for creating your own blessed implements for *impromptu* liturgical ceremonies and instructions on exorcisms. Taken together, in Sequeira's collective work, what one finds is a series of exercises for spiritual purification and the acquisition of Grace – a state of proximity and conversational familiarity with the Divine from which one is able to petition the Heavens –, and the pragmatic ends towards which this same Grace and spiritual purity may be applied for concrete this-world function and leverage.

To take a particular detail, looking at Sequeira's Novena of the Rock, a fundamental exercise for numerous purposes in his books, we see it completely follows the above-mentioned pattern: one starts with an expression of humility and repentance before the Divine; and gradually, based on Biblical and theological exegeses, this offering of humility and obedience is worked into a kind of deal where one is to acquire Grace and spiritual favour in exchange for such goods; finally, this ends with something that almost follows the pattern of a pact, meaning that both the practitioner and the Divine, or its representative, become obliged to each other and establish a trade relationship of spiritual goods.

This pattern of work isn't a novelty in any way, and is in fact the underlying mechanism of Catholic Prayer. Following Antonion Deça Erhassion's *Compendio de Devoções Utilissimas* (*Compendium of Most Useful Devotions*) there are firstly three types of prayer: Mental, Vocal and Missal.[90] The first of these is the one solely performed with one's thoughts, elevating the mind to the Divine. Vocal is done with words, such as the Our Father; and the Missal is composed of these two forms combined. In this final form, thought and contemplation of the Divine makes one erupt into words of Divine praise.[91]

Mental prayer can itself be further divided into three parts: meditation, prayer, and contemplation. In this scheme, prayer is the fruit of meditation, and contemplation the fruit of prayer. Besides this, this type of prayer can also be divided into six parts: Lesson, Preparation, Meditation, Action of Grace, Offering and Petition.[92]

Of particular relevance for the understanding of Sequeira's prayers are the two final parts of prayer. Offering is effectively a surrender to God, so as to be made into an instrument of his will, offering the worth of the Just and that of the blood of Christ shed in our benefit. Consequently,

90 Erhassison, *Compendio de Devoções Utilissimas Para Todo o Fiel Christão*, 251.
91 Erhassison, *Compendio de Devoções Utilissimas Para Todo o Fiel Christão*, 251.
92 Erhassison, *Compendio de Devoções Utilissimas Para Todo o Fiel Christão*, 251-252.

Petition is the supplication for His mercy towards sinners, and for the particular remedies for spiritual and temporal needs as well as the maintenance of Grace and the avoidance of sin.[93]

In this form, the particular exercise of Mass, being a prayer event, does also provide a powerful circumstance for particular petitions and devotions to be made. Prayer, in its various forms, is meant as a ritual for the creation of an environment of proximity with the Divine, and thus Mass, the very manifestation and reification of Divine presence on Earth, ends up being the most appropriate time for powerful petitioning. Catholic 'Witches' have long realized this.

The issue of the acquisition of Grace can be further explored by the recourse to Indulgences. These are an assuredly controversial aspect of Catholicism, but they ultimately translate the complexity of the union and shared treasure of the Church in its several parts of Church Triumphant, Militant and Suffering. While mortal sin can only be removed from an individual by full Confession, venial can be easily dealt with by Indulgences. These are a relaxation of temporal penalties taken from the common treasure of the Church, which consists mostly of the worth of Jesus Christ and the superabundance of satisfactions of the Virgin Mary, the Saints and the Just.

The superabundance of satisfactions attributed to the Saints and the Virgin comes from the unbalance such individuals, during their lifetime, had between worth and sin. They, having sinned very little or not at all,[94] carried with them a greater value than debt towards the Divine, thereby creating a common reservoir of extra worth for all faithful. The administration of this common treasure, accessible to all Catholics as a means to immediately pay for their minor sins, was given to the Pope by Christ, who distributes Indulgences according to an economy of sin and forgiveness. It should still be noted that Indulgences do not forgive sin in regards to its guilt, but rather its temporal penalty, which, even after forgiveness, will still require purging in this life or in Purgatory.[95]

As mentioned, the full forgiveness of mortal sin can only be accomplished with recourse to the worth of Christ (which Sequeira appeals to often) and not that of the Saints. Also, Indulgences and Grace can be acquired on behalf of others, namely for the Souls in Purgatory by applying these for the mitigation of their penalties. This once again translates the inherent union of the three bodies of the Church: the Saints of Church Triumphant intercede in the name of the living faithful and supply them with an abundant treasure of Indulgences, and the faithful of Church Militant, while taking care of their own salvation and worth, can relay this common worth to the Souls of Church Suffering.

On the particular form of aiding those of Church Suffering, two different methods can be used: either one works towards Indulgences

93 Erhassison, *Compendio de Devoções Utilissimas Para Todo o Fiel Christão*, 254-255.
94 Erhassison, *Compendio de Devoções Utilissimas Para Todo o Fiel Christão*, 25.
95 Erhassison, *Compendio de Devoções Utilissimas Para Todo o Fiel Christão*, 24.

which were specifically attributed by the Pope as being directed to the Souls in Purgatory, or one may issue an official offering towards these souls. This can either be a simple and explicit offering of a particular prayer or intention to the Souls, or it can become a complex form of spiritual devotion, resembling a contract by which, for a determined amount of time (which can escalate to one's full life) one offers the entirety of acquired worth and satisfactions to the Souls.

On the Virgin and the Saints

As the great cornerstone of Sequeira's system, and the supreme interceder and intermediate spirit in the Catholic pantheon stands the Virgin. While Christ is God made Man, and consequently infinitely closer to humans than God the Father, the Virgin stands simultaneously as a universally positive entity towards humans and as a figure of irreducible authority in the face of the Divine, who itself owes her the respect given to a mother as God the Son. She is thus able to hold the hand of the very creator God in favour of humans and consequently create a divinely validated mechanism for a humane cosmos truly based on love and compassion, able to bypass divine Justice/Punishment.

An easy way to comprehend the eccentric complexities of Catholicism, when compared to the various forms of Protestantism, is precisely through the idea of intercession. The infinite space between humans and the terrifying God is filled in Catholicism by an endless stream of intermediaries, all meant to appease and offer protection from the harshness of the Divine itself. The first of these stands as the very *raison d'être* of Christianity, namely, Jesus Christ, God made man. Below him stands the Virgin, Mother of God and humans, and below her the Saints, themselves divided into numerous categories of specific cosmic function.

Comparing the Virgin with other 'regular' Saints, these assuredly function on a lower level than her. While Mary was human in nature and substance, the dogma of Immaculate Conception, implying an existence inherently free from original sin, places her on an immediate superior level of Grace compared to all other humans. Hence, in her Assumption, her rising into Heaven in body and soul, there was no transubstantiation, meaning that Mary remains fully human, but merely one of ultimate perfection (without sin and, as the prayer goes, full of Grace) and capable of looking God in the eye and moving him to particular action. A good contrast to this situation can be seen in Enoch, who was equally taken into Heaven in body but was transformed into the Angel Metatron, thus losing his human nature and his inherent sin.

By contrast, Saints are born like any other human, burned with original sin and subject to any additional sin they may acquire in life. Thus they are simultaneously closer to humans in their flaws, but also occasionally removed from us by habit. Mary, as mother of God made man, is permeated by love, and stands as mother to all humans, thus her intercession is immediate and available, independently of the nature, character or circumstantial Grace of the human reaching out to her. In contrast, the process for the rising to Sainthood that a Saint goes through implies a certain level of harshness; there needs to be an active effort for the shedding of sin and that part of humanity associated with it (occasionally equated with sexuality or even the very sexual organs) to acquire this state which the Virgin did not need or required to go through.

The particularities of this process of Sainthood leads to a certain number of conditionings when approaching any particular Saint. While their nature is closer to humans, their irreducible humanity equally conditions their actions and position; the process or reason to approach a particular Saint, while proper for one, might be offensive to another depending on his particular process of acquiring Sainthood, or that part of themselves they had to cast out or highlight to reach such a state. The open natural love of Francis is not the same as the scholarly exercise of Augustine or Thomas of Aquinas, and this is not the same as the eremitism of Anthony the Anchorite - but all are equally Saints. The humanity of the Saints and Mary is what allows for dialogue and communication in a cosmos of strict unbreakable Aristotelian rules.

On the other hand, Angels are the manifestation of Divine Will; while they may be positive towards humanity, an Angel will never be able to see your point of view because you have no point of view it can see before the certain and clear-cut Will of God. Still, Mary and the Saints get to change that Will because they are not strictly conditioned by it. Not only do they converse and dialogue with us, but they converse and dialogue with the Divine itself.

Following the Virgin, what can be seen to occupy the most of Sequeira's pages is then the intercession of the Saints. While for the process of acquisition of Grace (and Grace can be considered to be an objective in itself), the Virgin and, to a minor extent, the Holy Heart of Jesus, or other members of the Holy Family, are the proper spirits or powers to be addressed, the Saints stand as minor spirits, relegated to mundane preoccupations, auxiliaries in temporal affairs and the guidance and inspiration of the faithful. This is one of the aspects that gives Sequeira's *Botica Preciosa* a particular 'grimoiric' aspect. Its initial sections present several purifications and methods to acquire Grace; once this is acquired, and a perfect 'embrace' by the full body of the Church and proximity to the Divine (mostly through the Virgin, the Queen of Heavens) has been acquired by the practitioner, he is given access to his brothers within the Church Triumphant: the Saints and the Blessed in Heaven.

While difficult to crack, the system for Saintly evocation Sequeira uses rises from concrete liturgical methodology tailored for 'mundane' applications typical of folk magico-religious preoccupations. In general, in Sequeira's system of Saintly work, for each Saint one is given an Antiphon followed by a prayer. It then stands, from the perspective of evocation, that what in this system is described as the actual calling to the Saint is the Antiphon, and the prayer stands as a petition made to either him, to God, or to both once the Saint has been called forth. Furthermore, as a conclusion to this extended section of his work, Sequeira further offers the instructions on how to fit these same Saint Antiphons and prayers to the general Novena of the Rock, allowing for literally hundreds of novenas to be made in which one calls and works with the Virgin of the Rock and the Saint in question simultaneously.

In terms of systematization, if enough of these Antiphon/prayer pairs are analyzed, one can very easily see that they follow a pattern, which, if one is not familiar with more ecclesiastic, theological or liturgical definitions may be hard to understand. As it goes, outside of a strict folk perspective, Saints are divided into several categories, with each category having its own functioning and place within the Church hierarchy in the union of Church Militant and Church Triumphant, plus a particular liturgical expression. These same categories can also be found, for example, in the calendar of the Saints, in front of the name of the Saint in question,[96] usually in the following way:[97]

Saint	S./SS.(p)	Confessor	C.	Hermit	H.	Priest	Pr.
Apostle	A./AA.(p)	Companion	Comp.	King	K.	Queen	Q.
Abbot	Ab.	Doctor	D.	Martyr	M./MM.(p)	Virgin	V.
Bishop	B.	Deacon	Dea.	Pope	P.	Widow	W.

Besides these categories, one can still mix and match them such as with Virgin Martyrs, Confessor Bishops and so on. A few more characterizers can be added to some particular Saints, indicating their job or function on Earth (Founder, Monk, etc.), or association to a particular Catholic order (Carmelite, Franciscan, etc.), making up an extremely wide variety of possible combinations.

Looking beyond personal pleas and petitions to Saints, worked by means of prayers coming into the more folkish aspects of Catholicism, these are also regularly worked into Masses, and the procedure to do so is dependent on their category. Given its possible variability, Mass can be divided into two sections: the Ordinary, which is a section which never changes in any Mass, and the variable part. The Liturgical devotions to the Saints fit into the variable part, and these are dependent on the times of the Liturgical year and the particular days and festivities of Saints. Furthermore, this Saintly section of the Mass has two main variations: the Proper and the Common.

The Proper is the variable part of Mass dedicated to a particular Saint, usually celebrated on his feast day. The Proper has particular elements and compositions describing the celebrated Saint, his works, miracles and

96 See the calendar of the Saints in Leitão, *Bibliotheca Valenciana*, 58-80.

97 Challoner, *The Garden of the Soul*, lxxx.

position. The Common is the variable part of Mass dedicated to a category of Saints as a whole. These are non-specific compositions, only specialized on the general characters of the Saint category in question or the general category of a Saint with no specific Proper.

In the function of Mass, the Proper of a Saint is offered first, being followed by the Common. Propers can be as multiple as Saints, and should one choose to take an active role in all of this, new Propers can be constructed based on personal devotion. However there are only fifteen different types of Saint Commons, with a few of these having alternative versions:

1. Apostle.
2. Martyr Bishop.
3. Martyr not a Bishop.
4. Martyr in Easter.
5. Several Martyrs.
6. Several Martyrs in Easter.
7. Confessor Bishop.
8. Doctor.
9. Confessor not a Bishop.
10. Abbot.
11. Virgin Martyr.
12. Several Virgins.
13. Virgin.
14. Holy Woman not a Virgin but a Martyr.
15. Holy Woman neither a Virgin nor a Martyr.[98]

The general order of Commons given above also roughly translates the hierarchical position of Saint categories in the Catholic pantheon, namely: Apostles[99]/Evangelists, Martyrs, Confessors (generally speaking these are members of the clergy in their various classes of Popes, Bishops and so on) and finally Virgins and Holy Women.[100]

Sequeira's Saint calling system is then based on the variable Mass, Saint Propers, and Commons. It can be observed that a great deal of the Saints present in his 'Vocations of the Saints' are called in by a personal Antiphon, mentioning aspects of their life or Celestial position and function, followed by the two lines: «℣ Pray for us Saint [NN] / ℟ So as we may be worthy of the promises of Christ». These two final lines are taken from the *Salve Regina*, which is an Antiphon in itself for the Virgin Mary, being one of the four Marian Antiphons, together with the *Alma Redemptoris Mater*, the *Ave Regina Cælorum* and the *Regina Cœli*. These personal Saint Antiphons should stand in Sequeira's system as Propers; a direct and personalized address to a particular Saint.

---

98 Challoner, *The Garden of the Soul*, lxxiv-lxxvi.

99 Contrary to what might be thought, this is not a closed category of the twelve Disciples of Christ. The title and category of Apostle can also be given to other Saints. This category mainly signifies a Saint who significantly helped in the spread of Christianity, such as Saint Francis Xavier, Confessor and Apostle of India.

100 It is the Patriarchy after all.

The Holy Trinity surrounded by Saints, author and date unknown. Read counterclockwise from the top (From God's right hand) the Catholic Hierarchy of Saints is also visible. First, closest to God the Son stands Mary, Queen of Heaven, below her stand Apostles (Peter and Paul are plainly visible), followed by Martyrs (a healed Saint Sebastian stands in the front), followed by Confessors (Popes, Bishops and Monks visible) and finally by Virgins and Holy Women. 'The Holy Trinity with Saints. Engraving.' . Credit: Wellcome Collection. CC BY.

On the other hand, a great deal of the Saints he presents are not given a personal Antiphon, but rather one which is repeated and offered to many other Saints of the same category, meaning, a Common. However, narrowing down Sequeira's thinking, it should be noted that regular Commons usually open with a section of a Psalm, thus, the use of Antiphons (a psalm-text) and the variability and particularities of the Commons he presents breaks away with general Commons and unambiguously places them specifically as Vespers (evening service) Commons, which only have eleven variations:

1. Apostle and Evangelist
2. Apostle and Evangelist in Easter
3. Martyr
4. Martyr in Easter
5. Several Martyrs
6. Confessor Bishop
7. Confessor not a Bishop
8. Virgin
9. Several Virgins
10. Holy Woman neither a Virgin nor a Martyr
11. The year's day of the Dedication of the Church

Following the 1725 *A Manual of Devout Prayers and Other Christian Devotions*, the Common opening Antiphons for the Anglican/Protestant Evensong prayer and the Catholic Magnificat, or Vespers, prayer, are as follows (except the one for the Dedication of a Church):

APOSTLE AND EVANGELIST

Apostle signifies envoy or ambassador, because the Apostles were the envoys or ambassadors of Jesus Christ, sent by him to preach the gospel to all nations, with a promise that he would be with them and their successors, *all days, even to the end of the world.* We are therefore to look on them as our fathers, since it was through them we received the precious gift of faith. We ought likewise on their festivals, in a particular manner, to give thanks to God for having made us members of his Apostolic and Catholic Church, and impartially examine the conduct of our lives, to see, if while we submit our reason and understanding to the truths the Apostles taught mankind, we bend our wills to the practice of those divine precepts they left behind them. This grace we ought to beg of God, on their festivals, through their powerful intercession.

The Divine Office For The Use of the Laity, i.

	Vernacular	Latin
Evensong	Our Lord sware, and it shall not repent him, Thou art a Priest forever.	Juravit Dominus & non pœnitebit eum, Tu es Sacerdos in æternum.
Magnificat	Be you strong in battle, and fight with the old Serpent, and you shall receive an everlasting Kingdom. Alleluia	Estote fortes in bello, & pugnate cum antique Serpente, & accipietis Regnum Æternum. Alleluia.

In the time of Easter

	Vernacular	Latin
Evensong	Thy Saints, O Lord, shall flourish as the Lilly, Alleluia. And they shall be as the savor of the Balm-tree in thy presence. Alleluia.	Sancti tui Domine florebunt sicut lilium, Alleluia. Et sicut odor balm sami erunt ante te, Alleluia
Magnificat	Ye Holy and Just rejoice in our Lord, Alleluia. God hath chosen you for his Inheritance. Alleluia.	Sancti, & justi in Domino gaudote, Alleluia. Vos elegit Deus in hæreditatem sibi, Alleluia.

MARTYR

The holy martyrs come next after the apostles, in whose honour the church hath instituted festivals. This honour is due to them, for having Borne testimony to the truths of the Christian religion before the Pagans, and for having sealed this their testimony with their blood, and given their lives for Jesus Christ. The church thanks God for the courage and constancy he gave them, and proposes their example to her children. It is true, we do not live amongst idolaters, against whom we have our faith to defend. But the number of libertines and bad Christians is very great,[101] before whom we ought not to be ashamed to shew, that we profess a religion that is holy, and for which we ought to be ready to lose all, even our very lives. Such is the grace of constancy and resolution we ought to beg of God thro' the intercession of the martyrs.

The Divine Office For The Use of the Laity, vi.

101 Heh!

	Vernacular	Latin
Evensong	He that shall confess me before Men, I also will confess him before my Father.	Qui me confessus suerit coram hominibus, confitebor & ego eum coram Patre meo.
Magnificat	He that will come after me, let him deny himself, and take up his Cross and follow me.	Qui vult venire post me, abneget semeripsum, & tollar erucem suam, & sequatur me.

In the time of Easter

	Vernacular	Latin
Evensong	Thy Saints, O Lord, shall flourish as the Lilly, Alleluia : and they shall be as the savor of the Balm-tree before thee, Alleluia.	Sancti tui Domine florebunt sicut lilium, Alleluia : & sicut odos balsami erunt ante te, Alleluia.
Magnificat	Ye holy and just rejoice in our Lord, Alleluia : God hath chosen you for his inheritance, Alleluia.	Sancti & justi in Domino gaudere, Alleluia : Vos elegit Deus in hæreditatem sibi, Alleluia.

SEVERAL MARTYRS NOT IN THE TIME OF EASTER

	Vernacular	Latin
Evensong	These are Saints, who have delivered their Bodies for the Testament of God, and have wash'd their Bodies in the Blood of the Lamb.	Isti sunt Sancti, qui pro testament Dei sua corpora tradideruns, & in sanguine Agni laverunt stolas suas.
Magnificat	The Souls of the Saints rejoice in Heaven, who have followed the steps of Christ; and because they have shed their Blood for his Love, therefore with Christ without end exceedingly they rejoice.	Gaudent in Cœlis animæ Sandorum qui Christi vestigial sunt secuti; & quia pro ejus amore senguinem suum fuderunt, ideo cum Christo exultant sine fine.

CONFESSOR

In the five or six first ages of the church, those were called *Confessors*, who confessed Jesus Christ before the Pagans; particularly if tortures accompanied this their confession, as was generally the case. In aftertimes the name of *Confessor* was given to such as confessed Jesus Christ by the purity and sanctity of their lives. There are different degrees of *Confessors*: some of them are *Bishops*, some *Priests*, and *Doctors* of the Church; and by their intercession we ought to beg of God pastors full of his spirit, and capable of teaching the truths entrusted to them. Others are *Monks* or *Solitaries*; and it is thro' their intercession we ought to beg of God the spirit of retirement and penance. Others lived in the world in different states and conditions. But they all lived without any attachment to the things of this world; and despised whatever is transitory, to give themselves up to God and his truths; and mortifying their bodies by penance, they underwent a sort of martyrdom in the perpetual mortification of their passions, and denial of their own will. It is to the imitation of these virtues that their feasts ought to animate us; and, on them, we ought to have recourse to God, that, thro' their intercession, we may obtain his enabling grace to follow their steps.

The Divine Office For The Use of the Laity, xxvii.

BISHOP

	Vernacular	Latin
Evensong	Behold a great Priest, who hath pleased God in his days, and was found just.	Ecce Sacerdos magnus, qui in diebus suis placuit Deo, & inventus est Justus.
Magnificat	Our Lord loved, and adorned him; a Garment of Glory he put on him, and at the Gates of Paradise he crowned him.	Amavit eum Dominus, & ornavit eum stolam gloriæ induit eum, etad portas Paradisi coronavit eum.
Magnificat, a Pope	Whil'st he was High-priest he feared not earthly things, but passed glorious to the Celestial Kingdom.	Dum esset summus Pontifex, terrena non metuit, sed ad cœlestia Regn gloriosus migravit.
Magnificat, a Doctor	O Most excellent Doctor, Light of the holy Church, blessed N. Lover of God's Law, supplicate the Son of God for us.	O Doctor optime, Ecclesiæ sanctæ lumen, beate N. Divinæ Legis amator, deprecare pro nobis Fillium Dei.

NOT A BISHOP

	Vernacular	Latin
Evensong	Lord, five talents thou didst deliver me; behold I have gained other five besides.	Domine, quique talenta tradidisti mihi; ecce alia quinque superlucratus sum.
Magnificat	This Man despising the World, and triumphing over earthly things, heaped up riches in Heaven by Word and Work.	Hic vir despiciens mundum, & terrena, triumphans, divitias cœlo condidit ore, manu.

VIRGINS

The state of Virginity is perfectly agreeable to the Christian scheme, whatever objections human policy may make against it. God himself, become incarnate, recommends it by word and example. St. Paul bestows the greatest encomiums on it; and in every age of the Church, those that preserved their Virginity, were always looked on as the noblest portion of the flock of Christ. On the festivals therefore of Virgins, we are to beg of God the grace of perseverance to the end for those who have voluntarily, by vow, undertaken that perfect state; as likewise for all, that purity of mind necessary in every state of life, and without which we cannot see God.

The Divine Office For The Use of the Laity, xliv.

	Vernacular	Latin
Evensong	This is a wise-Virgin, and one of the number of the prudent.	Hæc est Virgo sapiens, & una de numero prudentum.
Magnificat	Come, Spouse of Christ, receive the crown, which our Lord for ever hath prepared for thee.	Veni, Sponsa Christi, accipe coronam quam tibi Dominus præparavit in æternum.

SEVERAL VIRGINS

	Vernacular	Latin
Evensong	You wise Virgins, make ready your lamps behold the Bridegroom comes, go forth to meet him	Prudentes Virgines, aptate vestras lampades; ecce sponsus venit, exite obviam ei.
Magnificat	Virgins after her shall be presented to the King : They that are nearest her shall be brought unto thee	Addecentur Regi Virgines post eam : Proximæ ejus asterentur tibi.

HOLY WOMEN, AND NEITHER A VIRGIN NOR MARTYR

When we celebrate the festivals of those saints who were engaged in the married state, we ought seriously to meditate on the virtues by which they sanctified themselves in that state of life. A profound humility, purity of heart, and an exact compliance with the duties, and untired patience under the difficulties of that state of life, rendered them agreeable to God. These are the virtues the Church honours in these saints; and these are the virtues we ought to beg for all engaged in the married state, on the feasts of these holy women. The Church likewise honours some, who, after an irregular course of life for some time, received of God the grace of true repentance; and were so enflamed with the love of God, that the ardour of their love rendered them almost equal to Virgins. Let us beg of God, thro' their intercession, the spirit of true repentance, and that charity that covered a multitude of sins.

The Divine Office For The Use of the Laity, lv.

	Vernacular	Latin
Evensong	While the King was on his bed, my Nardus did give an odour of sweetness.	Dum esset Rex in accubitu suo, Nardus mea dedit adorem suavitaris.
Magnificat	She hath been open-handed to the needy, and hath extended her charity to the poor and hath not eaten her bread in idleness.	Manum suam aperuit inopi, & palmas suas extendit ad paupeem, & panem otiosa non comedit.

This is the Liturgical base of Sequeira's Saint calling system; a personalized and particular simplification of the use of Saint Propers and Vespers Commons in the form of Antiphons, followed by a prayer/petition. Besides all of this, and in line with the Liturgical structure he is deriving from, there are also a number of indications in a few of the Saints he offers which indicate that these callings are meant to be used on their specific feast day, like regular Propers.

However, looking deeper into his system, while Sequeria roughly follows the Catholic Magnificat Common Antiphons to call on his Saints, he is ultimately not too consistent with the system presented above or with himself. At times, instead of the actual Vesper Common Antiphon, he uses pieces of 'call-and-response' hymn contained in the Common of the same Saint category he is addressing (such as with Saint Agatha); other times he uses other Antiphons included in the body of the Common of one category of Saints and matches it with that of another category (such as with Saint Blaise, where he uses a minor Antiphon from the Evensong Common and matches it with the Easter Apostles and Evangelists/Martyrs Evensong Antiphon); or, occasionally, he will use pieces from the Antiphon of one category and match it with hymns from a contradictory category (such as with Saint Abraham and a few others, where he uses the Antiphon of a non Bishop Confessor and a piece of hymn from a Bishop Confessor). Also, it is clear that Sequeira took these Antiphons and prayers from a variety of sources and languages, as one can find several 'translator's false friends' in a few of them, and it is thus hard to make an evaluation of his system if we don't really know what Missal(s) he was using. Furthermore, the Antiphons used by Sequeira have probably gone through an unknown number of translations, not all of them 'official', meaning that, even if most of the Antiphons he presents are possible to identify with the above Magnificat ones, significant differences should be expected. While Sequeira's Saint calling procedures can certainly be said to roughly follow the above system (and the interested reader is advised to consult a good Missal for an introduction to the full procedure for Vespers Commons), the amount of variability he presents leaves out the possibility of fully understanding or systematizing his Antiphon composition and, consequently, his Saint calling methodology.

Regarding the finer aspects of practical application, given Sequeira's activity as a music teacher, it is likely that he intended all of these to be sung. Antiphons are typically sung as refrains during Christian ritual, in particular before and after Psalms. This may lead one to very interesting forms of working Saints, mixing their personal aptitudes and specializations, addressed in their Proper Antiphon, with Biblical Psalm magic to create very versatile and powerful techniques of spirit magic utterances. However, this practice contains a certain degree of difficulty in its proper execution, as the combination of singing Antiphons and Psalms depends of the proper use and control of Psalm tones, which ensure the smooth chanting continuity between Antiphons and Psalms in a Mass setting, likely following the Ecclesiastic modes, or the Gregorian modes of Protus or Dorian (D), Deuterus or Phrygian (E), Tritus or Lydian (F) and Tetrardus or Mixolydian (G). These are liturgical music theory issues I'm not an expert on.

The issue of Saints' work can also be brought forward on one other difficult aspect of Sequeira's proposed work. Coming from his Jacobeu tendencies, Sequeira constantly prescribes the frequent consultation and obedience to a spiritual director. This should be an ordained priest, specialized in Confession and knowledgeable about spiritual literature, exercises and meditations. Ultimately the whole issue of Grace and divine proximity is inseparable from this, it being, as already mentioned, the only way to remove mortal sin. From a theological Catholic perspective there is no way around this, as it is a specific capacity offered by Jesus to his Apostles (as described in John 20:21-23) and passed on and perpetuated through the clergy by Apostolic succession.

If we are opening the door to theological Saintly proximity and the acceptance of the union of the three bodies of the Church, an alternative might be proposed which can possibly revolutionize this process for the solitary Catholic or the uncomfortable occasional practitioner.

Priesthood, like any sacrament, is irremovable, and the several categories, functions and callings of Saints we observe in full use within the Catholic Church clearly indicate that Saints, passing unto death, still retained their priestly condition. It should then stand to reason that such a Saint could just as easily act as a spiritual director for a feverous devotee, but they should be prepared for the potentially harsh penitence demanded by a holy dead with no material preoccupation for absolution to be reached.

For this concrete transplantation of Confession and Absolution from the body of the Church Militant into that of the Church Triumphant, certain cares still need to be taken. First of all, you may be able to lie to a priest and trick him into Absolving you (not that this does you any good), but you can't trick a Saint. Secondly, the Saint in question needs to be a recognized and ordained priest (but not necessarily a Confessor); once again, you can't trick your way around this as there needs to be an actual material continuity between Jesus and the Saint in question made by the Sacrament of Holy Orders using Laying of Hands. Virgins and Holy Women are out, Nuns don't actually receive Holy Orders, and those cool legendary Saints everybody loves, like Cyprian, aren't a good choice. Third, similarly to the last case, Angels will not do, as a Confessor needs to be a human who is also subject to sin and understands the human state.

The point here is not to teach how to bypass Confession (although, as stated, Sequeira himself does offer a particular method to postpone it), but indeed this is one of the most problematic aspects of Catholicism (or Christianity in general) for the more heterodox practitioner, including those still calling themselves Christians. Confession is ultimately a personal and internal examination and process. The priest involved is merely serving a practical function, i.e. the recognition of your sincere contrite state, since only a priest ordained in Apostolic succession can give you Absolution. The argument is then to simply substitute one ordained priest for another, and furthermore, one for whom you actually have some guarantee has a perfect morality and character.

ON THE CURRENT BOOK

To conclude this introduction, having offered what I can on conceptualization, biography, history and reconceptualization, a final description of this book needs to be supplied. The current title, this *Precious Apothecary*, is a heavy-handed collection and compilation of most of the material produced by Ângelo Sequeira. This means that what is collected here is not a 'Complete Works' by any means; but a careful selection of all the material produced by Sequeira which could be included by a contemporary magical sensitivity in order to offer a book of frankly brilliant Catholic techniques for the acquisition of Grace, Saintly patronage and the consecration of liturgical tools and remedies.

Primarily, the current book is based on Sequeira's *Botica Preciosa*, to which has been added material from his *Pedra Iman*, *Penitente Arrependido*, *Livro do Vinde e Vede* and *Exercicios Devotos*. Unfortunately, no copy of the *Fructuoso Desvelo* has been located in any of the many consulted libraries. This book certainly still exists somewhere, as Ruben Borba de Moraes presents an image of its cover in his *Bibliografia Brasileira do Período Colonial*,[102] but he unfortunately does not offer the location of any such copy and I have been unable to find one. Still, we do have information on some of its content, namely that this had the means to 'enjoy the beatific vision in the company of our Saint [Fructuosus], patron against rabid dogs, and fevers' also containing 'various devotions, and prayers against Earthquakes'.[103]

The current collection has also been trimmed to remove all of Sequeira's excessively 'discursive' material, namely his sermons, reports from his missionary travels and his extensive narratives of miracles and wonders performed by his prescribed blessed remedies. To further add material to this already impressive collection, a few more processes and prayers have been taken from Erhassison's *Compendio de Devoções Utilissimas*. This last addition was made due to the observation that there is a significant agreement and coherence between this book and those of Sequeira (which it actually quotes somewhat frequently). In particular, the list of blessings and exorcisms given by Sequeira is seen to also feature in the *Compendio*, but in this these lists were actually more extensive, meaning that both were likely quoting a common source composed of 'open access' blessings, prayers and exorcisms.

With this, rearranged and reorganized, what is offered is a Catholic Grimoire. A book full of the extravagancies of Portuguese 18th century Catholicism, with exhalations of liturgical incense, flowers and oils, but also those of mountain air, rocks, water and morning dew.

102 Moraes, *Bibliografia Brasileira do Período Colonial*, 344.
103 Moraes, *Bibliografia Brasileira do Período Colonial*, 342-343.

N.S. DA LAPA
que se venera em Portugal
e no Rio de Janeiro re
nos seus semin.

Jesus, Mary, Joseph

In the name of the Father, and the Son and the Holy Spirit. Amen.

In the beginning God created the Heavens, and the earth, the firmament, and further elements, herbs, plants, the Sun, the Moon, the fish, the birds, the rational and irrational creatures, springs, cliffs, metals, and all on which our eyes may gaze, and our understanding perceive, so as with everything and by everything the Creator of all would be praised: *Benedicit omnia opera Domini Domino.* With that prodigious word *fiat* He created this entire universal, celestial, and terrestrial machine, so as to better reveal Himself by means of these exteriorities, as he did to David, when he wished to raise his thoughts to God, to know Him: *Consideravi opera tua & expavi*: I have heard of thy deeds, and was awed.

As time passed, God, seeing that the world was flooded in guilt, and in sin, so as to show His love, sent His only-begotten Son: *Sic Deus dilexit nundum, ut Filium suum unigenitum daret,* so as with His own blood to heal our infirmities of body and soul: *Ego veniam, & curabo eum.* And so great was the love of the Eternal Father, that to confirm this love, the Son incarnated in the most holy womb of the most holy MARY so as to communicate with the sons of men: *Deliciæ meæ esse cum filiis hominum,* suffering so many torments in his sacred Passion, and shedding so much blood as remedy, and medicine for our sins, and recommending his, and our Mother, the holiest MARY, that we are her children: *Mulier, ecce Filius tuus.*

And with the devotion of the Rosary she left us with the true medicine for all infirmities of the body, and soul, with holy roses, holy oils, holy waters, holy Rosaries, all a precious Apothecary, and precious Treasure for whoever wishes to use it. Being this thus placed and experimented, as I shall show with evidence, and ocular experience. I wonder what Solomon today, seeing the prodigies and miracles of Our Lady of the Rock, printed in the precious Apothecary, which exceeds all the sciences and marvels of nature, would say; if he should resuscitate to the sight of the fruits which are plucked from the roses of the Rosary and precious Treasure of the Rock!

No one doubts that Solomon was gifted with science infused with knowledge, and news of the virtues of all plants of the universe; that he penetrated the natural virtues of all flowers, with which he resolved to write many books so as in these to leave us the knowledge of herbs, and flowers, so we would not know disease, and infirmity in the creatures: *Locutus est Salomon de lignis à cedro usque ad hyssopum.* Thus, writing these books so as to give us our health, by opening these did remedies immediately appear, and the body's infirmities immediately disappear.

But as the creatures solely cared for the effects of medicine, and not its causes, nor the Author of the virtues of these remedies, for as soon as these saw themselves ill, immediately did they seek the books of Solomon so as to apply these medicines and become free from their bodies' aches, and they no longer remembered God, and they only remembered these books. The Prophet Ezekiel, seeing this ungratefulness, ordered these books to be burnt, where the precious Apothecary and precious Treasure of Solomon was kept.

The people complained over the lack of those books, and they cried when seeing themselves without remedy to heal their infirmities in the absence of those books, which due to an unfailing decree were devoured and burnt. But what would Solomon say, if in the sight of the Precious Apothecary of the Rock he was to resuscitate, and hear the praise of the virtues of roses, oils, flower, and holy waters, of the Rosary of the Apothecary of the Rock? What would he do, what would he say, if he should see in a single flower all the combined virtues of all the flowers? And consider in one sole plant the virtue of all plants.

For certain that, with amazement he would say: A flower such as this, a medicine such as this, I have never found in the entire world, nor could I penetrate, nor my science could investigate, and discover its virtue and for this did I not write it in my books, for all I found I have placed in them, and none was as this. It is certain that at this point Solomon, with his science, and prudence, would console the people missing his books, saying that with the sight of the precious Apothecary of the Rock, and precious Treasure of the Illuminated Rock, and filled with the holy roses, and holy oils, no longer would his books be missed.

This, what Solomon would say, is what I think our Lady of the Rock is saying: *Egrediamur in agrum; videamus si flores fructus parturient*, inviting us to this treasure up until now hidden in the fields, so as to see if its flowers do give fruit, and if these medicines do heal with holy Rosaries our infirmities, as best the Church advises in the blessing of the same roses: *Ut quibuscumque in infirmitate appositæ fuerint, ab infirmatate sanentur.*

It is the Holiest MARY the true precious Apothecary, the true Treasure, all comes to us from her hands, as so says Saint Bernard: *Omnia per manus Mariæ*, finally it is everything for everything: *Omnibus omnia facta est*, she is the one who frees us from all danger: *Sed à periculis cunctis libera nos simper, virgo gloriosa, & benedicta.*

And as in the apothecaries one finds a variety of remedies, in this one shall be given a recipe for the Saintly advocates of all infirmities so as the sick may choose the one most suited, and know that over all recipes, and vocations it is our Lady of the Rock who is the main advocate for all bodily and spiritual infirmities.

Christian Doctrine

I found it fair to include the Christian Doctrine, so as family men may teach it to their children, servants, and slaves. Books are filled with indulgences which are earned by those who teach these, and family men shall have to respond for many harsh debts for not teaching the Doctrine, Prayers, and Confession to those under their obligation.

Question: What Law do you profess?
Answer: The Law of Christ.

Q: And who is Christ?
A: He is God, and true Man, as God Son of the Eternal Father, and as Man Son of the Virgin Mary.

Q: Who is God?
R: He is an infinite, independent, all-powerful Lord, and Creator of all, who permeates the good with eternal glory, and punishes the wicked with eternal Hell.

Q: Is God solely one?
R: He is solely one in Divinity, and attributes, and trine in Persons.

Q: How many are, and who are the Persons of the Holiest Trinity?
A: They are three, Father, Son, and Holy Spirit, three distinct persons, and one sole true God.

Q: The Father is God?
A: Yes, and the Son is God, and the Holy Spirit is God, and all the three Persons are the same God.

Q: The Person of the Father, and the Person of the Son, and the Person of the Holy Spirit are the same Person?
A: No, for they are three distinct Persons, of which one is not the other.

Q: Are all Three the same God?
A: Yes, for God is solely one. In such a way that the true, and necessary intelligence of this Most High Mystery consists not only in believing, that each of these three Divine persons is God, and all three the same God, but that one such Person is not one other; for these are distinct as Persons, as while God, the three are the same God.

Q: Which of the three Divine Persons was first?
A: Neither was the Person of the Father before the Son, nor the one of the Son before that of the Holy Spirit, but all three were *ab æterno*.

Q: Which is greater?
A: None: all three are equal; for the Father is not greater than the Son,

nor the Son greater than the Holy Spirit: rather they are equal, for the same power, knowledge, love, and everything else, which is in one of the Persons, is the same, which is in all three, except that one is not the other.

Q: Which one of these was made man?
A: The Son, and only the Son; and this Son of God made man, is Christ, whose Law we profess.

Q: The Eternal Father is Christ?
A: No; for the Father was not made man, and Christ is God, and Man; and for this same reason is Christ not the Holy Spirit; for the Holy Spirit was not made man, but solely Christ the Son of God the Father, who is the second Person of the Most Holy Trinity made man.

Q: Which is greater, the Eternal Father, or Christ?
A: Christ as God is the same God as the Father; as a Person he is equal to the Father, but distinct; and as a Man he is lesser than the Father; and the same can be said of Christ in regards to the Holy Spirit.

Q: Why do you believe this?
A: For God so said, and this is taught by the Holy Mother Roman Catholic Church.

Q: What thing is the Holy Roman Catholic Church?
A: All the Christians, whose head is the Pope; and what this true Church determines, to this we are all obliged to believe in.

Q: How many are the Articles of Faith?
R: They are fourteen, seven referring to the Divinity, and the other seven to the Humanity of Our Lord JESUS Christ.

Q: Which belong to the Divinity?
A: The following:
The first is to believe that there is solely one all-powerful God.
The second is to believe that he is the Father.
The third is to believe that he is the Son.
The fourth is to believe that he is the Holy Spirit.
The fifth is to believe that he is the Creator.
The sixth is to believe that he is the Saviour.
The seventh is to believe that he is the Glorifier.

Q: Which belong to the Humanity?
R: The ones that follow:
The first is to believe that Christ was conceived of the Holy Spirit.
The second is to believe that he was born of the always Virgin Mary.
The third is to believe that he was crucified, killed, and placed in the sepulchre.
The fourth is to believe that he descended to Limbo, and took out the souls of the Holy Fathers.
The fifth is to believe that on the third day he returned from among the dead.
The sixth is to believe that he rose to Heaven, and is seated at the right hand of God the Father almighty.

The seventh is to believe that he shall return to judge the living, and the dead, and that he shall give Glory unto the good, and Hell unto the wicked.

Q: And these Articles, are they not the same as contained in the Creed?
A: Yes: but the Creed is more intelligible, to know and understand these articles.

Q: And what is the Creed of the Holy Mother Church?
A: It is in the following form:

I believe in God the Father almighty, Creator of Heaven, and Earth : and in Jesus Christ, his only Son, our Lord, who was conceived by the Holy Spirit : born of the Virgin Mary : he suffered under Pontius Pilate : was crucified, died, and buried : descended to the Hells: on the third day he rose again from the dead : ascended onto heaven, and is seated at the right hand of God the Father almighty, from where he shall come again to judge the living and the dead. I believe in the Holy Spirit, the Holy Catholic Church: the communion of the Saints : the remission of sin : the resurrection of the body, and in the eternal life. Amen.

Q: What does it mean, I believe in the communion of the Saints?
A: That I should believe, that in the Church there are the Just, and virtuous, and that in all the good works that some do, all those in grace and in the friendship of God participate in.

Q: How do you understand the Article of the Remission of Sin?
A: That Christ left in his Church the remedy to forgive us of all kinds of sin through Grace, which is communicated to us, both by means of the Sacraments, in which he deposited worth, and the satisfaction of his precious blood, and also by means of the act of contrition, which is given to us as our aid. And among the Sacraments, of those which forgive sin, one is Baptism, meant for the original sin, and for the current ones committed before Baptism; and after this, Penitence for sins, which the baptized commit; and these remedies, and this grace is offered by God for the entirety of the time which this life lasts.

Q: What is contained in the Article of Resurrection of the body?
A: That all good, and bad men, shall resurrect at the end of the World, returning the souls to their bodies, which are then once again formed, being these individually the same, that in this life they had.

Q: What does the Article of Eternal Life mean?
A: That there is a life, which lasts forever after this life; the soul by itself is immortal; the bodies shall be as such after resurrection, however, the good shall have a glorious life, which is proper life; the wicked an eternity filled with such excessive penalties, that it might have been better that they had no life rather than that true death.

Q: How many are the Sacraments of the Catholic Church?
A: These are seven.

Q: Which are they?
A: Baptism, by which we become children of God, in his Grace, and heirs to Glory.
Confirmation, which fortifies us in Faith.
Communion, in which we receive the body of Christ, and the whole Christ as real, and true, as he is in Heaven. And one should mention, that the whole Christ is in every host, and in any part of the host, no matter how small.
Confession, in which repenting our guilt with a firm purpose of never again offending God, we confess these, becoming once again children of God; which we lose when we commit any mortal sin.
Extreme Unction, which is used at the time of death.
Orders, which is what the priests receive.
Matrimony, which is when, legitimately and without impediment, a man and a woman are married.

Q: What effects have these Sacraments?
A: All give Grace; in such a way that a Sacrament is a thing which offers us Grace, and makes us friends of God; and all Christians should know, that the Sacraments are the greatest gift, which Christ left to his Church, and the greatest possession it has for us.

Q: How many are the Theological Virtues?
A: These are three, Faith, Hope, and Charity.
Faith is to believe in what God has said, for He said it, and our Holy Roman Mother Church affirms it.
Hope is a sure trust in the mercy of God, which shall save me by the worth of Christ, but through me doing the part he thus orders.
Charity is to love God above all things, for being him who he is, infinitely good, and to my fellow man as myself, for the love of God; and he who does not have the three virtues, it is certain, that he shall not be saved.

Q: How are their acts performed?
A: The acts of these virtues, which should be done often in life, are in this form.

Act of Implicit Faith

I believe, Lord, in all which the Holy Roman Catholic Church believes and orders, for thou have thus taught, and she thus teaches.

Act of Explicit Faith

I believe, Lord, that thou art one single true God in three Persons truly distinct, Father, Son, and Holy Spirit, all three equal in attributes, and perfections, and all three the same Almighty God, who permeates the good with eternal Glory in Heaven, and punishes the wicked with eternal penalties in Hell. I believe that the second Person of the Holiest Trinity, which is the Son, was made man by work of the Holy Spirit in the most pure loins of the always Virgin Mary, and that he was born, suffered, and died to save us. All this I believe, and in all else which the Holy Mother Church orders me to believe, for thus thou taught, and it teaches.

Act of Hope

I have hope, my God, in thy mercy, that thou shall save me by the virtue of Christ, while I do my part.

Act of Charity

I love thee, my God, over all things, for being thou who thou art, infinitely good, and to my fellow man as myself for thy love.

Q: How many are the Commandments of the Law of God, which a Christian should keep?
A: These are ten. The first three belong to the honour of God; the other seven to the benefit of our fellow men.
The first is to honour one sole God.
The second is to not swear in his holy name in vain.
The third is to keep the Sunday, and the feasts.
The fourth is to honour your father, and your mother.
The fifth is to not kill.
The sixth is to not fornicate.
The seventh is to not steal.
The eight is to not raise false witness.
The ninth is to not desire the wife of your fellow man.
The tenth is not to covet another's possessions.
These ten Commandments are enclosed in two; these are good to know as, love God over all things, and your fellow as yourself.

Q: And how many, and which are, the Commandments of the Holy Mother Church, which a Christian is obliged to keep?
A: These are five.
The first is to listen to Mass in the proper days and feasts.
The second is to confess at least once per year.
The third is to commune in Easter of Resurrection.
The fourth is to fast every Lent, and in the further days, which along the year, the Church commands.
The fifth is to pay the tithe and tributes.

Q: Which are the sins, and vices, from which a Christian should be parted from?
A: From all, and particularly the seven, which are called capital, for being the origin, and root of others, and these are the following seven:
The first is pride. It is defined as a disorderly appetite for one's own excellence.
The second is greed. It is defined as a disorderly desire for wealth.
The third is lust. It is defined as a desire for foul and dishonest delights.
The fourth is wrath. It is defined as a disorderly desire for revenge against whom we think offended us.
The fifth is gluttony. It is defined as a disorderly desire to eat, and drink.

The sixth is envy. It is defined as a sadness over another's possessions, and a sorrow over another's happiness.
The seventh is sloth. It is defined as a weakness of heart for good works, and a tiredness from spiritual things.

Q: Which is the prayer, which Christ taught us to pray to God?
A: The one Christ our Lord gave us is that of the Our Father, and it is in the following form:
Our Father, Who art in heaven, hallowed be Thy Name, Thy kingdom come, Thy will be done on earth, as in heaven, give us this day our daily bread, and forgive us our debts, as we forgive those who owe us, and lead us not into temptation, but deliver us from all evil. Amen JESUS.

Q: Should a Christian also invoke, plead, and ask the Saints?
A: Yes; for these are of worth, and an aid to us before God with their prayers, and they reach from the Lord many favours for their devotees.

Q: And with which prayers is it more convenient to pray, and request to the Virgin Mary our Lady?
A: With the following of the Hail Mary, and the Salve Regina, which the Church has established in the following way:

Hail Mary full of grace : the Lord is with thee : blessed art thou among women : blessed is the fruit of thy womb JESUS. Holy Mary Mother of God, pray for us sinners now, and at the hour of our death. Amen.

Hail, Queen, Mother of Mercy : our life, sweetness, and hope : to thee do we cry poor banished children of Eve : to thee do we sigh, mourning and weeping in this vale of tears : be then our advocate, turn thine merciful eyes toward us : and after this our exile show unto us the blessed fruit of thy womb JESUS. O clement, O merciful, O always sweet Virgin MARY. Pray for us Holy Mother of God, so as we may be worthy of the promises of Christ. Amen.

Practical way of confessing, and communing

The penitent shall say the Confession until where it says, by my guilt, by my great guilt; and he shall further say when he finishes all his sin: As such I plead, and pray &c.

As experience shows the little knowledge, with which men confess themselves, and the little news, which one has of the necessary things for this, it seems proper to offer here a brief summary of such an important and necessary thing.

For a man to confess himself, he should take the convenient time to examine his conscience; and this time, more or less, with prudent judgment of the last time he confessed; this examination should be done by going through the Commandments of the Law of God and the Holy Mother Church, through the bad inclinations that each one has, through the states, and people, with whom one deals, considering in these instances if one sinned in thoughts, words, and works, counting, more or less, the times one has sinned.

After this examination a Christian should know that there are still two things to be done. First, have the act of attrition, or contrition; and to do this better, make one and the other, which is always advisable.

The act of attrition is to have pain for sins over the penalties of Hell, or by their lowliness, with a purpose of atonement; and this is done when a Christian says with his heart, or in his heart: *It weighs me all my sins by the penalties of Hell, and I firmly propose to atone.* Or: *It weighs on me all my sins by their lowliness, and I firmly propose to atone.* This act of attrition with a confession is enough to place one in Grace, but it is not enough without confession.

The act of contrition is pain that one has over sins, for these being offences to the infinitely good God, whom one loves above all things, with a purpose to atone; and this is done when a Christian says with his heart or in his heart: *My Lord Jesus Christ, God, and true Man, Creator, and my Redeemer, for being thou who thou art, and because I love thee over all things, my whole heart weighs for having offended thee, and I firmly propose to not offend thee anymore; and for the sins, which I have committed against thee, I ask forgiveness, and this I hope to reach by the worth of thy precious blood, and most holy Passion. Amen.*

But as not all will easily understand all of these words, know that their substance is summed up in the two things already mentioned, the pain of having offended the infinitely good, and lovable God, and the purpose of atonement, and all one has to say is: *Lord, it weight my heart for having offended thee, for being an infinitely good God, and because I love thee over all things, and I firmly propose myself to never offend thee again.* This act of contrition is not only enough with a confession, but it is also of worth without it, in order to place a soul in Grace, and have its sins forgiven, having the intention to confess them, as one should have the obligation to do so, later; and thus this act of contrition should be done by every Christian many times, mainly when going to bed, for morning may not come; and every time one feels mortal sin. O Blindness of those in the hour, or moment of mortal sin, condemned to eternal penalties, and in the hatred of God, when so easily, and with so little words said with one's heart, they may return to His divine grace!

After the above-mentioned act of attrition, or contrition is done, the second thing is to confess all your sins; and for this, before the feet of a Confessor, say the general confession in the following form:

I sinner confess myself to God almighty, the Blessed and always Virgin MARY, the Blessed Saint Michael the Archangel, the Blessed Saint John the Baptist, the Saintly Apostles Saint Peter, and Saint Paul, to all the Saints, and to thee Father, that I have sinned many times in thoughts, words, and deeds, and by my guilt, by my great guilt. As such I plead to the Blessed and always Virgin Mary, to the Blessed Saint Michael the Archangel, the Blessed Saint John the Baptist, to the Saintly Apostles, Saint Peter, and Saint Paul, and to all Saints, and to the Father, that thou plead for me to God our Lord.

Say then all your sins in the form in which you remembered them in your examination, and the more that might occur to you, hoping greatly for reverence of God, that no Christian should avoid confessing any sin, no matter how great; for the ill-founded, and unreasonably ill idea one has of Confessors has condemned many souls; and it is a great disgrace, that where a Christian should go to seek the forgiveness of his sins, for lack of confession of one of these, he will carry back the same which he took, and one further greater one of sacrilege, and thus the hatred of God condemns him to eternal penalties by communing with JESUS Christ our Redeemer in mortal sin. O blindness! O abomination!

Confessed thus all its sins with the above-mentioned disposition, a soul arrives pure, and righteous to the sacred Communion, to which one should go with living faith, and great respect with what in it is communed, which is the same Christ, as true, and real, as he is in the high Heavens; and after Communion for some time, considering with the greatest fervour, and withdrawal possible, your soul prostrated at the feet of JESUS Christ, which you have in your bosom, giving him infinite grace for such high benefits, ask then for forgiveness of your sins, and that he may conserve you in divine Grace. *Amen.*

First column for after confession

Here comes, Lord, this ungrateful son, who lost respect for thee many times in thy presence; here he is already raised, by the regret of guilt, to recognize thee as Father with a true penitence for seeing thee on that Cross, where thou wert placed by my sins, and on it I see thee nailed so as I may not be punished : and thus, Lord, I propose, already for the future, to never again offend thee, and may my tears, and sighs be the impediment for offence, since I have already offended thee, so as with them drown, in the immense sea of the multitude of thy mercies my faults, and kindle my will, so as to see what I did not see, and to know that it shall not need to extend itself more than that loving heart, where by union of thy Grace I wish to make my residence forever; for when thou wishes to seek me, knock on the doors of thy heart, and in it thou shall find me safe, firm, constant, and manifest, and we shall be two souls in one single body, with thou casting thy blessing, and absolution of my faults : so as, purified with the fire of thy Divine love, I may enjoy thee in that glory forever.

Second column

But, O my God, I still see thy heart being the occasion of greater excesses of blazes of love, for with such excess thou seeks me! The excessive love, that thou has for me, caused the excess of leaving thy Eternal Father, and thou wert made Man by thy love for me, being this absence the attraction for another greater excess, which thou worked for thy same love; for thy love growing ever more thou wert not satisfied in making thyself a Man for the love of men, for thou gave thy very life for the life of men, shedding thy precious Blood in the tree of the True Cross. O what love, and what excessive love is this my Good JESUS, and my Redeemer? O soul of mine, how does thou receive this excessive love? How does thou see the Blood running down the Body of Christ, to wash us, and purify our soul? O soul of mine, how does thou not burn in the flames of such a love in the Blood, which is boiling for our heart? How does thou show thyself, O soul of mine, so cold, that thou resembles snow, while Christ shows himself as an enflamed Vesuvius of love? For Lord, I am already in flames, my soul and my spirit is already kindling, I am already dying for thee, aid me, comfort me, console me, favour me, for I am so certain that I am dying for thee now at thy feet, that I shall not rise up from them without the sureness of thy forgiveness. Look, Lord, that it is still missing this forgiveness for this sinner, who contrite arrives at thy feet. For if thou did not hear me, when I offended thee, thou does not wish to hear me now when I know of my sin? For, Lord, I know, thou shall use thy mercy, for I have thy word, signed with thy precious Blood, that thou shall forgive me, when, contrite, and regretful, I arrive at thy feet, and with my tears, as did the regretting Magdalene, I wash thy feet. O sacred feet of my Lord JESUS Christ, who walked so much to prevent my twisted steps of sin, guide me to the path of salvation, so as I may direct my thoughts solely to God, my JESUS, my Redeemer, to love him, and place him in my heart; to stay with him until death, and from death revive and enjoy him for all centuries of centuries.

Third column

O Divine Spirit, come down to aggrandize this poor soul, ennoble this house with thy Divine presence, come with thy Divine Grace, as thou did the Queen of Heaven, when thou came down over her to incarnate in her virginal loins, enter into this tepid heart, so as it may become thy eternal residence, ablaze it in thy fiery love; for as thou are a God of love, thou shall inflame my heart, which is already thine from this sacramental union. Come Father of the poor, Light of the Souls, rest of the afflicted, and consolation of tears, handsome guest, sweet refreshment, do not delay thy steps any longer, come with full hurry; that my soul, as a deer who desires the springs, desires thee, as a spring of Grace, so as to enjoy thee eternally; for as thou comes loving, and thou picked my heart for thy residence, remedy it in all flaws, and defects; increase the disposition, which I should have towards thy sacred Passion, may I not be missing anything, which may make me lose the grace I seek, concede to me thy gifts, prepare me, as a palace of the Holiest Trinity, in which thy magnificence is sustained, come, come, that I am surrendered, and ablaze, come as the fire of the Divine love, and purify me with the fires of thy Divine Grace. Take me united to thy heart to those heights, where thou reigns, and shall reign for all centuries of centuries. *Amen.*

Act of grace, for after Communion

O soul of mine, be proud of such a Sovereign guest, from whom came such a great good! May God be eternally praised, who aggrandized my soul. My God, my Divine Husband, I surrender to thy Grace, and I offer this to thee infinitely for having selected thy great residence in this poor heart; but now, that I am ennobled, for having thee inside my heart, and I shall never let thee go, and secure that I am as such, from this day forth I shall never not deserve thy presence; for I am so firm with it, that no matter how much the stars, the elements, the flowers, the beasts, the fish, the earth, and the creature may arm themselves against me to fall into sin, I say, and one thousand times I claim, that easier would it be for the Heavens and the Stars to fall, than I to fall into any other sin; for if the earth, before I united myself with thee, being in mortal sin, for thy mercy, and compassion did not swallow me; for if the beasts did not devour me; if the air did not consume me, if the fire did not burn me; if the other living creatures did me no harm; now, having thee at my side, what can they possibly do? What more can I fear? Now, that I enter to thank thee this mercy, and this forgiveness, and I shall have no other coldness, and care, besides that of knowing how to conserve, and contract a deal with thee, and a contract of society, and company, and we may be armed with arrows, and weapons of love; and as thou art with thy side open, and thy heart pierced, and also, so as to become two souls in a single body, I am with my heart pierced, and when thou wishes, seek me in thy heart, that I shall always be at thy side, inside thy Heart, and in it thou shall find me: for what shall I now fear, but seeing that door open, to enter secure through that my Heart, mine in all titles : mine, for thou art my Father, my Saviour, my JESUS, my Redeemer; mine, for thou suffered for me; mine, for thou redeemed me with thy precious Blood; mine, for thou gave thy Body, and Blood as true food, and drink; mine, by the title of filiation; mine, for on the Cross thou redeemed me; mine, because thou forgave me, because thou gave me life, and being; thou are entirely mine, and I am entirely thine, and from this point I shall never part : and as I am already in the possession of this Treasure, I only ask thee that thou gives me true knowledge for my regret, firmness, and constancy to establish in my chest a Temple, and in my Heart a Monstrance, so as thou may make in it a residence, enriching it with the treasure of Divine Grace, in which thou lives, and reigns for all centuries of centuries. *Amen.*

It is the work of an Angel to aid in Mass, and thus fathers, and masters should take care to teach this, and for this reason is supplied the customary method. Any young boy, or man, who aids in Mass, should first check if the casters have wine and water, and he shall prepare everything, and the bell, and he should aid Mass with all devotion, and infallibly they shall have, or place, their hands as the Priest has them, as this is the ways Our Lady of Immaculate Conception has them, and they shall not respond to anything without the Priest being done speaking, and whoever is hearing, he should be with both knees on the earth, and do not pray in such a way as with your lips you may bother the Priest.

Way of aiding Mass according to the Roman Church

Priest: Introibo ad altare Dei.

Minister: Ad Deum, qui lætificat juventutem meam.

P: Judica me Deus, & discerne causam meam de gente non sancta : ab homine iniquo, & doloso erue me.

M: Quia tu es Deus fortitudo mea : quare me repulisti, & quare tristis incedo, dum affligit me inimicus.

P: Emitte lucem tuam, & veritatem tuam : ipsa me deduxerunt, & adduxerunt in montem sanctum tuum, & in tabernacula tua.

M: Et introibo ad altare Dei, ad Deum, qui lætificat juventutem meam.

P: Confitebor tibi in cithara Deus Deus meus : quare tristis est anima mea? & quare conturbas me?

M: Spera in Deo, quoniam adhuc confitebor illi : salutare vultus mei, & Deus meus.

P: Gloria Patri, & Filio, & Spiritui Sancto.

M: Sicut erat in principio, & nunc, & semper, & in sæcula sæculorum. Amen.

P: Introibo ad altere Dei.

M: Ad Deum, qui lætificat juventutem meam.

P: Adjutorium nostrum in nomine Domini.

M: Qui fecit cœlum, & terram.

P: Confiteor Deo omnipotenti, beatae Mariae semper Virgini, beato Michaeli Archangelo, beato Ioanni Baptistae, sanctis Apostolis Petro et Paulo, et omnibus Sanctis, quia peccavi nimis cogitatione, verbo et opere: mea culpa, mea culpa, mea maxima culpa. Ideo precor beatam Mariam semper Virginem, beatum Michaelem Archangelum, beatum Ioannem Baptistam, sanctos Apostolos Petrum et Paulum, et omnes Sanctos, orare pro me ad Dominum Deum nostrum. Amen.

M: Misereatur tui omnipotens Deus, & dimissis peccatis tuis, perducat te ad vitam æternam.

P: Amen.

Minister: Confiteor Deo omnipotenti, beatæ Mariæ semper Virgini, beato Michæli Archangelo, beato Joanni Baptistæ, Sanctis Apostolis Petro, & Paulo, omnibus Sanctis, & tibi Pater, quia peccavi nimis cogitatione, verbo, & opere, mea culpa, mea culpa, mea maxima culpa. Ideo precor beatam Mariam sempre Virginem, beatum Michælem Archangelum, beatum Joannem Baptistam, Sanctos Apostolos Petrum, & Paulum, omnes Sanctos, & te Pater orare pro me ad Dominum Deum nostrum.

P: Misereatur vestri omnipotens Deus, & dimissis peccatis vestris perducat vos ad vitam æternam.

M: Amen.

P: Indulgentiam, absolutionem, & remissionem peccatorum nostrorum tribuar nobis omnipotens, & misericors Dominus.

M: Amen.

P: Deus tu conversus vivificabis nos.

M: Et plebs tua lætabitur in te.

P: Ostende nobis Domine misericordiam tuam.

M: Et salutare tuum da nobis.

P: Domine exaudi orationem meam.

M: Et clamor meus ad te veniat.

P: Dominus vobisum.

M: Et cum spiritu tuo.

P: Kyrie eleison.

M: Kyrie eleison.

P: Kyrie eleison.

M: Christe eleison.

P: Christe eleison.

M: Christe eleison.

P: Kyrie eleison.

M: Kyrie eleison.

P: Kyrie eleison.

P: Dominus vobiscum

M: Et cum spiritu tuo.

P: Per omnia sæcula sæculorum.

M: Amen.

Once finished the Epistle the Minister responds.

M: Deo gratias.

P: Dominus vobiscum.

M: Et cum spiritus tuo.

P: Sequentia Sancti Evangelii &c.[104]

M: Gloria tibi Domine.

Finishing the Gospel, the Minister responds.

M: Laus tibi Christe

P: Orate frates.

M: Suscipiat Dominus sacrificium de manibus tuis ad laudem, & gloriam nominis sui, ad utilitatem quoque nostram, totiusque Ecclesiæ suæ sanctæ.

P: Amen.

P: Per omnia sæcula sæculorum.

M: Amen.

P: Dominus vobiscum.

M: Et cum spiritu tuo.

P: Sursum corda.

104 Translator's note: usually this is an indication to read the opening of one of the Gospels. The most typical is the Gospel of John, up until vesicle 14 (*et Verbum caro factum est et habitavit in nobis et vidimus gloriam eius gloriam quasi unigeniti a Patre plenum gratiae et veritatis*).

M: Habemus ad Dominum.
P: Gratias agamus Domino Deo nostro.
M: Dignum, & justum est.
P: Per omnia sæcula sæculorum.
M: Amen.
P: Et ne nos inducas in tentationem.
M: Sed libera nos à malo.
P: Pax Domini sit sempre vobiscum.
M: Et cum spiritu tuo.
P: Ite, missa est, ou Benedicamus Domino.
M: Deo gratias.
P: Requiescant in pace.
M: Amen.
P: Á porta inferi.
M: Erue Domine animas eorum.
P: Requiem æternam dona eis Domine.
M: Et lux perpetua luceat eis.

Way of aiding Mass according to the Order of Carmel

P: Consitemini Domino, quoniam bonus.

M: Quoniam in sæculum misericordia ejus.

P: Confiteor Deo omnipotenti, beatæ Mariæ semper Virgini, beato Michæli Archangelo, beato Joanni Baptistæ, Sanctis Apostolis Petro, & Paulo, omnibus Sanctis, & tibi Pater, quia peccavi nimis cogitatione, verbo, & opere, mea culpa, mea culpa, mea maxima culpa. Ideo precor beatam Mariam sempre Virginem, beatum Michælem Archangelum, beatum Joannem Baptistam, Sanctos Apostolos Petrum, & Paulum, omnes Sanctos, & te Pater orare pro me ad Dominum Deum nostrum. Amen.

M: Misereatur tui omnipotens Deus, & dimittat tibi omnia peccata tua, liberet te ab omni malo, conservet te, & confirmet omni opere bono, & perducat ad vitam æternam.

P: Amen.

Minister: Confiteor Deo omnipotenti, beatæ Mariæ semper Virgini, omnibus Sanctis, & tibi Pater, quia peccavi nimis congitatione, locutione, opere, & omissione, mea culpa. Ideo precor beatam Mariam simper Virginem, omnes, Sanctos, & te Pater orare pro me ad Dominum Jesum Christum.

P: Misereatur tui omnipotens Deus, et dimissis peccatis tuis, perducat te ad vitam aeternam.

M: Amen.

P: Indulgentiam, ✠ absolutionem, et remissionem peccatorum nostrorum, tribuat nobis omnipotens et misericors Dominus.

M: Amen.

P: Adiutorium nostrum in nomine Domini.

M: Qui fecit cœlum, & terram.

And the responses are similar to the ones of the Roman Mass, except when one responds to the *Orare fratres*, and it is in this way:

P: Orare fratres.

M: Memor sit Dominus omnis sacrificii tui, holocastum tuum pingue fiat, tribuat tibi secundum cor tuum, & omne consilium tuum confirmet.

Right at the beginning of the Mass one prepares the chalice, and the Minister shall give the casters to the Priest, and when offering the water, the Minister says, *Benedicite*, and the Priest, giving him a blessing, responds. *Amen.*

Mass in the way of the Order of St. Dominic

P: Consitemini Domino, quoniam bonus.

M: Quoniam in sæculum misericordia ejus.

P: Confiteor Deo omnipotenti, beatæ Mariæ semper Virgini, beato Michæli Archangelo, beato Joanni Baptistæ, Sanctis Apostolis Petro, & Paulo, omnibus Sanctis, & tibi Pater, quia peccavi nimis cogitatione, verbo, & opere, mea culpa, mea culpa, mea maxima culpa. Ideo precor beatam Mariam sempre Virginem, beatum Michælem Archangelum, beatum Joannem Baptistam, Sanctos Apostolos Petrum, & Paulum, omnes Sanctos, & te Pater orare pro me ad Dominum Deum nostrum. Amen.

M: Misereatur tui omnipotens Deus, & dimittat tibi omnia peccata tua liberet te ab omni malo, conservet, & confirmet in omni opere bono, & perducat ad vitam æternam.

P: Amen.

Minister: Consiteor Deo omnipotenti, & beatæ Mariæ semper Virgini, & beato Dominico Patri nostro, & omnibus Sanctis, & tibi pater, quia peccavi nimis cogitatione, locutione, opere, & omissione mea culpa, precor te orare pro me.

P: Misereatur tui omnipotens Deus, et dimissis peccatis tuis, perducat te ad vitam aeternam.

M: Amen.

P: Indulgentiam, ✠ absolutionem, et remissionem peccatorum nostrorum, tribuat nobis omnipotens et misericors Dominus.

M: Amen.

P: Adjutorium nostrum in nomine Domini.

M: Qui fecit cœlum, & terram.

At the *Orate fratres* one does not respond, but in responding to the *Pax Domini &c* he should take the paten with the veil of the chalice, without touching it with his hand, and offer it to the Priest to kiss, who shall say: *Pax tibi.* And the Minister responds*: Et cum spiritu tuo.*

Prayers for the day

EXERCISE FOR THE MORNING

As soon as the creature awakes, immediately raise your heart to God, bless yourself, and pray three Hail Marys to the Holiest Hearts of Jesus, Mary, and Joseph, offering your heart to these Hearts, so as to assist this day united with them. Then say the following.

Prayer

I offer thee grace, Lord, for this time in life, which thou concedes to me: by the worth of thy beloved Son, and intercession of his Holiest Mother I ask thee to give me the grace to perfectly love thee, and my fellow man.

For when you rise

In the name of the Father, and the Son, and the Holy Spirit I rise, and I give thee great grace, Lord, for having preserved me with health to see the light of day, in which I may praise thee, and give thee grace for all the benefits I have received. I ask thee with humility, and with the devotion of my soul, that thou concedes to me thy holy grace, so as I may employ my thoughts, desires, words, and deed on this present day in the honour, and glory of thy Divine Majesty, and in the same way, for thy Divine clemency, and thy mercy, I may be guided by the Holy Angel of my Guard in the path of true Faith with love, and perfection, and my works may shine before thee for all days of my life. *Amen.*

Our Father, Hail Mary.

For when you dress

Dress me Lord, as a new man, so as I may live in sanctity, justice and truth. Cover my nakedness so as I may be humble, and honest, I ask that thy kindness bless, and defend me.

Afterwards make these Prayers to Our Lady, to which are many Indulgences conceded.

Blessed be, O Holiest Virgin Mary, Mother of God, Queen of Heaven, Door of Paradise, and Lady of the entire world. Thou art the singular Virgin. Thou art the only one conceived without original sin. Thou art that pure Virgin, who conceived Jesus Christ without stain by the Holy Spirit. Thou art the only Virgin, and chosen Mother, who birthed the Creator, and Saviour of the world. As such I ask thee to pray for me to Jesus Christ thy beloved Son, and our Lord, so as to free me from all evil. *Amen.*

Blessed be the Holy, and Immaculate Conception of the Blessed Virgin Mary. God save thee Daughter of God the Father, God save thee Mother of God the Son, God save thee Wife of God the Holy Spirit.

Our Father, Hail Mary.

Prayer of the Guardian Angel

O Glorious Angel, guardian of my soul, who from the Celestial Hierarchy thou wert given for my defense, I humbly, and devoutly ask thee to free and defend me from the adversary's cunning, and from the claws of the enemies of my soul, enlighten me on the path of salvation, and defend me from all dangers, and disasters, which may happen on this day, for thou has me in thy care. *Amen.*

Our Father, Hail Mary.

Protestation of Faith

I believe in God the Father, I believe in God the Son, I believe in God the Holy Spirit, I believe in the Mystery of the Holiest Trinity, and in all of which the Holy Catholic Church believes and teaches, for God has thus said, and revealed. I wish, my God, to have loved thee, and to love thee now, and for all moments of eternity, and that all men, and Angels love thee, if such is possible, as thou loves thyself. Cast onto us, Lord, thy blessing, and may this be from the Father, the Son, and the Holy Spirit. Amen Jesus.

For when you wash yourself

I very well know, Lord, that thou has washed the guilt from my soul with thy precious blood, and I waste this benefit, for I have offended thee so many times. I ask thee, my Lord Jesus Christ, that as I wash my body, thou washes me in the fountain of thy Divine grace, so as being clean, and pure I may serve, and love thee. *Amen.*

For when you leave your home

My God, place before my soul thy Holy Commandments, and councils, and govern my thoughts, words, and deeds in thy holy service. *Amen.*

When entering Church

I shall enter, Lord, into thy Holy Church, and I shall worship thee with fear, and reverence in thy Holy Temple, and I shall glorify thy Holy Name. Aid me my God, so as my supplication may not be unworthy of fulfilment for being shy, and weak. *Amen.*

For when you take the holy water

May this holy water be my spiritual health, and life, and through it may all my venial sins be forgiven. *Amen.*

EXERCISES FOR ANY TIME

At the start of any work

I ask thee, Lord, that thou anticipate with thy grace this work, and in it thou teaches, and aids me, so as all I may do I may start and end it for thee, and for thy greater glory. *Amen.*

For after it is finished

Receive, most clement Lord, this small service : and that which I have done right, see with benignity; and that which is wrong forgive me with pity, and mercy. *Amen.*

For before eating

Us, and that which each of us shall eat, may it be blessed by the Trine and Single God, Father, Son and Holy Spirit.

Here one should keep three things: Courtesy in sitting, in speaking, and temperance in eating, and patience in the error of the meal.

For after eating

Infinite grace, and infinite praise I give thee, my Lord Jesus Christ, for all the blessings, which from thy liberal hand I have received, and may all be in thy holy service, and the salvation of my soul. *Amen.*

Our Father, Hail Mary for the Souls.

For when the clock marks the hours

Praised be the hour, in which my Lord Jesus Christ incarnated, was born, died, resuscitated, raised to Heaven, and instituted the Holiest Sacrament of the Altar. My God, have mercy on my soul now, and in the hour of my death. *Amen.*

Before this Prayer one should pray one Hail Mary so as to earn one hundred days of Indulgences, which were conceded by reigning Pope Benedict XIV, and in praying it, or a Gloria Patri, when it marks the quarters, further fifty days. Afterwards one should say the following, which carries a great deal of Indulgences.

Blessed, and praised be the Holy, and Immaculate Conception of the Blessed Virgin Mary. God save thee Daughter of God the Father, God save thee Mother of God the Son, God save thee Wife of God the Holy Spirit. *Our Father, Hail Mary.*

For the ring of the Hail Mary[105]

Angelus Domini nuntiavit Mariæ, & concepit de Spiritu Sancto. *Ave Maria.*

Ecce ancilla Domini, fiat Mihi secundum verbum tuum. *Ave Maria.*

Et Verbum caro factum est, & habitavit in nobis. *Ave Maria.*

Prayer

Gratiam tuam, quæsumus, Domine, mentibus nostris infunde; ut qui, Angelo nuntiante, Christi Filii tui incarnationem cognovimus, per passionem eius et crucem, ad resurrectionis gloriam perducamur. Per eundem Christum Dominum nostrum. *Amen.*[106]

For those who don't know Latin

The Angel of the Lord announced to Mary, and conceived of the Holy Spirit. *Hail Mary.*

Here is the servant of the Lord, be it done unto me according to thy word. *Hail Mary.*

The Son of God was made man, and lived among us. *Hail Mary.*

Offering

I plead to thee, Lord, for all which I am obliged to ask thee, according to the intention of the Pontiff, when he conceded this Indulgence, which I intend to earn.

Examination of conscience for the evening

Having prepared the bed, place yourself on your knees, and going through the Commandments make an examination of your conscience, asking yourself for justification for what you laboured on that day, of the good you did not do, and the great deal you offended God in thoughts, words, and deeds. Make then a feverous Act of Contrition with great pain over your sins, and take some penitence, or mortification, such as placing your arms as a cross, or something similar. Immediately consider the great deal which Christ suffered for his love, and keep watch so as not to fall into mortal sin, for the judgment of God is hidden; and many who have thus laid in bed have risen in Hell.

105 Translator's note: 6 a.m. and 6 p.m., also called the hour of the Trinities.

106 Translator's note: this section is part of the 'Angelus' prayer, used in the 6 a.m., 12 noon, and 6 p.m. prayers.

For when you undress

My Lord Jesus Christ, who died on the Cross undressed : as I undress the vestments of the body, I ask thee to also undress me of bad habits, and stains on my soul, so as I may die with thee on the cross of mortification, and may enjoy the Blessedness in eternity among the chosen. *Amen.*

Our Father, Hail Mary for the souls of your dead, and also order yourself a great deal to Our Lady, so as she may free us from lowly dreams, to the Angel of your guard, and the saint of your name; and finally, laying down with honesty, consider the hard bed of the Cross, which was that of Christ, and in this way sleep.

Devotions to Our Lady

NOVENA OF THE LADY OF THE ROCK

PREPARATIONS

For every day before the start of the Novena.

FIRST DAY

Open, Lord, my mouth so as to praise thee, and to increase thy holy name: purify also my heart of all evil, perverse, and foreign thoughts, enlighten my understanding, inflame my will, so as being worthy, alert, and devout I may do this exercise, and be worthy of being heard before the presence of thy divine Majesty. For Christ our Lord. *Amen.*

Invocation to the Holy Spirit

Hymn

Come Creator Spirit,
To visit our souls,
And the hearts thou has created,
Fill them with Divine grace.
Thou art the celestial consoler,
Gift of God, most clear fountain,
Ardent fire, and charity,
Mystical sacrosanct anointment.
Thou art Lord of seven gifts,
And of the dexter sovereignty
Of the Father thou art the finger, and promise,
That thou offers precious words.
Kindle our senses
In thy loving flame
And to our weakness give
Virtue, that it may become strong.
Rout our enemies
Giving us the desired peace,
That in being our guide,
May no harm threaten us.
Through thee, the Father, and the Son

Our faith knows, and exalts,
Confessing that of both thou art
The uncreated aspiration.
Glory to the Father, and glory to the Son,
Who beats and breaks death,
And to thee Holy Spirit,
Be it eternally given. Amen.
℣Send Lord thy Creating Spirit.
℟And thou shall renew the face of the earth.

Prayer

God, thou who taught the hearts of the faithful with the illumination of the Holy Spirit, concede that we may know what is fair, and good, with the favour of the same Spirit, and always have the pleasure of his consolation. *Amen.*

Immediately one should sing, or say the following LITANY:

Kyrie eleison.
Christe eleison.
Kyrie eleison.
Christe audi nos.
Christe exaudi nos.

Pater de Cœlis Deus,	Miserere nobis.
Fili Redemptor mundi Deus,	Miserere nobis.
Spiritus Sancte Deus,	Miserere nobis.
Sancta Trinitas unus Deus,	Miserere nobis
Sancta MARIA,	Ora pro nobis.
Sancta Dei Genitrix.	Ora.
Sancta Virgo virginum,	Ora.
Mater Christi,	Ora.
Mater divina gratiæ,	Ora.
Mater purissima,	Ora.
Mater castissima,	Ora.
Mater inviolata,	Ora.
Mater intemerata,	Ora.
Mater amabilis,	Ora.
Mater Creatoris,	Ora.
Mater Salvatoris.	Ora.
Virgo prudentissima,	Ora.
Virgo veneranda,	Ora.
Virgo prædicanda,	Ora.
Virgo potens,	Ora.
Virgo clemens,	Ora.
Virgo fidelis,	Ora.
Speculum justitiæ,	Ora.
Sedes sapientiæ,	Ora.
Causa nostræ lætitaæ,	Ora.
Vas spirituale,	Ora.

Vas honourabile, Ora.
Vas insigne devotionis, Ora.
Rosa mystica, Ora.
Turris Davidica, Ora.
Turris eburnea, Ora.
Domus aurea, Ora.
Fœderis arca, Ora.
Janua Cœli, Ora.
Stella matutina, Ora.
Salus infirmorum, Ora.
Refugium peccatorum, Ora.
Consolatrix afflictorum, Ora.
Auxilium Christianorum, Ora.
Regina Angelorum, Ora.
Regina Patriarcharum, Ora.
Regina Prophetarum, Ora.
Regina Apostolorum, Ora.
Regina Martyrum, Ora.
Regina Confessorum, Ora.
Regina Virginum, Ora.
Regina Sanctorum omnium, Ora.
Regina sacratissimi Rosarii, Ora.
Agnus Dei, qui tollis peccata mundi Parce nobis Domine.
Agnus Dei, qui tollis peccata mundi Exaudi nos Domine.
Agnus Dei, qui tollis peccata mundi Miserere nobis.

Oremus

Gratiam tuam, quæsumus, Domine, mentibus nostris infunde, ut qui Angelo nuntiante, Christi Filii tui incarnationem cognovimus, per passionem ejus, & Crucem, ad resurrectionis gloriam perducamur. Per eundem Christum Dominum nostrum.

℟Amen.

Antiphon

OF OUR LADY

To thy favour, and presidency we call upon, Most Holy Mother of God, do not despise our pleas, which we make to thee in necessity; but free us from all dangers, glorious, and blessed Virgin.

℣Plead for us, Virgin Mother of God.

℟So as to be worthy of the promises of Christ.

Prayer

Infuse, Lord, thy grace into our souls, so as those of us who confess the incarnation of thy Son by the Annunciation of the Angel, by the Passion, and Cross of the same Christ may reach the glory of Resurrection. By the same Christ our Lord. *Amen.*

Antiphon

Tota pulchra es, Maria, & macula originalis non est in te. Tu gloria Jerusalem, Tu lætitia Israel, tu honourificentia populi nostri. Tu advocata peccatorum. Ó Maria, Virgo prudentissima, Mater Clementissima, Ora pro nobis. Intercede pro nobis ad Dominum Jesum Christum.

℣In conception tua, Virgo, immaculate fuisti.
℟Ora pro nobis Patrem, cujus Filium peperisti.

Oremus

Deus, qui per immaculatam Virginis Conceptionem dignum Filio tuo habitaculum præparasti : quæsumus, ut qui ex morte ejusdem Filii tui prævisa, eam ab omni labe præservasti, nos quoque mundos, ejus intercessione ad te pervenire concedas. Per eundem Christum Dominum nostrum.

℟Amen.

ACT OF LOVE OF GOD

My God, and Lord crucified on the cross, where for my disillusion I have come to seek thee so as not to have further excuse from my guilt, for seeing thee in that trunk covered in wounds, where, even after death thou gave the last drop of thy blood for the redemption of my sins, what should I say, except, that I come today with a most firm purpose of not offending thee further; already with the knowledge of the greatness, that for me thou has worked, I have no further recourse, but to repent : this I want, Lord, with the knowledge of the worth of thy sacred Passion to brand in my heart, and thus, Lord, I wish to, by all means, hold thee as my guard, and guide to my salvation, and in this way I come to ask for thy forgiveness by that crown of thorns, by those nails, by that spear, and by those wounds, and by that precious blood, by these ropes, so as with them tie and bind my heart, and my attention, my sighs, my thoughts so as to place them on this Cross, and in that loving heart, shouting, and asking for thy mercy. *Amen.*

Immediately after one should say nine Our Fathers, and nine Hail Marys, and a Gloria Patri, and the following Jaculatoria

Jaculatoria

O Most Holy Virgin of the Rock
Joachim, Anne, and Joseph,
I give thee my heart,
And my soul.

Antiphon

O how beautiful thou art, O how ennobled, and loved among the delights! Thy stature is similar to the palm, thy bosoms to the bundles, thy head to the Carmel, thy neck as an ivory tower.

℣Plead for us, Virgin Mother of the Rock.
℟So as we may be worthy of the promises of Christ.

Prayer

My Lord Jesus Christ, who with admirable providence wished that the Sacred image of thy Most Holy Mother of the Rock should be conserved free from the Saracens; and that after these had been expelled, this would miraculously appear for the benefit of the faithful, who may use this power, and suffrage : make it so, that our hearts enflamed in devoted affections, and our souls free from all enemies, we may appear purified in thy divine presence so as to be able to intuitively see in Heaven the most pure original of such a miraculous copy, and so as to enjoy the happiness of Blessedness, where with thy Eternal Father, and with the Holy Spirit, thou lives, and reigns forever without end. *Amen.*

Supplication of the Most Holy Mary

Sovereign Empress of Heaven, and earth, Queen of the Angels, Most Pure Mother of God, and Most Clement Mother of Sinners, ineffable Temple of the Holiest Trinity, joy of the Just, consoler of the afflicted, Succour of the abandoned, and Lady of the Rock, it is time, Lady, by the purest cleanliness of thy body, by the multitude of thy degrees of grace, and almost infinity of gifts, which ennoble, and adorn thy blessed soul, that we humbly ask with tears at thy feet, that by the life, which thou had as a mirror for thy true devotees and the Just, and by the incomprehensible dignity of being the Mother of God, by the glory, which thou enjoys among the courtesans of Heaven, and by the three hundred years, in which thou were hidden in a Rock because the Moors had taken Spain, and Portugal, after being restored by the Christians, thou miraculously appeared among some mountains, I ask thee to aid me with thy powerful patronage, so as I may resist with strength, and constancy the attacks of the Devil, and mainly his constant temptations, so as I may take the fruits I so desire from this Novena, I may achieve by means of thy patronage the following of my petition, (*make your petition here if you so wish*) and may I have saintly thoughts, and make saintly deeds, without concerning myself with earthly and transient things; but rather only consider the celestial things for greater honour, and glory of thy blessed Son, so as in thy, and his company we may rejoice in the company of the Angels for all centuries of centuries. *Amen.*

Offering

O Sovereign Lady of the Rock precursor of the eternal, and divine Son, high dome of Heaven, and strong wall against all of Hell, mirror of the divine grace, example of humility : I, with great affection offer thee these nine Our Fathers, and nine Hail Marys, and a Gloria Patri in honour of the nine months, in which in thy virginal womb thou carried thy greatly beloved Son, so as he may be swayed to accept these our supplications, directed for the goodness of the souls, and of all peoples, who praise thee by singing the Rosary,[107] accept Most Holy Mary our clamorous echoes, so as these may reach the presence of thy precious Son, that he may cast us his blessing, and may we rejoice, and reign in thy, and his company. *Amen.*

SECOND DAY

Everything as on the first day, and one says the Acts of Love of God below as was said on the first day.

ACT OF LOVE OF GOD

Most wounded Lord of my heart, here I come a second time to thy sacred feet all embarrassed to see my looseness in those prisons of thy arms, and sacred feet; thou with such despise nailed on that Cross, and me, which such confidence, and audacity loose in my vanities, and temporalities of the world : now I know that I have despised thy blood; then Lord allow that now that I know the ill, which I have done, and I come firm, and constant, offering my back to the world, and my soul, heart, and life to thy love, may I from this day forth feel such sweetness in my soul, that by this being from thee, may it live for thee, the heart, which is only meant to love thee, may it only love thee, the life, which is solely for thee, may it walk towards thee, let my mouth only praise thee, my tongue only praise thee, my thoughts only praise thee, my senses only praise thee, my deeds only praise thee, for these my heart, soul, life, mouth, tongue, thoughts, and senses, which shall praise thee, should not look upon the world anymore, and thus already trusting in thy wounds, and in thy divine grace do I ask for mercy. *Amen.*

Immediately after one shall say the nine Our Fathers, and nine Hail Marys as above, until the end of the Novena, as on the first day.

THIRD DAY

Everything as on the first day, except the Act of love of God.

ACT OF LOVE OF GOD

Most beloved Lord, a third time I come to ask thee to not despise my supplications; for all of these are directed to thy wounds, to where I come as a thirsty deer to quench my soul, asking forgiveness for my faults, trusting in thy divine mercy I shall bathe in the perennial fountain of thy grace, and find the right path for my tears, for my sailing in the goodness of my repentance, I know that thou as Father, and fountain of grace, shall not leave me on a dry dock, nor despise the torrent of my sighs. Behold, Lord, that I seek thee as a son after having lived so long away from thee (should life even be possible without thee) and I confess my guilt, and

107 Translator's note: the Portuguese word used here stands as *Terço*, technically this is one third of a full Rosary, or in other words, five mysteries, or one single turn around the Rosary beads.

drown my sins in the sea of my tears; for I immediately confess, Lord, that I am not worthy of calling myself thy son, however, Lord, thou did not cease to be a loving Father, for I know that thou shall receive me with festivities for seeking thee confessing my crimes, and for having lived outside of thee, and of thy grace, and from this day forth I shall only wish to live in thy company; contrite, and repented I ask from thy sacred passion for forgiveness from my faults, and mercy for my tears, and sighs. *Amen.*

Immediately say the nine Our Fathers, and nine Hail Marys of above until the end.

FOURTH DAY

Everything as on the first day, except the Act of love of God.

ACT OF LOVE OF GOD

Most beloved Lord, a fourth time this great sinner comes to thy sovereign feet crying tears without end over his faults, and he shall not rise without the security of absolution from his enormous sins, for he is already confessing them with all his heart, his tears testifying his repentance, and thus, Lord, I am he, who countless times has tasted thy wrath, living lost as a stray sheep from thy flock, submerged in the mouth of the infernal wolf, without fearing the horrors of Hell, nor loving thy kindness, for this is so immense, that I now know that thou wishes to save me for having conserved my life; perhaps, Lord, it is this knowledge that, from this day forth, makes me not have another care, nor another distraction, than that of thy love, and in it with thy divine grace I shall only employ my care, and wakefulness to be able to ask for thy mercy. *Amen.*

Immediately one shall say the nine Our Fathers, and the nine Hail Marys as above until the end.

FIFTH DAY

Everything as on the first day, except the Act of love of God.

ACT OF LOVE OF GOD

Beloved Lord of my soul, and love of my heart, here comes for the fifth time to refine this love, and true propose this so weakened soul, of which thou knows, Lord; for it comes with constant, and firm spirit of not offending thee further, repented, and contrite, one, and many times for its most enormous sins, he comes Lord, entirely penetrated by the pain of his faults with a most firm purpose of never offending thee again, and thus Lord as he comes humbled, and contrite do not despise his heart, but rather remember that in it thou may enter, and that from thy own heart shed so much blood; do not allow the preciousness of thy blood to go to waste, so as he may from this day forth reform his life with boredom towards mundane things, and only aspire to the celestial so as to praise thee eternally, coming forth thou with thy mercy. *Amen.*

Immediately one shall say the nine Our Fathers, and the nine Hail Marys as above until the end of the first day.

SIXTH DAY

Everything as on the first day, except the Act of love of God.

ACT OF LOVE OF GOD

My Lord Jesus Christ, God, and true Man, for being thou who thou art, worthy of being loved, does this sinner come to thy presence a sixth time already with all his heart, with all his soul, and with all his strength crying his crimes, and his guilt, confessing that with all his heart, and all his soul, and all his strength he has offended thee, because Lord, since I learned the way in which I have offended thee, I cannot have an excuse from this day forth, if as a miserable sinner I have offended thee, which thou does not permit, and it weighs in the core of my heart one, and a thousand times having offended thee from the moment in which I started sinning until this one, have compassion of this such weak soul, who comes to seek its remedy in the antidote of thy precious blood, offer thy arm to this fallen one, who wishes to rise up from the twisted steps of his sins, heal me Lord, so as I may, strengthened by thy smooth medicine, and strengthened in my entire heart, and in my entire soul, and with all my strength, ask for mercy. *Amen.*

Immediately one shall say the nine Our Fathers, and the nine Hail Marys as above until the end of the first day.

SEVENTH DAY

Everything as on the first day, except the Act of love of God.

ACT OF LOVE OF GOD

Most merciful Lord of my heart, the time has come, for the seventh time, for this unworthy soldier to approach thee, who ripped thy most beloved heart, but trusting in thy mercy, and in the greatest certainty of his repentance, insults his sins so as not to have further occasion to seek them out, for already knowing, Lord, that thou should only be sought for being the true love, and with it thou calls forth all sinners : then, Lord, here is the greatest of them all by thy sacred feet, confessing his crimes, and hearing from thy wounds the clamorous echoes, with which thou is calling; thy voice penetrate my heart, then Lord, rend, and rip, Lord, open Lord my heart, enter into it, so as in it I may find, worship, and adore thee in such a way, that I may never let thee go, and being always united with thee we become two souls in one single body, or make my heart into pieces, and may it be united with thine in such a way that it becomes identical by means of the union of thy love, so as I may ask, and reach thy mercy. *Amen.*

Immediately one shall say the nine Our Fathers, and the nine Hail Marys as above until the end of the first day.

EIGHTH DAY

Everything as on the first day, except the Act of love of God.

ACT OF LOVE OF GOD

Most clement Lord, and merciful love of my insides, here lies for the eighth time thy son already confounded by the wicked life, wishing for a better one, which thou art, for even if he discovered late the evil he was in, yet, O Lord, better late than never; for thou said that thou would convert to a heart, which had converted to thee : here I am Lord already converted, shedding tears of regret in the firmness of never offending thee again; for I am so firm, and constant in the trust of thy clemency, and thy grace, that it seems to me, that the Sun, the Moon, and the stars shall rather fall, than me falling more into sin : make my heart fall, torn into a thousand pieces, and may each piece be turned into new hearts so as all of these may cry tears of blood to testify the strength of my regret, the constancy of my firmness, and the true purpose of never again offending thee, and in this way I am already, Lord, surrendered, I am already contrite, I am all thine to ask for thy piety, and mercy. *Amen.*

Immediately one shall say the nine Our Fathers, and the nine Hail Marys as above until the end of the first day.

NINTH DAY

Everything as on the first day, except the Act of love of God.

ACT OF LOVE OF GOD

Lord, and only Lord, here comes for the last time this invalid to see if thy wounds, thy blood, thy grace have cured him; but so as to better recover, I wish to immediately make up with thee, and let us be friends, I wish to give thee my heart, so as thou may give me thine, and since we are on terms of contract, let us arm a contract to deal with thee, and may it be a contract of partnership, and company; enter with thy precious blood, and with thy heart, that I shall enter with my heart, my tears, my repentance, my pain, with my proposition of shedding my last blood drop to conserve our society, and company, making thy Most Saintly Mother as trustee, and a part of this society, and company, in which she is the greatest investor, and for this I shall never part from thee : Succour me, do not abandon me, do not leave me, take me with thee, aid me with thy mercy. *Amen.*

Immediately one shall say the nine Our Fathers, and the nine Hail Marys as above until the end of the first day.

GENERAL NOVENA FOR ALL THE FEASTS OF THE HOLIEST MARY

The same as the Novena of the Rock until the Litany.

Preparatory prayer for every day of the Novena

Most High Eternal God, I a most vile creature with all the affection of my soul give thee infinite grace for the unfailing privileges, with which thou exalted the Holiest Mary, and I ask thee to concede to me that this admirable Lady, which thou chose as Mother, and to whom thou denies nothing as her son, always attend me with merciful eyes, and aid me in all my labours, necessities, and afflictions, and take into heavy consideration the most important business of my salvation. And so as I may not deserve to lose such a loving, and important care, inflame me in her love, and incline my heart to imitate her admirable virtues, given as effective grace for this, and with it the approval of my supplication, and in particular the ones I make in this Novena, being for thy greatest glory, and of this sovereign Lady, through whose pleas, and worth I hope to achieve from thy clemency all these benefits, and afterwards the supreme happiness of seeing thee, and loving thee eternally in her most beloved company in that Glory. *Amen.*

Immediately after say with great devotion the following sighs, praying on each of them an Our Father, Hail Mary and Gloria Patri.

1. O purest Mary, Mother of God, and our Mother, I am joyful that thy Conception was immaculate, and preserved from the mortal guilt of Adam. O beloved Lady, I desire to love thee with the finest, and most excessive love in order to deserve thy greatest pleasure, and that by this singular benefit I should be made free from all guilt. *Amen.*

2. O most clement Mary, and my beloved Mother, concede to me, Lady, thy fine love, and reach for me effective aid, by which I may live as I should, and die as I want.

3. O purest Mary, and my most merciful Mother, may I be missing the whole world, and not be missing thy Succour, and patronage, that I shall have everything with it, and I shall be safe from all my enemies.

4. O sweetest Mary, and my most powerful Mother, exercise with me thy great power, saving me from the temptation of the Devil, and breaking his strength, may he never harm my soul.

5. O softest Mary, and my Mother of mercy, hurry in saving me from all the harm, which presses me in this world, for only from thee do I hope for its relief.

6. O most august Mary, and my beloved Mother, for thou so promptly aids those who invoke thee, concede to me thy sovereign Succour, which I beg for with my heart.

7. O immaculate Mary, and my most liberal Mother, enrich my poor soul with the precious stones of thy virtues, and make it as in them I may imitate thee with fervour, tenderness, and devotion.

8. O most glorious Mary, and my Mother of wisdom, enlighten the darkness of my soul with thy celestial light, and soften the dryness of my interior in such a way as I may live consoled with God, and constantly persevere in his service.

9. O most Blessed Mary, and my most beloved Mother, show that thou art this in the last hour of my death, softening its bitterness to me with thy most beloved company, and favouring me then with thy Succour, and patronage, in such a way as I may go with thee to immediately sing the Divine mercies in Heaven for eternity.

One concludes with a Salve Regina, and at the end of this the following prayer, and the same shall be done on all days of the Novena.

O Most Saintly Mother of God, Virgin Mary, my most clement Lady, consolation and refuge of all needy, remember that never has one heard that thou has not aided, and consoled any who has invoked thee, remedying with thy mercies their miseries; and thus with this great trust I come to thy feet to beg thee to not deny me thy grace, and love, for, after God, in thee I have placed all my trust, as the sole, and supreme hope of my salvation. Accept me, as mercy, Mother, under thy protection, for in thy merciful hands I completely place myself, and all my things. Concede to me this favour, and with it also what I ask for in this Novena. Hear my sighs, which most of all are meant to ask that thou concedes to me a most ardent love, and a feverous zeal for thy honour, and that in the hour of my death thou may assist, defend, and reach for me the final grace, so as by thy endless worth, patronage, and powerful intercession, and by the Mystery of thy admirable Name (*here one declares the mystery, according to the feast, ex. Conception, Assumption, &c, or the title, ex. Lady of Necessity, Mother of God, Carmel, &c*) I may deserve to see, praise, and enjoy thy softest company in Heaven, under the sight of the Holiest Son, who with the Father, and Holy Spirit lives, and reigns for all centuries of centuries. *Amen.*

SIGHS FOR THE NOVENA OF THE SORROWS OF THE HOLIEST MARY

The same as the previous Novena.

Pray an Our Father, Hail Mary and Gloria Patri.

1. O most sorrowful Virgin, Mother of God, and our Mother, how do I love thee so little, and do not break with sorrow, seeing what thy heart suffered!

2. O most afflicted Virgin, Mother of God, and our Mother, I wish, even at the cost of my life, to give thee some relief, when thou felt such cruel anguishes!

3. O most hurt Virgin, Mother of God, and Mother of sinners, how much my faults weigh on me, for they so much tormented thy Son, and caused thee such agony!

4. O inconsolable Virgin, Mother of God, and our Mother, who could suffer thy pain, so as taking them over myself, I could free thee from suffering such a cruel martyrdom.

5. O Holiest Virgin, Mother of God, and our Mother, give me one compassion of those which thou suffered, so as I may feel with my soul the immensity which thou tolerated without relief.

6. O most anguished Virgin, Mother of God, and our Mother, who with so much spirit suffered so much pain, give me valour to sustain mine with great strength, and constancy.

7. O saddest Virgin, Mother of God, and our Mother, by the pain, which pierced thy heart at the death of thy Son, reach for me a good death, so as I may achieve the eternal life in thy company.

8. O most merciful Virgin, Mother of God, and our Mother, by the anguishes thou suffered, seeing thy beloved Son dead, and broken in thy arms, aid me in my death, receiving my soul in thy hands, so as I may praise thee eternally.

9. O most painful Virgin, Mother of God, and our Mother, by the pain and penalties thou felt, when thou saw thyself without thy Son in the greatest loneliness, I ask thee to aid me in satisfying the obligation, which I have of truly feeling thy pain, and that for this may there be mercy on our souls, mercy, mercy, Holiest Virgin of Piety.

Salve Regina and the following Offering as in the previous Novena

O purest Mary, Mother of God, and Mother of sinners, Virgin Lady of Mercy, whose pain at the Passion and Death of thy Son was so great, that it pierced thy Holiest soul : I offer thee these prayers in memory of that cruel sword of pain, which before, and after thy Loneliness pierced thy painful heart. For all these penalties, anguishes, and pains, which thou suffered through the entire Passion, and Death of thy Son, and by that cruel spear, which thou saw being driven into him, being he already dead, and when afterwards thou had him in thy arms so full of wounds thy sight was blocked by a stone, with which his tomb was closed, I ask thee, Mother of Mercy, reach for us the forgiveness of our faults, since these were the cause of so much pain, so as we may enjoy thy sight, and that of thy Holiest Son for all centuries of centuries. *Amen.*

Immediately after sing the Hymn *Stabat Mater*, and its accompanying prayer, below, by which this Novena will be finished.

Pray seven Our Fathers, and seven Hail Marys to the sorrows of Our Lady, and one may also conclude with the Litany.

SIGHS OF THE NOVENA FOR THE JOYS OF THE HOLIEST MARY

The same as the previous Novena.

Pray an Our Father, Hail Mary and Gloria Patri.

1. O Queen of Heaven, be joyous, Alleluia, for that which thou deserved to carry in thy womb, Alleluia, he has resurrected as he promised, Alleluia.

2. O sweetest Mary, Alleluia, be joyous, Mother of love, that what thou saw with so much pain, resuscitated as he promised, Alleluia.

3. O most clement Mary, Alleluia, be joyous, shining Sun, that what thou saw as hurt, has resuscitated as he promised, Alleluia.

4. O most glorious Mary, Alleluia, be joyous, hurt Mother, that what thou saw without life, has resuscitated as he promised, Alleluia.

5. O most powerful Mary, Alleluia, be joyous, strong Woman, that what thou saw delivered to death, has resuscitated as he promised, Alleluia.

6. O softest Mary, Alleluia, be joyous, pure Virgin, that what thou saw in the grave, has resuscitated as he promised, Alleluia.

7. O most beloved Mary, Alleluia, be joyous, sad Dawn, that what thou cried so far, has resuscitated as he promised, Alleluia.

8. O immaculate Mary, Alleluia, be joyous, patient Mother, that thy absent Son has resuscitated as he promised, Alleluia.

9. O most beatific Mary, be joyous, beautiful Light, for thy Jesus has already resuscitated as he promised, Alleluia.

Salve Regina and the following Offering as in the previous Novena

O most beloved Mary, single Lady of the creatures, be one thousand times congratulated by the resurrection of that Son, whose Passion, and Death left thee so sorrowful : I am joyful, and I enjoy with full soul that ineffable jubilee, and pleasure, that in thy soul was caused by the sight of thy beatific Jesus, and in that supreme joy, which thou then had, I humbly offer thee these sighs, and prayers. I ask thee, most beautiful Virgin, by the immense softness, which lifted thy heart from so much pain, when thy venturous eyes saw such a sovereign sight, reach for me that I may live in such a way, that I may deserve to enjoy the fruit of the Sacred Passion of thy Son, and after this to eternally enjoy him and thee in Glory. *Amen.*

WAY OF PRAYING THE ROSARY OF THE VIRGIN OUR LADY

Offering of the Rosary

I offer this Rosary, which I intend to pray with the devotion, and attention I owe to the Holiest Mary our Lady in honour, and glory of God. The indulgences, which are conceded to me by means of this devotion, I apply for myself what is necessary for me, and further to the Souls of Purgatory of greatest need, especially to those to whom I am more obliged for any reason, and our Lord shall know to offer them, if he sees them in suffering; and I pray to the same Lord by the intention that the Holy Pontiffs had, when they conceded these Indulgences, which I intend to earn.

This Offering can be used for other prayers, such as the Rosary,[108] the Chaplet, &c. When one says 'I offer', one should name what one intends to pray, or if this is a visit to an Altar, a Chaplet, a Rosary, &c.

JOYFUL MYSTERIES

℣Deus in adjutorium meum intende.

℟Domine ad adjuvandum me festina.

℣Gloria Patri, & Filio, & Spiritui Sancto.

℟Sicut erat in principio, & nunc, & semper, & in sæcula sæculorum.

℟Amen. Alleluia.

From the Septuagesima until Easter instead of the Alleluia, one says Laus tibi Domine Rex æternæ gloriæ.

FIRST MYSTERY

Of Incarnation

We contemplate in this Mystery how the Blessed Virgin Mary Our Lady was greeted by the Angel Saint Gabriel and how she was told that she would conceive Jesus Christ our Lord, and Redeemer.

Our Father &c.

Jaculatoria

O Most Saintly Virgin of the Rock, Joachim, Anna and Joseph, I give thee my heart, and my soul.

℣Domine exaudi orationem meam.

℟Et clamor meus ad veniat.

108 Translator's note: once again this refers to a *Terço*. Carefully observed, all these 'Rosaries' are made up of five mysteries, meaning they are all technically Terços. In fact, for a full Rosary one may pray the Joyful, Sorrowful and Glorious Mysteries in a row and in that way make up the fifteen of a full Rosary.

Let us pray

O Queen of Virgins Holy Mary, by the most high Mystery of the Incarnation of Jesus Christ thy beloved Son, and our Lord, who is the principle of our salvation, concede that we learn of the great benefit, that this Lord gave us by being our brother, and in giving us to thee, who is his greatly beloved Mother, as our Mother. *Amen.*

SECOND MYSTERY

Of the Visitation

In this Mystery we contemplate how the Blessed Virgin Mary our Lady, hearing that her cousin Saint Elizabeth was pregnant, went with great hurry to the mountains of Judea, where she lived, and entering the home of Zechariah, visited Saint Elizabeth, and was with her for three months. *Our Father &c.*

Jaculatoria as above.

℣Domine exaudi &c.

Let us pray

O Virgin Mary, most clear mirror of humility, by the great charity, with which thou visited Saint Elizabeth, make it so as our hearts are visited by thy Most Saintly Son, in such a way, that clean from all sin we may praise him, and we may give him grace for eternity. *Amen.*

THIRD MYSTERY

Of the Birth of Jesus Christ

In this Mystery we contemplate how the Blessed Virgin our Lady, arriving at the hour of her most holy labour, gave birth to Christ our Redeemer in Bethlehem at the hour of midnight, and laid him down in a manger between two animals, as she couldn't find a room in the inns of Bethlehem. *Our Father &c.*

Jaculatoria as above.

℣Domine exaudi &c.

Let us pray

O Purest Mother of God, by thy virginal and joyful labour, with which thou gave thy only-begotten Son to the World, reach out to us that we may live so purely and saintly, that we may always sing the mercy of thy Son and thine without ceasing. *Amen.*

FOURTH MYSTERY

Of the Presentation

In this Mystery we contemplate how the Blessed Virgin, on the day of her Purification presented the Baby Jesus in the Temple, who was praised and given great grace by the just old Simeon, taking him in his arms. *Our Father &c.*

Jaculatoria as above.

℣Domine exaudi &c.

Let us pray

O admirable Virgin, great Mistress, and example of obedience, who presented at the Temple, the Lord of the same Temple; reach for us from thy beloved Son the grace, so as with the just Simeon, and the devoted Anne we may praise him day, and night. *Amen.*

FIFTH MYSTERY

Of the Boy God among the Doctors

In this Mystery we contemplate how the Blessed Virgin Mary our Lady having looked for the time of three days for her Son, who, without her knowing, had stayed in Jerusalem, finally found him on the third day in the Temple seated among the Doctors, disputing with them, being him of the age of twelve years. *Our Father &c.*

Jaculatoria as above.

℣Domine exaudi &c.

Let us pray

Blessed Virgin Mary, more than martyr, consoler of the afflicted, by the great joy thou had, when thou found thy Son in the Temple disputing among the Doctors, concede that we may know to seek this Lord in the Holy Catholic Church, and do not consent that by our sins we may be parted from him any more. *Amen.*

All say Salve Regina.

℣Domine exaudi &c.

Let us pray

Supplicationem fervorum tuorum Deus miserator exaudi, ut qui in societate sanctissimi Rosarii Dei Genitricis, & Virginis congregamur, ejus intercessionibus à te de instantibus periculis eruamus. Per Christum Dominum nostrum.

℟Amen.

SORROWFUL MYSTERIES

V Deus in adjutorium &c.
As in the first Rosary above.

FIRST MYSTERY

Of the Lord Jesus praying in the Garden

We contemplate in his mystery how Our Lord Jesus Christ prayed, and sweated so much blood in the Garden; that this flowed over the earth; he was in deathly agony, and was arrested by the cruel Ministers. *Our Father &c.*

Jaculatoria as above.

℣Domine exaudi &c.

Let us pray

O Most Saintly Virgin Mary, more than a Martyr, by that feverous prayer, which thy beloved Son prayed in the Garden to his Eternal Father, we ask thee to intercede for us, so as dominating our passions, we may always subject ourselves to the will of God. *Amen.*

SECOND MYSTERY

Of Jesus Christ tied to the column

In this Mystery we contemplate how our Lord Jesus Christ was tied to a column, and cruelly flogged in the house of Pilate, and he was flogged five thousand and some times. *Our Father &c.*

Jaculatoria as above.

℣Domine exaudi &c.

Let us pray

O Mother of God, source of perennial patience, for those floggings, which thy beloved Son took for us, concede that we may learn to mortify our rebellious senses, and cut out the occasions for sin with that sword of pain, which pierced thy soul. *Amen.*

THIRD MYSTERY

Of Jesus crowned with thorns

In this Mystery we contemplate how our Lord Jesus Christ was crowned with sharp thorns, and mocked by the cruel executioners. *Our Father &c.*

Jaculatoria as above.

℣Domine exaudi &c.

Let us pray

O Mother of the Eternal Prince, and King of Glory, by those thorns, which cruelly pierced his most saintly head, I ask thee to drive from our heart any moment of greed, and in the tremendous day of Judgment free us from confoundment, which we deserve by our sins. *Amen.*

FOURTH MYSTERY

Of Jesus with the Cross over his back

We contemplate in this Mystery how our Lord Jesus Christ, being condemned to death, as a greater affront to him, and greatest torment, took with great patience, the Cross, which was placed over his back. *Our Father &c.*

Jaculatoria as above.

℣Domine exaudi &c.

Let us pray

O Virgin Mary, mirror of patience, by that heavy Cross, with which thy Son, and our Lord took our sins over to himself, concede to us such valour, which in following him, we may take our cross with great patience until the end of our lives. *Amen.*

FIFTH MYSTERY

Of Jesus Christ crucified

We contemplate in this Mystery how our Lord Jesus Christ, after arriving on the Calvary mound, was undressed of his robes, and nailed to the Cross under the sight of his suffering Mother. *Our Father &c.*

Jaculatoria as above.

℣Domine exaudi &c.

Let us pray

O Blessed Mother of God, just as the most saintly body of thy Son was laid on the Cross, so may our desires towards everything, which is in thy service, be laid, and our hearts, so as we may always feel his most saintly Passion. And thou, most saintly Virgin, be served with the negotiation of our salvation by thy efficacious intercession. *Amen.*

All say a Salve Regina.

GLORIOUS MYSTERIES

℣Deus in adjutorium &c.
As in the first Rosary above.

FIRST MYSTERY

Of Jesus resurrected

In this Mystery we contemplate how our Lord Jesus Christ gloriously triumphed over death, and his torments, and resurrected on the third day immortal, and impassible. *Our Father &c.*

Jaculatoria as above.

℣Domine exaudi &c.

Let us pray

O Glorious Virgin Mary, by that ineffable joy, which thou had with the Resurrection of thy Son, we ask thee, do not consent that our hearts be taken by the false tastes of this world, but that all be committed to the true spiritual possessions. *Amen.*

SECOND MYSTERY

Of the Ascension of Christ to Heaven

In this Mystery we contemplate how our Lord Jesus Christ, forty days after His glorious Resurrection, rose to the Heavens accompanied by Angels at the sight of his most saintly Mother, and the sacred Apostles with great admiration from all. *Our Father &c.*

Jaculatoria as above.

℣Domine exaudi &c.

Let us pray

O Mother of God, consoler of the afflicted, as thy only-begotten Son, rising to the Heavens, cast a blessing over his Apostles, make it so, Lady, that we may deserve to reach his blessing, and thine, so as free from these mortal bodies we may rise to enjoy him up in Heaven. *Amen.*

THIRD MYSTERY

The coming of the Holy Spirit

In this Mystery we contemplate how Christ our Lord, seated at the right hand of his Eternal Father, ordered the Holy Spirit to his Apostles, as he had promised them, who, in the company of the Virgin Mary our Lady, were in the Cenacle of Jerusalem waiting the fulfillment of this promise. *Our Father &c.*

Jaculatoria as above.

℣Domine exaudi &c.

Let us pray

O Most Saintly Virgin, Tabernacle of the Holy Spirit, we ask thee that that soft Spirit, which thy beloved Son ordered to his Apostles, with which he filled them with consolation, and joy, teach us in this world to find the right path of salvation, by occupying ourselves always with the exercise of virtue, and good deeds. *Amen.*

FOURTH MYSTERY

Of the Assumption of the Lady of Heaven

In this Mystery we contemplate how the glorious Virgin Mary, twelve years after the Resurrection of our Lord Jesus Christ her Son, passed from this life, and was taken to Heaven by the same Lord, accompanied by all the Choirs of Angels. *Our Father &c.*

Jaculatoria as above.

℣Domine exaudi &c.

Let us pray

O Most Prudent Virgin, thou, who rising to the Heavens, filled the Angels with joy, and men with trust, be given to intercede in our behalf at the hour of our deaths, so as, free from the illusions and temptations of the Devil, joyful, and secure we may exit this life to enjoy the Blessedness in the other. *Amen.*

FIFTH MYSTERY

Of the Coronation of the Lady in Heaven

In this Mystery we contemplate how the glorious Virgin Mary with great festivities, and rejoicings from the whole celestial Court was crowned by her Son, from which all Saints received particular glory. *Our Father &c.*

Jaculatoria as above.

℣Domine exaudi &c.

Let us pray

O Queen of all Citizens of Heaven, be given to accept from us this Crown of roses, and concede to us, our most clement Lady, that in us such a desire to see thee crowned with such glory be kindled, that we may wish, and not intend for no other thing. *Our Father &c.*

All say Salve Regina.

Hymn

To be sung after the Rosary of our Lady

Clemency, my God
Succour my good,
Forgiveness, my Jesus,
Forgiveness, mercy
Repeat – Clemency, &c.
O how many offences
Confesses, Lord,
With great fear
My Wickedness
Repeat – Clemency, &c.
I am an ingrate,
Who with no respect
Cast thee out of my chest
With such mercilessness,
Repeat – Clemency, &c.
I am the prideful
Who outraged God
And I did not respect
Such great Majesty
Repeat – Clemency, &c.
Now I cry, and already feel,
The hurting pain,
That of my sins
I ask forgiveness.
Repeat – Clemency, &c.
For a vile whim
I wounded a Lord
Who is a fire of love
O great cruelty!
Repeat – Clemency, &c.
This rebellious soul
On the day of horror
To his Redeemer
What excuse shall he give.
Repeat – Clemency, &c.
Then sovereign
In the throne seated
With a clamorous shout
Thus will he tell me.
Repeat – Clemency, &c.
I already come to seek
The loving breast,
And a beautiful rest
My soul shall have.
Repeat – Clemency, &c.
In that sea of blood
I wish to be washed
And there my sin
Shall be extinguished
Repeat – Clemency, &c.
The sin be gone
From my heart,

Nor may Heaven
See me sin evermore.
Repeat – Clemency, &c.
I resolve, and promise
With the whole truth,
That thy kindness
I will not affront.
Repeat – Clemency, &c.
O Saintly Mary,
Joyful hope,
Firmness reach,
Constancy give me.
Repeat – Clemency, &c.
May I be saved by the cloak,
Of thy purity,
May false wickedness
From me flee.
Repeat – Clemency, &c.
Clemency, my God
Succour my good,
Forgiveness, my Jesus,
Forgiveness, mercy.
Repeat – Clemency, &c.
With thy aid
I await victory,
That from the Heaven glory
My soul shall have.
Repeat – Clemency, &c.

CHAPLET OF THE ROCK

℣Deus, in adjutorium meum intende.
℟Domine, ad adjuvandum me festina.
Sing one time:

Blessed, and praised be
The Holiest Name of JESUS Christ.
Invoked in life, and in death,
Consoles, comforts, gives grace, and gives light.

Repeat ten times:

Blessed, and praised be
The Holiest Virgin Lady of the ROCK
Invoked in life, and in death
Consoles, comforts, and from evil parts us.

℣Gloria, Patri, & Filio, & Spiritui Sancto.
℟Sicut erat in principio, & nunc, & semper & in sæcula sæculorum.
℣Amen.

Most Holy Jesus do not allow,
That I live, or die in mortal sin.
In mortal sin I shall not die.
That the Virgin of the Rock, shall save me,
Shall save me from the greatest affliction,
Calling for her in my heart.
Of my heart thou art the Virgin Mary,
Of my soul thou art the supreme joy,
Thou art the supreme joy Mother of men,
Of the Angels of the Saint thou art the whole good,
Thou art the whole good, and of the sinner,

Who fully contrite cries his horrors.
His horrors broken in great pain;
Deserve from thee the whole favour
Thy favour shall be eternal for me
To be free from the penalties of Hell,
From the Penalties of Hell I shall cry victory,
Content, and joyful there in thy glory.

CHAPLET OF JOYS

Make the act of Contrition, Offering and Application of Indulgences and the following prayer.

God save thee most beloved Daughter of God the Father, God save thee most dignified Mother of God the Son, God save thee most loving Wife of God the Holy Spirit, God save thee Holiest Temple of the Holiest Trinity.

Our Father and Hail Mary.

For the Mondays, and Thursdays of the year, or for any day, especially from the first Sunday of Advent until the Saturday before the Sunday of Shrovetide.

℣Deus in adjutorium meum intende.

℟Domine ad adjuvandum me festina.

℣Gloria Patri, & Filio, & Spiritui Sancto.

℟Sicut erat in principio, & nunc, & semper & in sæcula sæculorum, Amen.

From Shrovetide until Easter in place of the Alleluia one says: Laus Tibi, Domine, Rex æternæ gloriæ.

FIRST MYSTERY

In this first Mystery we contemplate the ineffable joy, which the immaculate Virgin Mary our Lady had in the Incarnation of the Divine Word.

Sing, or Pray an Our Father, and ten Hail Marys, with a Gloria Patri at the end, and say:

Lord God, mercy. Virgin Mother of God, and our Mother, mercy.

Jaculatoria

Lady, for this Sacred Mystery ask Jesus to free us from falling into sin.

The Choir should respond the same.

Offering

℣Dominus vobiscum.

Whether you are a priest or not.

℣Domine, exaudi orationem meam.

℟Et clamor meus ad te veniat.

Let us pray

O Immaculate Lady, Mother of God and men, we offer thee this first Mystery in memory of the excessive, and ineffable joy, which thou received, when the Angel Saint Gabriel announced to thee that thou would be Mother of the same God made man, greeting thee with the sweet words : God save thee full of grace, the Lord is with thee; and of the happiest years, which thou lived in the home of thy Holiest parents, and the ineffable joy, which thou had, when in thy purest womb thou conceived the Divine Word. For all of this be thou praised ten thousand million times by all the Angels, and the Blessed, and may they intercede for us, so as we may reach from thy Only-begotten the forgiveness of our faults, and the final grace, so as we may enjoy thy ineffable joy in Glory. *Amen.*

SECOND MYSTERY

In this second Mystery we contemplate the ineffable joy, which the immaculate Lady Virgin Mary had when visiting her cousin Saint Elisabeth.

Our Father, &c, as in the first Mystery.

Let us pray

O Immaculate Lady, Mother of God and men, we offer thee this second Mystery in memory of the joyful years, in which thou lived in the Temple, and the ineffable joy, thou had, when, after conceiving the Divine Word, thou visited thy Holy Cousin Elisabeth. For all this may thou be praised twenty thousand million times by all the Angels, and the Blessed, and may they intercede for us, so as we may reach from thy Only-begotten the forgiveness of our faults, and the final grace, so as we may enjoy thy ineffable joy in Glory. *Amen.*

THIRD MYSTERY

In this third Mystery we contemplate the ineffable joy, which the immaculate Lady Virgin Mary had in the birth of the Son of God.

Our Father, &c.

Let us pray

O Immaculate Lady, Mother of God, and men, we offer thee this third Mystery in memory of the joyful years thou lived until the twelfth of thy most beloved Jesus, and the ineffable joy, which thou had, when he was born as a man from thy purest loins. For all this may thou be praised thirty thousand million times by all the Angels, and the Blessed, and may they intercede for us, so as we may reach from thy Only-begotten the forgiveness of our faults, and the final grace, so as we may enjoy thy ineffable joy in Glory. *Amen.*

FOURTH MYSTERY

In this fourth Mystery we contemplate the ineffable joy, which the immaculate Lady Virgin Mary had in the adoration of the Three Holy Kings.

Our Father, &c.

Let us pray

O Immaculate Lady, Mother of God, and men, we offer thee this fourth Mystery in memory of the joyful years, thou lived until the thirtieth of thy beloved Jesus, and the ineffable joy, thou had, when the Three Holy Kings worshipped him in thy arms. For all this may thou be praised forty thousand million times by all the Angels, and the Blessed, and may they intercede for us, so as we may reach from thy Only-begotten the forgiveness of our faults, and the final grace, so as we may enjoy thy ineffable joy in Glory. *Amen.*

FIFTH MYSTERY

In this fifth Mystery we contemplate the ineffable joy, which the immaculate Lady Virgin Mary had when she found the Child God in the Temple.

Our Father, &c.

Let us pray

O Immaculate Lady, Mother of God, and men, we offer thee this fifth Mystery in memory of the joyful years, which thou lived until the Ascension of thy beloved Jesus, and the ineffable joy, which thou had when thou found him in the Temple disputing with the Doctors. For all this may thou be praised fifty thousand million times by all the Angels, and the Blessed, and may they intercede for us, so as we may reach from thy Only-begotten the forgiveness of our faults, and the final grace, so as we may enjoy thy ineffable joy in Glory. *Amen.*

SIXTH MYSTERY

In this sixth Mystery we contemplate the ineffable joy, which the immaculate Lady Virgin Mary had, when she saw her beloved Jesus resurrected.

Our Father, &c.

Let us pray

O Immaculate Lady, Mother of God, and men, we offer thee this sixth Mystery in memory of the joyful years thou lived until the mission, and division of the Saintly Apostles, and the ineffable joy, which thou had, when before the Magdalene, and the same Apostles, thy beloved Jesus appeared to thee, resurrected, and glorious. For all this may thou be praised sixty thousand million times by all the Angels, and the Blessed, and may they intercede for us, so as we may reach from thy Only-begotten the forgiveness of our faults, and the final grace, so as we may enjoy thy ineffable joy in Glory. *Amen.*

SEVENTH MYSTERY

In this seventh Mystery we contemplate the ineffable joy, which the immaculate Lady Virgin Mary had in her Assumption to Heaven.

Our Father, &c.

Let us pray

O Immaculate Lady, Mother of God, and men, we offer thee this seventh Mystery in memory of the joyful years, which thou lived until thy softest, and most beloved transit, and the ineffable joy, which thou had, when in body and soul thou wert taken into Heaven by the ministry of Angels, and placed on the throne of the Holiest Trinity at the right hand of thy beloved Jesus. For all this may thou be praised seventy thousand million times by all the Angels, and the Blessed, and may they intercede for us, so as we may reach from thy Only-begotten the forgiveness of our faults, and the final grace, so as we may enjoy thy ineffable joy in Glory. *Amen.*

Last Our Father, and three Hail Marys.

On this last Our Father we contemplate the last Most Sacred Wound at the side of Christ our Lord, and on the three Hail Marys the Death, Resurrection, and Crowning of his Holiest, and Immaculate Mother.

Sing, or pray an Our Father and three Hail Marys, with a Gloria Patri.

Offering

℣Domine, exaudi ortionem meam.

℟Et clamor meus ad te veniat.

Let us pray

O Immaculate Lady, Mother of God, and men, we offer thee this Our Father in memory of the Holiest Wound at the side of thy beloved Son Jesus Christ our Lord, from where the Divine Sacraments flowed from, by which we were spiritually recreated, and vivified in the society of the Roman, and Catholic Church our Mother; and these three Hail Marys after the memory of the joyful years of thy Holiest life in memory of thy precious Death, glorious Resurrection, and triumphant Coronation. For all this may thou be praised three thousand million times by all the Angels, and the Blessed, and may they intercede for us, so as we may reach from thy Only-begotten the forgiveness of our faults, and the final grace, so as in reward for this Chaplet of mystical roses, symbol of thy incomparable virtues, prerogatives, and excellencies, which we reverently offer thee on earth, thou may crown us in Heaven with the crown of Glory. *Amen.*

Antiphon

Hail, Queen, Mother of mercy, life, sweetness, and hope of ours, hail. We the exiled children of Eve cry to thee. To thee we beg, moaning, and crying in this vale of tears. Be our Patron, may thine eyes of mercy turn towards us. And after this exile reveal Jesus to us, blessed fruit of thy womb. O clement, O merciful, O always sweet. Virgin Mary.

℣Pray for us, Holy Mother of God.

℟So as we may be worthy of the promises of Christ. Amen Jesus.

℣Domine, exaudi orationem meam.

℟Et clamor meus ad te veniat.

Let us pray

O Immaculate Lady, Mother of God, and men, conceived without the stain of original sin from the first physical and real moment of thy animation, in which thou already displayed thyself as the Lady of conception of the Crown, symbolized in that prodigious woman, which appeared in Apocalypse with her feet on the Moon, dressed with the Sun, and crowned with stars, thy expressed figure in this purest Mystery : make it, purest Lady, that those who offer thee this Seraphic Crown of mystical roses, (which thou thyself revealed to the Seraphic patriarch) [109] be transformed by its benefit into joyful stars, may we deserve to be among the Blessed, which compose thy crown of accidental glory, with which thou were crowned in Heaven. Amen Jesus.

End with a Litany of Our Lady, a Station of the Holiest Sacrament, and a Novena to the Souls, or alternatively, devotions of little cost, and great benefit.

CHAPLET OF SORROWS

For the Fridays of the whole year, and for every day since Shrovetide until Easter.

Make the Act of Contrition, application of indulgences and everything else as mentioned in the Chaplet of Joys.

℣Deus in adjutorium meum intende.

℟Domine ad adjuvandum me festina.

109 Translator's note: Saint Francis of Assisi.

℣Gloria Patri, & Filio, & Spiritui Sancto.

℟Sicut erat in principio, & nunc, & semper & in sæcula sæculorum, Amen.

From Shrovetide until Easter in place of the Alleluia one says: Laus Tibi, Domine, Rex æternæ gloriæ.

FIRST MYSTERY

In this first Mystery we contemplate the penetrating pain, which the immaculate Virgin Mary our Lady suffered, when the Saintly elder Simeon prophesized the Passion, and Death on the Cross of her sweetest Son.

Sing or pray one Our Father and ten Hail Marys with a Gloria Patri at the end, and everything else which is mentioned in the Chaplet of Joys.

Offering

℣Domine, exaudi ortionem meam.

℟Et clamor meus ad te veniat.

Let us pray

O immaculate Lady Mother of God, and men, we offer thee this first Mystery in memory of the most innocent years thou lived in the house of thy Holiest Parents, and the penetrating pain, which thou suffered, when the Saintly elder Simeon prophesized to thee the Ascension, and Death on the cross of thy sweetest Son. For all this may thou be praised ten thousand million times by all the Angels, and the Blessed, and may they intercede for us, so as we may reach from thy Only-begotten the forgiveness of our faults, and the final grace, so as by the compassion, with which we accompany thee on earth, we may deserve to accompany thee in Glory. *Amen.*

SECOND MYSTERY

In this second Mystery we contemplate the penetrating pain, which the immaculate Virgin Mary our Lady suffered, when it was revealed to her, and ordered to her chastest Husband, the escape from Egypt with her sweetest Son.

Our Father, &c.

Let us pray

O Immaculate Lady, Mother of God, and men, we offer thee this second Mystery in memory of the most innocent years, thou lived in the Temple, and by the penetrating pain thou suffered, when by an internal uttering of the Most High, and an external by thy chastest Husband thou wert told of the escape from Egypt with thy sweetest Son. For all this may thou be praised twenty thousand million times by all the Angels, and the Blessed, and may they intercede for us, so as we may reach from thy Only-begotten the forgiveness of our faults, and the final grace, so as by the compassion, with which we accompany thee on earth, we may deserve to accompany thee in Glory. *Amen.*

THIRD MYSTERY

In this third Mystery we contemplate the penetrating pain, which the immaculate Virgin Mary our Lady suffered with the loss of the sweetest Son.

Our Father, &c.

Let us pray

O Immaculate Lady, Mother of God, and men, we offer thee this third Mystery in memory of the most innocent years, that thou lived until the twelfth of thy Sweetest Son, and the penetrating pain, which thou suffered, when, returning to Jerusalem, on the night of the first day thou found thyself without him, and thou thought him in the company of thy chastest Husband Saint Joseph. For all this may thou be praised thirty thousand million times by all the Angels, and the Blessed, and may they intercede for us, so as we may reach from thy Only-begotten the forgiveness of our faults, and the final grace, so as by the compassion, with which we accompany thee on earth, we may deserve to accompany thee in Glory. *Amen.*

FOURTH MYSTERY

In this fourth Mystery we contemplate the penetrating pain, which the immaculate Virgin Mary our Lady suffered, when she saw her sweetest Son with the Cross on his back walking towards the Calvary.

Our Father, &c.

Let us pray

O Immaculate Lady, Mother of God, and men, we offer thee this fourth Mystery in memory of the most innocent years, which thou spent until the thirtieth of thy sweetest Son, and the penetrating pain, which thou suffered, when on the street of bitterness thou found him with the Holiest Cross on his back, so oppressed with its weight, that he fell three times over the earth, and so weak, that he admitted that the Cyrenian help him carry it. For all this may thou be praised forty thousand million times by all the Angels, and the Blessed, and may they intercede for us, so as we may reach from thy Only-begotten the forgiveness of our faults, and the final grace, so as by the compassion, with which we accompany thee on earth, we may deserve to accompany thee in Glory. *Amen.*

FIFTH MYSTERY

In this fifth Mystery we contemplate the penetrating pain, which the immaculate Virgin Mary our Lady suffered when she saw her sweetest Son crucified and expiring on the Cross.

Our Father, &c.

Let us pray

O Immaculate Lady, Mother of God, and men, we offer thee this fifth Mystery in memory of the most innocent years, which thou spent until the Ascension of thy Sweetest Son, and the penetrating pain, which thou suffered, hearing the blows, with which he was nailed on the Cross, and raised up high, seeing him hanging from it, and finally dying. For all this may thou be praised fifty thousand million times by all the Angels, and the Blessed, and may they intercede for us, so as we may reach from thy Only-begotten the forgiveness of our faults, and the final grace, so as by the compassion, with which we accompany thee on earth, we may deserve to accompany thee in Glory. *Amen.*

SIXTH MYSTERY

In this sixth Mystery we contemplate the penetrating pain, which the immaculate Virgin Mary our Lady suffered, when she had her sweetest Son taken down from the Cross into her arms.

Our Father, &c.

Let us pray

O Immaculate Lady, Mother of God, and men, we offer thee this sixth Mystery in memory of the innocent years, which thou lived until the mission, and division of the Sacred Apostles, and the penetrating pain which thou suffered, when thou had in thine arms, and clasped to thy chest the Holiest body of thy sweetest wounded and disfigured Son being he the beauty of Heaven, and earth. For all this may thou be praised sixty thousand million times by all the Angels, and the Blessed, and may they intercede for us, so as we may reach from thy Only-begotten the forgiveness of our faults, and the final grace, so as by the compassion, with which we accompany thee on earth, we may deserve to accompany thee in Glory. *Amen.*

SEVENTH MYSTERY

In this seventh Mystery we contemplate the penetrating pain, which the immaculate Virgin Mary our Lady suffered in the loneliness from her sweetest Son.

Our Father, &c.

Let us pray

O immaculate Lady Mother of God, and men, we offer thee this seventh Mystery in memory of the most innocent years, which thou lived until the softest, and loving transit, and the penetrating pain, which thou suffered in thy loneliness, being internally, and externally penetrated by the bitterness of thy sorrowful soul, and renewing the species of the Mysteries of the Passion, and Death of thy Sweetest Son. For all this may thou be praised seventy thousand million times by all the Angels, and the Blessed, and may they intercede for us, so as we may reach from thy Only-begotten the forgiveness of our faults, and the final grace, so as by the compassion, with which we accompany thee on earth, we may deserve to accompany thee in Glory. *Amen.*

Finally one last Our Father, and three Hail Marys, and a Salve Regina, the same as the Chaplet of Joys, and in the same way to conclude.

CHAPLET OF GLORIES

For Wednesdays, Saturdays, and Sundays, or for every day from Easter until the Saturday before the Sunday of Advent.

Make the Act of Contrition, application of indulgences and everything else as mentioned in the Chaplet of Joys.

℣Deus in adjutorium meum intende.

℟Domine ad adjuvandum me festina.

℣Gloria Patri, & Filio, & Spiritui Sancto.

℟Sicut erat in principio, & nunc, & semper & in sæcula sæculorum, Amen.

From Shrovetide until Easter in place of the Alleluia one says: Laus Tibi, Domine, Rex æternæ gloriæ.

FIRST MYSTERY

In this first Mystery we contemplate the ineffable glory of the Dignification, which the immaculate Virgin Mary our Lady enjoys in Heaven, exceeding in it all the Angels and Saints.

Sing, or pray an Our Father and ten Hail Marys, with a Gloria Patri.

Offering

℣Domine, exaudi ortionem meam.

℟Et clamor meus ad te veniat.

Let us pray

O Immaculate Lady, Mother of God, and men, we offer thee this first Mystery in memory of the happiest years, which thou lived in the house of thy Holiest Parents, and of the ineffable glory of Dignification, which thou enjoys in Heaven, whose plenitude is so superabundant, that thou exceeds all the Angels, and the Blessed. For all of this may thou be praised ten thousand million times by all the Angels, and the Blessed, and may they intercede for us, so as we may reach from thy Only-begotten the forgiveness of our faults, and the final grace, so as glorifying thee on Earth, we may rise to enjoy this thy Glory in Heaven. *Amen.*

SECOND MYSTERY

In this second Mystery we contemplate the ineffable glory of Illumination, which the immaculate Virgin Mary our Lady enjoys in Heaven, diffusing through all the Celestial Paradise her brilliant lights.

Our Father, &c.

Let us pray

O Immaculate Lady, Mother of God, and men, we offer thee this second Mystery in memory of the happiest years, in which thou lived in the Temple, and of the ineffable glory of Illumination, which thou enjoys in Heaven, for with the brilliant rays of thy glorification, thou illuminates it better than the material Sun illuminates the entire world. For all this may thou be praised twenty thousand million times by all the Angels, and the Blessed, and may they intercede for us, so as we may reach from thy Only-begotten the forgiveness of our faults, and the final grace, so as glorifying thee on Earth, we may rise to enjoy this thy Glory in Heaven. *Amen.*

THIRD MYSTERY

In this third Mystery we contemplate the ineffable glory of Adoration which the immaculate Virgin Mary our Lady enjoys in Heaven, being revered by the whole Celestial Court.

Our Father, &c.

Let us pray

O Immaculate Lady, Mother of God, and men, we offer thee this third Mystery in memory of the happiest years, which thou lived until the twelfth of thy most beloved Jesus, and the ineffable glory of Adoration, which thou enjoys in Heaven, where by the entire Celestial Curia thou art worshipped, obeyed, and revered, as Mother of the supreme King. For all this may thou be praised thirty thousand million times by all the Angels, and the Blessed, and may they intercede for us, so as we may reach from thy Only-begotten the forgiveness of our faults, and the final grace, so as glorifying thee on Earth, we may rise to enjoy this thy Glory in Heaven. *Amen.*

FOURTH MYSTERY

In this fourth Mystery we contemplate the ineffable glory of Potestative Impetration, which the immaculate Virgin Mary our Lady enjoys in Heaven, achieving from the Holiest Trinity all she may desire for her devotees.

Our Father, &c.

Let us pray

O Immaculate Lady, Mother of God, and men, we offer thee this fourth Mystery in memory of the happiest years, which thou lived until the thirtieth of thy beloved Jesus, and the ineffable glory of Potestative Impetration which thou enjoys in Heaven, where thou has thy will identified in such a way with that of the Most High, that all, which is of thy agreement, thou impetrate, and achieve for thy servants. For all this may thou be praised forty thousand million times by all the Angels, and Blessed, and may they intercede for us, so as we may reach from thy Only-begotten the forgiveness of our faults, and the final grace, so as glorifying thee on Earth, we may rise to enjoy this thy Glory in Heaven. *Amen.*

FIFTH MYSTERY

In this fifth Mystery we contemplate the ineffable glory of Remuneration, which the immaculate Virgin Mary our Lady enjoys in Heaven, for according to their approval are her faithful devotees rewarded in this life and in the eternal one.

Our Father, &c.

Let us pray

O Immaculate Lady, Mother of God, and men, we offer thee this fifth Mystery in memory of the happiest years, in which thou lived until the Ascension of thy beloved Jesus, and the ineffable glory of Remuneration, which thou enjoys in Heaven, where with thy will thou rewards, and gifts in the present life, and in the future life the worth of thy faithful servants. For all of this may thou be praised fifty thousand million times by all the Angels, and Blessed, and may they intercede for us, so as we may reach from thy Only-begotten the forgiveness of our faults, and the final grace, so as glorifying thee on Earth, we may rise to enjoy this thy Glory in Heaven. *Amen.*

SIXTH MYSTERY

In this sixth Mystery we contemplate the ineffable glory of Habitation, which the immaculate Virgin Mary our Lady enjoys in Heaven at the right hand of her beloved Jesus on the throne of the Holiest Trinity.

Our Father, &c.

Let us pray

O Immaculate Lady, Mother of God, and men, we offer thee this sixth Mystery in memory of the happiest years, which thou had until the mission and division of the Holy Apostles, and of the ineffable glory of Habitation, which thou enjoys in Heaven placed on the throne of the Most Blessed Trinity at the right hand of thy beloved Jesus, so absorbed, penetrated, and deified in the inaccessible light of Divinity, by which thou art a delectable object to the Three Persons, and with supreme fruition thou art seeing, and knowing as the Son (which thou generated in thy immaculate womb) proceeds from the Father, and from the Father, and the Son proceeds the Holy Spirit. For all this may thou be praised sixty thousand million times by all the Angels, and the Blessed, and may they intercede for us, so as we may reach from thy Only-begotten the forgiveness of our faults, and the final grace, so as glorifying thee on Earth, we may rise to enjoy this thy Glory in Heaven. *Amen.*

SEVENTH MYSTERY

In this seventh Mystery we contemplate the ineffable glory of Augmentation, which the immaculate Virgin Mary our Lady enjoys in Heaven, for she is never diminished, but is always accidentally growing.

Our Father, &c.

Let us pray

O immaculate Lady, Mother of God, and men, we offer thee this seventh Mystery in memory of the happiest years, which thou lived until thy softest, and most loving transit, and of the ineffable glory of Augmentation, which thou enjoys in Heaven, where, like thy beloved Jesus, thou art dressed in the light of Divinity, from whose incomparable glory art all the Celestial Spirits congratulated with thee, and from this mutual congratulation is continuously renovated, growing, and augmented thy accidental glory. For all this may thou be praised seventy thousand million times by all the Angels, and the Blessed, and may they intercede for us, so as we may reach from thy Only-begotten the forgiveness of our faults, and the final grace, so as glorifying thee on Earth, we may rise to enjoy this thy Glory in Heaven. *Amen.*

Finally one last Our Father, and three Hail Marys, and a Salve Regina, the same as the Chaplet of Joys, and in the same way to conclude.

LITANY OF OUR LADY

Translated into the Vernacular

Lord, have mercy on us.
Christ, have mercy on us.
Lord, have compassion on us.
Christ, hear us.
Christ, Succour us.
God the Father up in Heaven, where thou art, have compassion on us.
God the Son, Redeemer of the world, have compassion on us.
God the Holy Spirit, have compassion on us.
Holiest Trinity, who art one sole God, have compassion on us.

Holy Mary	Pray for us.
Holy Mother of God,	Pray.
Holy Virgin of virgins,	Pray.
Mother of JESUS Christ,	Pray.
Mother of divine grace,	Pray.
Purest Mother,	Pray.
Chastest Mother,	Pray.
Mother without blemish,	Pray.
Mother without corruption,	Pray.
Lovable Mother,	Pray.
Admirable Mother,	Pray.
Mother of the Creator,	Pray.
Mother of the Saviour,	Pray.
Most prudent Virgin,	Pray.
Virgin worthy of veneration,	Pray.
Celebrated Virgin,	Pray.
Powerful Virgin,	Pray.
Clement Virgin,	Pray.
Faithful Virgin,	Pray.
Mirror of Justice,	Pray.
Seat of Justice,	Pray.
Cause of our rejoicing,	Pray.
Spiritual vase,	Pray.
Honourable vase,	Pray.
Vase of notable devotion,	Pray.
Mystical rose,	Pray.
Tower of David,	Pray.
Tower of ivory,	Pray.
House of gold,	Pray.
Ark of the Covenant,	Pray.
Gate of Heaven,	Pray.
Morning Star,	Pray.
Health of the Infirm,	Pray.
Refuge of the sinners,	Pray.

Consoler of the afflicted, Pray.
Succour of the Christians, Pray.
Queen of the Angels, Pray.
Queen of the Patriarchs, Pray.
Queen of the Prophets, Pray.
Queen of the Apostles, Pray.
Queen of the Martyrs, Pray.
Queen of the Confessors, Pray.
Queen of the Virgins, Pray.
Queen of all the Saints Pray for us.
Lamb of God, who takes the sin from the world, hear us Lord.
Lamb of God, who takes the sin from the world, have compassion on us.

℣Pray for us, Virgin Mother of God.

℟So as we may be worthy of the promises of Christ.

Prayer

Divine, and almighty Lord, be moved to illuminate with the lights of thy grace our understanding so as all those, who have the happiness of knowing the highest Mystery, announced by the Angel, of the Incarnation of thy beloved Son, may also have joy by his Cross, and by the worth of his most sacred Passion, by the glory of Resurrection, for the love of the same JESUS Christ. *Amen.*

MARIAN REMEDIES

Blessings which should be done every day in the morning, and evening, to Our Lady with the following salutation

God save thee, Mother of God, full of grace : show me, Lady, thou who art my Mother, and give me light, and grace, so as I may show, in everything, that I am thy son, for which concede to me, and cast onto me thy holy blessing, and together with the Father, and the Son, and the Holy Spirit. *Amen.*

Pray three Hail Marys, in the praise of the virginal purity of the Mother of God to acquire the virtue of chastity, saying in the following way:

Virgin before birth, Hail Mary. Virgin during birth, Hail Mary. Virgin after birth, Hail Mary.

Offering

O Purest Virgin, Mother of God, and our Mother, I offer thee these Hail Marys in the praise of thy purest Conception, and of the highest dignity of Mother of God, to which the Most High sublimated thee : and I ask thee to take me in thy consideration, and give me a great bother towards all vices, and faults, and a great love for the virtue of Chastity, and Humility, receiving me under thy Succour, and protection, as thy son, and slave, so as in this way I may be free from my enemies, and have the grace to serve, and love thee for all centuries of centuries. *Amen.*

Devotion of Our Lady of Conception, so as to concede to us the gift of Purity

Antiphon

Girdle me, purest Virgin, with the belt of purity, and extinguish from my body all the sensual violence, so as the virtue of continence, and chastity may be preserved in me.

℣Make me worthy of praising thee, Holy Virgin.

℟Give me strength against thy enemies.

Let us pray

For thy holy virginity, and Immaculate Conception, O purest Virgin, purify my flesh, and my heart. In the name of the Fa✠ther, and the So✠n, and the Holy ✠ Spirit. *Amen.*

When saying: in the name of the Father, &c, make three Crosses over your heart.

Each time this devotion is prayed devoutly, one shall profit for two hundred days of indulgences.

Effective remedy to move the heart with the sorrows of the Holiest MARY for a true act of love of God.

Hymn, which the Church usually recites in the sorrows of the Holiest MARY, which we should pray every Friday of the year, and in any other time, so as we may meditate on the sorrows of the Holiest MARY : the vernacular of the Hymn Stabat Mater dolorosa.

Next to the painful Cross
Was the constant Mother,
Seeing the agonizing Son hanging.
Her tender soul
Moaned with the stabbing
Penetrating pain of the sharp sword.
From the only-begotten Son
O how sad, and how afflicted
The blessed mother was seeing death!
Her bosom in anguish
In pain suspended
In the Son's the most intense martyrdom.
What human heart
Would not cry,
Seeing the pain, which the Virgin suffered!
Who would suspend the pain
Seeing the pierced Mother
In the torment of the Son tormented!
By fault of her people
Saw that crucified
He died by a thousand blows shattered.
She saw on the affrontful log
The beloved Son die
In a sad, and more than human abandonment.

Sweet Mother fountain of love,
With thee in just sorrow
Make my eyes rivers of water.
Make it so as ardently
For the one who so much loves me
My heart be ablaze in a living flame.
Those divine wounds
Make it so in a gentle way
They imprint on my chest.
From thy beloved Son
The punishments, he suffered,
Share them with my chest, who deserves them:
And crying with thee,
I may always feel
From thy Son the death in my life.
Of always accompanying thee
By the Cross may I be able
To Cry for the death of JESUS
In thy company
Enlightened pure Virgin,
May my chest be a sea of bitterness.
In it the death of Christ,
Be bitterly imprinted,
So as to feel what Christ feels.
By compassionate affection
By those wounds hurt,
Feeling only love, may it lose sense.
And that ablaze love
There in the terrible day
May I deserve thy pain.
Make it so as defended
From the cross I achieve venture,
Which the torment of Christ assures me.
And when this ends
Its transitional duration
In Paradise may I have the glory.
Amen.

℣Pray for us most painful Virgin.

℟So as we may be worthy of the promises of Christ.

Let us pray

Lord God, whose passion and sword of pain prophesized by Saint Simeon pierced the sweetest soul of the Virgin MARY thy Mother : concede to us that venerating, and feeling the pain of the same Lady together by the intersection of all the Saints, who faithfully accompanied thy Cross, we may achieve the happy effect of our redemption. Thou, who lives, and reigns for all centuries of centuries. *Amen.*

Seven Our Fathers, and seven Hail Marys.

Remedy for the consolation of the infirm : when any Priest wishes to operate that work of mercy in visiting the infirm

He shall say:

℣Pax huic domui.

℟Et omnibus habitantibus in ea.

Immediately place the stole on, and with a light say over the infirm:

℣Adjutorium nostrum in nomine Domini.

℟Qui fecit Cœlum, & terram.

℣Sit nomen Domini benedictum.

℟Ex hoc nunc, & usque in sæculum.
℣Dominus vobiscum.
℟Et cum spiritu tuo.
℣Sequentia sancti Evangelii secundum Mattheum.
℟Gloria tibi Domine.

In illo tempore : Cum introiisset Jesus Capharnaum accessit ad eum Centurio, rogans eum, & dicens : Domine, puer meus jacet in domo paralyticus, & male torquetur; & ait Jesus : Ego veniam, & curabo eum; & respondens Centurio ait : Domine, non sum dignus, ut intres sub tectum meum, sed tantum dic verbo, & sanabitur puer meus nam; & ago homo sum sub potestate constitutus, habens sub me milites, & venit; & servo meo : Fac hoc, & facit. Audiens autem Jesus, miratus est, & sequentibus se dixit : Amen dico vobis, non inveni tantam fidem in Israel; & dixit Jesus Centurioni : Vade, & sicut credidisti, siat tibi; & sanatus est puer ex illa hora.

℟Laus tibi Christe.
℣Dominus vobiscum.
℟Et cum spiritu tuo.
℣Sequenti sancti Evangelii secundum Marcum.
℟Gloria tibi Domine.

In illo tempore : Recumbentibus undecim discipulis, apparuit illis Jesus; & exprobavit incredulitatem eorum, & duritiam cordis, quia his, qui viderant eum resurrexisse, non crediderunt, & dixit eis : Euntes in mundum universum, prædicate Evangelium omni creaturæ : qui crediderit, & baptizatus fuerit, salvus erit : qui vero non crediderit, condemnabitur. Signa autem eos, qui crediderint, hæc sequentur : In nomine meo dæmonia ejicient : linguis loquentur vobis : serpentes tollent; & si mortiferum quid biberint, non eis nocebit : super ægros manus imponente, & bene habebunt.

℟Laus tibi Christe.
℣Dominus vobiscum.
℟Et cum spiritu tuo.
℣Sequenti sancti Evangelii secundum Lucam.
℟Gloria tibi Domine.

In illo tempore : Surgens Jesus de synagoga, introivit in domum Simonis, socrus autem Simonis tenebatur magnis febribus, & rogaverunt illum pro ea : & stans super illam, imperavit febri, & dimisit illam, & continuo surgens ministrabat illis. Cum autem sol occidisset, omnes, qui habebant infirmos variis languoribus, ducebant illos ad Jesum; at ille singulis manus imponens, curabat eos.

℟Laus tibi Christe.
℣Dominus vobiscum.
℟Et cum spiritu tuo.
℣Initium Sancti Evangelii secundum Joannu.
℟Gloria tibi Domine.

In principio erat Verbum, & Verbum erat apud Deum, & Deus erat Verbum. Hoc erat in principio apud Deum. Omnia per ipsum facta sunt : & sine ipso factum est nihil, quod sanctum est; in ipso vita erat, & vita erat lux hominum : & lux in tenebris lucet, & tenebræ eum non comprehenderunt. Fuit homo missus à Deo, cui nomen erat Joannes. Hic venit in testimonium, ut testimonium perhibéret de lumine, ut omnes crederent per illum. Non erat ille lux : sed ut testimonium perhibéret de lumine. Erat lux vera, quæ illuminat omnem hominem venientem in hunc mundum. In mundo, erat, & mundus per ipsum factus est, & mundus eum non cognovit. In propria venit, & sui eum non receperunt. Quotquot autem receperunt eum, dedit eis potestatem filios Dei fieri, his, qui credunt in nomine ejus : qui non ex sanguinibus, neque ex voluntate carnis, neque ex voluntate viri, sed ex Deo nati sunt. ET VERBUM CARO FACTUM EST, & habitavit in nobis, & vidimus gloriam ejus, gloriam quasi unigeniti à Patre, plenum gratiæ, & veritatis.

℟Laus tibi Christe.

Immediately placing your hands over the infirm say:

Per Evangelica dicta, & per impositionem manuum nostrarum extinguatur in te omnis infirmitas, & virtus diaboli in nomine Patris ✠ & Filii, ✠ Spiritus Sancti ✠ Amen. Kyrie eleison. Christe audi nos. Kyrie eleison. Christe audi nos. Kyrie eleison.

Pater noster, qui es in cælis: sanctificetur nomen tuum; adveniat regnum tuum; fiat voluntas tua, sicut in caelo, et in terra. Panem nostrum cotidianum da nobis hodie; et dimitte nobis debita nostra, sicut et nos dimittimus debitoribus nostris; et ne nos inducas in tentationem; sed libera nos a malo.

℣Salvum fac servum tuum.
℟Deus meus speratem in te.
℣Domine exaudi orationem meam.
℣Dominus vobiscum.
℟Et cum spiritu tuo.

Oremus

Domine Jesu Christe, qui præsentia majestatis tuæ Socrum Simonis, servum Centurionis, & filiam Archisynagogi ab infirmitate liberasti; exaudi nos propitius, & præsta, ut hæc creatura tua sana fiat ab omni infirmitate, & languore per virtutem tui sanctissimi nominis Jesu, cui honour, & gloria in sæcula sæculorum. *Amen.*

When the bells ring, either in the morning, or at midday, or at the Trinities, which are the Hail Marys, one should pray in the following way the three Hail Marys, to which our Holiest Father Benedict XIII, by a decree on the 14th of September of 1724 conceded plenary indulgencies in one day out of every month, or any one may choose, to all who pray the following vesicles on their knees.

Angelus Domini nuntiavit Mariæ, & concepit de Spiritu Sancto.

Say the first Hail Mary.

Ecce ancilla Domini, fiat mihi secundum verbum tuum

Say the second Hail Mary.

Verbum caro factum est, & habitavit in nobis.

Say the third Hail Mary.

This same indulgency was confirmed by the Holiest Father Benedict XVI, currently reigning, in a Brief issued on the 20th of April of 1742, and besides this he conceded further one hundred days of indulgences for each time this is done; however, one should be warned that from Saturday afternoon until Sunday one should pray standing, and from Holy Saturday until the eve of the Trinity also, and not on one's knees, in memory of the Resurrection of our Lord JESUS Christ, and during this time, those who know, instead of the vesicles above of the *Angelus Domini*, pray the following vesicles.

Regina Cœli lætare, alleluya,
Quia quem meruisti portare, alleluya,
Resurrexit sicut dixit, alleluya,
Ora pro nobis Deum, alleluya.
℣Gaude, & lætare Virgo Maria, alleluya.
℟Quia surrexit Dominus verè, alleluya.

Oratio

Deus, qui per resurrectionem Filii tui Domini nostri Jesu Christi mundum lætificare dignatus es : præsta quæsumus; ut per ejus genitricem Virginem Mariam, perpetuæ capiamus gaudia vitæ. Per Christum Dominum nostrum. *Amen.*

Devotions to our Lord Jesus Christ

Devotion to the Holiest Heart of Christ our Lord

What one should pray to the Holiest Heart of Jesus Christ our Lord is a Chaplet, which is made up of thirty-three small beads, and five large beads, according to the age of this same Lord, in such a way that you place one large bead at the beginning, and another at the end, and the others divided into three Decades.

Before one passes to the large beads say:

Sweetest name of Jesus, make my heart accommodate to thine.

When going through this same bead say:

I worship thee, my Jesus, that in the Garden thou wert most afflicted, and in the Sacrosanct Sacrament thou art still today despised by ungrateful men : I confess, my God, that thou art the only Lord, only thou art Holy, only thou art the Most High.

When going through the small beads say:

I worship thee, Holiest Heart of Jesus, ablaze my heart in the Divine Love, in which thou burns.

At the end pray an Our Father, and a Hail Mary, and the following.

Prayer

My Lord Jesus Christ, who in the Holiest Sacrament of the Altar with the ineffable love of thy sweetest Heart thou gave thyself fully as spiritual nourishment for men : conceded to us, that those, who detest the sacrileges, which in this Sacred Mystery we commit against thee, in this way inflame our love of this same Holiest Heart, so as we may eternally aggrandize thy mercies in Glory. *Amen.*

These prayers should be done on your knees in front of the Image of the Holiest Heart of Jesus, which is a heart among flames, with a crown of thorns, sustaining a cross, and with the wound from a spear, which pierced it.

Devotion to the Holiest Name of Jesus, which has many Indulgences

℣Deus in adjutorium meum intende

℟Domine ad adjuvandum me festina.

℣Gloria Patri, & Filio, & Spiritui Sancto.

℟Sicut erat in principio, & nunc, & semper & in sæcula sæculorum. Amen.

All say, with their heart.

We have sinned, Lord, which greatly weighs on us, have mercy of us.

℣From the rise to the setting of the Sun.

℟Is the Name of the Lord worthy of praise.

Hymn

Jesus, Jesus, Jesus Christ,
Jesus, Jesus, Holy Jesus,
Jesus in the mind of the Father,
Jesus in the mouth of the
Angel.
Jesus, Jesus, Jesus Christ,
Jesus, sovereign Jesus,
Jesus, ab æterno Jesus,
Jesus, without when, nor where.
Jesus, Jesus, Jesus Christ,
Jesus, Incarnate Jesus,
Jesus, and birthing Jesus,
And Jesus circumcised.
Jesus, Jesus, Jesus Christ,
Jesus, and my Jesus I call,
Jesus, and Jesus dying,
Jesus, and Jesus reigning.
Jesus, Jesus, Jesus Christ,
Jesus, Sacrosanct Jesus,
In Heaven, on earth, and Hell
Jesus worshipped Jesus.
Jesus, to thee who wert born
From the Virgin, remaining
Virgin,
Be with the Father in glory,
And with the Holy Spirit.

Colloquium

Jesus, name above all names, I confess thee, Jesus.
Ineffable Jesus, I praise thee, Jesus.
Incomprehensible Jesus, I worship thee, Jesus.
Sovereign Jesus, I worship thee, Jesus.
Admirable Jesus, I glorify thee, Jesus.
Jesus, first name of my Lord Jesus Christ, may the Angelic Choirs praise thee, Jesus.
Jesus, name of the Divine Word, second Person of the Holiest Trinity dressed of human nature, the Heaven, and the earth aggrandize thee, Jesus.
Jesus, name of my Saviour, may the entire orb magnify thee, Jesus.
May the glory be only thine, eternal Jesus.
May the virtue only be thine, Jesus brighter than the Stars of the Firmament in the mind of the Eternal Father before the world was made.
To thee the majesty, Jesus of infinite excellence among all creatures.
O Jesus, name from Heaven, and given to the Child Jesus on the eighth day of his Birth.
O Jesus written in the purest blood in the cleanest paper of the sacrosanct humanity.
O Jesus signed in the book of life.

O Jesus written with five letters by five wounds.
O Jesus sculpted in the most precious, and fundamental stone of the Church.
Thou, Jesus, may all the creatures, the Angels, and men praise.
Thou, Jesus, may all creation profess.
Thou, Jesus, may all humble themselves.
And I never forget thee.
Never cease.
Never may I be prevented from saying in all places, and in all parts, and in all times praised be Jesus Christ forever, and for all centuries of centuries.

℣Gloria Patri, & Filio, & Spiritui Sancto.

℟Sicut erat in principio, & nunc, & semper & in sæcula sæculorum. Amen.

Antiphon

On the eighth day the Child was circumcised, and was called Jesus, which name was pronounced by the Angel before he was conceived in the womb.

℣Be the name of Jesus blessed.

℟From now, and for all centuries.

Let us pray

God, who in thy only-begotten Son thou made the Saviour of the human kind, and thou ordered him to be called Jesus : propitiously concede to me, that from him, whose Holy Name we venerate on earth, we may enjoy also his sight in Heaven. For the worth of the same Jesus Christ, who lives, and reigns with thee for all centuries of centuries. *Amen.*

Litany

Lord, have compassion on us.
Christ, have compassion on us.
Lord, have compassion on us.
Christ, hear us.
Christ, heed us.
God the Father, up in Heaven, where thou art, Have compassion on us.
God Holy Spirit, Have compassion on us.
Holiest Trinity, who art one single God, Have compassion on us.
Jesus, Son of the living God, Have mercy on us.
Jesus, splendour of the Father, Have mercy on us.
Jesus, purity of the eternal light, Have mercy on us.
Jesus, King of Glory, Have mercy on us.
Jesus, Son of Justice, Have mercy on us.
Jesus, Son of the Virgin Mary, Have mercy on us.
Jesus most admirable, Have mercy on us.
Jesus, strong God, Have mercy on us.

Jesus, Father of future centuries,	Have mercy on us.
Jesus, Angel of the great council,	Have mercy on us.
Jesus most powerful,	Have mercy on us.
Jesus most patient,	Have mercy on us.
Jesus most obedient,	Have mercy on us.
Jesus, soft, and humble of heart,	Have mercy on us.
Jesus, lover of chastity,	Have mercy on us.
Jesus, our lover,	Have mercy on us.
Jesus, lover of peace,	Have mercy on us.
Jesus, Author of life, Jesus, example of virtues,	Have mercy on us.
Jesus, zealot of our souls,	Have mercy on us.
Jesus, our God,	Have mercy on us.
Jesus, our refuge,	Have mercy on us.
Jesus, Father of the poor,	Have mercy on us.
Jesus, treasure of the faithful,	Have mercy on us.
Jesus, good Shepherd,	Have mercy on us.
Jesus, true light,	Have mercy on us.
Jesus eternal Wisdom,	Have mercy on us.
Jesus, infinite Goodness,	Have mercy on us.
Jesus, our guide, and our life,	Have mercy on us.
Jesus, joy of the Angels,	Have mercy on us.
Jesus, King of the Patriarchs,	Have mercy on us.
Jesus, Master of the Apostles,	Have mercy on us.
Jesus, Doctor of the Evangelists,	Have mercy on us.
Jesus, strength of the Martyrs,	Have mercy on us.
Jesus, light of the Confessors,	Have mercy on us.
Jesus, purity of the Virgins,	Have mercy on us.
Jesus, crown of all the Saints,	Have mercy on us.
Be propitious to us,	Forgive us, Jesus.
Be propitious to us,	Hear us, Jesus.
From all sin,	Free us, Jesus.
From thy wrath,	Free us, Jesus.
From the snares of the Devil,	Free us, Jesus.
From the sensual spirit,	Free us, Jesus.
From the eternal death,	Free us, Jesus.
From the despise of thy Divine inspirations.	Free us, Jesus.
By the Mystery of thy Holy Incarnation,	Free us, Jesus.
By thy Birth,	Free us, Jesus.
By thy childhood,	Free us, Jesus.
By all thy Divine life,	Free us, Jesus.
By thy labours,	Free us, Jesus.
By thy agonies, and Passion,	Free us, Jesus.
By thy Cross, and abandonment,	Free us, Jesus.
By thy falls,	Free us, Jesus.
By thy Death, and burial,	Free us, Jesus.
By thy Resurrection,	Free us, Jesus.
By thy Ascension,	Free us, Jesus.

By thy joys, Free us, Jesus.
By thy glory, Free us, Jesus.
Lamb of God, who takes the sin from the word, Forgive us Lord.
Lamb of God, who takes the sin from the world, Hear us Lord.
Lamb of God, who takes the sin from the world, Have mercy on us.
Jesus, hear us.
Jesus, heed us.

Let us pray

O Lord JESUS, thou, who said if we asked, we would receive, if we sought, we would find, if we knocked, it would open to us : we ask thee that if such is thy will, make us conceive the true affections of thy Divine love, so as in this way we may love thee with all our heart, and confessing with our mouth, and deeds, may we never end thy praising. *Amen.*

For each time, that one says the Holiest Name of Jesus with devotion, one earns twenty five days of Indulgences. And those who lower their head, when saying this Holiest Name, profit twenty days.

Remedies for the souls in Purgatory

Prayer for the souls in Purgatory

Fidelium Deus omnium Conditor, & Redemptor, animabus famulorum, famularumque tuarum remissionem conctorum tribue peccatorum : ut indulgentiam, quam sempre optaverunt, piis supplicationibus consequantur.

Remedy to inflame the devotion towards the souls in Purgatory

Devout exercises. Many and grave Authors contend among themselves whether it is more useful to apply all the profits of faith, and labours, for the souls of Purgatory, or to make some partition, taking for oneself what one needs, and applying the remaining for the souls. If in all one does, one should always seek the greatest pleasure of God, it is in this where our greatest convenience is, it seems that in this particular case one should follow the example of Saint Catherine of Siena, placing everything in the hands of God, by which both opinions may be conciliated, and the blessed souls not any less obliged to their devotees; for, as being so saintly, these should desire that these should operate thus, and in everything which is in the greatest pleasure of God, and thus, without fear of any harm a devotee may offer them this gift in the following way.

My God, and my Lord, should it be more in thy pleasure, and my worth, that all, which I profit, be applied for the soul in Purgatory, thus shall I desire, and I apply all the labours, which with thy grace I may perform in this life. And if a partition is necessary, taking onto myself what I may need, thus do I desire, if such is more to thy pleasure, and will.

Method of making a vow

For greatest honour, and glory of God, one in essence, and trine in persons, for some degree of imitation of my sweet Redeemer JESUS Christ, and to show my cordial slavery to the mother of mercy Holiest MARY, loving mother of all souls in Purgatory. I (NN) intend to be the redeemer of those poor souls, imprisoned for debts and faults towards the divine justice, and for lack of satisfactory works, and in this way, in which I licitly may, and without sin, free and spontaneously, I swear to redeem that soul, or souls, which the same Virgin, my beloved mother, may so desire, as I renounce, and make a donation of my satisfactory labours, proper, or participated both in life, as in death, and after my death. As such I make and confirm this vow. And should I not have enough satisfactory labours to pay the debts of that soul, or souls, chosen by the same mother of mercy, and to satisfy my own for my sins (which I detest with all my heart with the firm purpose of never sinning again) I oblige myself, and wish to pay in the prison of Purgatory myself with penalties all which may be missing in satisfactory labours; and I sign this, citing as witnesses all the living in the three Churches Triumphant, Penitent, and Militant.

In ______ at the ______ of the month of ______ of the year of ______

I ______

Pontiff Benedict XIII by Decree of the 11th of April of 1726 concedes to those who make this vow the following indulgences.

Every Altar, and any Mass is privileged to remove one soul from Purgatory for each Priest, who makes this vow, applying for the mentioned redemption at least the fruit of the sacrifice for charity, and the same is valid for the Celebrant.

Any person from one, or the other gender, who makes this vow, every Mass they may hear on every Monday of the year, and in the days in which they commune for the redemption, shall be as if celebrated on a Privileged Altar.[110]

All the people, who make this vow, all indulgences are applicable for redemption, even if this is not declared in the concession.

Pope Paul V conceded that those who, after communion say five times: *Praised be the Holiest Sacrament*, shall remove five souls from Purgatory, and Pontiff John XXII conceded many indulgences to those who say the following prayer on their knees after communion.

Soul of Christ, sanctify me,
Body of Christ, save me,
Blood of Christ, inebriate me,
Water from the chest of Christ, purify me,
Passion of Christ, comfort me,
O good Jesus, hear me,
Sweat from the face of Christ, wash me,
And do not allow that I be parted from thee,
And from the infernal enemy defend me,
At the hour of death call me,

110 Translator's note: *Altare Privilegiatum*, a concrete physical Altar which grants plenary indulgences to the souls in Purgatory upon every Mass performed on it. The practice was discontinued by Paul VI in 1967.

And order me to come to thee,
So as with the Angels I may praise thee
For all centuries of centuries amen.
Our Father, and Hail Mary

One may finish these graces after communion by praying a station of the Holiest Sacrament in a Cross (should this be possible) for the souls of Purgatory, and with the following Acts, which can be made in any other occasion, and time, not without great utility, and worth, should these be made with fervour.

Sighs, and Acts of Love of God

O supreme kindness of my God, who loves thee, as thou deserves to be loved with infinite love! O how I wish, that the whole world would serve thee, and that all sinners would be thy lovers!

O who had as many hearts for thy praise, as creatures thou created to serve thee, so as with all of them love, and glorify thee, fulfilling the debt, which they cannot pay, and which I owe!

O my singular beloved, who shall love thee without ceasing! O how may I always, and without beginning, love thee, for thou loved me in the infinite before I was created!

O soul of mine, if love should be paid with love, pay what thou owes to thy God. Immediately move to love him without ceasing, for he loved thee as such since the beginning of eternity!

O my Lord, who shall love thee as much, as thou loves me! I love thee, as thou wants to be loved; I love thee more than the whole of creation.

O sweetest JESUS of my soul, dominate this my heart, and consume all which in it is unpleasant to thee, and convert it into the living fire of thy love, so as I may not love anything before thee!

O gentlest JESUS of my life, who since its first moment until death is in thy presence continuously, and feverous acts of love!

O my JESUS, and my entire good, who knows thee, like thou knows me, so as my soul may love thee, as thou loves me!

O who had, Lord, the heart as kindled in thy love, that it will become ablaze, and consumed!

O Most Holy Virgin MARY of the Rock, my beloved mother, how little, my Lady, do I love thee, and how much does thou deserve to be loved! O who could have all the love of the Angels, and Saints to love thee. O single hope of my soul, who does love thee how thou deserves to be loved, and could make all creatures love and serve thee!

O Lady of my most merciful Rock, take hold of my heart, which is better, and safer with thee than with me : make it truly love thee so as to fulfil what I owe, and thou desires, so as all thy true devotees, singing the

Rosary may enjoy thee for all eternity in the company of the Holiest Trinity, Father, Son, and Holy Spirit. *Amen.*

Another vow, or table of spiritual banquet in favour of the Souls of Purgatory, adorned with various exercises, and Indulgences for the same blessed Souls

In this way I place down, licitly, and without any sin, free, and spontaneously and make a vow to redeem that soul, or souls, who the Virgin Mary Mother of God may desire, renouncing myself, and making a donation of my satisfactory, or participatory works. And in the hands of this same Lady I make a vow to God to redeem that most needed soul in Purgatory, and those five souls, which in this world were the most devout of the Holiest Rosary, (*or the Carmel, or the Conception, or as one may wish*) together with the souls of my parents, relatives, or those God knows should participate, always in first place; and when there is a stalemate, I want this to be an election of these according to the order, which God knows I would choose, should I see them suffer. In this universal renunciation I reserve in favour of my soul all the interpenetration, and Indulgences, which are necessary for me, if only the last plenary Indulgence, which, from this moment on I always apply to myself; and I also reserve the liberty to apply for the living, and dead all the interpenetration, and Indulgences, in any time, when these won't be of use to those they are applied to, and from this moment forever I apply, in the same way, all other things which I may do, or have done, and which may not have an effect on whom I apply them to, and all else I may, to the souls explicated in this vow, and in the same order. And in this way I make a universal renunciation, and donation of all interpenetration, and plenary, and partial, Indulgences, which by any means may be conceded to me, for the already mentioned souls; and I always apply each plenary Indulgence for one particular soul in Purgatory of the nominated ones, and in the explicated order. And once these souls are redeemed, I wish that other souls be redeemed in the same order, and for this I make the intention from this moment forever to plead to God, and I pray for all the intentions of the Holy Pontiffs and all my prayers, and works, according to their intentions in the concession of the Indulgences, and Jubilees. This renunciation, application, and donation, without any obligation of mortal sin, I make for the time of (*here one says the time of this vow, ex. for one's entire life, or until some confessor absolves him of the vow, or as one may freely desire*) both in life as in death. And if my mentioned satisfactions are not enough for what is mentioned, and in order to pay for me, I oblige myself to pay in Purgatory what I may be missing in honourable satisfactory works, and in praise of Jesus, Mary, and Joseph. *Amen.*

The Holiest Father Benedict XIII, incomparable devotee of the Holy Souls of Purgatory, approved with Apostolic authority this vow of renunciation of personal and participatory satisfactions, and conceded three privileges, or indulgences to those who may do this for the entire duration of the vow, as is mentioned in his Decree given in Rome on the 23rd of August of 1728, and these are the following:

1. All Priests, who make the above vow, saying Mass, be it regular, or for a Saint, or for the Dead, the Altar shall become for this Priest an *Altare Privilegiatum*, which means that he will take one soul out of Purgatory.

2. All those, who make this vow, shall remove as many souls from Purgatory according to as many Masses as they hear on Mondays. This same grace is also conceded in the days in which they commune in favour of the Souls in Purgatory.

3. Every person, who makes such a vow, may apply for the Souls in Purgatory all the Indulgences, which may be conceded, even if who is conceding these does not have this faculty.

One should know that the exercise of the banquet of the Souls of Purgatory consists in picking on each year, or month, one day, and on this day in the morning make the mentioned vow, or renew it, and have said, or hear Mass, confession, and communion, and if you can, make everything else, which you may do so freely, and in this same day one may ask each of his friends to give him some delicacy for his banquet, meaning, hear Mass, pray the Rosary, Chaplet, Station, and whatever each one may choose to do freely, for the Souls in whose favour you made the vow, and make your banquet in that day. It is inexplicable, and incomparable the profit one earns with this devotion.

NOVENA
DAS
ALMAS,
OU SAUDAC,OENS
DE S. GREGORIO PAPA.

SAUDAC,AM I.

O' Senhor meu JESU Chriſto, eu vos adoro ſuſpendido neſ-ſa Cruz, ſupportando a coroa de eſpinhos em voſſa ſacroſanta ca-

NOVENA OF THE SOULS OR SALUTES OF ST. GREGORY POPE

OFFERING OF THE NOVENA

My God, and my Lord, I offer thee these prayers in praise of the Sacred Death, and Passion of my Lord Jesus Christ, and I plead for me, and for all the intentions of the Holy Pontiff, and further obligations, which I should pray in justice, or charity. I apply all I can, and the Indulgences, which are conceded to me, for the Souls in Purgatory, especially for those in the most need, which the Mother of God knows I have chosen, should she see them suffer, observing the order of justice, and charity.

Or one may do as Saint Catherine of Siena, placing all in the hands of God saying: Lord, if it is in thy greater pleasure, and my worth that all which I may profit be applied for the Souls, that is what I wish, and execute as such. If any partition be needed, then I do that which thou may wish.

FIRST SALUTE

O my Lord Jesus Christ, I worship thee suspended on that Cross, bearing the crown of thorns over thy sacrosanct head : I plead to thee, that that most noble Cross be the shield, which shall free me from the Ministers of thy Justice. Amen. *P. N. A. M.*

SECOND SALUTE

O my Lord Jesus Christ, I worship thee on that Cross wounded, and sore; where thou were given vinegar and gall to drink over the greatest bitterness of my sins : I plead to thee, that those precious wounds be my remedy, and the cure for my soul. Amen. *P. N. A. M.*

THIRD SALUTE

O my Lord Jesus Christ, I worship thee by that bitterness, which for me, miserable sinner, thou suffered on the Cross, mainly in that hour, when thy most noble soul left thy blessed body : I plead to thee, that thou have mercy on my soul, when it leaves this mortal prison, and take it to enjoy its eternal life. Amen. *P. N. A. M.*

FOURTH SALUTE

O my Lord Jesus Christ, I worship thee laying on the sepulchre, anointed with myrrh, and sweet balms : I plead to thee, that thy precious death be my harsh life. Amen. *P. N. A. M.*

FIFTH SALUTE

O my Lord Jesus Christ, I worship thee descending into Limbo to free the souls, who were awaiting in this for thy relieving arrival : I plead to thee, that thou does not allow that my soul enter into those infernal prisons, and dark jails. Amen. *P. N. A. M.*

SIXTH SALUTE

O my Lord Jesus Christ, I worship thee resurrected among the dead, rising up to Heaven, and sitting on the right hand of the Eternal Father : I plead to thee, that thou makes me worthy of following thee in this Glory, and be presented to thy divine presence. Amen. *P. N. A. M.*

SEVENTH SALUTE

O my Lord Jesus Christ, benign Shepherd, keep the Just in grace, justify the sinners, be moved by all the faithful, and lovingly favour this great sinner. Amen. *P. N. A. M.*

EIGHTH SALUTE

O my Lord Jesus Christ, I worship thee coming for Judgment, calling the Just to Paradise, and condemning the sinners : I plead to thee, that thy painful Passion free us from those penalties, and through them take us to eternal life. Amen. *P. N. A. M.*

NINTH SALUTE

O Most Beloved Father, I offer the innocent death of thy precious Son, and the love of thy divine heart, for all the guilt, and penalty, which

I miserable sinner, and the most depraved of all sinners incurred, for the faults I earned, and for all my relatives, and friends, living, and dead : I plead to thee, that thou have mercy on us. Amen. *P. N. A. M.*

For the intercession of St. Gregory Pope

O Lord my Jesus Christ, who admirably revealed the Mystery of thy most saintly Passion to thy Blessed servant Saint Gregory : I ask thee, that to this miserable sinner thou concedes that he perfectly reach that remission from sin, that this same venerable Pontiff with abundant Apostolic authority liberally conceded to all those who truly repented, and meditate on the progress of thy Passion, thou who lives, and reigns for all centuries of centuries. Amen.

Pray one Station to the Holiest Sacrament for the souls.

Offering

My God, and my Lord JESUS Christ, prostrated by thy sacred feet, I offer thee this Station, united, and incorporated with all the worth of thy painful Passion, and Death, so as to deserve thy mercy, and compassion, and to know the multitude of thy benefits, which thou art doing for me, without stopping nor ceasing for one single moment; and thus, Lord, it is my intention to earn the Jubilee, and all the Indulgences, which for the worth of thy sacred Passion are conceded to me in Rome, and in any other parts, and places, which the Pontiffs have increased, for the benefit of the souls, which may want to use them.

I ask thee, by thy very self, and by the Exaltation of the Catholic Faith, peace, and concord among Christian Princes, Captives, Moors, and Infidels, and for all those who suffer the afflictions, pains, and agonies of death, that thou concedes to them eternal life in thy company: and I apply, as suffrage for the Souls in Purgatory, and for all my friends, relatives, and benefactors, and for the Ecclesiastic and Secular Justice, so as all in general may praise thee, may fear thee, and may I love thee as thou deserves to be praised, feared, and loved. I ask thee by all the good works I have done, and by those of my fellow men. Guide me on the way to Heaven: accept all which I offer them. *Amen.*

ROSARY FOR THE SOULS

JOYFUL MYSTERIES

1. Jesus Son of David, by thy Holy Incarnation have mercy on the Souls, who art imprisoned in Purgatory.

2. Jesus Son of David, by the visitation of thy Holiest Mother to Saint Elisabeth, have mercy on the Souls, who art imprisoned in Purgatory.

3. Jesus Son of David, by thy Holy Birth, have mercy on the Souls, who art imprisoned in Purgatory.

4. Jesus Son of David, by thy Presentation in the Temple have mercy on the Souls, who art imprisoned in Purgatory.

5. Jesus Son of David, by the sacred pleasure of thy Holiest Mother, when she found thee in the Temple, have mercy on the Souls, who art imprisoned in Purgatory.

Prayer of the Holy Shroud

Lord God, who left us the signs of thy Passion in the Holy Shroud, with which thy Holiest Body was wrapped, which was brought down from the Cross by Joseph : concede to us, merciful Lord, that by thy death, and burial we be taken to the Glory of Resurrection, in which thou lives, and reigns with God the Father in unity of the Holy Spirit for all centuries of centuries. Amen.

℣Requiem æternam dona eis Domine.
℟Et lux perpetua lucea eis.

Oremus

Fidelium Deus omnium conditor, & Redemptor, animabus famulorum, famularumque tuarum, remissionem cunetorum tribue peccatorum, ut indulgentiam, quam sempre optaverunt, piis supplicationibus consequantur. Qui vivis et regnas in sæcula sæculorum.

Our Father, Hail Mary.

℣Jesus Son of David, give eternal rest to the Souls, which are imprisoned in Purgatory.
℟And may the eternal light illuminate them. Amen.

SORROWFUL MYSTERIES

1. Jesus of Nazareth, King of the Jews, for all that great pain, which thou felt, when after having sweated drops of blood on the Garden thou wert arrested, and tying thy Holiest hands, they placed a rope around thy neck, have mercy on the Souls, who art imprisoned in Purgatory.

2. Jesus of Nazareth, King of the Jews, by the floggings, and shames, which thou suffered, when naked, and tied to the column they mistreated thy delicate body, have mercy on the Souls, who art imprisoned in Purgatory.

3. Jesus of Nazareth, King of the Jews, by the terrible pain, which thou felt in thy Divine head, when they crowned thee with thorns, have mercy on the Souls, who art imprisoned in Purgatory.

4. Jesus of Nazareth, King of the Jews, by that pain, which thou felt, when, condemned to death as an evildoer, thou carried the Cross on thy back, whose weight, and great load, made thee fall over the earth, have mercy on the Souls, who art imprisoned in Purgatory.

5. Jesus of Nazareth, King of the Jews, by the pain, and affronts, which thou suffered nailed to the Cross; by the love, which thou showed thy enemies; by the gall, and vinegar, which thou wert given to taste; and by the death, which thou received, have mercy on the Souls, who art imprisoned in Purgatory.

Say the Prayer of the Holy Shroud and all which follows, except the following:

℣Jesus Son of David, give eternal rest to the Souls, which are imprisoned in Purgatory.

℟And may the eternal light illuminate them. Amen.

GLORIOUS MYSTERIES

1. Jesus Son of the living God, by the highest Mystery of thy glorious Resurrection have mercy on the Souls, who art imprisoned in Purgatory.

2. Jesus Son of the living God, by the Mystery of thy Ascension, and rising to the Heavens, have mercy on the souls, who art imprisoned in Purgatory.

3. Jesus Son of the living God, by the coming of the Holy Spirit, which thou promised, have mercy on the Souls, who art imprisoned in Purgatory.

4. Jesus Son of the living God, by the glorious Assumption of thy Holiest Mother, have mercy on the Souls, who art imprisoned in Purgatory.

5. Jesus Son of the living God, by the Coronation of thy purest Mother, on which she was elected Queen of the Heavens, and earth, have mercy on the Souls, who art imprisoned in Purgatory.

Say the Prayer of the Holy Shroud and all which follows, except the following:

℣ Jesus Son of David, give eternal rest to the Souls, which are imprisoned in Purgatory.

℣And may the eternal light illuminate them. Amen.

Way of visiting the Stations of the Cross

Offering

Sovereign, and Most High Lord, I offer to thy Divine Mercy all which in this holy exercise I may do, and meditate. In it I desire to unite all to the infinite worth of my Lord JESUS Christ, and it is my intention to earn all, and any indulgences, which are given to it by the Vicars of thy Church; of which I offer one of the plenary ones in remission of all my sins, and of the faults, which I have earned from them. All the rest I apply to the souls in Purgatory, and firstly by my greatest obligations, secondly in the order of justice, and charity, and as it may be more pleasant to thy divine eyes. I plead to thee, Lord, by thy Church, extirpation of heresy, peace, and concord among Christian Princes, and for all that, which the Pontiffs conceded to these indulgences.

FIRST STATION

✠

✠✠✠

✠

First ✠ Station

Made up ✠ of 26 steps

✠✠

✠✠✠

✠✠✠✠

JESUS beaten, crowned with thorns and sentenced to death

In this so painful place,
Jesus Christ they beat
And then sentenced him
As a deceiving traitor.

O my beloved JESUS here thou has me at thy feet, worthy of so many Hells, as the offences, which I have given thee. These prisons, these floggings, these wounds, these thorns, and this sentence is only because of my wickedness, of my excesses, and my faults. For all of these instruments I ask thee, that breaking the chains of the lack of resolution of loving thee, and arresting the recklessness of my actions in the fear of offending thee, I may suffer with resignation the affronts of this life, and the floggings of adversity, so as punishing me, may all the sentence of eternal death be removed, which could be placed against me by my sins, and make me free from its infernal prisons and may I enjoy thee in Heaven. *Amen.*

Lord I have sinned, have mercy on me.
Six Our Fathers, and six Hail Marys.

SECOND STATION

✠

✠✠✠

✠

Second ✠ Station

Made up ✠ of 26 steps

✠

✠✠

✠✠✠

✠✠✠✠

Our Lord JESUS Christ received the Cross on his shoulders

Sentenced the Redeemer,
A Cross was destined for him,
With furor they took him
To die as an evildoer.

O King of Glory, and Lord of the World, how high was the price for the rescue of my daring! If my sins created that Cross, may I take the weight of that Cross, and feel the weight of my sins. Let that Cross come to my shoulders, so as I may feel the weight of the punishment, for I so far have not known the weight of sin. And if until this moment I have fled with my body from the cross of penitence, and of labour, give me grace, so as embracing my cross I may take all labour with pleasure, and make penitence from all my faults. Only in this way may I relieve thee of these penalties of dolorous pain, and I shall deserve to accompany thee in the glories, with which thou art glorified in Heaven. *Amen.*

Lord I have sinned, have mercy on me.
Six Our Fathers, and six Hail Marys.

THIRD STATION

✠

✠✠✠

✠

Third ✠ Station

Made up ✠ of 80 steps

✠

✠✠

✠✠✠

✠✠✠✠

JESUS falls the first time under his Cross

Have compassion, and mercy
Of thy God, who greatly surrendered
He has already fallen with the weight
Of thy infamous wickedness.

O God of my soul, O Lord of Heaven, and the earth! If in this thou art seeking me prostrated, so as to raise me from guilt, how is it possible that I do not fall at thy feet, seeking the hand of thy mercy, to raise me from the falls in which I have so blindly plunged? Give me, my beloved Father, the powerful hand of thy grace, so as rising, resolved from the fall of my sins, I may no longer trip in the unruliness of my excesses, and embracing the cross of penitence, constantly walk in the observance of thy precepts, and may I enjoy them in the eternal happiness of the Blessed. *Amen.*

Lord I have sinned, have mercy on me.
Six Our Fathers, and six Hail Marys.

FOURTH STATION

✠

✠✠✠

✠

Fourth ✠ Station

Made up of 70 steps

✠

✠✠

✠✠✠

✠✠✠✠

JESUS encounters his Holiest Mother

Mary her beloved Son
Saw with great bitterness
Sighing with tenderness
For seeing him so hurt.

O hurt Mother of my Lord JESUS Christ, I am the one who with my great faults was the cause of thy great pains : I am the one who until now never felt the offence of thy Son, and for this, he, and thou, art so hurt in that meeting. At the feet of thy mercy, and thy piety I come to seek forgiveness for my sins, even if due to my ungratefulness, and my misery I may recognize, that I am unworthy of thy mercy, and of his mercy. Remember, that thou art Mother, and he is Father : as a Mother reach to me the grace to cry the offences, which I have done to such a loving Father; and he as Father may take me on the path, to which I may meet thee up in Heaven. *Amen.*

Lord I have sinned, have mercy on me.
Six Our Fathers, and six Hail Marys.

FIFTH STATION

✠

✠✠✠

✠

Fifth ✠ Station

Made up of 71 steps

✠

✠✠

✠✠✠

✠✠✠✠

JESUS is aided by Simon to carry the Cross

Simon to carry
The Cross he aided Christ,
And in it he taught us
How we should imitate him.

O most merciful Lord, that I being the one who should carry the weight of this Cross alone, for the infamous load of sin is mine alone, thy Charity is so blazing that it orders me to follow thy steps, as Simon, so as to aid thee in carrying it on this path. Here art my shoulders, place over them this Cross, that with it I wish to follow thee during my whole life, so as afterwards I may love thee for all eternity in glory. *Amen.*

Lord I have sinned, have mercy on me.
Six Our Fathers, and six Hail Marys.

SIXTH STATION

✠

✠✠✠

✠

Sixth ✠ Station

Made up of 191 steps

✠

✠✠

✠✠✠

✠✠✠✠

JESUS cleaning his face with Veronica

From Christ the mortal sweat
A woman pressed,
In a fine cloth printed
The image of the Saviour.

O unique beauty of the Heavens and the earth! My faults placed thy face in a state of necessity for that kindness. O uglyfied glory of the Angels! The breakings of my disconcerted life undid the gentle beauty of that sovereign face. O I wish that my heart would break with pain, and from it the purest blood would flow out, and making this as ink, such a beautiful image could be drawn on my soul! Give me this pain my Divine grievance, that my regretful heart is at thy feet. Draw this image with the brush of thy grace, so as I may be worthy of being in the same glory. *Amen.*

Lord I have sinned, have mercy on me.
Six Our Fathers, and six Hail Marys.

SEVENTH STATION

✠

✠✠✠

✠

Seventh ✠ Station

Made up of 330 steps

✠

✠✠

✠✠✠

✠✠✠✠

JESUS falls a second time

If being strong he has fallen,
My soul, my good God,
Judge in that thy labour
How much has thou offend him.

O Holiest Lord, thou fell with such weakness at my feet, and I in so many precipices proudly risen against thee! Thou, being God, fallen to the dirt of the earth, and I being dirt of the earth, without falling to the feet of God? Make it so, God of my soul, that in one term the strength of my rebelliousness may fall to the earth, so as the proud elevations of my vainglory being trampled on, I may recognize with true humility the great weight of my sins, and never cast thee out of the city of my soul because of them, and for thy grace may I praise, and enjoy thee with the Angels in the city of the eternal praise of glory. *Amen.*

Lord I have sinned, have mercy on me.
Six Our Fathers, and six Hail Marys.

EIGHTH STATION

✠

✠✠✠

✠

Eighth ✠ Station
Made up ✠ of 348 steps

✠

✠✠

✠✠✠

✠✠✠✠

JESUS suspends the tears of the daughters of Jerusalem

Daughters of Jerusalem
Who lament my ills,
Thou would be wrong not to cry
Also thy sins.

O my beloved Redeemer, since in the middle of such penalties, and torments thou taught me the way of crying, take from the stone which is this hard heart, with the rod of contrition and strikes of sorrow one single stream of copious agonies, so as it may never cease to cry the faults, which thou art forced to walk with so many guilts. Only in this way can I make thy torments pleasing company, and I shall not cry eternally absent from thee, and from thy glory. *Amen.*

Lord I have sinned, have mercy on me.
Six Our Fathers, and six Hail Marys.

NINTH STATION

✠

✠✠✠

✠

Ninth ✠ Station

Made up of 171 steps

✠

✠✠

✠✠✠

✠✠✠✠

JESUS fallen under the Cross a third time

Behold, be warned, sinner,
At thy peerless vigor,
For it is capable of casting down
The Creator three times.

O Almighty God, single good of the creatures, my depraved swellings, and looseness, and my insolence are what brings thee dragged in so many falls. O how much it weighs on me, my JESUS! Give me grace so as I may rise from all those I have given in thoughts, words, and deeds; and embracing myself with thee, may I not only take the Cross from thy shoulders, which afflicts thee, and raise thee from the earth, on which thou art fallen; but I also cry with regret the weight of my guilt, which oppressed thee so much, and walk with thee to the mount of eternal happiness. *Amen.*

Lord I have sinned, have mercy on me.
Six Our Fathers, and six Hail Marys.

TENTH STATION

✠

✠✠✠

✠

Tenth ✠ Station

Made up ✠ of 18 steps

✠✠

✠✠✠

✠✠✠✠

JESUS stripped of his clothes, and given gall and wine to drink

They wounded thy Redeemer
With tyrannical mercilessness,
And from these atrocities
Countless abundances emerged.

O most patient Lord, how unjustly the world rewards thee! Thou gives it the Holiest Sacrament, thy blood to drink with all the pleasures, and it offers thee bitter gall. Thou gives it the dressing of grace, which removed it from guilt, and it strips thee with such rabid barbarity. Ungrateful world. For the love and suffering, which on this occasion thou hast shown, I ask thee the grace, so as I may never again drink the delights, which the world offers me with the gall of the guilt of all vanities; and strip me of all vanities, which art offences to thee; of all disorderly affections, and of all the habits of my faults, and may I only have taste for the bitterness of thy Holiest Passion, dressing myself with thy very self, so as to enjoy thee in the militia of glory. *Amen.*

Lord I have sinned, have mercy on me.
Six Our Fathers, and six Hail Marys.

ELEVENTH STATION

✠

✠✠✠

✠

Eleventh ✠ Station

Made up ✠ of 12 steps

✠✠

✠✠✠

✠✠✠✠

JESUS nailed to the Cross

With hands and feet they nailed
On the cross the greatest Love;
O my JESUS, with how much pain
Thy members they dislocated

O single happiness of my soul, if thy love forced thee to be nailed with hands and feet to that Cross, so as in this way thou could further assure me in the greatest expressions of that same love, what reason could there be, which could free me from the obligation to die in that same cross crucified, so as to offer justified satisfaction of my thankful actions! I am resolute to crucify myself in that holy Wood with all my disorderly passions, so as these may never again be the occasion for the taking of thy life. Make it so, as for thy love I may force them to all die on that Cross, since it was because of them that thy love forced thee to die on it. And having the glory of dying crucified with thee on earth, I shall also have the happiness of seeing thee glorious in that glory. *Amen.*

Lord I have sinned, have mercy on me.
Six Our Fathers, and six Hail Marys.

TWELFTH STATION

✠

✠ ✠✠✠ ✠

✠✠✠ ✠ ✠✠✠

✠ ✠ ✠

✠ ✠ ✠

✠ ✠✠ ✠

✠✠ ✠✠✠ ✠✠

✠✠✠ ✠✠✠✠ ✠✠✠

JESUS lifted, and killed on the Holy Cross

If here our Beloved shall die,
How does thy life continue,
If he was the sweetest gift
Where shall thou put thy care.

O God of my soul! I know, and confess that my most grave sins were the cruel executioners of thy Death, and the singular occasion, as among so many affronts thou expired. They, Lord, took thy life, and they placed thee on that Cross with so much confusion, injury, despise, irritation, beastliness, rigor, barbarity, and affront. And I am the one who, knowing all of this, still has a heart : and I am the one who, knowing all of this, still dares to come close to thee with life, and not die of pain, of fright, of sorrow, of confusion, and of sentiment! O my offended Divine, for those wounds, for those nails, for those thorns, for that Cross, for that blood, and for that death, make it so as I may die for everything which is not loving thee; that in a single sweep I may be stripped of all the thoughts which are not to serve thee; that on a single turn I nail in the cross of my fear all my cares, and affection; and that in a single turn I may rise to the glory of dying to myself, and to the world, so as to only live eternally to love thee. *Amen.*

Lord I have sinned, have mercy on me.
Six Our Fathers, and six Hail Marys.

THIRTEENTH STATION

✠

✠✠✠

✠

Thirteenth ✠ Station

Made up ✠ of 13 steps

✠✠

✠✠✠

✠✠✠✠

JESUS taken down and off the Cross

Soul of mine, have mercy
And accompany, with regret,
The Mother who lives afflicted
In the saddest Solitude.

O Holiest Mother, O afflicted and unconsoled Lady, my sins are the cause of thy sentiment, and my horrible disconcertment is the one who made the sword, which pierced that painful heart. All of this weights on me, and I have a great pain, and I desire with tears of blood to satisfy that dead, and offended Majesty, and accompany thee in thy pain. Make it so, Mother of mercy, that the pain which on that occasion thy beloved heart felt penetrate my own, so as crying, day and night my faults, I may satisfy that God, who I have offended, and I may enjoy thee, and him also, in the rest, which awaits me in paradise. *Amen.*

Lord I have sinned, have mercy on me.
Six Our Fathers, and six Hail Marys.

LAST STATION

✠

✠✠✠

✠

Last Station
Made up of 30 steps

✠

✠

✠✠

✠✠✠

✠✠✠✠

JESUS deposited in the Holy Sepulchre

Over a cold, and strong stone
Lies finished, and entombed
A King, who being a Soldier,
Was killed with the same death.

O most Sacred Mother of my Lord, hurt wife, and faithful Lady, how thy justified sentiments make me feel, and hurt my heart with tears, with which I see the light of thy eyes drowned! How can I relieve thee in this absence, so as the greatness of thy pain, which thou feels, could immediately end! I have, hurt Lady, all the guilt of thy injury, and thy pain, of thy anxiousness, of thy sentiment, of thy sorrow. But being today hurt I desire to cry thy sorrow, thy sentiment, and thy pain. Make it so, which in a single turn, and forever I may die to the world, to sin, and to myself: and that, entombing myself in the abyss of my misery, and my nothingness, I may resuscitate with the grace of thy Son to a new life, so as walking in that observance of his precepts, the fruits of his Passion, and precious blood may not be wasted on me. *Amen.*

Lord I have sinned, have mercy on me.
Six Our Fathers, and six Hail Marys.

Now contemplate, in your soul, all the torments of the Passion of the Redeemer, so as you may see how much you owe to your God, and so as you may commit from this moment on to love him.

Seven were the falls, which our beloved JESUS suffered, from the Garden to the house of Annas.

All respond with kindness: Praised be forever such a good Lord.

The kicks that he suffered were one hundred and forty, and four. *Praised be &c.*

The punches were one hundred and fifty. *Praised be &c.*

The slaps were one hundred and two. *Praised be &c.*

The blows to the chest, and the body, two hundred and two. *Praised be &c.*

Seventy-eight times they dragged him by a rope, which he carried around his neck. *Praised be &c.*

Three hundred and fifty times they dragged him by the hair, and twenty seven times they dragged him thought the dirt. *Praised be &c.*

The floggings he took were over five thousand; and three times he was at the throes of death. *Praised be &c.*

Four times they violently placed the crown of thorns on him, which cut down to his sacred head with a thousand tips. *Praised be &c.*

Three times he fell on the ground with the Holy Cross. *Praised be &c.*

His heart was afflicted with seventy two anguishes. *Praised be &c.*

Having his hands and feet nailed to the cross, they gave seventy two blows with a hammer. *Praised be &c.*

In the course of his Passion he gave one hundred and nine sights. *Praised be &c.*

The drops of blood he shed were two hundred and thirty thousand. *Praised be &c.*

The tears which he cried for our sins were six hundred thousand and two hundred. *Praised be &c.*

Praised be forever such a good Lord, who desired to suffer such for men, and for their sins, being these the cause of his death, and his torments! Let us cry at his feet our ungratefulness, and let us say to him with pain, and sorrow.

ACT OF CONTRITION

Most Beloved Lord JESUS Christ, my Redeemer, and Saviour, single joy of my soul, and merciful Father of infinite mercy. I know, Lord, and confess, that, even if I were to love thee with all the love that the Just, and the Seraphim have for thee, and that which thy Most Holy Mother loves thee, this still would not correspond to the love by which thou offered thy life, nor would it satisfy in the slightest way thy Holy Passion. But alas, that the satisfaction of this love was always the faults, and the correspondences for those finenesses ended in crucifying thee with affront. It weights on me, Lord, all which I have committed, for being thou who thou art, supremely good, and worthy of being loved. I propose with thy grace to emend my life, and I hope, that thou shall forgive me, by thy love, by thy death, by thy Blood, by thy wounds, by thy worthy, and by thy mercy. JESUS of mine, mercy, my JESUS.

Spiritual Remedies

Remedy, or medicine which was used by a priest so as not to endure the penalties of Purgatory

Caesarius[111] tells us in his dialogues, that on the day, and moment, in which a priest of his Prelate expired, he appeared to him and told him that one could go to Heaven without passing through Purgatory; for while he was alive he prayed this Prayer in front of the crucified Lord.

Prayer

My Lord Jesus Christ, by that great bitterness, and passion thou suffered on the Cross, and especially when thy Most Saintly soul was parted from thy Most Saintly body, I ask thee to have mercy upon mine, when it leaves my body. Jesus of Nazareth, King of the Jews, have mercy on me, and give me a good death by thy most holy death. *Amen.*

Prayer, which was made by Saint Teresa of Jesus in order to reach spiritual fervour

O God of my soul, what hurry we have in offending thee, and thou even greater in forgiving us! What cause may there be, Lord, for such a restless daring; having already understood thy great mercy, and forgetting that thy justice is just? The pains of death surround me. Oh, oh, oh, what grave thing sin is, which was enough to kill God with pain, how surrounded by it art thee my God, where can thou go that these may not torment thee! From all sides all mortally wound thee. O all of thee who art consumed in delights, and contentment, and pleasures, and to always do thy will, have pity on thyselves; remember, thou shall always be subjected to the endless furies of Hell, look, look, the Judge pleas to thee, that he shall condemn thee, and that thou shall not have a single safe moment in life, for thou do not wish to live forever. O harshness of the human heart, soften them by thy immense mercy, God of my soul, JESUS.

111 Translator's note: most likely Caesarius of Heisterbach (before 1180 – after 1240), author of *Dialogus Miraculorum*.

The greatest devotion, and of much greater pleasure to God, which is given by the Missionary Reverent Friar Joseph Gavarri in his *Instructions*[112] claiming this devotion to be so powerful, that with it we may earn more than if we prayed five hundred thousand Rosaries, and if we gave the whole earth as alms; and for this one should pray it with care, devotion, and with full pain : all of this in order to have a good death, making this great devotion every day, twelve times, which are twelve perfect acts of contrition.

It weighs on me, Lord, with all my heart, for being thou who thou art, of how much I have offended thee, and I firmly propose to correct myself.

Prayer composed by Saint Augustine to be said by he who is contrite of his sins, for each time he shall earn eighty thousand years of indulgences, and by saying it for forty days shall reach full remission from his sins. Boniface VII conceded it, and Benedict XI confirmed it.

Prayer

God, who for the redemption of the world wished to be born, be circumcised, despised by the Jews, sold by Judas with a kiss of peace, arrested as an innocent lamb, affronted, sacrificed, presented before the judges Annas, Caiaphas, Pilate, and Herod, be accused with false witness, affronted with floggings, and offences, spat, crowned with thorns, slapped, wounded with a rod, thy face covered, undressed of thy vestments, risen, and nailed to the Cross, called a thief, given gall and vinegar to drink, be wounded on thy most holy side with a spear, which I an unworthy sinner mention, and by thy holy Cross, and death I ask thee, my Lord Jesus Christ, have it as good to free me from the punishments of Hell, and take me to where thou took the good Thief, crucified with thee, who with the Father, and the Holy Spirit thou lives, and reign forever without end. *Amen.*

Our Father, Hail Mary &c.

Great remedy to stop the contagious plague

The most eminent Cardinal Dom Friar Francisco Gonzaga of the Order of Saint Francis, and Bishop of Mantua, in the Chronicle he wrote of the mentioned Order, part 3. most. 8, and it is mentioned in the Roman Breviary, that there was a great plague in the city of Coimbra, and fearful of this destruction, and neighbouring it, the Nuns of the Monastery of Saint Claire of the Order of Saint Francis, founded that it was by the Queen Saint Elizabeth, and where today her saintly body lays, and I had

112 Translator's note: Joseph Gavarri, an Aragonese Franciscan Friar active in the 17th century. The book mentioned is his *Instrucciones Predicables y Morales, No Comunes, que Deven Saber los Padres Predicadores, y Confessores Principiantes, y en Especial los Missoneros Apostolicos*, from 1677.

the pleasure of seeing the bier where the silver coffin is kept, which contains that great treasure of the glorified body of the Queen Saint, and I with great devotion kissed it, and with adoration, and my eyes with tears saw, and worshipped it. There the Nuns immediately took care to leave that place, and go to a safer one, less contagious; and while these deliberated in the way of exit, a poor man appeared at their gate, and he asked them the cause of their sadness and worry, with them offering the cause of their determination and its urgent causes, and he gave them a piece of paper, which he was carrying in his hand, in which was written the Antiphon Stella Cœlis &c. with the following prayer, recommending that they sang it greatly every day (as I also recommended in the Seminaries, which I founded in the fields of Guaitacazes, and the city of Rio de Janeiro, to be sung every morning), and that within a few days their monastery would be free from the plague, of which it was already suffering. The poor man then disappeared never to be seen again, and the Nuns afterwards understood through devout conjecture that this should be the Apostle Saint Bartholomew. The Convent was free from illness, and the Nuns remained peaceful, without moving, and the city also, given the mentioned devotion, and in a short time such an evil contagion was extinguished.

This is the Antiphon, *in Latin, as was given, and afterwards in vernacular*

Stella Cœli extirpavit, quæ lactavit Dominum, mortis pestem, quam plantavit primus parens hominum. Ipsa Stella nunc dignetur sydera compescere, quorum bella plebem cædunt diræ mortis ulcere. O piissima Stella maris, à peste succurre nobis. Audi nos Domina, nam Filius tuus nihil negans te honorat. Salvat nos Jesu, pro quibus Virgo Maria te orat.

℣Ora pro nobis Sancta Dei Genitrix

℣Ut digni efficiamur promissionibus Christi.

Oremus

Deus misericordiæ, Deus pietatis, Deus indulgentiæ, qui misertus est super afflictionem populi tui, & dixisti Angelo percutienti populum tuum : Contine manum tuam : ob amorem illius Stellæ gloriosæ, cujus ubera pretiosa contra venenum nostrorum delictorum, quam dulciter suxisti, præsta auxilium gratiæ tuæ, ut ab omni peste, & improvisa morte secure liberemos, & à totius perditionis incursu misericorditer salvemur. Per te Jesu Christe, Rex sæculorum. ℟Amen.

Antiphon in vernacular[113]

Star of Heaven, who breastfed the Lord, who drove away the plague of death, who planted the first father of men. This same Star now permit the stars to slow down, whose wars shall kill the people with wounds of cruel death. O most merciful Star of the Sea, free us from the plague. Hear

113 Translator's note: this Antiphon and its corresponding prayer is usually referred to as the 'Star of Heaven'. Through Ângelo Sequeira's work it has become quite popular in folk circles in Portugal and Brazil. This is usually printed or written on a piece of paper and nailed to the front door to keep disease and plague away.

us, Lady, since thy Son, who doesn't deny thee anything, honours thee. O Jesus save us by the pleas the Virgin thy Mother offers thee.

℣Plead for us Holy Mother of God

℟So as we may be worthy of the promises of Christ.

Let us pray

God of mercy, God of compassion, God of forgiveness, who wert moved by the affliction of thy people, and thou told the Angel, wounding them : Restrain thy hand : by the love of that glorious Star, on whose precious breasts thou so sweetly suckled against the poison of our sins, offer the aid of thy grace, so as we may surely be free from all plague, and sudden death, and be mercifully saved from attacks of perdition. For thee, O Jesus Christ King of glory, Saviour of the world, who lives, and reigns forever without end. *Amen.*

Effective remedy to achieve from God freedom from sudden death

Make a Cross ✠ *over your forehead saying*: Free us, Lord, from sudden and unexpected death.

Make a second Cross ✠ *over your mouth, and say*: Free us, Lord, from sudden and unexpected death.

Make a third Cross ✠ *over your chest, and say*: Free us, Lord, from sudden and unexpected death, and pray one Our Father.

Make a Cross ✠ over your forehead, another over the mouth, and another over the chest, and at each time repeat the following words: Free us, glorious, and blessed Virgin from sudden and unexpected death, and pray one Hail Mary.

Devout prayers, which were used by the Holy Father Benedict XIII to reach the Grace of not dying a sudden death from God, proposed to the faithful by the Holiness of Pope Clement XII on the occasion that in the city of Rome sudden deaths were occurring, which would cease with the use of these prayers

Most Merciful Lord Jesus, by thy agony, and bloody sweat, and by thy Most sacred Death I ask thee to free me from sudden and unforeseen death.

Most benign Lord Jesus, by the most affrontful flagellation, and coronation of thorns, and by thy Cross, and Sacrosanct Passion, and by thy infinite kindness humbly I ask thee not to allow me to die suddenly, and go from this life without the Holy Sacraments.

Most beloved Jesus, my Lord, and my God, for all the labours, and pains, and by thy most precious Blood, by thy Holiest Wounds : sweetest Jesus, by those last words, which thou said on the Cross : *My God, My God, ut quid dereliquisti me?* for that clamour, with which thou expired : *Pater, in manus tuas commendo spiritum meum*, ardently do I ask thee to not take me from this world suddenly. From thy Divine hands this creature comes, entirely formed, and reformed : do not call it before time, so as it will not have need for penitence, and concede to me to have a happy transit, and thy grace, so as I may love thee with all my heart, and praise thee for all eternity. *Amen.*

My Lord Jesus Christ, for those five wounds, which thy Divine love made onto thee on the Cross, Succour thy servants redeemed by thy most precious blood.

By the Mystery of the Holy Incarnation, and Passion, Resurrection, and thy Ascension, and for thy Holiest Mother free us, Lord Jesus Christ, from all evil. *Amen.*

Those who do not know how to read may carry these Prayers with them, and pray an Our Father and a Hail Mary on each day.

Remedy for a good death, which was taught by Our Lady to Saint Mechtilde : it is contained in her life chap. 55.[114]

Pray a Hail Mary.

O my Lady Holy Mary, as God the Father with omnipotence made thee most powerful, in this way I plead to thee, so as thou may assist me in the hour of my death, to cast, and part from me all contrary powers. *Pray another Hail Mary.*

O my Lady Holy Mary, as God the Son gifted thee with so much knowledge, and clarity, that thou illuminates the entire Heaven, so in the hour of my death enlighten my soul with knowledge of faith, and strengthen it, so as it may not be perverted by any error, or ignorance. *Pray another Hail Mary.*

O my Lady Holy Mary, as the Holy Spirit infused in thee a great flood of love, so may thou in the hour of my death distil in me the sweetness of this divine love, by which all bitterness may become most gentle.

Mary, Mother of grace, Mother of mercy, free us from the enemy, and receive me in the hour of my death.

To thee, my Jesus, by the glory, that thou wert born from a Virgin Mother, and lives with the Father, and the Holy Spirit for all centuries of centuries. *Amen.*

℣Hear, Lady, my prayer.

℟And may my clamour reach thee.

Let us pray

My Lord Jesus Christ, we ask the Virgin thy Mother to intercede for us now, and in the hour of our deaths, before thy clemency whose sacred

114 Translator's note: Saint Mechtilde of Hackeborn, a Benedictine (Cistercian) nun from the 13th century, a visionary and devotee of the Hail Mary and the Sacred Heart of Jesus. The book mentioned is likely *The Book of Special Grace.*

soul in the hour of thy Passion was pierced by a sword of pain for the love she had for thee, who lives, and reigns with the Father, and the Holy Spirit for all centuries of centuries. *Amen.*

Jesus of Nazareth, King of the Jews, have mercy on me, and give me a good death. *Amen.*

Most evident remedy for the dying to say, or hear, for the fears of death, and Drexel[115] says God revealed this to his friends

My Lord God, I am that miserable creature, which thou created by thy immense kindness, and thou redeemed from the captivity of the Devil by the affrontful death of thy only-begotten Son. Only thou has dominion over me, only thou can save me by thy infinite mercy, in which I place my hope.

Remedy to aim all our senses to the service of God, and the wellness of the souls, and which was prayed every day by His Holiness the Pope Innocent XI and Alexandre VII; and to which the Cardinals Conti, Vicenti Bichi being nuncios in this Court of Lisbon conceded forty indulgences, and remission from sin to those who prayed it

I worship thee, Most holy, and undivided Trinity, Father, Son, and Holy Spirit: three Persons, and one sole true God.

I humble myself in the presence of thy Majesty, recognizing that I am nothing.

I firmly believe, and I am prepared to offer up one thousand lives, if I had so many, by the commission of the Mysteries, which thou revealed in thy sacred Scripture; and by means of thy Catholic Church which thou gave us to believe.

In thee I place all my hope, and all I may have of spiritual, or corporeal good in this and the next life, all this I desire, and hope, and wish to reach by thy hand, my God, my life, and only hope of mine.

From this day forth, and forever I give thee my body, and soul, all my potencies, memories, understanding, and will, and all my senses.

I protest, and will not consent, but rather I shall place all my strength to never consent that no single thing, nor the slightest offence against thy Majesty be made.

I firmly propose to employ myself fully, in all that I am, and am worth, and with all my strength in thy service, and for thy greater glory.

I am prepared to receive all the adversities, and labours, which from thy paternal hand may come, so as in this way give thee pleasure and contentment.

---

115 Translator's note: most likely Jeremias Drexel, a Jesuit writer from the 17th century.

I desire to fully commit, in all that I am, to thy service, and seek that all may serve, glorify and love thee as my God, and creator.

It pleases me immensely thy eternal happiness, and I am joyful in the greatest glory, that thou has in Heaven, and on earth.

I give thee infinite grace by the countless benefits, which to me, and to the whole world thou hast given, and thy benign providence is continuously giving every day.

I love thy infinite kindness by love of itself with all the affection of my soul, and heart. And should it be possible, I wish I could love thee with all the love with which the Angels, Saints, and Just love thee, with whose love I unite, and gather my most imperfect love, that I have for thee.

From this day forth, and forever I offer to thy Majesty in unity with the gifts of life, Passion, and Death of Christ, the always Blessed Virgin, and of all the Saints, all my works bathed, and united with the most precious blood of our Redeemer Jesus Christ.

I intend to earn as many indulgences as I can from all actions, which on this day I may work; and I apply these as suffrage for the souls in Purgatory.

I also have the intention, and wish to offer all I can in penitence, and satisfaction for my sins.

God, and my Lord, by being thou who thou art, and infinitely worthy of all love, and gifts, I offer myself as much as I can, and my sins weigh me greatly, and I am bothered by these more than by any other evil, and of them I humbly ask for forgiveness; and I make firm the intention of never offending thee again.

In thy most just wounds I take refuge, O good Jesus! In them shield me, and defend me from this day unto forever, until thou concedes to me the grace of seeing thee, and loving thee eternally. Amen. JESUS, MARY, JOSEPH, in thy hands I deliver my soul, and my heart.

All for the greater glory of God, and of the immaculate most holy Virgin his Mother.

Effective remedy for a God-loving soul, considering the greatest torments, which the Lord suffered in his sacred passion, to convert to God. This was revealed by this same Lord to several Saints in the following words

Wife of mine, so as thou may once again be animated to suffer for my love, I wish to tell thee something of how much I have suffered for thee. And so turn thy ear to my voice, listen, and reflect. Thou should know that, crying for the sins of the world, I have shed seventy-two thousand, and two hundred tears. By the great charity, with which I love men, I sweated in the Garden, after having made sacrament, ninety-seven thousand three hundred and five drops of blood. I have received in my holy body five thousand four hundred seventy-five wounds. On my divine neck I was given one hundred and twenty-five blows, and on my mouth these same slaps.

I was spat on the face thirty-two times, on the chest forty-two, and on my head eighty-five. My feet were stomped, and hurt one hundred and seventy-two times. My legs took thirty-two blows, and my chest forty. I was cruelly cast on the ground three times. My beard was disarranged fifty-eight times. In the coronation of thorns I was made three hundred wounds, and I shed from these wounds eighty-one thousand and two hundred drops of blood. I moaned, and mourned for thy sins ninety times. I had deathly tremors one hundred and seventy-two times. The deathly sufferings I endured were six thousand six hundred and sixty-six.

By the great pains, and anguishes, which I had, I was seen as dead nineteen times. I received in my most holy body five thousand five hundred blows. Almost did my soul separate from my body once in the agony of the Garden, another at the column, another time when I was nailed to the Cross. While nailed on it three more times, on the first the earth trembled, on the second the stones broke and the cliff under the Temple broke; on the third I said goodbye to my most holy soul, and committing my spirit into the hands of my Eternal Father, suffered a most affrontful death with great leisure for men. This is the revelation by the very words of this same Lord.

Devotion of the Most Holy Virgin, to which Pope Sixtus IV conceded plenary indulgences; and which can be applied for the souls in Purgatory, having the Bull of the holy Crusade.

God save thee, most beloved Daughter of God the Father.

God save thee, most dignified Mother of God the Son.

God save thee, most lovable Wife of God the Holy Spirit.

God save thee most sacred Temple of the Holiest Trinity. Our Father, Hail Mary.

Effective remedy against violent death by lightning, bolts, and thunder

Antiphon

Sub tuum præsidium confugimus, Sancta Dei Genitrix, nostras deprecationes ne despicias in necessitatibus nostris, sed à periculis conctis libera nos semper Virgo gloriosa, & benedicta.

℣Ora pro nobis Sancta Dei Genitrix.

℟Ut digni efficiamus promissionibus Christi.

Oremus

Protege Domine famulos tuos subsidiis pacis, & Beatæ Mariæ semper Virginis patrociniis confidentes à cunctis hostibus redde securos. Per Christum Dominum nostrum. *Amen.*

In vernacular

Antiphon

To thy favour, and presidency we refer to, Most Holy Mother of God, do not despise our pleas, which we make to thee in need; but free us always from all danger, glorious and blessed Virgin.

℣Pray for us, Virgin Mother of God.

℟So as we may be worthy of the promises of Christ.

Prayer

Defend, Lord, thy servants with the gifts of peace; and make free, and safe from their enemies all those faithful, who trust in the patronage of the Blessed always Virgin MARY. For Jesus Christ our Lord. *Amen.*

Devotions to beat any temptation from the Devil

Make three Crosses, one over your forehead, another over your mouth, and another over your chest, saying at each of them: Jesus of Nazareth, King of the Jews, have mercy on me; and continue saying: *Gloria Patri &c.* It is also very useful to use this devotion in the morning and evening.

Make another three Crosses over your heart, saying the following words on each Cross: Christ wins, Christ reigns, Christ rules, Christ defend me from all evil.

Invoke the Holiest Names of Jesus, and Joseph with great devotion, which is a most effective remedy.

Devotion to beat the three ordinary temptations

Our Virgin Lady gave through Saint Brigit three greatly devout prayers to easily beat the three ordinary temptations of thoughts, words, and deeds, and these are the following.

Prayer to resist sensual and fitly thoughts

Jesus Christ, Son of God, knower of everything, aid me, so as I may not take pleasure in bad thoughts.

Prayer to resist the temptation of words

Jesus Christ, Son of God, who were silent before the Judge, keep my tongue under control, so as I may take care as to when, and to whom I may speak.

Prayer to resist the temptation in deeds

Jesus Christ, Son of God, who were tied, govern my hands, and all my members, and my deeds, so as these may go on a good path.

Effective remedy for the exercise of the Novices to free them from the temptations of the Devil and may we triumph over him

O Death! O Judgment! O Eternity! O Hell! O Paradise!

Make the sign of the Cross, saying: Remember thy Novitiate, and do not sin eternally.

Then say three times: O Eternity! O Eternity! O Eternity!

Say a few more times: O Death! O Judgment! O Eternity! O Hell! O Paradise!

And thus continuing, repeat the above-mentioned things five times, and as many times as might be your wish, saying once again at the end:

Remember thy Novitiate, and do not sin eternally.

Experience has shown, and today also shows, the advantageous efficiency of these marvellous words in all sorts of people, mainly to repress the impulses of the flesh, and it is true that many boys confess that by saying these words, not only did they abandon sin, but also the desire to sin. Say them to yourself whenever you wish to work any deed: What thing do I wish I would have done at the hour of my death, in the day of my judgment, when I am alone before the judging God?

Efficient Remedy to reach the ultimate perfection, which was taught by our crucified Lord JESUS Christ

1. Despise the world, and thyself with profound humility.
2. Despise sin, and thyself.
3. Penitence, and total mortification of pleasure.
4. Great patience, and esteem for work.
5. Perfect obedience, and resignation in the hands of God.
6. Love God, and your fellow man.
7. Poverty, detachment from all possessions, and affections for the earth.

Holiest words against lightning, storms, and thunder

Christ the King came in peace,
And God was made man,
The Word was made flesh,
Christ was born from the Virgin,
Christ through them went in peace,
Christ was crucified,

Christ was killed,
Christ resurrected,
Christ rose,
Christ rules with empire,
Christ reigns,
Christ defend us from all lightning,
Christ is with us,
Thou art unmovable.
Our Father, Hail Mary, Creed.

Prayer that the Apostle of the Orient St. Francis Xavier did for the five wounds

My Lord Jesus Christ, love of my heart, by those five Wounds, which were opened on thee on the Cross by the love of men, Succour thy servants, who thou redeemed with thy precious blood. *Amen.*

Remedy, and easy method, and even more practical way to perform mental prayer, even for those who may not know how to read, and for all people, who might say that they don't have the time for mental prayer, and they think that it is a difficult thing

It is certain that prayer is an elevation of the understanding towards God, meaning, it is a rising of the mind to God, joining the five senses to God, and with all of these as if in the presence of God, invoking his aid, crying for the support of our Lady, meditate, so as to aid in your understanding of death, judgment, Hell, and Glory; consider any of these points for the whole time your devotion, and your fervour determines; further consider the greatness, immensity, and infinity of God, the greatness of his works, of the Heavens, the Sun, the Moon, and the Stars; fountains, tides, rivers, fish, flowers, fruit, and the formation of men, considering how all was the work of the hand of the Almighty; and on any if these points you have the occasion to praise, and love God with all your heart, soul, and all your strength, considering that he created everything from nothing, and men from mud, and that this God, who redeemed us with his precious blood, shall judge us on judgment day, offering Heaven as a prize to the good, and Hell as punishment for the wicked. Consider the Passion of Christ, and the ugliness of sin, and the ungratefulness of men.

On your knees in front of the crucified Lord, and our Lady to the side, wherever you may find this, and persignating,[116] say what follows:

Come Holy Spirit, fill the hearts of the faithful, and kindle in them the fire of thy love.

116 Translator's note: making the sign of the Cross.

℣Send Lord thy Creating Spirit.
℟And renew the face of the earth.

Prayer

God, who taught the hearts of the faithful with the illumination of the Holy Spirit, concede that we learn what is just, and good with the favour of the same Spirit, and always have the pleasure of his consolation. *Amen.*

Offering

My God, and my Lord JESUS Christ, Eternal Father, and Redeemer of souls redeemed by thy precious blood, we offer thee ourselves, our souls, our hearts, our powers, our senses, and all we have, so as from all of this thou may do what thou so wishes, and should we do anything, which is in thy liking, we offer it to thee humbly with all the worth of thy Mother MARY Holiest Queen of Heaven, and earth, so as aided by thy divine love, we may continue in this exercise and from it take the fruit of the tree of true life, which is thee, my God, my Creator, and my Redeemer.

Let us make the act of Faith with all five senses, believing that we are in the presence of God, who is with the same majesty, greatness, and immensity, as he is in Heaven manifested to the Angels, and the Blessed, and that these assist him by praising without ceasing, and that the celestial, earthly, and infernal creatures prostrate themselves on their knees solely by the articulation of the name of JESUS, our true God, who is here as perfectly, as he is in Heaven, here he is in us, and outside of us, here is our body, our soul inside of our loving God, more than a fish in the waters : all which is in our interior is seeing, and for all the good, which we may work, is aiding us, here he is more firmly, than if we would see him with our eyes, for the eyes can be fooled, but God, who thus said, cannot lie.

Act of humility

My God, and my Lord JESUS Christ, we art here surrendered to thy sovereign feet, and to them prostrated we learn of our wickedness, and thy mercy : now, Lord, humbly do we ask forgiveness for our guilt, and tears so we may wash our souls, and we may reach this fountain of divine grace. *Amen.*

Act of love of God

It weighs on me, Lord, with all my heart having offended thee for being thou who thou art, infinitely good, and worthy of being loved; and because I love thee, and regard thee above all things, I firmly propose myself to, with thy divine grace, never offend thee again, and I hope for the forgiveness of my faults by the worth of our Lord JESUS Christ. *Amen.*

Act of feverous love of God

O my Lord JESUS Christ, and my loving God, we offer thee everything which we work on during this holy exercise for thy greatest honour, and glory, and of the Holiest Mary our Mother, for the good of our souls, and the ones in Purgatory. O Most Holy Virgin Queen of Heavens, and the earth, advocate of sinners, aid us, support us, and guide us. O Angels of God, and of our guard, assist us, awaken us, teach us, so as we may take from this the fruit, and gain for our souls. O custodian angel Saint Gabriel, Saint Michael Archangel, Saint of our name, and all further Saints of Heaven, aid us so as we may be in the presence of God our Lord with humility, and reverence, with which we should be.

Here meditate on some point mentioned above, according to your understanding, and for the time you can.

Action of grace

We give thee infinite grace Almighty God, and our Lord, for the great benefits thou hast done, and does to thy Holy Mother Roman Catholic Church, and in particular for those who died, and all those in our obligation.

Supplication

Already thankful, Lord, we ask thee with all humility, and with open hearts, and contrite, for thy mercy, and in common with all miserable sinners, and in particular, the remedy for all our spiritual, and temporal necessities, and the grace to overcome vice, and passions, which wage the greatest war, and thus, Lord, we ask for the increase of the Holy Mother Roman Catholic Church, for the High Pontiffs, and further Prelates of this, for peace, and agreement among Christian Princes, for the extinction of heresy, and for all our companions, and benefactors, friends, and enemies, acquaintances, living and dead, and for all the Just, so as thou may conserve them in thy grace, and for all those who art in mortal sin, and for all those in the agony of death, and roaming over the waves of the sea, and on the lands of infidels, especially for the blessed souls, who art in the sufferings of Purgatory, have mercy on them and us, most merciful Lord, for all centuries of centuries. *Amen.*

And immediately say the Litany of Our Lady above, and if you so desire, the Novena to the Souls, especially on Fridays, and during disciplines, &c.

Remedy so as a Nun may reach from God, her Divine Husband, the virtue of Chastity, and any other creature, as did the Saint Count Elzéar with the following Prayer

God, who has promised to aid all those with goodwill : I plead to thee, that thou give me the grace to conserve with perseverance the affection of purity, and chastity, so as this may increase grace by grace, and casting out the yoke of contagion, we switch it by the yoke of sainthood, and may I walk in thy presence with pure, and sincere heart, until I reach the eternal crown in Heaven, and sing the praises of thy goodness for all centuries. *Amen.*

Remedy for the spiritual renovation of a Nun's vows every time you wish to do so, and for after or before confession

Many Saints say that the day in which a Priest professes, being in grace, he attains that state in which he was after baptism; and the same (according to some Doctors) each time he renews his professions, having esteem for having done it, and thus it is an excellent act of love for God to renew it each day, and this can be done in the following way.

My most beloved Jesus, as an action of grace for the benefit, which thou offered me by removing me from the century,[117] and I say, if I was the Queen of the world, and of a hundred thousand worlds, with thy saintly grace I would despise them for thy love; and if in my hand I had one, and one hundred thousand times the power to return to it, and enjoy all the honours, wealth, and delights, for as many women as exist and will exist, and thy Majesty may come to create, enjoy, and if of all of this I could licitly enjoy until the day of Judgment, of everything I would deprive myself for thy love, and I would once again sacrifice myself, as I do now, with the intention of obliging myself, even if I have no such obligation. I (NN) make my profession, &c. saying the same words, which I said when I professed. And the same may any person do, who has made a vow of chastity.

Practices, which should be done, as an advice, by Nuns for honest and good enjoyment

Disciplines, cilices, and bodily harshness are the first tools for spiritual life.

A beginner in perfection without a master for prayer is a ship without a pilot, which has no helm.

Having too much fun, and keeping chastity is wanting to mix darkness and light.

Great bodily and spiritual enjoyments only a miracle can join.

Whoever wants to extensively deal with God, should not deal with men, but only the strictly necessary and briefly.

For each one his obligation is to quickly walk towards perfection.

Spending too much time in prayer is to fail obligation, it has more illusions than perfection.

---

117 Translator's note: mundane non-priestly life.

Whoever brings God by his side in the present, walks modestly, sternly and is silent.

Perseverance in prayer during darkness and harshness is a most valorous end, and solid sainthood.

To regret by guilt is proper of thieves; but to regret without it is a thing of a strong saint.

A penitent, who is not obedient, of virtue and sainthood, has only appearance.

Whoever does not wish to err in corporal penitence, should resign himself to the will of his spiritual Father.

The pleasure of prayer is greatly delicious, but the bitterness of loneliness is more advantageous.

Repeated stitches on a poor and ragged habit are the practices of Christ in a religious breast.

Doing much good, without suffering much evil is the doing of a spiritual man.

In vain one shall flee from the Cross if truly he seeks Jesus.

A curious cell, and richly adorned, is not of a poor Nun, but of a relaxed person.

Whoever wants to enjoy the spiritual life, should communicate his entire life to his spiritual Father.

Canticle of our Lady or the Magnificat,[118] *which is useful to pray every day on your knees, for having been composed by our Lady, and this is used to ask for the virtue of humility, and the support of the Most Holy Mary*

Magnificat anima mea Dominum.

Et exsultavit spiritus meus in Deo salutari meo.

Quia respexit humilitatem ancillæ suæ; ecce enim ex hoc beatam me dicent omnes generationes.

Quia fecit mihi magna qui potens est : & sanctum nomen ejus.

Et misericordia ejus á progenie in progenies timentibus eum.

Fecit potentiam in brachio suo : dispersit superbos mente cordis sui.

Deposuit potentes de sede; & exaltavit humiles.

Esurientes implevit bonis : & divites dimisit inanes.

Suscepit Israel, puerum suum : recordatus misericordiæ suæ,

Sicut locutus est ad patres nostros : Abraham, & semini ejus in sæcula.

Gloria Patri, et Filio, et Spiritui Sancto,: sicut erat in principio, & nunc, et semper : & in Sæcula sæculorum. *Amen.*

---

118 Translator's note: also known as the Song of Mary, or Canticle of Mary. This is one of the earliest, if not the earliest, Marian hymns. It has been used in liturgy since around the fourth century and it is still used in the Vespers Mass. It grants partial indulgences.

Following is the Magnificat in vernacular[119]

Magnify * my soul to the Lord : And my spirit rejoiced * in God, who is my health;

Because he attended to the humility of his servant, * and for that all generations shall call me Blessed.

For the Almighty did great things with me, * and his holy name.

And his mercy shall extend from generations unto generations * to those who fear him.

In his arm he manifested his power : * he destroyed the greedy with the spirit of his heart.

He deposed the mighty from their chairs, * and he raised the humble.

To those in hunger, he filled with goods, * and he left void those who were rich.

He received his servant Israel, * and agreed to his mercy.

As he said to our father Abraham, * and his generation for all centuries.

Glory be to the Father, to the Son, and to the Holy Spirit, *, as it was in the beginning, is now, and ever shall be, and for all centuries of centuries. *Amen.*

Remedy to reach the pleasing of the Holiest Mary, which she herself revealed to one of her devotees, wanting him and all his family to practice the following devotion, for being in gratitude for the immense graces, with which the Holiest Trinity exalted her when she was taken into Heaven so as to prepare for us a better seat.

On your knees, and with profound reverence, pray one Our Father and Hail Mary with a Gloria Patri, and say

I worship thee, O Eternal Father, with the whole of the heavenly Court, as my God, and Lord, I give infinite grace in the name of the Holiest Mary, beloved daughter of thine, for all the graces, and favours, which thou gave her, especially by the power, with which thou took her up to Heaven.

Make another reverence, with an Our Father, Hail Mary and Gloria Patri, say

I worship thee, O Eternal Son, with the whole of the heavenly Court, as my God, and Lord, I give infinite grace in the name of the most beatific Virgin Mary, thy beloved mother, for all the graces and favours, which thou gave her, especially by the supreme wisdom, with which thou took her up to Heaven.

---

119 Translator's note: an English version of the *Magnificat* isn't particularly difficult to find at this point. Still, I'll be translating this version from the Portuguese presented by Ângelo Sequeira, which means that there should be considerable differences from this instance and the 'official' translations out there.

Make another reverence, with an Our Father, Hail Mary and Gloria Patri, say

I worship thee, O most Holy Spirit paraclete, with the whole of the heavenly Court, as my God, and Lord, I give infinite grace in the name of the most holy Virgin Mary, thy most beloved Wife, for all the graces, and favours, which thou gave her, especially by the divine charity, with which thou kindled her holiest, and purest heart in her glorious Assumption to Heaven.

Conclude with the following salute, which was given to Saint Bernard by an Angel, in which the Holiest Mary promised to assist in the hour of death whoever greeted her with it every day. This is in the *Chronica da Arrabida*, p.II, book.5, ch.1XV, n.1010[120]

God save thee, Mary, servant of the Holiest Trinity most humble.
God save thee, Mary, Daughter of the eternal Father most holy.
God save thee, Mary, Wife of the Holy Spirit most lovable.
God save thee, Mary, Mother of our Lord Jesus Christ most worthy.
God save thee, Mary, sister of the Angels most beautiful.
God save thee, Mary, promise of the Prophets most true.
God save thee, Mary, Doctor of the Apostles most prudent.
God save thee, Mary, consolation of the Martyrs most strong.
God save thee, Mary, flowing fountain of the Confessors most smooth.
God save thee, Mary, honour, and crown of the Virgins most joyful.
God save thee, Mary, health, and consolation of the living, and the dead most ready : be with me in all my tribulations, necessities, anguishes, and infirmities, and reach for me the forgiveness of my sins; most of all, do not fail me in the hour of my death, most pious, and beatific Virgin Mary.

Remedy to burn in the flames of Divine love in the hearts of Jesus, and Mary, which was revealed by Sister Maria Villani, as is told in her life,[121] to support in life, and in death, those who utilize it.

Hail Mary.

I salute thee, divine heart of my Jesus, as the sweetest fruit of the virginal womb of Mary, and I offer thee her purest heart with all the services which she gave thee in life, and I offer thee infinite grace by the excessiveness, with which thou enriched the lovable heart of thy holiest Mother. *Hail Mary &c.*

I salute thee, most sacred heart of Mary, and of thy only-begotten Son in union with that most ardent love, by which thou loved each other so much, and I give thee grace for the services, that thou offered thy Jesus,

---

120 Translator's note: this refers to the book *Espelho de Penitentes e Chronica da Santa Maria da Arabida*, from 1737, by Friar José de Jesus Maria Antonio da Piedade. A chronicle of Arrabida and the friars of the local convent.
121 Translator's note: this refers to the book on the life of Maria Villani, Dominican, written by Antonio Jacinto Zuazo, from 1692, *Espejo del amor divino, en la vida de la Ven. madre Sor María Villani, Religiosa del Sagrado Orden de Prodioadores y fundadora del Monasterio del Divino Amor, de Nápoles.*

and to him by the great privileges by which he enriched thee. *Hail Mary &c.*

Eternal Father, and sovereign God, and my Lord, I offer thee the two purest, and holiest hearts of thy Son, and his most lovable Mother, as unique gifts of thy delight, and in sweet union with them I offer thee also my filthy, and miserable heart, and as ask thee by the great deal, by which these loved thee, purify it fully, and kindle mine, so as I may always love, serve, and praise thee, as I should. *Amen.*

Conclude with the following salute translated from French, which is said that the Holiest Mary promised, to whoever is in grace, to augment the divine love in their heart : and that to those in mortal sin, she would knock on their soul so as these could repent &c

God save thee, Mary, Daughter of God the Father.
God save thee, Mary, Mother of God the Son.
God save thee, Mary, Wife of the Holy Spirit.
God save thee, Mary, splendorous Lily of the Holiest Trinity.
God save thee, Mary, pleasant Rose of the whole celestial Court.
God save thee, Mary, Virgin of virgins, most powerful virgin, filled with sweetness, and humility, from whom the eternal, and supreme King of Heaven wished to be born, and to be fed by thy milk.
God save thee, Mary, Queen of the Martyrs, whose Holiest soul was cruelly wounded by the sword of pain.
God save thee, Mary, Lady, and Mistress of the World, to whom was given all the power in Heaven, as on earth.
God save thee, Mary, Queen of my heart, my Mother, my guide, my sweetness, and all my hope.
God save thee, Mary, most lovable Mother.
God save thee, Mary, most admirable Mother. Mary filled with grace, the Lord is with thee. Mary, blessed art thou among women. Blessed is the fruit of thy womb Jesus Christ. Blessed is thy husband the Lord Saint Joseph. Blessed is thy Father the saintly Patriarch Saint Joachim. Blessed is thy Mother the glorious Saint Anne. Blessed is thy cousin Saint Elizabeth. Blessed is thy lovable adoptive Son Saint John Evangelist.[122] Blessed is thy beloved nephew Saint John the Baptist. Blessed is thy glorious Angel, and Ambassador Saint Gabriel. Blessed is the glorious archangel Saint Michael. Blessed is the Eternal Father, who picked thee. Blessed is thy Son, who loved thee. Blessed is the Holy Spirit, who took thee as his wife, and with a pure heart may thou be praised, and make us worthy of thy blessing, O Holiest Virgin, and of thy most lovable Son. *Amen.*

122 Translator's note: there is a consistent and constant confusion in the writings of Ângelo Sequeira between John the Apostle and John the Evangelist. Although these are quite easy to identify, I will maintain these original attributions.

Petition of loving supplication, which should be done before confession, and in any time in which any Christian may want to come to the presence of God, in front of the crucified Lord

Lord, and single Lord. I am the prodigal son, who walks blind through the path of perdition after so many falls, I fell now upon myself to see my misery, and blindness, and because of this I come in the way to confess my faults, and crimes in thy presence, and publically say, that I am not worthy of being called thy son any longer; however if I lost, due to my disobediences, the right of being thy son, thou did not lose being my loving, and merciful Father, for thou art still calling me, and inviting me to forgiveness, and to the celestial banquet, and thus I already know the multitude, and ugliness of my faults, and because of this, moved by the impulse of thy Divine grace, and immense mercy, I have in the way, which was possible to me, disposed to my conscience with that care, diligence, and exams, to arrive at thy presence in this venerable place of the Sacrament of Penitence, and thus, Lord, I am already resolved to leave this deceitful world, and all my sins, for knowing that it is all a deceit, and blindness of the Devil, who has brought me fooled and blind until this point : I come, Lord, vexing my sins, and I want to deal with them, offending them, as if my principal enemies : thou, Lord, very well knows how I come, and how my heart is; for, Lord, while I know the evil I have done, enlighten, and animate my contrite, and humiliated heart so as thou shall not despise it, but rather, Lord, inflame my affection, may they all be, and solely, for thee, so as in this way I may know, confess, and cry all of my sins, clearly and distinctly, without the Devil further fooling me; and as thou knows of my sins, I wish to confess them in the same way, in which I committed them, and thou wert offended, for I come very contrite and regretful, and all I am missing is thy mercy, and thy grace, so as with more confidence I may present them without fear of shame to the Confessor, and tell of all of them with the full circumstances, and occasions, re-incidences, and habit of sin; and thus, Lord, enlighten my understanding, so as I may know that thy mercy is extended to all my sins for forgiveness, and that if I don't confess them in the way in which I have committed them that I shall not be saved, and that with this knowledge I may resolve to cry them, and confess them, without any of the circumstances being missing, that may make me unworthy to reach the fruits of this Sacrament, which is to save myself, and I want to offend them, so as I may no longer seek them. Now, Lord, now that I trust in thy mercy, I wish to remember all of them, and the smallest of thoughts so as with tears of blood I may confess, and detest them, and thus, Lord, it is already time to ask thee with all my soul, with all my strength, and with my entire heart broken into pieces, forgive my sins for that crown of thorns, and for those wounds, for that Blood, for those nails, for the spear, for the slaps, for the offences, for the floggings, I ask thee, I beg thee, and I supplicate by the intercessions of the Holiest Mary of the Rock, patron of sinners, for the Angels in the Court of Heaven, for the souls in

Purgatory, and for all my devotions, by the Saint of my name, by the patron of this land, and by the Angel of my guard, I ask thee once again to animate me, and aid me to make this confession, to purge, and clean my soul of the leprosy of sin with all the proper circumstances, and to further secure myself, I ask thee by thy own self, give me fervour, constancy, firmness, knowledge, regret, Faith, Hope, Charity, tears, hurts, and moans to drown in the immense sea of thy divine grace the confoundment of my faults, and crimes so as to give glory, and joy to Heaven, and confoundment, and sadness to Hell, victory to Heaven, and war to Hell, for Lord, I already know that a greater celebration is done in Heaven for a penitent soul who repents, than for ninety souls together, for thou said, that thou did not come to call the Just, but rather the sinners : here thou has prostrated before thy feet the greatest of them all, and as he is the greatest, so too will thy glory be in forgiving him, and to see prostrated before thy feet thy greatest enemies. O sacred feet of my beloved JESUS, lift me up, for in the sea of my tears I have no footing, and in it I shall drown all my sins so as to leave comforted, joyful, and animated in that fountain of mercy, and divine wounds, and in them I hope, Lord in thee I trust, Lord, and in them I shall reach, Lord, for the worth of thy sacred passion, forgiveness, and remission for my faults, glory, and grace to my soul. *Amen.*

Remedy to cry, and to move God to forgiveness, and also for before confession

My most beloved, and most merciful Lord, if thou wants, and desires tears, here thou has me as a fountain of tears flowing to that sea of mercifulness to reach the forgiveness of my crimes, and a love for my heart, so as it will not be possible to incline it to the world anymore. And thus, Lord, as I can do something which is so great for me, and so small to thee, which is so easy for thee, and so hard for me, as is the heeding of my tears so as I may benefit from thy infinite mercy. Remember, my God, the great things thou did for me, and do not abandon what I ask of thee. How is it possible Lord, that thou suffered me when I sinned, and that now thou does not want to forgive me when I cry for my sins, and that I know my crime? For, Lord, I learned, and thou shall forgive, for I have thy word, and witnesses of it, for through David thou said that if a sinner should cry the sin in their heart as he did, who washed his bed with tears, and watered the land with the same tears, and had no other sustenance day or night than his tears, here thou has it now, Lord, another repenting David, to whom thou said that if the sinner cries his sin, he would reach the forgiveness of his faults. Thy Son thou delivered to death so as to save me, now that I come to thy presence JESUS, thou does not want to receive me? Lord, see how much thou worked for me, that thou parted from thy suffering Son so he would die, and be crucified for me. Now with this, Lord, what shall thou do? What does thou think of, Lord? If this worm shrouded in guilt causes thee boredom, give good use to thy death so as with it thou may resurrect this miserable and great sinner, so as thy forgiveness may be greater, by seeing an insolent, and transgressor of thy divine law prostrated at thy feet. Do not become accustomed, Lord, to be bothered by the sinner, for thou has seen many with thine eyes of piety and mercy. Do not forget, or make thyself deaf, when I cry, when I ask, when I sigh, when I regret, for I do not call for a God who closes his ears to sinners, I do not cry to a rigorous God, I do not plead to a severe God, I do not sigh for an unloving God, I do not regret for an unjust God, but rather to a merciful God, to a pious God, to a loving God, to a compassionate God, who created me, fed me, who redeemed me, who suffered and died to save me; because, Lord, now at last, I very much know the great deal thou did, and worked for me, and the blood thou shed for me, the offences thou suffered for me, the affronts thou suffered for me, the slaps for me thou took; for I already know thy love, I wish to cry, I wish to repent, I wish to emend, may thy wounds, thy pain, thy agonies be in my worth, Our Lady of the Rock be in my worth, be in my worth that blood, which I see on thy body, Lord, let it be the incentive for my heart to melt in fountains, and rivers of tears so as my life be nothing else but cries, sights, moans, wanting, and repenting from all of my sins so as to drown them in the torrent of my tears, and purify my soul in that sea of blood, and mercy, and from this place I shall not rise except when secure of thy forgiveness, which I cry for, my God, for thy mercy, mercy, Lord, mercy, Lord.

And immediately say the following Sonnet to the crucified Lord before confession:

To thee, I run to, thy holy arms,
  In that sacrosanct Cross uncovered,
  Who to receive me thou art open,
  Who not to punish me thou art nailed.
To thee, divine eyes eclipsed,
  With so much blood, and tears covered,
  Which to forgive me thou art open,
  And to not see me thou art closed,
To thee, nailed feet for not fleeing,
  To thee, lowered head for calling me,
  To thee, shed blood for anointing me:
In thy side I want to unite myself,
  To thee, precious nails I want to tie myself,
  So as to be united, tied and firm.

Remedy to move God to mercy, and for before confession

Lord, and my God, what is lost in hearing me? What does thou lose in seeing me? What honour escapes thee in forgiving me? The Angels, and Saints in Heaven are joyful, and the demons condemned in Hell saddened.

Make a new celebration in Heaven, the good shall praise thee, the wicked shall be newly animated. Who shall blame thee, for having purified me from my faults? Thou can surely see me, thou can surely see my misery, then how can thou not have compassion for me? For, my God, thou sees the good end for the souls, who thy Son redeemed : in the same way see thyself revered, and beloved by thy creatures, would thou wish to forgive, and allow me to truly love thee : May thou see thus thy wives in Heaven. May all the Just know how much thou loves them, being called in by their love, thou art saddened by all : may thou see thy Son desired, and loved by the whole world : may thou thus see all the sinners converted, and fulfil me, and I ask for whatever more thou may wish to give me, which is all I desire, thy mercy. *Amen.*

Confession, and prostration of the Catholic Faith for the awakening of the soul to the pain of sin, and the love of God, and particularly at the hour of death

Let the Heavens with all the Angels, and Saints, who enjoy the eternal life, hear the confession I make of the Catholic faith, and the prostration of offences, made against my God, and Benefactor, and against this same Heaven, from where I justly live in exile. Let the earth hear me with those who live in it, and may all creatures be witnesses to the correction of my life, and take the example of my wickedness; and those who might be scandalized by my faults, see my correction, and public satisfaction, and example. Be the Hells vigilant with all the evil spirits, and the disgraced souls so justly condemned to the eternal fire, for they shall not convert to their God, and not persevere in his love, that I take punishment from his head. And at last may all know that this letter of true prostration, and offering of my soul to God, and those who see this final, and last will, as I (NN) miserable sinner, and of full judgment, say, that having received from my Eternal Father a great wealth, and riches from the Heavens throughout my life I have despised, dissipated, and lost these, and the esteem, the excellence, and the nobility which is to be a son of God. I declare that I am his servant by title of creation, for he created me in his image, and likeness, so as to serve, know, and love him, by title of redemption, by the desire to bring down from Heaven this Divine Shepherd to seek my soul, as a lost sheep, and finding me in the power of the demons, so as to rescue me he bought me with his blood, suffering thirty-three years of excessive labour : by title of donation, for in baptism I made the solemn promise of renouncing all pomp, and the laws of the Devil, and the world; and then the same Almighty God being a supreme Lord, and King of Glory, and I his enemy, son of wrath, and prisoner of the Devil, without seeing my lowliness, besides his kindness, he had it as good that I be baptized in the name of the Holiest Trinity, with the Father giving me the title of son, and the Son the merits, and effects of his Passion, and blood, and the Holy Spirit receiving my soul as a wife.

Pitiful me, who did not know how to esteem this, nor how to conserve myself in such honour, and instead of a continuous, and perpetual thanking of so many benefits I was always ungrateful, instead of spending my life in love, and in his praise, I have spent it in offending him with so many faults. Woe is me, that for so many of these I shall have earned the penalties of Hell, as an ingrate, and traitor.

His kindness was so invincible with my evils, that when I was living in the greatest forgetfulness, he remembered me with public inspirations : when I was dead he called me, sometimes with threats, others with kindness, others with afflictions, and labours, and the whole of my life is a penitence for my wickedness, and this was neglected by his kindness, and invincible patience. He has waited for my penitence my entire life (blessed be God for infinite centuries) for while I have been alive I have known myself as ungrateful, and treacherous. I was conceived in sin, and in sin I was born, and in sin I have spent my life, always multiplying, and adding sin to sin. Miserable me, disgraceful me, if the same God, whom I offended does not receive me in his grace, and concede to me the last remedy, O as me!

For as a delinquent I present myself in front of the tribunal of justice, and I confess my sins, and evil, which are more than the sands, and the waters of the sea : I judge myself worthy of eternal punishments : I consent to the sentence : I confess that by justice I deserve one thousand Hells. However if I am permitted an appeal in such a rigorous court, and to supplicate for mercy, and to the same supreme judge, I appeal, and supplicate to my Creator, and Father of mercy to this same tribunal of grace. I take as my attorney JESUS Christ his son, who by the laws of his infinite mercy, and his grace may defend me. I present his worth, his life, his Passion, and death, his example, his actions, and all he did in the time of thirty-three years, not for himself, for he had no needs, but rather for my remedy, and salvation. And thou Queen of Heaven Virgin of the Rock, life, sweetness, and our hope, and mother of mercy be my patron. I nominate as my defender the Angel of my guard, who knows all my steps, and needs, be in my worth the Saints to whom I have devotion, who art (NN) and kneeling before his Divine Majesty, my Lord, and my God, moved by faith, and filled with hope, trusting in charity, I beg thee, to see with the eyes of mercy, that I was made by thy hands, do not condemn me, nor destroy me, for thou did not create me for such an end, but rather to enjoy thee, and praise thee in Heaven. Do not listen to the accusations of my enemies, for these are liars, false, and thy enemies. Do not listen to them, may they not feel that thou favours their bad intentions, give me thy light, and grace, so as I may always understand thy will, and execute it, which from this day forth I determine, and promise to obey thee in everything, and to do penitence over the past. Do not destroy me now that I seek thee, for thou pleaded, and called to me while I still offended thee. Do not condemn me, nor abandon me now, that I wish to serve thee, for thou does not abandon those who seek thee. And should there be a time which with weakness, or my illness, or with the cunning, and trickery of the Devil I say, or imagine, a contrary thing to those which I here confess, I immediately declare it void. And I wish that what I propose here, be firm, and valuable forever, and from now on forever, and from then to now I remit myself to this Catholic protestation, in which it is my will to live, and die with the desire to reach Heaven, where I may know, serve, and praise my God, and my Creator, and Redeemer without defect, and without sin in the company of the Saints for all centuries of centuries. *Amen.*

General prescription of the vocations of the Saints

Remedy to avoid the excessive crying of children, of which Saint Abraham Abbot is the patron

Antiphon

This Saintly man despising the world, and triumphing over the things of the earth, with his works, and words made his treasure in Heaven.

℣The Lord took the Just through the straight path.

℟And showed them the Kingdom of Heaven.

Prayer

God, who for the salvation of the souls wished that thy servant Saint Abraham Abbot would be useful for all : concede to us that bathed in tears of regret, and in the sweetness of thy love, interceding by thy worth, we may achieve the eternal pleasures. For Jesus Christ our Lord, who lives, and reigns for all centuries of centuries. *Amen.*

Remedy against breakings, and sufferings of pain, and plague, of which Saint Adrian Martyr is the patron.

Antiphon

This Saintly man, and Martyr Saint Adrian was cruelly beaten in the presence of the tyrant Emperor, and his body torn to pieces for the wholeness of our Faith.

℣Pray for us blessed Saint Adrian.

℟So as we may be worthy of the promises of Christ.

Prayer

God, who for the augmentation of our Faith illuminated thy blessed servant Saint Adrian strengthening his heart in the constancy of the spirit : propitiously concede to us, that by his worth, and by imitating his virtues, we may emend life in reformation of our vices. For Christ our Lord, who lives, and reigns with thee for all centuries of centuries. *Amen.*

Remedy against stones, arthritic gout, dry cough, and colic of which Saint Aelred is the patron

Antiphon

This Saintly man despising the world, and triumphing over the things of the earth with works and words made his treasure in Heaven.

℣The Lord took the Just through the straight path.

℟And he showed them the Kingdom of Heaven.

Prayer

God, who for the relief of thy creatures, thou wished that thy blessed servant Saint Aelred became the remedy for pain; propitiously concede to us that, by his intercession, thou may see it proper to mellow the pain we suffer. For Jesus Christ our Lord. *Amen.*

Remedy against breast pain, of which Saint Agatha is the patron

Being the blessed Agatha in her prison with her hands risen in prayer to the Lord, she said: My Lord Jesus Christ, true Master, I give thee many graces, for having given me the valour to beat the torments of my terrible guards : allow, Lord, that I may happily enjoy thy undying glory.

℣Grace was diffused in thy lips.

℟And for this God blessed thee forever.

Prayer

Almighty God, and Lord, who among the many marvels of thy power thou also communicated the victory of martyrdom to the fragility of the female sex : propitiously concede to us, that those who worship the birth of the blessed Saint Agatha, Virgin, and thy Martyr, may seek to imitate her so as to reach thy grace. For Jesus Christ our Lord, who with the Father, and the Holy Spirit lives, and reigns for all centuries of centuries. *Amen.*

Remedy to conserve good fame and against false witness, and for chest pain, of which Saint Agnes is the patron

Antiphon

Being the blessed Saint Agnes in the midst of the flames, with her hands high, she raised to the Lord, saying: Almighty, lovable, venerated, and tremendous God, I praise thee, and eternally glorify thy name.

℣Grace was diffused in thy lips.

℟For this God blessed thee forever.

Prayer

Almighty, and eternal God, who chose the weak things of the world to confound the ones who are strong : propitiously concede to us, who venerate the blessed Virgin, and Martyr Saint Agnes, that we may reach by her intercession thy grace. For Christ our Lord. *Amen.*

Remedy for the childbirth of women in the greatest danger, of which Saint Albert is the patron, and also for intermittent fever, malignant fever, and for any kind of fever, for which one should bless his water to give to the sick

Saint Albert Sicilian of the sacred, illustrious and most ancient Religion of our Lady of the Carmel, hero of great sainthood, and by his rare virtues, and miracles even the very Heavens sang his praises, when the Angels came down from Heaven to canonize him singing Mass on his funeral: *Os justi meditabitur.*

Any Priest may bless the water of Saint Albert, by putting on a stole, and with the following blessing.

℣Adjutorium nostrum in nomine Domini.
℟Qui fecit Cœlum, & terram.
℣Dominus vobiscum.
℟Et cum spiritu tuo.

Oremus

Fidelium Deus omnium fortitudo, & salus, qui socrum Beati Petri Apostoli tui febribus magnis detentam pio rogationis intuitu perfecte sanasti; sanctifica ✠ & benedic ✠ creaturam hanc aquæ in tuo sacrissimo nomine (& reliquiis, should there be any), & meritis sanctissimi Confessoris tui Alberti, quem spreto sæculo ad almæ tuæ Genitricis Religionem vocare dignatus es : & concede ejus gloriosis meritis, atque intercessionibus, ut quicumque febrium vexatione gravantur, per hujus aquæ sumptionem humilem à cunctis animæ, & corporis languoribus liberentur, atque Ecclesiæ tuæ repræsentari mereantur, gratiarum tibi actiones in ea jugiter referendo. Qui vivis, & et regnas in sæcula sæculorum.

Should there be any relic of the Saint make three crosses with it over the water, ✠ and otherwise simply make three Crosses.

Benedic ✠ Domine meritis Sancti Alberti creaturam ✠ hanc aquæ, qui glorioso tuo corpore benedixisti ✠ aquas Jordanis : & præsta, ut omnes gustantes ex ea, tam corporis, quam animæ recipient sanitatem. Qui vivis, & et regnas in sæcula sæculorum.

Immediately after say the Antiphon.

O Alberte norma munditiæ, puritatis, & continentiæ, ora Matrem misericordiæ, ut in hac valle miseriæ nos defendat à pravo scelere, ut exut mortali corpore, perfruantur æterna requie.

℣Ora pro nobis Beate Alberte.

℟Ut digni efficiamur promissionibus Christi.

Oremus

Deus, qui Beatum Albertum Confessorem tuum, spreto sæulo, ad almæ tuæ Genitricis Mariæ Religionem vocare dignatus es, ut ejus meritis, ac exemplis digne tibi fervientes, cum ipso in æterna gloria perpetuo te perfrui mereantur. Qui vivis, & et regnas in sæcula sæculorum.

Immediately after say the following Antiphon.

Antiphon

Vacant ægri vigilantes ad Alberti limina : surdi, claudi consequenter invocantes numina : febres fugat : morbos curat omnes : sanat noxium : ventos placat : maris sedat tædium.

℣Jesu dulcis Alberti meritis.

℟Tuam nobis infunde gratiam

Oremus

Concede, quæsumus omnipotens, & misericors Deus, ut per virtutem benedictionis hujus aquæ, & per meritum passionais Domini nostri Jesu Christi, & per intercessionem Beatæ Mariæ Virginis, & Beati Alberti, & omnium Sanctorum, & sanctarum Dei omnes fideles, qui piè, & devotè aquam istam gustaverint, & valeant, & in tuo sancto servitio sempre permanere. Per Dominum nostrum Jesum Christum, Filium tuum : qui tecum vivit et regnat in unitate Spiritus Sancti Deus, per omnia sæcula sæculorum. *Amen.*

Remedy for the purity of the soul, and stimulus of the flesh, for obedience, poverty, and humility, of which Saint Aloysius Gonzaga, who today is in Rome, and Italy, performing a thousand prodigies, and is generally venerated by all, is the patron

Antiphon

Be joyous good, and faithful servant, because thou wert so in the things of small value : I gave thee others of greater importance.

℣The Just shall blossom as a lily.

℟And shall always flourish in the presence of the Lord.

Prayer

All-powerful God, and Lord, who by the Holiest Virgin Mary advised the blessed Aloysius Gonzaga to enter into the Company of JESUS, thy son, and thou enriched him with celestial gifts : concede, that by his intercessions we may perfectly fulfil thy will in all things. By the same Jesus Christ thy Son our Lord, who lives, and reigns with thee for all centuries of centuries. *Amen.*

Remedy for pain, and wounds of the legs, and arms, of which Saint Amaro is the patron

Antiphon

Amaro set ablaze in the fire of charity and obedience earned to walk dry over the waters.

℣Pray for us blessed Saint Amaro

℟So as we may be worthy of the promises of Christ.

Prayer

Almighty God, and Lord, who adorned with virtues the blessed Saint Amaro : be propitious unto us, that, as he by the worth of charity, and obedience walked over the waters, so may we follow thy paths. For Jesus Christ our Lord, who with thee lives, and reigns for all centuries of centuries. *Amen.*

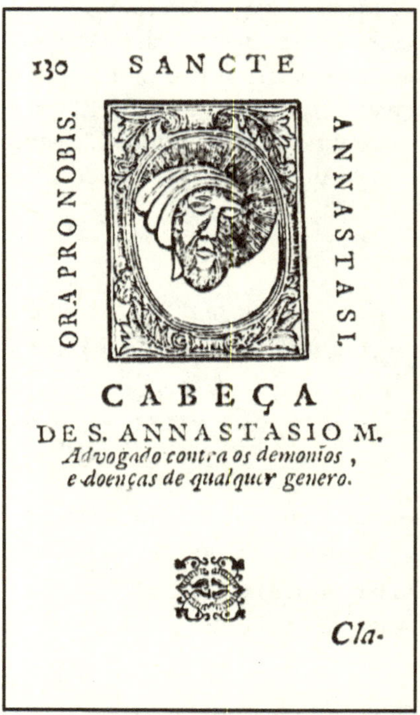
130 SANCTE

ORA PRO NOBIS.

ANNASTASI.

CABEÇA

DE S. ANNASTASIO M.

Advogado contra os demonios, e doenças de qualquer genero.

Cla-

Head of Saint Anastasius Martyr
Patron against demons, and illnesses of any kind

Unfailing remedy against the Devil, and against his malefica, and in the Council of Nicea was resolved that demons fled from the aspect of Saint Anastasius, and as such it is convenient to carry a medal for this end

Antiphon

JESUS Christ promised his disciples, that in his name they would cast out demons, and no poison, even after being drunk, could do them any harm, freeing them from all evil. This did Saint Anastasius execute in this world in the name of the same Lord.

℣Pray for us, O blessed Anastasius.

℟So as we may be worthy of the promises of Christ.

Prayer

O true God, and total virtue of those who await thee, who from the loneliness of Mount Carmel thou called the blessed Anastasius to achieve the palm of martyrdom; concede to us that, with his examples we become fully enflamed in the tolerance of torment, which may lead us to salvation: Which we ask thee by our Lord Jesus Christ thy only-begotten Son. *Amen.*

Hymn

O Saint Anastasius Martyr,
Who wert of the Persian nation,
And abandoning the magical art,
Thou increased in science.

By the confession of Faith
Thy head was severed,
And being taken to Rome,
It is venerated by the whole Church.
℣Pray for us, glorious Anastasius.
℟So as we may be free from all evil.

Let us pray

To thee, my God, we ask for the worth of thy faithful servant Anastasius to free us from the suggestions, and harm of the enemy, for thou conceded to him the special grace of being the patron against the powers of Hell. For Christ our Lord. *Amen.*

Remedy for the virtue of chastity, and constancy in torments, of which the Apostle Saint Andrew is the patron.

Antiphon

God save thee precious Cross, which in the body of Christ thou wert consecrated. Before the Lord was crucified on thee, thou freighted men; but now with pleasure I receive thee by the divine love, which shines from thee. Joyful, and secure I come before thee, so as thou, with rejoicings may receive me.

℣Pray for us blessed Saint Andrew.

℟So as we may be worthy of the promises of Christ.

Prayer

Lord God, humbly do I plead to thy Majesty, so as just like Saint Andrew Apostle, Preacher of thy Church, constantly preached thy faith, so may he forever be our intercessor in thy presence. For Jesus Christ our Lord; who with the Father, and the Holy Spirit lives, and reigns for all centuries of centuries. *Amen.*

Remedy for the hastening of legal processes, and to offer justice to those who need it, and against the ill of apoplexy, of which Saint Andrew Avellino, Holy Priest, is the patron

Antiphon

This Saintly man despising the world, and triumphing over the things of the earth with works, and words made his treasure in Heaven.

℣The Lord took the Just through the strait path.

℟And showed them the Kingdom of Heaven.

Prayer

Almighty God, who in the heart of thy blessed servant Saint Andrew Avellino, thy Confessor, thou deposited the treasure of thy wisdom : make it so, and we ask thee by his intercession, and supplication that thou hasten our pleas with a final sentence of thy mercy, so as we may go and enjoy thee in those celestial hierarchies. For Christ our Lord. *Amen*

Saint Andrew, Apostle

Remedy against sorcery, of which Saint Angelus Martyr, Carmelite, is the patron, and for the infirmities, which proceed from diabolical art, and to conserve the good fame of the Missionaries

Prayer

O illustrious Martyrs Saint Angelus, whose heroic virtues wert in such a way deserving in the presence of God, who conceded to thee the singular prerogative that thou would be the best defence in order to free thy devotees from all, and any malefic, without the arts of the Devil overcoming thy patronage. Receive me then in the number of those who enjoy this great happiness, and concede to me continuous triumph over the works of the Devil, in such a way that by thy great earnings the same Lord may concede to me a joyful death, not one occasioned by my enemies, but only that given especially by him, when he finds me in a state of grace, so as to achieve eternal life in thy divine presence. *Amen.*

Way of blessing the palms of Saint Angelus for all infirmities

℣Adjutorium nostrum in nomine Domini.
℟Qui fecit Cœlum, & terram.
℣Sit nomen Domini benedictum.
℟Ex hoc nunc, & usque in sæculum.
℣Dominus vobiscum.
℟Et cum spiritu tuo.

Oremus

Deus Creator, & Conservator generis humani, largitor æternæ salutis, & dator gratiæ spiritualis, benedictione tua santa bene ✠ dic has palmas, quas cum devotione, ac veneratione Sancti Angeli Ordinis Beatæ Mariæ Virginis de monte Carmelo, & Martyris tui hodie tibi præsentamus, & petimus benedici, & infundi in eis per virtutem Sanctæ ✠ Crucis, benedictionem cœlestem, aut qui eas ad domos, vineas, vel agros mittendas talem signaculo Sanctæ ✠ Crucis benedictionem accipiant, ut quibuscumque locis appositæ fuerint, vel cum devotione habuerint, infirmatates eradicentur, discedant diaboli, contremiscant, & fugiant persidi cum suis ministris de locis illis, nec amplius sibi servientes, inquietare præsumant. Per Dominum nostrum Jesum Christum, Filium tuum : qui tecum vivit et regnat in unitate Spiritus Sancti Deus, per omnia sæcula sæculorum. *Amen.*

Saint Angelus

Remedy of the Lady Saint Anne patron of the miserable, and for everything. Saint James taught the following devotion

Place in front of an image of the Saint a lit candle, pray every day, and above all on Tuesdays, for being her dedicated day, three times the Our Father, the Hail Mary, and Gloria Patri; and at the end of the Gloria Patri add on each of the three times:

Saint Anne, aid the miserable.

Prayer

Taught by the Holy Spirit

God save thee Blessed Anne, who deserved to be the Mother of she who is Mother to the Divine Word. Reach for me, from this Lord, the grace, so as I may always triumph over the ministers of Hell. Always be in my aid, and company, so as I may deserve to live eternally with thee in the sight of Jesus, and Mary. *Amen.*

Most efficient remedy for lost things, and against lost slaves, and further afflictions of the soul, and for the ill of roundworms, of which Saint Anthony of Lisbon is the miraculous patron, credit of the Portuguese nation, and admiration and amazement of the World.

Responsory

Si quæris miracula, which was made by Saint Bonaventure

Si quæris miracula, mors, error calamitas, dæmon, lepra fugiunt, ægri surgunt sani : * Cedunt mare, vincula, membra resque, perditas petunt, & accipiunt juvenes, & cani. ℣Pereunt pericula, cessat & necessitas, narrent hi, qui sentiunt, dicant Paduani. * Cedunt mare, vincula, membra resque, perditas petunt, & accipiunt juvenes, & cani. Gloria Patri, & Filio, & Spiritui Sancto. * Cedunt mare, vincula, membra resque, perditas petunt, & accipiunt juvenes, & cani.

In vernacular

If thou seeks miracles; death, error, tribulation, the Devil, and leprosy flee : and the infirm rise sane.

All respond: The sea obeys, and the prisons, members, and lost things, plead, and he receives the young and the old.

Dangers fall, and necessity ceases, let those who know tell of it, let the Padovani say it.

All respond: The sea obeys, &c.

Glory be to the Father, the Son, and the Holy Spirit.

All respond: The sea obeys, &c.

S. ANNA.

Anna Dei Matris Mariæ sanctissima mater,
2. *Præmonitu sobolem concipit Angelico.*

Lady Saint Anne

Antiphon

O Star of Portugal, and Spain, precious stone of poverty, form of purity, fear of the infidels, new light of Italy, teacher of truth, as the Sun shines in Padua with a sign of clarity.

℣Pray for us Blessed Antony.

℟So as we may be worthy of the promises of Christ.

Prayer

Lord God, may the commemoration of Saint Anthony thy Confessor, and Doctor bring joy to thy Church, garnished with the spiritual blessings, so as we may deserve to enjoy the eternal pleasures for the love of JESUS Christ our Lord. *Amen.*

SIGHS FOR THE TREZENA OF SAINT ANTHONY[123]

The same as the Novena of Our Lady of the Rock until the Act of Love of God.

FIRST DAY

FIRST SIGH

God save thee, my Glorious Saint Anthony, Monstrance of the Divine Holy Spirit : reach for me from Him the gifts, and aids of his grace.

Immediately say thirteen Our Fathers, Hail Marys, and Gloria Patri.

Offering

O my Most Glorious, and most beloved Saint Anthony, I offer thee this prayer, and sigh in honour, and veneration of thy heroic virtues, and admirable sainthood, and I humbly ask thee to reach from God our Lord, and from his Mother the Holiest MARY, with whom thou art of such worth, a most firm resolution of following thy examples, and imitate thy actions, so as directing the steps of my life by those of thy Holiness, I may walk secure in the valley of tears to eternal happiness. I also pray to thee that thou also reach from the same Lord the remedy for all my needs, both spiritual, as corporeal. Through thee I hope to reach these benefits from the Most High, and I am most certain that thou shall not fail with thy protection one who, as me, has so much trust in the singularity of thy Succour. With it I ask thee to be in my worth also at the hour of my death, so as coming out with victory from the infernal combats, and being my spirit free from the prisons of this mortal life, I may forever enjoy the perfect freedom of the children of God under his sight in thy company. *Amen.*

Pray the Response in Latin.

Antiphon

Ó Lingua benedicta, quæ Dominum sempre benedixisti, & alios benedicere fecisti, nunc manifeste apparet, quanti meriti extitisti apud eum.

℣Ora pro nobis Beate Antoni.

℟Ut digni efficiamur promissionibus Christi.

Oremus

Ecclesiam tuam, Deus Beati Antonii, Confessoris tui deprecatio votiva lætificet, ut spiritualibus sempre muniatur auxiliis, & gaudiis perfrui mereatur æternis. Per Christum, Dominum nostrum. *Amen.*

123 Translator's note: similar to a Novena, but made up of thirteen days.

Prayer

Be thy Church open, Lord, to the supplication of thy Blessed Saint Anthony, thy Confessor, so as it may forever be strengthened with his spiritual aids, and deserve to enjoy the eternal pleasures. For Jesus Christ our Lord. *Amen.*

SECOND DAY

All as in the first day.

SECOND SIGH

God save thee, my Glorious Saint Anthony, most beloved Son of the Holiest MARY, make me also a worthy son of such a sovereign Mother.

Immediately say thirteen Our Fathers, Hail Marys, Gloria Patri and as on the first day until the end.

THIRD DAY

All as in the first day.

THIRD SIGH

God save thee, my Glorious Saint Anthony, Seat of the Baby Jesus : achieve for me from him the unfailing innocence of that age.

Immediately say thirteen Our Fathers, Hail Marys, Gloria Patri and as on the first day until the end.

FOURTH DAY

All as in the first day.

FOURTH SIGH

God save thee, my Glorious Saint Antony, Mirror of virtue : make it so as to thy sight I may compose my soul, and purify it of its stains.

Immediately say thirteen Our Fathers, Hail Marys, Gloria Patri and as on the first day until the end.

FIFTH DAY

All as in the first day.

FIFTH SIGH

God save thee, my Glorious Saint Anthony, Most Beloved of sainthood : beg to the Lord of all, that I may be thy perfect imitator.

Immediately say thirteen Our Fathers, Hail Marys, Gloria Patri and as on the first day until the end.

SIXTH DAY

All as in the first day.

SIXTH SIGH

God save thee, my Glorious Saint Anthony, Restorer of lost things : do not allow me to be lost on the path to my eternal salvation.

Immediately say thirteen Our Fathers, Hail Marys, Gloria Patri and as on the first day until the end.

SEVENTH DAY

All as in the first day.

SEVENTH SIGH

God save thee, my Glorious Saint Anthony, shining Light of the universe : enlighten my blindness, so as I may not live engulfed in the darkness of so many vices, and sins.

Immediately say thirteen Our Fathers, Hail Marys, Gloria Patri and as on the first day until the end.

EIGHTH DAY

All as in the first day.

EIGHTH SIGH

God save thee, my Glorious Saint Anthony, Preacher of truth : conserve me firm in the Holy Faith, and I promise to obey the Gospels, which thou preached.

Immediately say thirteen Our Fathers, Hail Marys, Gloria Patri and as on the first day until the end.

NINTH DAY

All as in the first day.

NINTH SIGH

God save thee, my Glorious Saint Anthony, City placed over the mountains of perfection : receive me inside thee, so as I may be safe from the infernal enemies.

Immediately say thirteen Our Fathers, Hail Marys, Gloria Patri and as on the first day until the end.

TENTH DAY

All as in the first day.

TENTH SIGH

God save thee, my Glorious Saint Anthony, blazing torch of the Divine love : inflame my heart in this fire, so as I may always burn in its loving flames.

Immediately say thirteen Our Fathers, Hail Marys, Gloria Patri and as on the first day until the end.

ELEVENTH DAY

All as in the first day.

ELEVENTH SIGH

God save thee, my Glorious Saint Anthony, Salt of the earth : preserve me from the corruption of sin, may its contagion never infect me.

Immediately say thirteen Our Fathers, Hail Marys, Gloria Patri and as on the first day until the end.

TWELFTH DAY

All as in the first day.

TWELFTH SIGH

God save thee, my Glorious Saint Anthony, Ark of the Testament : make it so as I may enjoy the softest Manna of the Celestial Glory forever.

Immediately say thirteen Our Fathers, Hail Marys, Gloria Patri and as on the first day until the end.

THIRTEENTH DAY

All as in the first day.

THIRTEENTH SIGH

God save thee, my Glorious Saint Anthony, Glory, and jewel of Portugal : make it as this thy home, and thy countrymen may love and venerate thee, and God, who wished to reveal himself in thee so admirable.

Immediately say thirteen Our Fathers, Hail Marys, Gloria Patri and as on the first day until the end.

Remedy, and Exorcism for round worms of Saint Anthony

Potestas Dei Pa✠tris, sapientia Dei Fi✠lii, & virtus Spiritus ✠ Sancti liberet, & sanet te, creatura Dei ad infirmatate lumbricorum. *Amen.*

In nomine Jesu Christi Nazareni con✠juro vos ascarides, seu lumbricos, ut conversi in aquam recedatis à corpore isto in honorem Dei, & devotionem Sancti Antonii de Padua, qui oret pro nobis. *Amen.*

Per signum Santæ Cru✠cis, quo signo te, efficiaris sanus ab omni infirmitate, & vermes isti procul moriatur, & exeant à corpore tuo, ut in Domino gaudentes dicamus : Dum appropiant super te nocentes, ipsi infirmati sunt, & ceciderunt. *Si quœris miracula, &c.*

Remedy for breakings, of which Saint Apollinaris, Bishop and Martyr, is the patron

Antiphon

This Saint fought until death for the law of God; and remained strong against the words of the impious; for he was founded over a firm rock.

℣The Just shall blossom as a lily.

℟And shall always flourish in the presence of the Lord.

Prayer

O Almighty God, rewarder of the faithful souls, who consecrated this day with the martyrdom of thy Priest the blessed Saint Apollinaris : propitiously concede to us that, by his worth we emend our lives, so as, reformed, and strengthened we may rise to that glory. For Christ our Lord. *Amen.*

Remedy for toothaches, of which Saint Apollonia is the patron

After the priest consecrates the host, immediately pray a Hail Mary with great devotion to Saint Apollonia considering the pain of the holy passion of our Lord Jesus Christ.

Antiphon

Come Wife of Christ, receive the crown which was prepared by the Lord forever.

℣Pray for us Saint Apollonia.

℟So as we may be worthy of the promises of Christ.

Prayer

Eternal God, Saint Apollonia suffered for love, that her teeth were pulled, and she was burnt with flames, concede to me the grace of the celestial freshness against the fire of vice, and give me healthy Succour against toothache by her intercession. Amen JESUS.

Remedy for intelligence in the liberal arts, and all sciences, of which Saint Augustine is the patron, and for the reformation of life, and for tears

Antiphon

O Master of Masters, and Angel of the Doctors, O great Doctor; light of the Church, lover of the divine law teach us to love God.

℣O blessed Saint Augustine luminous splendour of the Church, pray for us.

℟So as we may be worthy of the promises of Christ.

Prayer

O Almighty God, who, for the splendour of thy Church, and the confoundment of the heretics thou illuminated with such science, and worth, thy blessed servant Saint Augustine; make it so, and this we ask, that by his intercession, and copious tears of regret, we may cry our faults, and with his example we may deserve to reach the true science so as with it we may learn to love thee. For Christ our Lord, who lives, and reigns with thee for all centuries of centuries. *Amen.*

Remedy for the passion of fear, and diabolical visions, and murmuration, and the plague, of which Saint Bartholomew Apostle is the patron

Antiphon

Thou art firm in battle, and thou fights the ancient enemy, and thou shall receive the eternal Kingdom.

℣Along the whole earth the sound of thy fame was heard.

℟And in the ends of the earth his words.

Prayer

Almighty and eternal God, who for the remedy of thy creatures thou sublimated thy Apostle Saint Bartholomew with such suffering of pain, and constancy of martyrdom : propitiously concede to us, that by his worth, and his great intercession we may be free from diabolical visions, and persecutions from our enemies, and from all plague in that glory. For Christ our Lord. *Amen.*

Saint Bartholomew, Apostle

Remedy for snake bites, and so as these do not bite, and against spiders, and venomous critters, and against sorcery, and plague, and stone pain, of which the great Patriarch Saint Benedict is the patron, and also the supplication of his medal

Antiphon

O Most holy Confessor of the Lord, father of Monks, intercede for us to the Lord, who is the true health of all.

℣Pray for us blessed Saint Benedict.

℟So as we may be worthy of the promises of Christ.

Prayer

Almighty God, who in order to enrich thy Church with the gifts of sainthood of thy servant the blessed Saint Benedict, thou elevated him to the highest sainthood : propitiously concede to us, that by means of his relevant merits, and intercession we may be free not only from venomous bites, and sorceries, as also from the snares of demons our enemies. For Christ our Lord, who lives, and reigns with thee for all centuries. *Amen.*

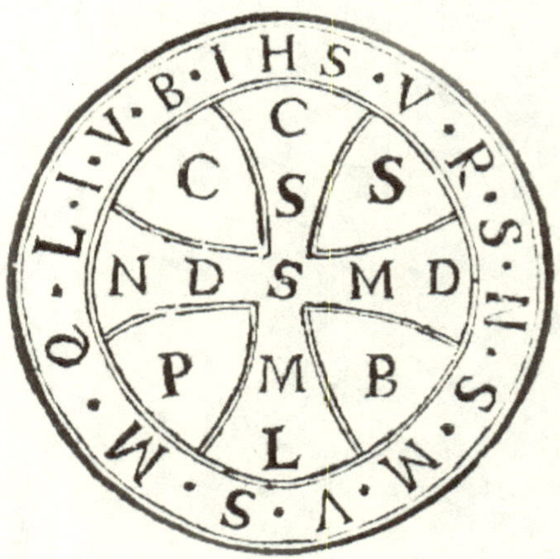

Explanation of the letters of the cross of Saint Benedict, which are found in his Medal

Each of these letters is worth a word. One starts reading the ones around from the top, turning towards the right, and they say the following: *Jesus : Vade : Retro : Satanas : Nunquam : Suadeas : Mihi : Vana : Sun : Mala : Quæ : Libas : Ipse : Venena : Bibas.* In vernacular: *JESUS. Be : Gone : Satan, Never : Tempt me : With vanities : These are : Evil : Drink : The poison : Thyself.*

The ones which are found in the middle of the Cross, starting from the letter on the left towards the right, say the following: *Non : Draco : Sit : Mihi : Dux.* These are in vernacular: *May : The dragon : Never : Be my : Lord.*

And from the top to the bottom one reads: *Cruz : Sancta : Sit : Mihi : Lux. In vernacular: The Holy : Cross : Be : My light.*

The four letters which are in the four corners or angles say: *Crux : Sancti : Patris : Benedicti.* In vernacular: *Cross of : The Holy : Father : Benedict.*

22

ESTA CRUZ
Sendo benta, tem as meſmas virtu-des, que a Veronica de S.Bento.

PALAVRAS SANTISSIMAS
Contra os Rayos, Tempeſtades, e Trovoens.

CHriſtus Rex venit in pace.
Et Deus Homo factus eſt.
Verbum Caro factum eſt.
Chriſtus de Virgine natus eſt.
Chriſtus per mediũ illorum ibat in
Chriſtus Crucifixus eſt. (pace.
Chriſtus Mortuus eſt.
Chriſtus

THIS CROSS
Being it blessed, has the same virtues as the medal of Saint Benedict.

Remedy against bones, and thorns, or fish bones, and to reach humility, of which Saint Benedict, Black Saint, and greatly venerated in Brazil, and patron of the faithful, is the patron

Antiphon

O Lover of humility, master of the Doctors, health of the infirm, rooter of vices, hope of the afflicted, garden of fragrant roses, celestial target, arrow of divine love, vase with the purple lilies of thy passion.

℣Pray for us, most glorious Saint Benedict.

℟So as we may be worthy of the Promises of our Lord Jesus Christ.

Prayer

God, who filled thy blessed Confessor Saint Benedict with celestial gifts, and with sovereign virtues, and signs and made him into thy enlightened Church : propitiously concede to us, that by his pleas, and merits we may achieve thy sovereign benefits. By the merits of our Lord Jesus Christ thy Son, who lives, and reigns with thee in the unity of the Holy Spirit, God for all centuries of centuries. *Amen.*

Remedy for headaches, and for the sciences, for the devotion of our Lady, for fevers, and all disease, of which the sweet Saint Bernard, credit of sainthood, and shield of faith, and despiser or earthly thing, and lover of chastity is the patron

Antiphon

This Saintly man despising the world, and triumphing over the things of the earth in works, and words, made his treasure in Heaven.

℣The Lord took the Just through the straight paths.

℟And showed them the Kingdom of Heaven.

Prayer

O Eternal God, who for thy greater glory, and honour illuminated with such worth thy blessed sweet Saint Bernard, gifting him with the gifts of science, and purity : concede to us that, through his intercession we may reach the necessary science in order to know how to love thee eternally, seeing ourselves free from all bodily, and spiritual infirmities so as in that Empirium we may enjoy thee for all eternity. For Christ our Lord. *Amen.*

Effective remedy for the dangers of the throat, and constancy in torments, of which Saint Blaise is the patron

Antiphon

This Saint fought until death for the law of God; and he prevailed strong against the word of the wicked; for he was founded over a firm rock.

℣Thou crowned, Lord, this one with honour, and glory.

℟And thou made him into the best work of thy hands.

Prayer

God, and Lord, who gives us joy with the yearly celebration of thy blessed Martyr and Pontiff Saint Blaise : propitiously concede, that by his intercession, and constancy we may be free from danger, and infirmities of the body, and soul, so as free and unencumbered we may praise thee in that glory forever. For Christ our Lord. *Amen.*

Remedy to reach the sciences, humility, and docility of spirit, and feverous devotion for communion, of which Saint Bonaventure is the patron

Antiphon

O excellent Doctor, light of the Holy Church, lover of the divine law, intercede for us with the Son of God.

℣With glory and honour thou crowned him, Lord.

℟And thou constituted him above the works of thy hands.

Prayer

Almighty Lord, who for the light of the Church, and director of the souls who aspire to the ultimate perfection, thou illuminated thy blessed servant Saint Bonaventure with the gifts of science, and virtue : propitiously concede to us, that just as we had on earth a Saintly Doctor, in Heaven may we have an intercessor, so as by means of his rogations and worth we may assist thee in that glory. For Christ our Lord, who lives, and reigns for all centuries of centuries. *Amen.*

Remedy in order to take a firm resolution in abandoning sin, and offer one's life to God, of which Saint Boniface is the patron

Antiphon

Saint Boniface Martyr resolved to abandon Rome, his home, for Jerusalem so as to rise by means of martyrdom to the celestial homeland, showing in this resolution the goodness of his name.

℣The Lord took the Just through the straight path.

℟And showed them the Kingdom of Heaven.

Prayer

O Almighty God, and merciful Lord, who for the good spirit of the sinners thou strengthened thy servant Saint Boniface so as to offer his blood, and his very life for thee : concede to us his imitation, the resolution in abandoning sin by his intercession, may we also deserve the crown of martyrdom to triumph in that Court of glory. For Christ our Lord. *Amen.*

Remedy for headaches, of which Saint Brigit is the patron, and for the consideration of the Passion of Christ

Antiphon

Come, Wife of mine, to receive the glory, which is prepared for thee for all eternity.

℣Grace was diffused in thy lips.

℟For this God blessed thee forever.

Prayer

Lord, and Almighty God, who were served in revealing to thy servant Saint Brigit the secrets of Heaven through thy only-begotten Son; we ask that by her worth, thou frees us from headache, and further dangers of this life, so as we may enjoy the vision of thy eternal glory. For Christ our Lord. *Amen.*

Remedy for humility, and sciences, and tears, and the resolution to abandon the world, of which Saint Bruno is the patron

Antiphon

This Saintly man despising the world, and triumphing over the things of the earth in works, and words, made his treasure in Heaven.

℣Pray for us blessed Saint Bruno.

℟So as we may be worthy of the promises of Christ.

Prayer

Almighty God, who enlightened the life of the blessed Saint Bruno, adorned with great worth, and despising the world : propitiously concede to us, so as by his intercession, and glorious death, filled with miracles, we may despise the earthly things, and embrace the celestial in thy company. For Christ our Lord. *Amen.*

General Remedy of Saint Cajetan, Saintly Priest, patron of necessities, and spiritual, and temporal tribulations, and of all infirmities, and poverty

Responsory

If thou seeks miracles,
Which Saint Cajetan rains over us,
The marvellous hand heals
Disease, wounds, and pain.
    From flowers,
From his oil always flee
Deliriums of the understanding,
Lucifer, storms, and death.
    If his prodigies are recognized
By all who are under the Heavens,
And Naples publishes it,
Happily holding his body.
    From flowers,
From his oil always flee
Deliriums of the understanding,
Lucifer, storms, and death.
    To the Father, Son, Love,
Triune God who accomplishes anything,
Give the World eternal glory,
All the peoples worship.
    From flowers,
From his oil always flee
Deliriums of the understanding,
Lucifer, storms, and death.
℣Pray for us blessed Saint Cajetan.
℟So as we may be worthy of the promises of Christ.

Let us pray

Almighty, and eternal God, who blessed Saint Cajetan, thy Confessor, so as in thy providence he would despise all the earthly things, and thou filled him with celestial goods : concede to the ones who venerate his memory, who experience the effects of this same providence, and always aspire to the eternal. For the worth of Christ our Lord. *Amen.*

Remedy for hernia, and demonic infestations, of which Saint Calogerus is the patron

Antiphon

This Saintly man despising the world, and triumphing over the things of the earth, with his works, and words made his treasure in Heaven.

℣The Lord took the Just through the straight path.

℟And showed them the Kingdom of Heaven.

Prayer

O God Almighty, who elected the glorious Saint Calogerus thy Confessor to cast out demons, putting them under his feet : propitiously concede to us, that by his worth, and his intercession we may be free from the snares of the Devil, and of any further necessities, so as we may go and enjoy thy presence in that glory. For Christ our Lord. *Amen.*

Remedy for the agonies of death, and fervour for Ministers, who may aid the agonizing to die well, and of which Saint Camillus de Lellis, founder of an Order of Priests, is the patron

Antiphon

I shall come, and I shall heal them of all their infirmity with the oil of charity, and with the holy fear of God.

℣Pray for us, Saint Camillus de Lellis.

℟So as we may be worthy of the promises of Christ.

Prayer

My God, who honoured the Blessed Saint Camillus with the singular prerogative of special charity to aid the souls of the faithful in the last agonies of death : by the worth of this Saint we ask thee, that thou infuses a blazing spirit into thy love, so as in the hour of death we may deserve to beat our enemy, and receive a crown of glory from Heaven. For Christ our Lord. *Amen.*

Remedy to drive away demons, and for malignant fevers, and to move one to offer alms to the poor, of which Saint Catherine of Siene is the patron, and to reach the sciences, and resolve the most difficult questions, and to reconcile friendships

Antiphon

This is the knowing Virgin, and one among the numbers of the prudent, who knew how to investigate the paths of the Kingdom of Heaven.

℣Grace was diffused in thy lips.

℟And for this God blessed thee forever.

Prayer

O God, and almighty Lord, who with the freedom of thy infinite mercy gifted thy blessed servant Saint Catherine with so many gifts, and excellences : propitiously concede, that by her intercession, and her miracles, we be free from the deceits of demons, and from the pains of Hell, so as we may resolve to abandon not only this deceitful world, but also its ignorance, and enter into that glory. For Christ our Lord. *Amen.*

Remedy for headache, and so as Musicians may properly sing the praises of God, and play their musical instruments and the organ, and for constancy in Martyrdom, of which Saint Cecilia is the patron

Antiphon

The glorious Virgin Saint Cecilia always brought the Gospel of our Lord Jesus Christ in her heart, and she did not cease during the night, or day, the divine colloquiums, and her prayer.

℣Grace was diffused in thy lips.

℟And for this God blessed thee forever.

Prayer

O Almighty God, who to be praised in Heaven, and on earth with such solemnity thou illuminated thy blessed servant Saint Cecilia, animating her in the instruments of martyrdom, and music : propitiously concede to us, that by her feverous intercession, and her relevant worth, and her imitation, and her voice we may make the best harmony among praises, and joys, so as to praise thee in alternate choirs in that glory. For Christ our Lord. *Amen.*

Remedy for tiredness, and for strengths, of which Saint Christopher is the patron, and for the stone, fire, hunger, plague, storms, earthquakes, wherever his body or image may be

Antiphon

He, who wants to go to Heaven take up his Cross, and follow me.

℣The Just shall blossom as a lily.

℟And shall always flourish in the presence of the Lord.

Prayer

O Lord, who are almighty in everything, and to show thy power thou illuminated so much Saint Christopher, gifting him with effort, and constancy so as to carry thee on his back, and suffer the martyrdom by thy love : propitiously concede to us, that by his intercession, and his relevant worth we may also be effortful in the resolution, and in spirit in order to deserve, and enjoy thy glory forever. For Christ our Lord, *Amen.*

Saint Christopher

Remedy for hydropsy, and malignant fevers, and to drive away demons, and for fervour in prayer, and respect, and devotion to the Temples, and the Holiest Sacrament, and humility, and conformity, and observance of the rules of Religion, and fires, of which that most bright light of the world, and example of patience, loud clarion of the Divine, Seraphic trumpet, and enlighten virtue of purity, and virginity, the founder Saint Clare is the patron

Antiphon

This clear light of the world, Royal banner of Faith; and most enlightened, and adopted daughter of the Most Holy Mary, who knew how to escape the delights of the home of her parents for the rigours of religion to deserve the honour and glory of God.

℣Grace was diffused in thy lips.

℟And for this God blessed thee forever.

Prayer

O eternal, and Almighty God, who with so much clarity illuminated with splendors thy blessed servant Saint Clare, gifting her of prerogatives, and excellences and sainthood : propitiously concede to us, that by her relevant worth, and her intercession, and doctrine we may imitate her in virtue, and be free from infirmities of the body, and soul, and despise the earthly possessions for the celestial, so as we may clearly see thee in that glory. For Christ our Lord. *Amen.*

Remedy for Chastity, and for all necessities

of which Saint Comba, Portuguese, and who is venerated with Novenas, mainly on Fridays, in which many Masses are said, and this is in a hermitage close to the Royal Monastery of Celas in Coimbra : she is also patron against intermittent fever, and malignant fever, as are witnesses the countless people who have used her patronage, and the signs, which are made of this are in this Hermitage, near the altar, which on the side of the Gospel there is a door, where one enters into a room, or kitchen, which is behind this Altar, where it is tradition that she was first buried. In here there is a round ditch, where the infirm, and those with fever, with full devotion go, and they take from that earth, which is placed inside small pouches and place these around the neck, invoking the favour of the patronage of the Saint; and in this way God our Lord by her worth, and pleas, gives them back their health, and they return the earth to this Heritage; and hanging those nominas, as a trophy of health, in a Cross which is close to the Altar and is placed there as a memory of the countless benefits which are made there; the earth which has been taken from that place is so much, that one now has a deep and wide ditch, to which one must go down a few steps.

Antiphon

This Holy Virgin, and Martyr, escaped the persuasions of her father, so as not to wed on earth, she hid in a ditch, and passing fire over her, she burned in the fire of divine love, offering her life in the branches of an olive tree to distill the oil of charity, and shine in the presence of God, announcing peace in the olive tree, Saint Comba is the imitation of the dove with the olive branch in Noah's Ark.

℣The shed oil is thy name.

℟For this do the Virgins love thee.

Prayer

O Almighty God, who with the oil of thy charity, and infinite mercy thou illuminated thy blessed servant Saint Comba with so much constancy, and resolution to offer her own life for thy love : concede to us that by her intercession, and her imitation we may also shed our blood on the tree of the true Cross so as to reach the peace, which we desire, and with it we may enjoy thee in that glory. For Christ our Lord. *Amen.*

Remedy for the usefulness of medication, and for suffering of pain, of which are patrons Saint Cosmas, and Saint Damian

Antiphon

O how pleasant it is to God that all live united in God, for of these is the Kingdom of Heaven, who despise the life of the world, and arrive at the prize of Heaven, and wash their stoles in the blood of the Lamb.

℣Pray for us Saint Cosmas and Saint Damian.

℟So as we may be worthy of the promises of Christ.

Prayer

O God, and almighty Lord, who held with the antidote of thy blood thy servants Saint Cosmas, and Saint Damian, freeing them from the infirmity of sin : propitiously concede to us, that by their worth we may be free from all evil, and comforted, and feed with the medicine of thy precious blood, and we may arrive to enjoy the true life in thy presence. For Christ our Lord. *Amen.*

Remedy so as elections are well done, and for chastity, and against false witnesses, and lying, of which Saint Damasus Portuguese Pope, from the town of Guimarães in this Kingdom of Portugal is the patron

Antiphon

O priest, and Pontiff, Master of virtues. Good Pastor among the people, pray for us to the Lord.

℣God loved the Just, and adorned him.

℟Dressing him with the stole of eternal glory.

Prayer

Almighty, and Eternal God, who among many thou were served to elect thy blessed servant Saint Damasus to the Pontifical chair, freeing him from many false witnesses : propitiously concede to us that by his intercessions, and his worth thou may free us from mundane falsehood, electing us to the place of eternal rest in thy presence. For Christ our Lord. *Amen.*

Remedy for constancy in Faith, and the science of Mathematics, and earthquakes, of which Saint Dionysius the Areopagite is the patron

Antiphon

The Kingdom of Heaven is of those who despised the life of the world, and came to the prizes of the Kingdom, and washed their vestments in the blood of the Lamb.

℣The Just shall blossom as a lily.

℟And shall always flourish in the presence of the Lord.

Prayer

Almighty, and eternal God, who for thy greater honour, and glory, and the good of thy creatures in thy holy passions, in the dark hour of our enemies, thou gave the first light to thy blessed Saint Dionysius the Areopagite, and after the preaching of thy Apostle Saint Matthew thou gave him the final light : concede to us, that by means of his conversions, and his worth, thou gives us as much light, so as we may see him, and imitate him in his virtues so as to enjoy thy glory. For Christ our Lord. *Amen.*

Remedy for fever, and further infirmities, and for the perfection of the Monastic state, and to reach the patronage of our Lady of the Rosary, of which Saint Dominic, the great Apostle of the Rosary, the flower of the Saints, the credit of Christendom, is the patron.

Antiphon

O Light of the Church, Doctor of Truth, Flower of the Rosary, and Rose of patience, Wall of chastity, Preacher of patience, Apostle of the Rosary, intercede with God for all thy devotees.

℣The Just shall blossom as the palm.

℟As was the Balm-tree multiplied.

Prayer

O Almighty God, who illuminated thy Church with the worth and doctrines of thy holy blessed servant Saint Dominic : concede to us, that by his intercessions we may deserve thy temporal and spiritual aid, so as to be free from infirmities of the body, and the deceits of the Devil, rising to that glory to praise thee in it eternally. For Christ our Lord. *Amen.*

Remedy for fever according to the devotion of the glorious Father Saint Dominic, founder of the enlightened, and never excessively praised Order of the great and many times great Order of the Preachers

A Priest should read, and cast this in the way of a nomina, and the sick person should have a Mass said in honour of Saint Dominic.

Jesus Mariæ filius sit tibi salus, clemens, & propitious, Amen. Benedictus Redemptor omnium, qui saluti providens hominum, mundo dedit Sanctum Dominium. Ó Beate Dominice, qui tot signis claruisti in ægrorum corporibus, nobis opem ferem Christi, ægris medere moribus. Ora pro nobis, Beate Dominice, ut digni efficiamur promissionibus Christi. Concede quæsumus omnipotens Deus, ut qui peccatorum nostrorum pondere premimur, Beati Dominici Confessoris tui patrocinio sublevemur. Amen ✠ Christus vincit, ✠ Christus regnat, ✠ Christus imperat, ✠ Christus ab omni febre te defendat. Amen. Pater est pax, ✠ Filius est vita, ✠ Spiritus Sanctus est remedium salutis. ✠ Fiat ✠ fiat ✠ fiat tibi, ut cupis. ✠ Jesus Nazarenus Rex Judæorum, ✠ Jesus Christus spinis coronatus te sanat. *Amen.*

Remedy for the respect of Priests, for humility, chastity, epilepsy, fainting, and accidents, of which Saint Edward King of England is the patron, and for secrecy

Antiphon

This Saintly man despising the world, and triumphing over the things of the earth in works, and words, made his treasure in Heaven.

℣The Just shall blossom as the palm.

℟As was the Balm-tree multiplied.

Prayer

Almighty God, and God of mercy, who to better reign with thee in thy Kingdom thou crowned, and adorned thy blessed servant Saint Edward with so many treasures of humility, and chastity: make it so, and we ask thee by his intercession, and prodigies, that we may imitate him, so as we may also reign, free from accidents, and faintings of this world, in that Kingdom of thy glory. For Christ our Lord, who lives, and reigns for all centuries of centuries.

Remedy against the danger of the sea, of which Saint Elesbaan is the patron

Antiphon

When thou sailed over the waters, the Lord said, thou shall always find me there to defend thee, and never shall thou be toppled by the sea.

℣Prodigious Saint, make it so as to achieve.

℟Triumph over the seas those who sail them.

Prayer

Almighty God, and Lord, who being admirable in thy Saints, thou offered thyself as particularly powerful knowledge in the blessed Emperor of Ethiopia Saint Elesbaan, professor, which he was of the primitive virtues of austerity and the sacred Religion of thy Holiest Mother Lady of the Carmel : concede to us by thy infinite clemency, that as by thy intercession one hundred and twenty thousand people become miraculously free from shipwreck, when the enemy of thy ineffable name armed under the waves of the Red Sea an unavoidable trap; thus, through thy patronage, and the worth of this same Saint, may we, his devotees, who profess thy divine law, manage to triumph over the cunnings of thy infernal enemy : in such a way as while we live in the world, we may navigate the storm, and the dangers of the sea safely until, after death, we may arrive with happiness to the port of glory, where thou lives, and reigns forever. *Amen.*

Remedy against fire, of which Saint Elijah, Prince of the Patriarchs, is the patron

Antiphon

O Elijah, thou who marvellously ended the power of death, and restored life to those who could no longer expect similar benefit, which thou did in the name of God.

℣Blessed art those, who manage to see thee.

℟And also those, who had the honour of thy friendship.

Prayer

Concede to us, O Lord Almighty God, that as the blessed Elijah (thy Prophet, and father of all who profess the Carmelite institute), before the common death of all men, thou took in a triumphant chariot to Paradise, where he assisted as if he was in Heaven; in this same way make it so, that by his intercession, that while we live, we may always have a spirit highly implemented in the celestial things, and that, together with the Saints we may be joyful in seeing, that with the Just we shall resuscitate for eternal glory. For Jesus Christ our Lord. *Amen.*

Remedy for giving alms, and to cure cancers, and to reach the gift of humility, and charity, of which Queen Saint Elizabeth is the patron. Her body is kept in the chapel of the Convent of Saint Clare in Coimbra, and I had the consolation of kissing the silver urn in which her saintly body is deposited

Antiphon

Thou glory of Jerusalem, thou joy of Israel, thou who art the supreme honour of thy people.

℣He spread, and gave to the poor.

℟His justice remains forever.

Prayer

Most clement God, who among other major gifts thou honoured the blessed Queen Saint Elizabeth with the prerogative of pacifying the furor of war : preciously concede to us, that by her intercessions, we may be free from the infirmities of this world, and that after the peace of this mortal life, which we ask with supplications, we may arrive to enjoy the eternal one in thy glory.

For Christ our Lord. *Amen.*

Remedy for poverty, and for paralysis, and so as Goldsmiths make their works perfect without burdening their conscience, and so as Prelates flee from simony, of which Saint Eloy is the patron

Antiphon

This Saintly man despising the world, and triumphing over the things of the earth, with his works, and words made his treasure in Heaven.

℣The Lord took the Just through the straight path.

℟And showed them the Kingdom of Heaven.

Prayer

O Almighty God, who to better illuminate thy Church thou elected the best artifice to crown with the glory of thy divine grace : propitiously concede to us, that by his work, and miracles we may perfect our consciences, and purify our souls so as to present thee our works perfect in that glory. For Christ our Lord. Amen

Remedy for the purity of the soul until death, of which Saint Emerentia, mother of the Lady Saint Anne, is the patron

Antiphon

Come, O my chosen, and in thy heart I shall place my throne to assist from it; for the King of Heaven was greatly pleased with the beauty of thy soul.

℣Come O Great-grandmother of Christ, and receive the crown of glory.

℟That this same Lord prepared thee so as with it he adorned thee for all eternity.

Let us pray

O my Lord JESUS Christ, thou had such a pure Great-grandmother, who still in the conjugal state loved chastity, as if she professed : wishing to conserve herself pure, while the divine will was not revealed to her, which she promptly obeyed with so much glory, by which she was the fruitful root, from where the tree of life sprang forth, of which thou wert the most fragrant flower, who filled the Heavens, and the earth with virtues : concede to us, Lord, by the intercessions of Saint Emerentia such a purity of conscience in life that, dying purified we may deserve to assist thee eternally in blessedness, where thou lives, and reigns for all centuries of centuries. *Amen.*

Remedy for cancers, and hemorrhoids of which Saint Fiacre, Confessor, is the patron

Antiphon

This Saintly man despising the world, and triumphing over the things of the earth, with his works, and words made his treasure in Heaven.

℣The Lord took the Just through the straight path.

℟And showed them the Kingdom of Heaven.

Prayer

O Almighty God, and Lord, heed our pleas, that through the intercessions of thy blessed servant Saint Fiacre, thy Confessor, we publish, may we be free from this ill by the worth of thy servant, who pleased thee so much : propitiously concede to us, that trusting in this hope, we may enjoy thee in that glory sane and safe. For Christ our Lord. *Amen.*

Remedy of the Cord of Saint Francis. This is used to cast out demons, and dangerous births, and other infirmities, and sending off ships, and boats into the sea.

Many horrible fires were miraculously stopped, and suspended, by casting into them the Cord of our Father Saint Francis with living faith, being that this belonged to any Priest his child. In dangerous births, one has the same daily experience of marvellous successes, by tying the holy Rope around a creature. The annals of the mentioned Order say of many people, who, dying in the disgrace of God by their enormous faults, as the eternal sentences of the divine tribunal were issued against them, never could demons, executors of the Divine Justice, approach their bodies, without these being first separated from the holy Habit and Cord.

Besides the remedies of the Cord of Saint Francis, he is the patron of humility, and of all acts of virtue.

Antiphon

God save thee, our Father Saint Francis, light of the nations, form and rule of the Franciscans, mirror of the virtues, path of Heaven, Master of good costumes, intercede for us with the Son of God.

℣Thou taught, Lord, thy blessed servant Saint Francis.

℟With the stamp of the wounds of thy passions.

Prayer

O God, who illuminated, and increased thy Church with the worth of thy blessed servant Saint Francis in his new creation : concede to us that in his imitation we may despise the earthly things, and deserve the Heavenly gifts. For Christ our Lord. *Amen.*

Remedy to despise dignities, honours, and vanities of the world, and to reach the love of God, of which Saint Francis Borgia is the patron

Antiphon

This Saintly man despising the world, and triumphing over the things of the earth, with his works, and words made his treasure in Heaven.

℣The Lord took the Just through the straight path.

℟And showed them the Kingdom of Heaven.

Prayer

O Lord Jesus Christ, prime and example of true humility, we ask thee, that as thou perfected the blessed Saint Francis, thy glorious imitator, and despiser of the honours of the world : concede that through his intercession we may learn to despise the dignities, and honours of the world, so as we may enjoy that glory. For Christ our Lord. *Amen.*

Remedy to have progeny, particularly male, and for all necessities, and lack of water, of which Saint Francis of Paola is the patron

Antiphon

Saint Francis of Paola, great in virtue, great in miracles, great intercessor for male progeny, reach from God all which is good for my salvation.

℣Pray for us Saint Francis.

℟So as we may be worthy of the promises of Christ.

Prayer

O Almighty God, height of the small, who sublimated thy blessed servant Saint Francis, thy Confessor, with the glory of thy Saints : propitiously concede to us, that by his worth, and his imitation we may deserve to achieve the fulfillment of our petitions in order to happily enjoy thee in that glory. For Christ our Lord. *Amen.*

Remedy for Missionaries to preach with patience, and suffering, and for the conversion of peoples, of which Saint Francis of Sales is the patron

Antiphon

This great Saint in seventeen years was despised in his Missions, and in one single afternoon he converted so many thousands of souls, showing God who thus mortified, and vivified him.

℣The Lord took the Just through the straight path.

℟And showed them the Kingdom of Heaven.

Prayer

God, who for the salvation of the souls thou wanted that the blessed Saint Francis, thy Confessor, and Pontiff, became all for everyone : propitiously concede to us, that bathed in the sweetness of thy love, and directed by his advice, interceding by his worth, we may achieve the eternal pleasures. For our Lord Jesus Christ, who lives, and reigns with thee in the unity of the Holy Spirit, God, for all centuries of centuries. *Amen.*

NOVENA OF SAINT FRANCIS XAVIER

Novena of Saint Francis Xavier, Apostle of the Orient, patron of Missionaries, and against storms, and all disease, and for the conversion of the gentiles, and for these reasons it is not fair that in this Precious Apothecary, and Precious Treasure of the Rock this medicine might be missing, or this universal recipe, and precious stone of the greatest treasure of India, that enflamed and famed Missionary, and Apostolic Nuncio of the Orient, of Japan, and the Indies, that new vase of election, that perfect and tireless imitator of the true Doctor of the people Saint Paul, admiration, prodigy, and palm of the universe, who illuminated the Court of Lisbon, when he came to it, and from it he went on to India in the company of Martim Afonso de Sousa, this was never enough praised, holy, and recognized light, useful for the whole world, and a thousand times good to the Company of JESUS, Saint Francis Xavier, it would not be fair, like I said, if I did not prescribe as medicine for recitation a remedy for everything as this Novena in the same form as the Revered Father Marcello Francisco Mastrili[124]composed it, and is done in Santo Antão,[125] and in the whole Kingdom of Portugal, and State of Brazil, and India, where he is recognized, praised, and many Churches, Chapels, and Altars, records, images and medals have been dedicated to him, beloved and venerated for his miracles, and prodigies by the whole world.

News of the origin of this Novena, and how it is accepted by God, and Saint Francis Xavier

Father Marcello Francisco Mastrili created this Novena when Saint Francis Xavier gave him the grace of working on him such a stupendous miracle, in this way: being the good Priest Marcello already without solution, and dying from the blow of a hammer, which fell over his head in his Church of the Company of JESUS in Naples, from where he is from, the Father Saint Francis Xavier appeared, and spoke to him in a pilgrim's garb, asking him, if he wanted health : and the patient responded, that if such was for the glory of God : The Saint then asked if he wanted to go to India, and the patient responded yes : the glorious Saint told him to make a vow of going, and to say this with him, as he did; and after they were done, the Holy Father told him to approach the relics to his wound; and in doing so the Saint said that the ill was in another part of the head, pointing to this with his hand, and placing those there, the Saint said: Thou art sane, and disappeared, and also the ill and weakness, and his head, which was bald in the location of the wound, was covered with equal hair. The patient asked for his vestments and some food, and he immediately rose sane, and valiant, and left for India to the amazement of the Princes, and people who saw him in Europe; and he went on to offer

124 Translator's note: a 17th century Jesuit Martyr active in the Philippines.

125 Translator's note: the Jesuit College of Saint Antão, in Lisbon (dedicated to Anthony the Anchorite).

his life for the Faith in Japan in one of the great martyrdoms, eager to be with his beloved Saint.

The year of one thousand six hundred and fifty-eight arrived, in which this new, and great miracle was worked by the Saint in another Priest of the same Company, Alexander de Felippuci, natural of the city of Macerata in Marche, this Novena was further confirmed, and for good reason. It was the case that this good Priest, in July of one thousand and six hundred and fifty-seven, fell with such a deadly disease, which seemed like all diseases together, with such a cruel, and pronounced cough, by which there was not a single instant during the day or night, but only for the briefest time, in which he could rest without coughing between one breath and the other, over thirty times and with such strength, that he was ripped with pain, and with such untoned grunts, which could be heard in a great distance, frightening the most learned Medics, not knowing the illness, all greatly admired that such an infirm could still live; and he was sighing for death, so as to be free from this torment, without having been able to speak for many days.

This torment continued until the eve of the third of March, when the glorious Saint, who wished to restore him to health with an admirable miracle, brought to his memory the countless miracles he operated, and the Novena, with which the Saint was obliged. The patient committed himself in this worth, and inside his soul he began the Novena, which he immediately made to the glorious Apostle Saint Francis Xavier, by whose means he reached health in the way we shall mention. By which method all should follow, starting on the third of March, so as to achieve a good result for their just petitions, with great trust. And this was in the following way, which the same priest described, and left written by his own hand.

WAY OF PERFORMING THE NOVENA OF SAINT FRANCIS XAVIER

Kneeling in front of an image of the glorious Saint, also taking as intercessors during the nine days the nine Choirs of Angels, taking particular esteem, and memory of the nine principal virtues of the Saint, perform in the following way, which is what was noted by the devout Father Felippuci.

Should you not have communed on this first day, make the act of contrition, so as these works are made in grace

Act of Contrition

Lord my God, Father, Son, and Holy Spirit, for being thou, my God, infinitely good, and because I love thee above all things, it weighs in my entire heart having offended thee : I propose, with thy grace, to correct myself, and confess my sins, and I ask thee for their forgiveness, which I hope to achieve by the worth of JESUS Christ my Redeemer. *Amen.*

Saint Francis Xavier

FIRST DAY OF THE NOVENA

Glorious Saint Francis Xavier, should it be for the glory of God, thine, and for the salvation of my soul upon my death, assist me with thy great mercy. And should thou reach health, life, and the dispatch I ask for me, let it be for the same glory of my God, and thine, and for the salvation of my soul, and of many others.

I offer thee, my Lord, so as thou gives me the grace, which I ask, the worth of the blessed Angels, and that Angelic purity of soul, and body of the glorious Saint Francis Xavier, so as by his intercession thou makes me worthy of this virtue, and the benefit, of which I ask in this Novena.

Here pray three Our Fathers, and three Hail Marys, and say the following Holy Prayer.

Most Blessed Father Saint Francis Xavier, who takes thy praise from the mouths of the innocent children, humbly do I beg for thy benign charity by the most precious blood of JESUS Christ, and by the immaculate Conception of the Holiest Virgin his Mother, and our Lady, that whenever God desires to take me to himself, that thou reaches for me from his infinite goodness, that my heart be withdrawn from all distractions of the world into a most ardent love of him, and desire for eternity, forgetful of everything, that which so far has disturbed me, and that I may only seek, and perfectly reach what most matters, which is death, and to rest in peace, piously, religiously, and saintly, in the embrace of the Virgin Mary, in the wounds of JESUS, in the softest kiss of my God in thy presence, by whose intercession I hope for this favour : and while the eternal disposition of divine providence increases my life, my protector and most prodigious patron, awaken thy power, and come; support me with thy mighty arm, so as what life and health I may have, that I may owe them, not to the forces of nature, not to the art of medicine, or human remedies, but to thy intercession before JESUS, and MARY. Here, softest father, I place before thee all my desire, thou knows, and very well sees my heart and suffering.

And immediately one makes the petition of grace, and favour and anything else one may wish to reach from the Saint. Which should be done with more or less delay according to each one's devotion, and one finishes with the following Antiphon, and Prayer.

Antiphon

Euge serve bone, & fidelis, quia in pauca fuisti fidelis, supra multa te constituam, intra in gaudium Domini tui.

℣Justum deduxit Dominus per vias rectas.

℟Et ostendit illi regnum Dei.

Deus, qui glorificantes te, glorificas, & in Sanctorum tuorum honoribus honoraris : concede propitius, ut qui Beati Francisci Xaverii gloriosa merita colimus, ejus pia patocinia sentiamus. Per Dominum nostrum Jesum Christum, Filium tuum : qui tecum vivit et regnat in unitate Spiritus Sancti Deus, per omnia sæcula sæculorum. *Amen.*

SECOND DAY

In front of an image of the Saint say

God my Lord, I offer thee the worth of all the Archangels, the second Choir of the Blessed Angels, and that love of thine, with which the blessed soul of my Saint Francis Xavier despised all the things of the earth, as a most holy Archangel, for loving thee and only having esteem for thee, and the souls of the whole world for the love of thee. For the love of this great servant of thine fulfil this petition, that I only ask so as to serve and love thee.

Three Our Fathers, and three Hail Marys and the Prayer of the Most Blessed Father above, and the Antiphon and the Prayer Deus qui.

THIRD DAY

My Lord, who with the most holy Spirits called Thrones, as the Throne of great respect thou rests on; I offer thee their worth, and that mortification of thy great Throne, and rest of Saint Francis Xavier, who to enthrone thy glory always despised his own, and in confessing thee denied himself; as respect for him hear my plead, which I offer here, and fulfil it for thy greater glory.

Three Our Fathers, and three Hail Marys and the Prayer of the Most Blessed Father above, and the Antiphon and the Prayer Deus qui.

FOURTH DAY

My Lord, the Dominions, Blessed Spirits, fourth Choir of Angels, who so much dominate their will so as to solely fulfil thine, be with the Divine Majesty my strength, and the obedience, and reverence, with which Saint Francis Xavier, with angelic dominion obeyed thee, and those in thy palace, his Prelates : concede to me Lord, this subjection for respect, and thy love, and to all my superiors, also fulfilling the petition that by the hand of Saint Francis Xavier I offer thee.

Three Our Fathers, and three Hail Marys and the Prayer of the Most Blessed Father above, and the Antiphon and the Prayer Deus qui.

FIFTH DAY

God, and my Lord, the fifth order of Angels, who are the Principalities, who with the Divine Majesty have a most principal union, wishing to unite all souls with thee. This was always the care of my glorious Saint Francis Xavier thy most principle, as united with thy Divine Majesty, by which nothing can separate him from thee. Give me this saintly union, Lord, that always united with thee in living grace, and may I die in it, interceding for me these Principalities of glory, and the most principle Saint, and my Lord, for whose respect, and love also fulfil this my petition, that by his hands, and his love I offer.

Three Our Fathers, and three Hail Marys and the Prayer of the Most Blessed Father above, and the Antiphon and the Prayer Deus qui.

SIXTH DAY

This day is consecrated by the Powers, most high Angels, to thy Majesty of theirs, and mine Lord God : these are of great power, and spirit in the workings of thy glory. This virtue was in thy most powerful, and divine Xavier most admirable, with which thou honoured him, for there was never a danger of failing with thy love. Trusting in thy merciful support I offer thee these powerful worths asking thee that by them thou gives spirit to my will to win, for thy love, over all dangers to salvation; hear this petition I offer thee by means of this glorious Priest.

Three Our Fathers, and three Hail Marys and the Prayer of the Most Blessed Father above, and the Antiphon and the Prayer Deus qui.

SEVENTH DAY

My Lord, and God of Virtues, who are the seventh order of the Saintly Angels : these consecrate this seventh day; with them accompany the virtues of the most virtuous Saint Francis Xavier, in particular the loving and saintly affability of his dealings with his God, and with his brothers, by which he could affect all to serve thee, and love thee, towards salvation : for these and other virtues, my Lord, concede to me the same favour in all my dealings with my God, and may my bothers be for God, being this the same end for this request I ask of thee.

Three Our Fathers, and three Hail Marys and the Prayer of the Most Blessed Father above, and the Antiphon and the Prayer Deus qui.

EIGHTH DAY

With divine knowledge do they believe, my Lord, the Cherubim of this eighth day, as their name indicates, which means, the most wise. Their loving wisdom did this human Cherubim learn, thy Saint Francis Xavier, so much of thy favour did he reach in thy Divine Majesty to love thee. For the respect of both of these make me this favour of listening to my pleas, and mercifully approve my petition.

Three Our Fathers, and three Hail Marys and the Prayer of the Most Blessed Father above, and the Antiphon and the Prayer Deus qui.

NINTH DAY

Most loving Lord of mine, the Seraphim ablaze in thy divine love make this final day most holy with that love, with which they are always loving, and desiring to love thee more, as their continuous desire demonstrates. Thou knows, my God, how much thy Seraphim Xavier follows them, who always for thy service, and thy love, and so as all could love thee forever, desired to fly higher in thy love; he asked this from thee with his 'more and more'. By the intercession of these Seraphim make my heart ablaze in thy love, that in order for me to love and please thee, let nothing ever be difficult for me. And as to so much love thou never denied any petition he might make, so by him fulfil my petitions, by which in the end of this Novena thou does not remove me from thy presence, and all of those who perform it may be consoled with thy divine favour, as I am expecting from thy mercy, and thy intercessions.

Three Our Fathers, and three Hail Marys and the Prayer of the Most Blessed Father above, and the Antiphon and the Prayer Deus qui.

In this final day of the Novena one should make confession, and communion, preparing oneself with the greatest possible diligence to please God our Lord, and the Saint, and reach from him the good fulfillment of his petitions, mainly by having a great trust in his benignity; for in this way did Father Felippuci reach perfect health, which happened in the following way.

After having done this entire devotion for nine days, in this final one he confessed, and communed with the greatest reverence, and devotion possible, and he already found himself very much improved, even if not completely sane, nor with his speech free; he then asked that the relic of the Holy Father Francis Xavier be brought to him; and as the Most Holy JESUS wished to offer all the glory of miraculous health to his servant Saint Francis Xavier, when the patient kissed the holy relic, he healed him, and he was completely free, as if he had never been ill. And from that point until he passed through Portugal to go to India, never again did he cough, as he himself said, enjoying a rare health. And in appreciation of such a great, and particular benefit, from that day forth he was called Francis Xavier Felippuci.

FOR THE TENTH DAY

His Holiness Pope Alexander VII, having had news of the piety with which the faithful in Portugal, and particularly in the famous Lisbon, and in the College of Santo Antão of the Company of Jesus solemnly prayed this Novena of the Apostle Saint Francis Xavier, liberally conceded plenary indulgences, and remission from all sins to all faithful who throughout this Novena, and also the following day, which is the twelfth of March, in which the Saint was canonized, visited the mentioned Church of Santo Antão, and at the Altar of the Saint, being confessed, and communed, offered there some prayers for the intention of his Holiness, and assisted in some of the spiritual exercises, which in that same church are done in reverence for that same Saint.

Furthermore, His Holiness conceded, that any faithful, who during any of these ten days so wished by his own devotion to confess once again, and commune, and make the same exercises, and pious works, he may earn seven years of indulgences, and this same number of quarantines. And as such, it is most wise to confess, and commune on the first day, and on the last of the Novena, or the tenth; and one is warned that in order to earn the jubilee, it is not necessary to make this devotion during the whole ten days, only the nine, unless one wishes to also earn the indulgences conceded on the tenth day.

Also be warned that, people who don't know how to read may satisfy this obligation of prayers by praying ten Our Fathers, and ten Hail Marys in reverence of these ten days, and of the ten years that this Priest was in India, and by the intention of His Holiness. His Novena can be prayed on any time of the year.

Warning, so as this Novena is done perfectly

The good Father Francis Xavier Felippuci, when he made the Novena, kept these warnings, and he recommended them a great deal, so as one may achieve the desired fulfilment from the hand of the Holy Father Francis Xavier.

The first warning: that in each of the ten days of the Novena one should seek to imitate one of the virtues of the Saint.

Second: that in each of the days one should do some work for the benefit of someone else, be it bodily alms, or a spiritual one of giving a good advice, consoling the afflicted, &c.

Third: that in each day one should offer the Saint some mortification, such as a fasting, the cilice, disciplines, less pleasures.

Fourth: that the senses be restrained, speaking little, not seeing open spaces, and not hearing murmurings.

Fifth warning, and very important: in each of these days one should read, or hear of something of the life of the great Saint. And as the days of the indulgence are ten, it is very much appropriate to, on each day, read one year of the life of the Saint in India, which are ten.

The Holy Pontiff also shows that he celebrates these ten years with the ten days of indulgences he conceded.

Sixth: one should be warned that people who are not in the state to go and fulfil the Novena at the Church, and at the Altar of the Saint, and should they do further pious works, which should be noted, in a whole, or in part, should talk with their Confessor so as he may change this obligation into some other one; and in this way they may gain the grace, and reach the desired fulfilment.

And to end such a saintly work, offer the glorious Saint Francis Xavier the commemoration with which the Catholic Church also celebrates him, by saying the Prayer with which His Holiness celebrated him, and published him as a Saint on the first Mass, which was said of him on the day, and solemnity of his canonization at the twelve of March of one thousand and six hundred and twenty-two, which was in this way:

Antiphona

Euge serve bone, & fidelis, quia in pauca fuisti fidelis, supra multa te constituam, intra in gaudium Domini tui.

℣Justum deduxit Dominus per vias rectas.
℟Et ostendit illi regnum Dei.

Oratio

Deus, qui glorificantes te glorificas, & in Sanctorum tuorum honoribus honoraris : concede propitius, ut que B. Francisci Xaverii gloriosa merita colimus, ejus pia patrocinia sentiamus. Per Dominum nostrum Jesum Christum, Filium tuum : qui tecum vivit et regnat in unitate Spiritus Sancti Deus, per omnia sæcula sæculorum. *Amen.*

Should there be any spiritual consolation in saying the commemoration of the Saint as a Prayer, which the Holy Church prays on his Mass, and Office, you should say the following:

Antiphon

Euge serve bone, & fidelis, quia in pauca fuisti fidelis, supra multa te constituam, intra in gaudium Domini tui.

℣Justum deduxit Dominus per vias rectas.
℟Et ostendit illi regnum Dei.

Oratio

Deus, qui Indiarum gentes Beati Francisci prædicatione, & miraculis Ecclesiæ tuæ aggregare voluisti : concede propitius, ut cujus gloriosa merita veneramur, virtutum quoque imitemur exempla. Per Dominum nostrum Jesum Christum, Filium tuum : qui tecum vivit et regnat in unitate Spiritus Sancti Deus, per omnia sæcula sæculorum. *Amen.*

Sonnet

Which Saint Francis Xavier wrote to the crucified Lord, in Vernacular

I am not moved, Lord, to want
The Glory, which thou has promised me,
Nor does the fearful Hell move me,
So as to stop offending thee.
Thou moves me, Lord, it moves me to see thee,
Nailed to that Cross, and mocked,
Thy body so badly wounded moves me,
And that death, which I see thee suffer.
My soul in loving thee such is clear,
That even without Heaven, I would love thee,
And without Hell, I would fear thee.
For loving thee it expects nothing,
For if what I desire from thee, I did not desire,
The same that I want thee, I would want.

Remedy for secrecy, and penitence, and humility, and obedience for Nuns, and resignation of will, religious poverty, and purity, and to drive away demons, of which Saint Gertrude the Great is the patron, who had the gift of prophesy

Antiphon

God prepared the heart of Saint Gertrude so as in it have his seat, and his rest.

℣Grace was diffused in thy lips.

℟And for this God blessed thee forever.

Prayer

O God, and almighty Lord, who edified, and elected a pleasant place for thee in the heart of the blessed Virgin Saint Gertrude : propitiously concede to us, that by her miracles, and her feverous prayers together with her intercession we may know to elect the best state, accompanying this with humility, obedience, poverty, and chastity so as we may triumph in that glory. For Christ our Lord, who lives, and reigns for all centuries of centuries. *Amen.*

Remedy so as not to be afraid, nor embarrassed in the telling of one's sins, and saying the sins denied in confession, and to free one from serpent bites, and cast out demons, and for the dangers of ships, and boats at sea, of which Saint Giles Abbot is the patron.

Antiphon

This Saintly man despising the world, and triumphing over the things of the earth, with his works, and words made his treasure in Heaven.

℣The Lord took the Just through the straight path.

℟And showed them the Kingdom of Heaven.

Prayer

O God, and almighty Lord, who by thy infinite mercy illuminated thy blessed servant Saint Giles with so many prodigies, and despises to the world : concede to us, that by his worth, and in his imitation, placed in a grave, where he did so much penitence, may we also deserve to escape this world into that glory. For Christ our Lord. *Amen.*

Remedy for the illnesses of children, which are called impetigo, or fire, and for the infirmities of cough, fever, of which Saint Godfrey is the patron

Antiphon

This Saintly man despising the world, and triumphing over the things of the earth, with his works, and words made his treasure in Heaven.

℣The Lord took the Just through the straight path.

℟And showed them the Kingdom of Heaven.

Prayer

O God, and almighty Lord, heed our pleas, that through the intercession of thy blessed servant Saint Godfrey we make, so as by means of his worth we may be free from all evil : propitiously concede to us that these innocent may see themselves free from this ill, by the intercession of thy servant, so as we all may praise thee in that glory. For Christ our Lord. *Amen.*

Remedy for good marriages, and for breakings, and wounds, and words, of which the great Saint Gonçalo is the patron

Antiphon

Blessed be God, O good servant; and faithful, for thou wert so in things of little worth, and I delivered others of greater worth, said the Lord.

℣The Just shall blossom as a lily.

℟And shall always flourish in the presence of the Lord.

Prayer

Almighty God, and Lord, who admirably enflamed in the love of thy holy name the spirit of the blessed Saint Gonçalo : we ask thee to concede to us, that as we follow his example, may we always meditate on thee, and make with diligent care all which is pleasant to thee. For Christ our Lord. *Amen.*

Remedy to reach forgiveness from sin at the hour of death, of which the Saint Good Thief is the patron. This is part of the Breviary of the Mercedarian Fathers

Antiphon

The Thieve saw Christ crucified, and called him as King, saying: Lord, remember me, when thou leaves for thy Kingdom.

℣Pray for us blessed Thief.

℟So as we may be worthy of the promises of Christ.

Prayer

Almighty, and merciful Lord, who justifies the impious, we humbly plead to thee, that with the benign intention, with which thy only-begotten Son tended to the Good Thief, thou calls us to the true penitence, and by that, which thou promised him, thou gives us eternal glory. For Christ our Lord. *Amen.*

Remedy against stomach pain, of which Saint Gregory the Great is the patron, and for the conversion of the gentiles, and so as books for the honour and glory of God may be written

Antiphon

O excellent Doctor, light of the holy Church, Saint Gregory, lover of the divine law intercede for us to the Son of God.

℣The Lord took the Just through the straight path.

℟And showed them the Kingdom of Heaven.

Prayer

O Almighty God, who gave all the prizes of thy eternal blessing to the soul of thy servant Saint Gregory : concede to us that by his relevant worth, with which thou so much gifted him to the sciences, and charity, that converted by his imitation, we may also praise thee for all eternity in that glory. For Christ our Lord, who lives, and reigns with thee for all centuries of centuries. *Amen.*

Remedy for self despising, and for humility, and obedience, of which Saint King Henry is the patron, and to be wealthy and raise temples

Antiphon

I shall be like a prudent man, who raised his house over a rock.

℣Thou crowned, Lord, this one with honour, and glory.

℟And thou made him into the best work of thy hands.

Prayer

O God, who this day transferred thy blessed servant Saint Henry from the greatest empire on earth to the Kingdom of Heaven : we humbly ask thee, that as thou made him forewarned in the fertility of thy grace, and made him beat the delicacies of the century, so may thou also make us in his imitation flee from the sweetness of this world, and arrive at thy presence free from all sin. For Christ our Lord. *Amen.*

Remedy so as married couples have children, and for continuous penitence, and to drive away demons, and give sight to the blind, of which Saint Hilarion is the patron, and for conformity in the hour of death

Antiphon

Saint Hilarion, admiration of penitence, terror of demons, horror of Hell, always defeated the snares of the Devil.

℣Pray for us Saint Hilarion.

℟So as we may be worthy of the promises of Christ.

Prayer

O God, and almighty Lord, who strengthened, and animated thy blessed servant Saint Hilarion in the desert with copious abundance of thy divine grace : propitiously concede to us, that by his feverous supplication, and his worth we may know to imitate him, and fulfil our supplications, so as we may be free from all dangers, and snares of the Devil, and see thee in that glory. For Christ our Lord. *Amen.*

Remedy against dangerous births, and headache, and fervour in prayer, of which the great Patriarch of the never too much praised Company of JESUS Saint Ignatius of Loyola is the patron

Antiphon

This Saintly man despising the world, and triumphing over the things of the earth in works, and words, made his treasure in Heaven.

℣The Lord took the Just through the straight path.

℟And showed him the Kingdom of Heaven.

Prayer

Almighty God, and Lord, who in order to propagate the greater glory of thy name strengthened a new Succour for the Church Militant by means of the blessed Saint Ignatius : concede to us, who are militant in this world, that with his aid, and example we may deserve to be crowned with him in Heaven. For Jesus Christ thy Son, our Lord, who with thee lives, and reigns in the union of the Holy Spirit for all centuries of centuries. *Amen.*

Remedy for the ill of the heart, of which Saint Inácio Martyr is the patron

Antiphon

Blessed is the man, who suffers the temptation; for knowing to flee with experience, he shall receive the crown of glory which was promised by God to whom knows how to love him.

℣Thou crowned, Lord, this one with honour, and glory.

℟And thou made him into the best work of thy hands.

Prayer

O God, and almighty Lord, look upon our infirmity, and tend to the ills, which afflict our hearts, so as by his worth, and by his intercession, free from all evils, we may reach the goods of glory. For Christ our Lord. *Amen.*

Remedy for war, of which the Apostle Saint James is the patron

Antiphon

Thou art firm in battle, and thou fights the ancient enemy, and thou shall receive the eternal Kingdom.

℣They shall announce the works of God.

℟And his works shall be known.

Prayer

Be present, Lord, to thy people, thou, who are sanctified, and our guard : so as by means of thy intercessions and worth, we may be free from the battles of this world, and victorious we may reach thy Kingdom. For Christ our Lord, who lives, and reigns with thee for all centuries of centuries. *Amen.*

Remedy against lighting, and for isolation, of which the great Saintly Doctor Saint Jerome is the patron, and in order to have the true science

Antiphon

O marvellous Doctor, splendour of the Holy Church, blessed Saint Jerome, lover of the divine law, intercede for us to the Son of God.

℣God loved the Just.

℟And adorned him by dressing him with the stole of eternal glory.

Prayer

O God, who wert served in electing the Great Doctor, the blessed servant Saint Jerome, to expose the sacred Scripture; we ask thee, and make it so, that by his example, which he gave us in his works, and words, and his worth, by thy aid, may we be free from all evil, and reach that glory. For Christ our Lord, who lives, and reigns for all centuries of centuries. *Amen.*

Saint James, Apostle

Remedy for patience, of which Saint Joachim, father of our Lady, is the patron

This is a great devotion to the lord Saint Joachim for all those under his protection so as through it operate prodigies, and admirable portents. And as it is most brief, I advise that it be done every day. And it is as follows: one Our Father, for the pleasure he had in being the grandfather of the Son of God incarnate : one Hail Mary for the pleasure he had in being the father of the Holiest Virgin, and one Gloria Patri for the greatest of all pleasures of a pure heart, which was to be related to the Holiest Trinity by flesh, and blood, through his Holiest Daughter who gave birth to the Eternal Word.

Antiphon

Let us praise this glorious Saint in his generation, for he reached from the Lord the blessing of all the peoples, and in him as head he confirmed his promise.

℣Powerful shall be thy progeny on earth.

℟The generation of the Just shall be blessed.

Let us pray

God, who, among all the Saints, thou wished that the blessed Saint Joachim became the father of the Holiest Virgin mother of thy only-begotten Son.: concede, we ask, that by the patronage of this glorious Saint, whose feast we celebrate, we may enjoy perpetually. For the worth of the same Lord Jesus Christ thy Son, who lives, and reigns with thee for all centuries of centuries. *Amen.*

Remedy for headache, and so as Missionaries may preach solid truths, and to reach the spirit of poverty, of which the great Precursor of Christ Saint John the Baptist is the patron

Antiphon

This child, who was born for us, is more than a Prophet : for this is the one who calls the Saviour of the world : Among those born of women no other was born greater than Saint John the Baptist.

℣This child is great in the presence of the Lord.

℟For his mother is also with the same Lord.

Prayer

We ask thee, Lord concede to us, that we may seek thee through the path of salvation, and following the doctrine of thy blessed Precursor Saint John, we may arrive safely to enjoy Jesus Christ, who he predicted, and by his worth we may have the resolution of praising thee eternally in that glory. For Christ our Lord. *Amen.*

Saint Joachim

Saint John the Baptist

SIGHS FOR THE NOVENA OF SAINT JOHN THE BAPTIST

FIRST DAY

The same as the Novena of Our Lady of the Rock until the Act of Love of God.

FIRST SIGH

O my Glorious Saint John the Baptist, by the ineffable pleasure, which thou had, when in the sixth month of thy conception, the Divine Word sanctified thee, conceding thee the perfect use of reason, reach for me the knowledge of how to love with my heart the same Lord who gave it to me.

Our Father, Hail Mary, Gloria Patri.

Antiphon

Puer, qui natus est nobis, plus quàm Propheta est : hic est enim, de quo Salvator ait : Inter natos mulierum non surrexit maior Joanne Baptista

℣Iste puer magnus coram Domino.

℟Nam & manus ejus cum ipso est.

Oratio

Deus, qui præsentem diem honorabilem nobis in beati Joannis Nativitate fecisti; da populis tuis spiritualium gratiam gaudiorum, & omnium fidelium mentes dirige in viam salitus æternæ. Per Deominum

SECOND DAY

All as in the first day.

SECOND SIGH

O my Glorious Saint John the Baptist, for the reverence, with which while still in thy mother's womb thou worshipped the Word incarnate on thy knees, reach for me that I worship my God with such fervour, that I may recover much of which I have so far lost.

Our Father, Hail Mary, Gloria Patri.

THIRD DAY

All as in the first day.

THIRD SIGH

O my Glorious Saint John the Baptist, for the admirable obedience, with which, by command of the Most High, thou wert born into the light of the world, that thou so much feared by the knowledge thou had of its dangers, reach for me that I may live with such carefulness, that I may escape its snares, and deceits.

Our Father, Hail Mary, Gloria Patri.

FOURTH DAY

All as in the first day.

FOURTH SIGH

O my Glorious Saint John the Baptist, by the ineffable pleasure, which thou had, when newly born thou saw thyself in the arms of the Mother of God, and wrapped in blankets, and cloths, which the same Lady made with her own purest hands, reach for me a true love, and devotion towards her.

Our Father, Hail Mary, Gloria Patri.

FIFTH DAY

All as in the first day.

FIFTH SIGH

O my Glorious Saint John the Baptist, by the resignation with which thou suffered the escape from the cruelty of Herod to the desert, and in it the death of thy Mother Saint Elizabeth becoming alone at the age of four years, reach for me the great conformity in the labours, which the Lord may send me.

Our Father, Hail Mary, Gloria Patri.

SIXTH DAY

All as in the first day.

SIXTH SIGH

O my Glorious Saint John the Baptist, by the virtues, which thou exercised in the desert, and the benefit, which in it thou received from the Most High, and from thy beloved Aunty the Holiest Mary, reach for me such a purity of life, that I may never stain it with the slightest fault.

Our Father, Hail Mary, Gloria Patri.

SEVENTH DAY

All as in the first day.

SEVENTH SIGH

O my Glorious Saint John the Baptist, by the excellence thou had in baptizing thy very Redeemer, and that he baptized thee, and by the humble fidelity, with which thou exercised the office of his Precursor, reach for me a true humility, so as I may be in everything faithful in the service of my God.

Our Father, Hail Mary, Gloria Patri.

EIGHTH DAY

All as in the first day.

EIGHTH SIGH

O my Glorious Saint John the Baptist, by the joyful conformity, with which thou tolerated being despised, and flogged in the prison by order or Herod, reach for me such a zeal of honour from God, and for the salvation of the souls, that without any fear of the world I my exercise in it with fervour, and diligence.

Our Father, Hail Mary, Gloria Patri.

NINTH DAY

All as in the first day.

NINTH SIGH

O my Glorious Saint John the Baptist, by the pleasure, thou had, when in prison the Redeemer of the world, and his Holiest Mother, appeared to console thee, and witness the martyrdom of thy beheading, assist me in the hour of my death in such a way that I may know thy powerful patronage.

Our Father, Hail Mary, Gloria Patri.

Remedy to acquire, or conserve good fame, and for secrecy, of which Saint John Nepomucene is the patron

Antiphon

This Saint fought until death for the law of God; and remained strong against the words of the impious; for he was founded over a firm rock.

℣With glory and honour thou crowned him, Lord.

℟And thou constituted him above the works of thy hands.

Prayer

God, who by the invictus sacramental silence of Saint John Nepomucene with a new crown of martyrdom thou adorned thy Church : concede to us by his intercessions, and example, that we may keep a careful tongue, and rather tolerate in this world all evils, than the determent of our soul. For Christ our Lord. *Amen.*

Remedy for poison, of which Saint John the Evangelist is the patron, and to reach the love of God

Antiphon

This is the beloved disciple of Christ, who in the supper of the Lord sat at his side : blessed Apostle, to whom the mysteries of Heaven were revealed.

℣He is worthy of great praise, the blessed Saint John

℟Who rested on the chest of the Lord on the night of the Supper.

Prayer

O almighty Lord, who illuminated thy Church with the science, and doctrine of thy blessed servant Saint John Evangelist, thy beloved disciple : propitiously concede to us, that by his intercession, and his worth we may be free from all poison, and we may know the celestial things to enjoy them in thy presence. For Christ our Lord. *Amen.*

Remedy for pain, and for the hour of death, and headache, and lost things, of which Saint Joseph is the patron

Antiphon

O Son of mine, (said the Holiest MARY to Jesus) why did thou cause us such distress? I, and Joseph thy father with great pain from thy absence wert seeking thee.

℣I seated under the shade of whom I wanted.

℟The fruit of this tree are most sweet to me.

Saint John the Evangelist

Prayer

My God, who with ineffable providence thou elected the glorious Saint Joseph for husband of thy Holiest Mother : concede to us, we beg thee, that we may deserve to have this Saint as an intercessor in Heaven, who we venerate as our protector on earth, thou, who lives, and reigns for all centuries of centuries. *Amen.*

Daily exercises according to Bernardino de' Bustis[126] *so as to have a good death*

Deus in adjutorium[127] &c.

Gloria Patri &c.

O Glorious Patriarch Most Saintly Joseph, by those great consolations, which among the mortifications of the infirmity thou had, thou wert assisted at the bedside, tending to thee as if thou wert his legal father, by the legislator of the world JESUS Christ : I plead to thee, that my deathly infirmity be placed under thy legislation for the relief of my tribulations, and agonies, so as thou shall make all of them merciful in the presence of the same Lord, so as I may achieve from him a precious death.

Our Father, Hail Mary.

O Illustrious Husband of the Queen of Heaven, by that intense love of God, which enflamed thy heart, when shortly before thy innocent spirit parted from thy body, thou said to JESUS Christ: *I shall die greatly joyous for the firm hope, which I have, that thou shall soon offer freedom to those who die in thy grace*; and I plead to thee, that from this same Lord thou reaches for me in that last hour such an ardent charity, that I may die for him, and then with him live in blessedness.

Our Father, Hail Mary.

O most chaste man, who by the excellence of thy virtues thou seemed more like an Angel than a man : for those last wills, and words, which from the mouth of the Author of life thou heard in the instant of thy death, as JESUS Christ said to thee: *Be gone now, O my beloved father : be gone from this valley of miseries, and take to the Just, who await for me, this good news, that shortly I shall come for them to take them to my Kingdom*; I plead to thee, that thou reaches for me from this same Lord such an effective aid in the hour of my death, and that truly contrite I may leave this banishment to return to the celestial homeland, where in thy company, and in that of the Holiest Mary I may offer the Most Blessed Trinity the grace of such an incomprehensible benefit.

Our Father, Hail Mary.

126 Translator's note: a 15th and 16th century Italian Theologian and writer, greatly devout of the Virgin Mary.
127 Translator's note: Psalm 69.

Saint Joseph

Remedy for the contrition of tears, and to move the heart to not sin any further, looking upon our Lady of Piety

Antiphon

O all of thee, who walk through this path, heed and see, if there is any pain such as this my pain.

℣May my eyes be weakened by so many tears.

℟And all my entrails wert disturb with excessive pain.

Prayer

O Lord Jesus Christ, whose sword of the cruelest passion in this way penetrated the soul of the beatific Mother, which made her into a greater Martyr : concede to us, and we ask thee, that we may in this world meditate on the memory of her pain, so as we may arrive to contemplate thy joys up there in Heaven. For Christ our Lord, who lives, and reigns for all centuries of centuries. *Amen.*

Remedy so as seamen may have good wind, of which Saint Lawrence is the patron, and for fire, and for chastity

Antiphon

It is most worthy to praise Saint Lawrence, so as he may guide us free from the storms of this world, and safely into the port of glory.

℣Pray for us Saint Lawrence.

℟So as we may be worthy of the promises of Christ.

Prayer

Almighty God, who wert served in conceding to thy blessed servant Saint Lawrence the extinguishing of the flames of our vices, and the beating of the fires of his torments : propitiously concede to us, that by his intercession we may have favourable wind, and we may sail through the torments of the seas of this world until arriving at the port of thy glory, the celestial homeland. *Amen.*

Remedy against stone pain, of which Saint Liborius is the patron

Antiphon

Heal us, Lord, with the rogations, and perpetual pleas, and the aid of the blessed Saint Liborius, so as we may be free from these insufferable pains.

℣Pray for us Saint Liborius.

℟So as we may be worthy of the promises of Christ.

Prayer

God, who illuminated thy blessed servant Saint Liborius with special privileges to cure the pain of stones, and sands, and with other countless miracles : propitiously concede to us, that by his intercessions we may deserve to be free from similar pain, and enjoy the eternal rest. For Christ our Lord. *Amen.*

Remedy for the eyes, of which Saint Lucy is the patron

Antiphon

O Blessed Saint Lucy, be joyous in the Lord, be joyous for that which the eyes never saw, nor the ears heard, nor the heart imagined, and thou deserved to receive.

℣Grace was diffused in thy lips.

℟For this God blessed thee forever.

Prayer

O Almighty God, who with so much splendour, and clarity of thy grace thou illuminated thy blessed servant Saint Lucy for her unblemished life : make it so as by her worth, and the miracles we have seen we be taken through the paths of truth, and certainty of this world to that celestial City of glory. For Christ our Lord. *Amen.*

Remedy against epileptic accidents, or falling sickness, and vertigo. Against the dangers of the roads, fevers, and all castes of sorceries, and sudden death, and for those who are sentenced to death, of which the Saint Mage Kings Caspar, Melchior, and Balthazar are the patron, and so as Preachers do not get lost in sermons

Antiphon

The Mage Kings, seeing the star, mutually said: This is the sign of the great King; let us go, and seek him, and offer him gifts, gold, incense, and myrrh. Alleluia.

℣The Kings of Tharsis, and of the Island shall offer him gifts

℟The Kings of Arabia, and of Sabah shall bring their gifts.

Prayer

God, who on this day thou wished to manifest thy only-begotten Son to the peoples, guiding them through a star : propitiously concede to us, by those, who already by means of the Faith know thee, that we may be taken to contemplate the beauty of thy greatness. For the love of the same Lord Jesus Christ thy Son, who lives and reigns with thee for all centuries of centuries. *Amen.*

Remedy for women who are rearing to have milk, and to be free from wild beasts, and fire, of which Saint Mammes, Martyr, is the patron

Antiphon

This Saint fought until death for the law of God; and he prevailed strong against the word of the wicked; for he was founded over firm rock.

℣Thou crowned, Lord, this one with honour, and glory.

℟And thou made him into the best work of thy hands.

Prayer

O Almighty God, we ask thee, and make it so as by the intercession of thy blessed Saint Mammes, thy Martyr : propitiously concede to us, that by his worth we be made free from all dangers of this world, and fed with thy doctrine, which is the milk of thy divine grace, and enjoy thee in that glory. For Christ our Lord. *Amen.*

Remedy against scrofula of which Saint Marcouf, Abbot, is the patron

Antiphon

This Saintly man despising the world, and triumphing over the things of the earth, with his works, and words made his treasure in Heaven.

℣The Lord took the Just through the straight path.

℟And showed them the Kingdom of Heaven.

Prayer

O God, and almighty Lord, who illuminated thy blessed servant Saint Marcouf Abbot with so many miracles : propitiously concede to us, that by his intercession we may be free from this evil so as to enjoy thee in that glory. For Christ our Lord. *Amen.*

Remedy against mange, and itch, of which Saint Marinus, Martyr, is the patron

Antiphon

He, who wants to go to Heaven take up his Cross, and follow me.

℣The Just shall blossom as the palm.

℟As was the Balm-tree multiplied.

Prayer

O God, and almighty Lord, who magnified thy servant Saint Marinus Martyr with so many prerogatives of sainthood : propitiously concede to us that by his intercessions we be made free from these persecutions, and perfidious considerations so as to enjoy thy glory. For Christ our Lord. *Amen.*

Remedy against the blackfly, worm, and any other critters, who destroy the vines, and further plants, of which Saint Martha, Martyr, is the patron

Antiphon

Come Wife of Christ, receive the crown which was prepared by the Lord forever.

℣Grace was diffused in thy lips.

℟And for this God blessed thee forever.

Prayer

O God, and almighty Lord, who favoured thy blessed servant Saint Martha Virgin with so much charity : concede to us that by her worth we may reach the abundance of thy charity, blossoming in this life to pick the fruits in that glory. For Christ our lord. *Amen.*

Remedy against fires, of which Saint Martial is the patron

Antiphon

The Lord loved, and adorned him, and dressed him with the stole of glory, and at the gates of Paradise crowned him.

℣The Lord took the Just through the straight path.

℟And showed them the Kingdom of Heaven.

Prayer

We ask thee Lord that thou hears our pleas, which we present in the solemnity of thy Confessor Pontiff Saint Mammes, and him, who was worthy to serve thee, interceding by his worth, may free us from fires, and absolve us of all sin, so as to reach that glory. For Christ our Lord. *Amen.*

Remedy against intermittent fevers, and further infirmities, and against critters, which destroy crops, of which the Holy Martyrs of Morocco are the patrons. I had the fortune of seeing, and worshiping their bones in the great sanctuary of Coimbra

Antiphon

The bodies of the Holy Martyrs of Morocco Berard, Peter, Accursius, Adjutus, and Otho were taken to the Santa Cruz of Coimbra, where they gave their lives by shedding their blood for the faith of JESUS Christ.

℣The Lord took the Just through the straight path.

℟And showed them the Kingdom of Heaven.

Prayer

O God, and almighty Lord, who illuminated the principles of the Friars Minor with the greatest martyrdoms of thy blessed Saints Berard, Peter, Accursius, Adjutus, and Otho, polishing with these five precious stones thy five wounds in the Holy Cross of Coimbra; make it so, and we ask thee propitious, that by their intercession we may pass from this life free from all evils unto the City of glory, so as in it, in the company of the Saints, we may enjoy thee for all eternity. For Christ Our Lord. *Amen.*

Remedy to reach the favours of God, of which The Holiest MARY is the patron

Antiphon

Holy Mary, aid the miserable, aid the pusillanimous, consul the sad, pray for the people, intercede for the priestly state, and for the devout female gender, so as all may experience thy consolations, and relief by means of thy patronage.

℣Pray for us Saint Mary Mother of God.

℟So as we may be worthy of the promises of Christ.

Prayer

God, and almighty Lord, who wert served in filling thy Mother the Holiest Mary with so many degrees of grace, for the support, and patronage of the sinners : make it, and we ask for thee auspiciously, that by her worth, and her intercessions we may also deserve to be protected in thy presence so as to have it in the last day, and we may enjoy her sight in those heights, where thou lives, and reigns for all centuries. For Christ our Lord. *Amen.*

Remedy to reach the gift of tears, and regret of faults, and the love of God, of which Saint Mary Magdalene is the patron

Antiphon

Mary anointed the feet of Jesus, and cleaned them with her hair, and her house was filled with the scent of the unguent.

℣Grace was diffused in thy lips.

℟And for this God blessed thee forever.

Prayer

O God, and almighty Lord, who wert so moved by the tears, and regrets of thy blessed servant Saint Mary Magdalene : propitiously concede to us, that as thou resurrected Lazarus after four days, may we also be her intercession, and worthy make us rise from the ugliness of sin, and with tears of regret may we arrive to see thee in that glory. For Christ our Lord. *Amen.*

Remedy for the dangers of the sea, and to be happy in journeys, and free from storms, of which the great Saint Mary of Perpetual Succour

of the Royal, and Military Order of Mercy, Redemption of the Captives is the patron

Antiphon

When thou sails over the waters, the Lord said, thou shall always find me there to defend thee, and never shall thou be toppled by the sea.

℣Prodigious Saint Mary, make it so as to achieve

℟Triumph over the seas those who sail them.

Prayer

God, who sees, that we cannot subsist by our frail constitution so much danger : propitiously concede to us, that by intercession of thy blessed servant Saint Mary we may be free from the waves of this life, so as we may arrive to that port of eternal salvation. For Christ our Lord. *Amen.*

Remedy to reach a good death, and to reach the patronage of the invictus and great Angel Saint Michael, and to reach everything from God, of which this great lover, and greatly beloved by God, is the patron

Antiphon

Blessed Angel Saint Michael, by the zeal, and honour of the Holiest Trinity, Father, and Son, and Holy Spirit, whose praise, empire, divinity and strength we venerate, be our guide, and our guard in this war, which the Devil of Hell is arming and doing against us.

℣Pray for us, O most blessed Michael, Prince of the Church of Christ.

℟So as we may be worthy of the promises of Christ.

Prayer

O most glorious Prince Saint Michael Archangel, Captain of the celestial spirits, receiver of the saintly souls, destroyer of evil spirits, the most noble of the Citizens of Heaver after Christ, admirable guide after the Holiest Mary, first with God above all the angels, great in virtue, and excellence : intercede for all of us, who call upon thee, free us from all adversity of the body and soul, and the bind in front of the court of the just Judge, and protect us in the last battle of death, send the holy Angels to our defence, defend us from the infernal dragon, and the cunnings of the demons, receive our souls in peace, and guide them to the Paradise of pleasures, and concede this to us by the love of that ineffable charity, and most ardent love, which thou has for our Lord Jesus Christ, who with him thou reigns, and lives for all centuries of centuries. *Amen.*

Devotions to the Angels

Those who pray twenty-seven times the Hail Mary, and nine times the Our Father in honour of the nine Choirs of Angels divided between the three Hierarchies, which means three Hail Marys, and one Our Father to each Choir, concluding at the end with four Our Fathers, the first for Saint Michael, the second for Saint Gabriel, the third to Saint Raphael, and the last to his Guardian Angel, the Archangel Michael promised that, by doing this devotion before communion, he would give one Angel from each of the nine Choirs to accompany you for when you receive the Holy Communion; and to those who perform this everyday he promised continuous assistance from the Angels throughout life, and that after death he would free their souls, and those of their relatives, from the penalties of Purgatory : this the same Archangel Michael reveals to his devotee Antonia de Stomaco, as is mentioned in her life, book 3, chapter 74.

Special devotion to the Archangel Michael

Antiphon

Glorious Prince Saint Michael, Guide, and Captain of the Celestial armies, Receiver of the souls, Destroyer of the wicked spirits, Citizen of the Lord, Governor of the Church of God after Christ, and of great excellence, and virtue, and all those who invoke thee free them from all adversity, and be in our worth in the service of God with thy precious office, and most dignifying intercession.

℣Pray for us Most Blessed Michael, Prince of the Church of Christ.

℟So as we may be worthy of the promises of the Lord.

Prayer

Almighty, and eternal God, who by thy supreme clemency, for the human health thou marvellously charged the Glorious Saint Michael Archangel as Prince of thy Church : concede to us that with his healthy aid we may deserve to be here defended from all enemies, and that in the hour of our death we may be free, and safe, and be presented before thy Divine and sovereign Majesty. For the worth of Christ our Lord. *Amen.*

The Archangel Michael

Remedy to reach relief in tears, and consolation in afflictions, and for the reconciliation of enemies, and dangers at sea, of which Saint Monica, mother of Saint Augustine, is the patron

Antiphon

My soul shall praise God until death, for he freed me from the affliction of my soul, and heard my moans, and heeded my tears.

℣Grace was diffused in thy lips.

℟And for this God blessed thee forever.

Prayer

O Almighty God, consoler of the sad, and health of the afflicted, who mercifully received the tender tears of the blessed Saint Monica in the conversion of her Son Augustine : concede that by the intercession of either one or the other we may cry our sins, and reach the indulgence of thy grace. For Christ our Lord. *Amen.*

Remedy for poor and abandoned damsels, of which Saint Nicholas of Myra is the patron

Antiphon

God loved Saint Nicholas, and adorned, and dressed him with the stole of glory, and at the gates of Paradise crowned him.

℣The Lord took the Just through the straight path.

℟And showed them the Kingdom of Heaven.

Prayer

O God, who illuminated with countless prodigies thy blessed Pontiff Saint Nicholas : we ask thee, and make this so by his worth, and his pleas that we be free from the fires of Hell. For Christ our Lord. *Amen.*

Remedy against plague, of which Saint Onuphrius is the patron

Antiphon

This Saintly man despising the world, and triumphing over the things of the earth, with his works, and words made his treasure in Heaven.

℣The Lord took the Just through the straight path.

℟And showed them the Kingdom of Heaven.

Prayer

Almighty God, that with thy eyes of mercy thou looked upon the labours, who for the love of thee thy servants suffer, allowing these labours so as to further increase their worth, by those of Saint Onuphrius we ask thee to give worth, and constancy to all of us so as to carry with patience all the tribulations, freeing us from fever, preparing us with true, and legitimate disposition to, dignified, receive thee in sacrament : who lives, and reigns for all centuries of centuries. *Amen.*

Remedy for ear pain, of which Ovidius, Archbishop of Braga, is the patron

Antiphon

Let us reach the patronage of the blessed Saint Ovidius, so as to favour us with his patronage.

℣Pray for us Saint Ovidius.

℟So as we may be worthy of the promises of Christ.

Prayer

O Almighty God, turn thy ears to our pleas, which by the intercession of thy blessed servant Saint Ovidius we make to thee : propitiously concede to us, that thou, hearing our clamours, removes us from the pains which we suffer, so as to enjoy thee in that glory. For Christ our Lord, who lives and reigns for all centuries of centuries. *Amen.*

Remedy for patience, and the suffering of floggings, and offences, and unjust prisons, and so as Missionaries may preach with spirit the truths, and be able to convert, and for the sciences, of which the Great Doctor of the Peoples, the Apostle Saint Paul is the patron

Antiphon

Saint Paul says, three times I was flogged, one time I was stoned, three times I suffered martyrdom in the name of Christ. I planted, Apollo watered; however, God is the one who made all.

℣Thou art the vase of election, Saint Paul Apostle.

℟Preacher of the truth in the world universe.

Prayer

God, who taught the world universe with the preaching of the blessed Saint Paul : give us, and we ask thee, that we may know to celebrate his conversion, and by his intercession we may be converted to thy love, so as free ourselves from the persecutions of this world, we may pick the fruits of our labour in the tree of life in thy, and his company, raptured into those Heavens. For Christ Our Lord. *Amen.*

Remedy so as the doors of Heaven open for us, and we may grow in the Faith, and reach the gift of tears, and all we may desire, of which the glorious Prince of the Apostles, and Patriarchs the Lord Saint Peter is the patron

Antiphon

Thou art Peter, and over this rock I shall found my Church, and the doors of Hell shall not prevail against it. I shall give thee the keys to the Kingdom of Heaven. All which thou binds over the earth, shall also be bound in Heaven: that which thou unbinds over the earth, shall also be unbound in Heaven.

℣Pray for us Saint Peter.

℟So as we may be worthy of the promises of Christ.

Prayer

Almighty God, who delivered the keys to the Kingdom of Heaven to the blessed Apostle Saint Peter, thou also gave him the power to bind, and unbound : concede to us, that by the aid of his intercession we may be made free from the binds of our faults, who lives, and reigns with God the Father in the union of the Holy Spirit for all centuries of centuries. *Amen.*

Remedy against shipwreck, and dangers at sea, and critters, which condemns the farms, of which Saint Peter González is the patron

Antiphon

This Saintly man despising the world, and triumphing over the things of the earth, with his works, and words made his treasure in Heaven.

℣The Lord took the Just through the straight path.

℟And showed them the Kingdom of Heaven.

Prayer

O God, and almighty Lord, heed our pleas, that by the intercessions of thy blessed servant Saint Peter we make, that by means of his worth we be made free from all dangers : propitiously concede to us, that triumphing over the dangers of the sea of this world, we arrive at that safe port of glory. For Christ our Lord. *Amen.*

Saint Peter, Apostle

Remedy against hail, which destroys the sowing rows of which Saint Peter Martyr is the patron

Antiphon

Perfect Martyr, Doctor of truth, and vase of purity, rule of sainthood, ask for forgiveness for my sins, and grace so as we may enjoy the presence of God.

℣The Just shall blossom as the palm.

℟As was the Balm-tree multiplied.

Prayer

We ask thee, Lord, and make it so as we may be favoured by the devotion of thy blessed servant Saint Peter Martyr, which by the prerogative of the same faith, deserved to reach the palm of martyrdom. For Christ our Lord.

Remedy to reach a good death, and the redemption of the captives, of which the great Patriarch of the Royal, and Military Order of Mercy Saint Peter Nolasco is the patron

Antiphon

The Lord ordered the redemption of his people, by which he sent Saint Peter Nolasco his servant.

℣Pray for us Saint Peter Nolasco.

℟So as we may be worthy of the promises of Christ.

Prayer

O almighty Lord, who divinely, as an example of thy charity for the redemption of the faithful, taught Saint Peter Nolasco to fertilize thy Church with a new family : concede to us, that by his intercessions we may be free from the captivity of sin, and with perpetual freedom we may enjoy that celestial homeland. For Christ our Lord. *Amen.*

Remedy to reach all which may be asked from God, of which the great Saint Peter of Alcantara is the universal patron, and against intermittent fever, and also fevers

Antiphon

O ineffable man, who living in the flesh, walked in spirit, and not desiring anything in the world, always had his familiarity in Heaven.

℣Pray for us Saint Peter.

℟So as we may be worthy of the promises of Christ.

Prayer

God, who illuminated thy blessed servant Saint Peter, thy Confessor, with the benefit of the admirable penitence, and of his highest contemplation : propitiously concede to us, that by his favourable worth, mortified in flesh, we may deserve to participate in the celestial gifts. For Christ our Lord. *Amen.*

Remedy against earthquakes, and the collapse of buildings, and to reach a good death, of which Saint Philip Neri is the patron

Antiphon

This is the one, who despising the word, reached Heaven for the conversion of the peoples, and he made many prodigies during his life.

℣Pray for us Holy Father Philip.

℟So as we may be worthy of the promises of Christ.

Prayer

Almighty Lord, who illuminated the blessed Saint Philip, thy Confessor, to conserve the health of the souls with the fire of thy divine love, and with admirable gifts of grace : propitiously concede to us, that contrite with our entire hearts we may be free from all imminent dangers to the body, and the soul, and we may deserve to reach that eternal life. For Christ our Lord. *Amen.*

This is also a special patron to reach a good death from God; and so as all may achieve his protection in that terrible trance, we cast the following Prayer, which was printed in Rome for this same purpose, which should be prayed every day.

Prayer

Most devoted to the blessed Saint Philip Neri to reach a good death

Blessed be the holiest name of our Lord Jesus Christ, and the Holiest Virgin MARY his mother, and of Saint Philip, and of the whole celestial Curia forever. *Amen.*

Saintly Father Philip, aid me, this miserable sinner, so as sudden death may not come over me, and I pass from the world unprepared; pray for me to the blessed Virgin MARY by the most bitter death of thy only-begotten Son our Lord Jesus Christ, so as by the detestation of sin, and the Devil, and by the renunciation of his works, by the true contrition, by the penitence, and dignified satisfaction, and acceptance of God, and the love of my fellow man, reconciled with Christ may I pass from this world, and by thy intercessions, Saint Philip, remember in the final hour, when the vital spirits fail, our pleas, which we do now; and aid me so as to be able to call the name of JESUS, and of the blessed Virgin MARY, so as we may be free in that last hour from the ministers of the Devil, and place us with Christ, and with his faithful servant friends.

Antiphon

Holy Father Philip, benignly receive our pleas, and make me leave the path of sin, and teach me, and aid me in following the path of sainthood, and move the celestial glory, so as thy holy prayer may reconcile me with Christ, and free me from the horrors of death.

℣Pray for us Saint Philip.

℟So as we may be worthy of the promises of Christ.

Prayer

We ask thee, Lord, that the intercession of the blessed Saint Philip, thy Confessor, may free us from adversity, so as through his intercessions we may devoutly deserve that before the day of our death we may receive the most glorious Sacrament of the sacrosanct body of our Lord Jesus Christ, and by the true, and pure confession we may receive the remission from sin. *Amen.*

Three Our Fathers, and three Hail Marys.

JESUS, MARY, I give thee my heart, and my soul.

This Jaculatoria used to be said by the Saint many times during the day. The same should be done by whoever has the fortune of being a devotee of such a great Saint.

Remedy against deafness, and further ear issues, of which Saint Quentin Martyr is the patron

Antiphon

Saint Quentin great Martyr, and zealot of the honour of God, who shed his blood to cultivate, and rule his heart for great honour, and glory of God.

℣The Just shall blossom as the palm.

℟As was the Balm-tree multiplied.

Prayer

O God, and almighty Lord, hear our pleas, that by means of thy blessed servant Saint Quentin Martyr, whom thou honoured with so much glory : propitiously concede to us, that by his pleas, our voices be heard, and free from all evil, and may we come to hear thy praise in that glory. For Christ our Lord. *Amen.*

Remedy against rabid dog bites, and to reach firmness, and consistency in the love of God, of which Saint Quiteria Virgin and Martyr is the patron

Antiphon

Come, Wife of Christ, receive the crown which was prepared by the Lord forever.

℣With thy presence, and with thy beauty.
℟Be ready, go forward, and reign.

Prayer

We ask thee, mighty God, concede to us, for thou adorned the blessed Saint Quiteria with virginity, and martyrdom; and as with thy virtue she bound the Devil, and converted a countless amount of peoples; in the same way, by her continuous pleas, may we be free from the infernal enemy, and from all danger, and infirmity. For Jesus Christ thy Son our Lord, who with thee lives, and reigns, in the union of the Holy Spirit for all centuries of centuries. *Amen.*

Remedy for the infirm, and so as journeys are successful, of which the Angel Saint Raphael is the patron

Antiphon

O glorious Prince, Saint Raphael Archangel, remember me; here and everywhere beg on our behalf to the Son of God.

℣The Angel was near the altar of the Temple.
℟Having the golden thurible in his hand.

Prayer

O God, who gave the blessed Saint Raphael Archangel as a companion to thy servant Tobias to guide him on the path : concede to us, who are thy servants, that we may always be protected in his guard, and favoured with his aid until we arrive at those heights. For Christ our Lord. *Amen.*

Remedy for the impossible, of which Saint Rita of Cascia is the patron

Antiphon

I greet thee wife Rita,
Who among the thorns of pain
Thou wert born the vase, and greatest rose,
For Christ's divine love.
℣Thou marked, Lord, thy servant Saint Rita
℟With the seal of thy charity, and passion.

Prayer

Lord God, who to the Blessed Rita gave so much grace, so as she would imitate thee in love for thy enemies, so as her heart, and forehead would carry the signs of thy charity, and Passion : by her intercession, and worth we ask for the grace to love our enemies, and penetrated by the thorn of piercing, and the pain of thy death, to contemplate the torments of thy holiest passion. Thou, who lives, and reigns without end for all centuries of centuries. *Amen.*

Remedy for the plague, and wounds, of which Saint Roch is the patron

Antiphon

God save thee holiest Roch, born of noble blood, marked by the Cross of Christ thou heals the infirm.

℣Pray for us blessed Saint Roch.

℟So as we may be worthy of the promises of Christ.

Prayer

Almighty, and merciful God, and Lord, who by the worth, and pleas of thy blessed Confessor Saint Roch thou made all general plagues graciously cease in men : propitiously concede to us, that by his supplications thou makes all plague cease, so as humbly we may seek thy mercy, so as we may be free from the plague, and infirmity, and we may eternally see thee. For Christ our Lord. *Amen.*

Remedy to lead a penitent life, for discipline, fasting, abstinence, mortifications, of which Saint Rose of Lima, first flower of America, is the patron, and for the eyes

Antiphon

Come beloved Wife of Christ, receive the crown of roses, and stars which thy divine Husband prepared for thee on earth to reign, and triumph in Heaven.

℣Grace was diffused in thy lips.

℟And for this God blessed thee forever.

Prayer

O Almighty God, rewarder, and Author of all goods, who wished that thy blessed Saint Rose, covered with the dew of celestial grace, and with the beauty of patience, and with chastity blossomed to the Indians : concede to us, who are thy servants, who, running to the scent of thy softness, may deserve to be the soft scent of Christ. For Christ our Lord. *Amen.*

Remedy for chastity, of which Saint Rose of Viterbo is the patron

Antiphon

Come, Wife of Christ, receive the crown which was prepared by the Lord forever.

℣Grace was diffused in thy lips.

℟And for this God blessed thee forever.

Prayer

Almighty God, and Lord, who added the blessed Saint Rose to the number of thy Holy Virgins : we ask thee to concede to us that by her pleas, and worth we may be purified from all faults, and enjoy eternal union with thy divine Majesty. For Christ our Lord. *Amen.*

Remedy against immoderate blood flow, of which Saint Sabina Martyr is the patron

Antiphon

Come Wife of Christ, receive the crown which was prepared by the Lord forever.

℣Grace was diffused in thy lips.

℟And for this God blessed thee forever.

Prayer

God, who among the many miracles of thy power thou also offered the victory of martyrdom to the female gender : propitiously concede to us, that by our praising of the commemoration of the life of thy blessed Saint Sabina Martyr, with her example we may walk towards thee. For Christ our Lord.

Remedy for a creature to enjoy the word of God, and for rain, of which Saint Scholastica is the patron, and to reach the gift of tears

Antiphon

Saint Scholastica asking her brother the Patriarch Saint Benedict, to spend the night in her house so as they could speak of the things of God the entire night, and not wanting this Saint to spend the night outside of his cell, she looked up at Heaven and it immediately started to rain so as the conversation would not be interrupted.

℣Grace was diffused in thy lips.

℟And for this God blessed thee forever.

Prayer

O Almighty God, who brought onto Heaven the blessed soul of Saint Scholastica in the form of a dove in order to show us the path of innocence : concede to us, that by her worth, and her supplications we may live without guilt, and reach that glory. For Christ our Lord. *Amen.*

Remedy against the plague, and to conserve secrecy, of which Saint Sebastian is the patron

Antiphon

O blessed Sebastian, great is thy faith, intercede for us to the Lord Jesus Christ, so as we may be free from the sudden plague, and of all dangers of the body, and soul.

℣Pray for us blessed Sebastian.

℟So as we may be worthy of the promises of Christ.

Prayer

God, who the blessed Saint Sebastian thy Martyr strengthened with the virtue of constancy in his passion : concede to his imitation our despise, by thy love, of the prosperities of the world, and the fear of its adversities. For Christ our Lord. *Amen.*

Devotion of Saint Sebastian against the plague, and contagious ills

Almighty God, who knows our infirmity, agony, anxiety, and tribulations in this life : make it so as in all of this Saint Sebastian may be of worth to us, and may free us from everything by his intercession. *Amen.*

Remedy for the ill of paralysis, of which Saint Servulus Confessor is the patron

Antiphon

This Saintly man despising the world, and triumphing over the things of the earth, with his works, and words made his treasure in Heaven.

℣The Lord took the Just through the straight path.

℟And showed them the Kingdom of Heaven.

Prayer

O God, and almighty Lord, who illuminated thy blessed servant Saint Servulus with so much virtue : propitiously concede to us, that by his worth, and his intercession we may be free from the ills of this life to reach the good of thy glory. For Christ our Lord. *Amen.*

Remedy for cripples, and against the gout of the feet, and hands, of which Saint Stapinus, Bishop, is the patron : this remedy is confirmed by repeated experience of those who call on it.

Father Theofilo Reynando[128] has the following antiphon, and prayer, and he says that he found it in Germany, while going over some old papers.

Antiphon

O Saint Stapinus, Confessor, and Pontiff of Christ, splendorous in virtue. Pray to God for all of those, who call thee, so as we may not be vexed with the ill of gout in our bones : be our intercessor, so as, sane and free we may live in this vile life through thy intercessions; and after the end of this life we may deserve to be placed on those eternal seats. *Amen.*

℣Pray for us blessed Saint Stapinus.

℞So as we may be worthy of the promises of Christ.

Prayer

O Almighty God, and eternal Lord, who raises the broken and those made lame, by the deprecations of thy most glorious Confessor, and Pontiff Saint Stapinus, and thou makes them free, and sane from all pain of gout of the hands, and feet those who suffer : concede to us, who beg, freedom, not looking at our wickedness; but rather by the worth, and intercessions of thy most glorious Confessor, and Pontiff Saint Stapinus may we be free from all vexations of the gout, and from all evil. For Christ our Lord, who lives and reigns for all centuries of centuries. *Amen.*

Remedy to reconcile animosities, and for constancy in martyrdom, and danger at sea, of which the First Martyr Saint Stephen is the patron

Antiphon

Saint Stephen filled with grace, and strength made many miracles for the people.

℣The Christians buried Saint Stephen.

℞And made over him a great cry.

Prayer

Give us, Lord, what we ask of thee, so as we may imitate the one we honour, so as we may learn, and may know how to love our enemies : for we celebrate his birth, who also knew how to pray, and ask for all of those, who pursued him, our Lord Jesus Christ, thy Son, who lives, and reigns for all centuries of centuries. *Amen.*

128 Translator's note: a Jesuit Theologian from the 17th century, also referred to as Théophile Raynaud or Theophili Raynaudi.

Remedy to preserve the fear of God, of which Saint Stollanus, father of the Lady Saint Anne, is the special patron

Antiphon

Fear the Lord, all those who live the path of sainthood, for nothing is wanting in those who fear him.

℣Pray for us Saint Stollanus.

℟So as we may be worthy of the promises of Christ.

Let us pray

Almighty God, and Lord, who as a prize for the heroic virtues of the glorious Saint Stollanus, especially by the great deal that he always knew to fear thee, thou gave him the singular prerogative of being the principal of the temporal generation of thy only-begotten Son, for having married Saint Emerentia, and having as a daughter the Lady Saint Anne, mother of the Virgin Mary, and grandmother of JESUS Christ : concede to me, and to all of us who are devotees of this glorious saint as a prize for this daily memory we offer, an equally perfect observance of all virtues, and such a worthy fear of thy divine justice, that through thy infinite mercy, we may achieve after a good death the happiness of eternal life. By the same Lord, who lives, and reigns with thee for all centuries of centuries. *Amen.*

Remedy against the stone pain, of which Saint Syria Virgin is the patron

Antiphon

Come Wife of Christ, receive the crown which was prepared by the Lord forever.

℣Grace was diffused in thy lips.

℟And for this God blessed thee forever.

Prayer

O God, and almighty Lord, hear our pleas, by means of the intercession of thy blessed Saint Syria Virgin : propitiously concede to us, that by her pleas we may be free from these pains, and may enjoy thee in those heights. For Christ our Lord. *Amen.*

Remedy for purity, for constancy, against lies, dishonesty, and for the sciences, and to reach the perfect state of the Nuns, of which the great Doctor, and Matriarch Saint Teresa of Ávila, famous flower of sainthood, and collector of the miracles of Mount Carmel is the patron

Antiphon

This flower of Carmel, honour, and glory of Ávila, loud trumpet of sainthood, example of humility and patience, was created by God for the good of the souls.

℣Grace was diffused in thy lips.

℟And for this God blessed thee forever.

Prayer

O God of infinite love, who with so many prerogatives, and countless prodigies published to the world thy great servant Saint Teresa of Ávila : propitiously concede to us, that as thou adorned her for the goodness of the souls, and to show that in her enflamed heart there was thy love, and thou with a dart ordered her to remove her heart; so may thou also remove this heart, and in it make a residence, so as by her intercession we may see each other united in that glory. For Christ our Lord. *Amen.*

Remedy for people who fall into fires, of which Saint Thecla is the patron

Antiphon

Saint Thecla Virgin, and Martyr, to thy aid, and rulership we run to, so as thou may intercede to the Lord to free us from the eternal fire.

℣Pray for us Saint Thecla.

℟So as we may be worthy of the promises of Christ.

Prayer

O God of infinite power, and immense mercy, who with so much charity, and fervour thou decorated thy blessed servant Saint Thecla : make it so, and we ask thee, that by her worth we may shed so many tears, as these may put out the fire of sin to be free from the eternal fires, and we may find ourselves in that eternal light. For Christ our Lord. *Amen.*

Remedy so as to establish ourselves in our true Catholic Faith, and in the Mysteries of the Holiest Trinity, of which Saint Thomas Apostle is the patron

Antiphon

For thou has seen me, Thomas, thou believed : blessed are those who, not seeing, believed.

℣Along the whole earth the sound of thy fame was heard.

℟And in the ends of the earth his words.

Prayer

Give us, and we ask thee, Lord, that thou glorifies us with the solemnities of thy blessed Saint Thomas, thy Apostle so as we may always be favoured by his patronage, and we may follow the Faith with equal devotion. For Christ our Lord *Amen.*

Remedy so as Missionaries may reach the science for their doctrines, and Writers may write their books for the greater honour, and glory of God, and the good of the souls, of which Saint Thomas Aquinas, light of the world, and Angelic Doctor is the patron

Antiphon

O perfect Doctor, maximum, and Angelic, splendour of the holy Church, O blessed Saint Thomas, lover of the divine law, plead for us to God.

℣The Lord loved, and adorned the blessed Saint Thomas.

℟And dressed him with the stole of glory.

Prayer

O God, who illuminated thy Church with the admirable erudition, and thou fertilized it with the saintly works of thy blessed servant Saint Thomas, thy Angelic Doctor : propitiously concede to us, that by his pleas, and doctrines we may have true knowledge of everything, which he taught, and so as to know how to rise to that glory. For Christ our Lord. *Amen.*

Prayer

Which the Angelic Doctor Saint Thomas Aquinas prayed before his study, lesson, or preaching

Veni, Sancte Spiritus, reple tuorum corda fidelium, & tui amoris in eis ignem accende : qui per diversitatem linguarum multarum gentes in unitate sidei congregasti.

℣Emitte spiritum tuum, & creabuntur.

℟Et renovabis faciem terræ.

Saint Thomas Apostle

Oremus

Deus, qui corda fidelium Sancti Spiritus illustratione docuisti : da nobis in eodem spiritu recta sapere, & de ejus consolatione gaudere.

Another Prayer

Aures, & oculos cordis mei Domine Jesu Christe aperi, ut audiam, & intelligam sermones tuos, & paream tuæ voluntati. Peregrinus ego sum in terra, mandata tua me celato patefac oculos meos, ut quæ sunt admirabilia in lege tua, intelligam. A mihi sedium tuarum assistricem sapientiam, quæ intellectum meum illuminet, cor meum purificet, affectum meum inflammet ad cognoscendum, & amandum te Dominum Deum meum in omnibus, & super omnia.

Prayer

Of Saint Thomas, which he frequently said before entering into lectures, and before he wrote, and before preaching, which was also said by João Franco[129] when he was writing his twelve volumes of sermons, so erudite and esteemed by the world, and the Master of life, and further books, &c

Creator ineffabilis, qui de thesouris sapientiæ tuæ tres Angelorum hierarchias annotasti, & eas super Cœlum Empyreum miro ordine collocasti, atque universi partes elegantissimè disposuisti. Tu, inquam, qui verus fons luminis, & sapientiæ dicereis, atque supereminens principium : infundere digneris super intellectus mei tenebras tuæ radium claritatis, duplices, in quibus natus sum, à me removens tenebras, peccatum scilicet, & ignorantiam. Tu, qui linguas infantium facis disertas, linguam meam erudias, atque in labiis meis gratiam tuæ benedictionis infundas. Da mihi intelligendi acumen, retinendi capacitatem, & addicendi modum, & facilitatem, interpretandi subtilitatem, loquendi gratiam copiosam : ingressum instruas, progressum dirigas, & egressum compleas. Tu, qui es verus Deus, & homo. Qui vivis, & regnas Deus, per omnia sæcula sæculorum. *Amen.*

Remedy for cough, and flux, of which Saint Tuda Bishop, and Martyr, is the patron

Antiphon

Whoever wishes to come to me, despise himself, take his cross, and follow me.

℣The Just shall blossom as the palm.

℟As was the Balm-tree multiplied.

129 Translator's note: a Portuguese Dominican Theology Master and Inquisition consultant. The work mentioned is his twelve volumes of *Sermões Varios.*

Prayer

O Lord of infinite mercy, who illuminated thy blessed servant Saint Tuda thy Martyr with so much prodigies : propitiously concede to us, that by his feverous intercession we may be free from this affliction, and pain, so as sane and free we may see ourselves in that glory. For Christ our Lord. *Amen.*

Remedy so as not to die without the Sacraments, and to shed one's blood for the Faith, of which the eleven thousand Virgins, and Saint Ursula, patrons of Brazil, are the patrons

Antiphon

O prudent Virgins, set up thy lamps : here comes thy Husband, go out to meet him.

℣Grace was diffused in thy lips.

℟And for this God blessed thee forever.

Prayer

Give us, and we ask thee, Lord our God, that we may venerate with tireless devotion the palms, and martyrdom of the Holy Virgins, and thy Martyrs Ursula and her companions, so as we may celebrate with pure understanding, and with devout benevolence. For Christ our Lord. *Amen.*

Remedy for falling, of which Saint Venantius is the patron

Antiphon

Whoever wishes to come to me, let him despise himself, take his cross, and follow me.

℣The Just shall blossom as the palm.

℟As was the Balm-tree multiplied.

Prayer

God, who consecrated this day with the triumph of the blessed Saint Venantius, thy Martyr : hear the pleas of thy people, and make it so we may venerate his worth, and imitate the constancy of his faith so as we may be free from all dangers, so as we may fall on ourselves to rise up victorious to those heights. For Christ our Lord. *Amen.*

Remedy for constancy of martyrdom, and to have the resolution to offer one's life to God, of which Saint Vincent Martyr, patron of Lisbon, is the patron

Antiphon

To these belongs the Kingdom of Heaven, those who despised the life of the world, and reached the prizes of Heaven, and washed their stoles with the blood of the Lamb.

℣With honour, and glory, thou crowned him, Lord.

℟And thou made him into the best work of thy hands.

Prayer

Lord God, heed our supplication, so as we, who know that by our sins were the defendants of thy justice, may we be free from punishment, which we deserve, by the intercession of thy blessed servant Saint Vincent. For Christ our Lord. *Amen.*

Remedy against vanity, and to reach everything one may ask from God, mostly the Missionaries, of which Saint Vincent Ferrer is the patron

Antiphon

Saint Vincent Ferrer, miracle of miracles, prodigy of prodigies, admiration, and amazement of sanctity, love of Christ, intercede for us to the Son of God.

℣Instrument of honour, and glory of God

℟Saint Vincent Ferrer raised in Heaven

Prayer

Almighty God, and Lord, thou who illuminated thy Church with the doctrine and virtues of thy blessed Confessor Saint Vincent : concede to us that we be instructed by his examples, and by his patronage be free from all evil. For Christ our Lord. *Amen.*

Remedy to reach alms, and to make the spiritual exercises, general confessions, and for Missionaries to preach with spirit, of which the great Saint Vincent de Paul, founder of the Congregation of the Mission, is the patron

Antiphon

Saint Vincent applied himself right, straight and truly in the presence of his God to the whole culture of the ministry of the house of the Lord, according to the laws, and ceremonies, seeking his God with all of his heart.

℣Pray for us Saint Vincent.

℟So as we may be worthy of the promises of Christ.

Prayer

God, who to evangelize the poor, aid the miseries of the lost and infirm, and promote the splendour of the Ecclesiastic state thou renewed the spirit of the Son in the Apostolic charity, and humility of Saint Vincent de Paul : concede that by his intercession, that being free from the miseries of our sins we may always be pleasant to thee with the same charity, and humility. By the same Lord Jesus Christ thy Son, who lives, and reigns with thee in the union of the Holy Spirit for all centuries of centuries.

Remedy against the labours, and persecutions of the new foundations of Convents, and Seminaries, of which Saint Zacharias, one of the founders of the Orders of the Dominicans, and Franciscans in Portugal, is the patron

Antiphon

The Lord loved, and adorned him, and dressed him with the stole of glory, and at the gates of Paradise crowned him.

℣The Lord took the Just through the straight path.

℟And showed them the Kingdom of Heaven.

Prayer

God, and almighty Lord, who was served to elect thy blessed servant Saint Zacharias for the new foundation : make it so, and we propitiously ask thee, that by his worth, and his intercession we may found in our hearts thy divine love, so as enriched, and founded with this treasure we may enjoy thee in thy celestial home, for all centuries. *Amen.*

Remedy against thunder, lightning, plague, and corrupt air, of which Saint Barbara is the patron

Antiphon

God save thee, O glorious Virgin.
Singular, and general Barbara,
From the high Paradise the most enflamed,
Pleasant to God, blossoming Rose,
Which thou wert in all ages
Pleasant Lilly, flower of chastity.
God save thee, beautiful creature,
All gallant, all beautiful, and pure,
That as the most esteemed
In the fountain of purity thou art washed,
Becoming sweet, soft, and softer,
And with the further virtues, of which God knows.
God save thee, O wise, who with understanding

Thou does not know how to offend, the one who gave thee life.
With such a great sense, and such care,
Who ignorant of guilt, and sin
Thou hears the voice of the Husband, who harmoniously
Calls thee to the crown at every hour.
God save thee, O Barbara, who even if human
Thou beats on earth the lights of Diana,
When with her rays
She distributes light to the World, to the Heavens fainting,
And seeking Endymion the most glorious,
With singing thou follows thy Husband.
God save thee, O blessed
Barbara, prepared for everything
For the noble celestial betrothal
Which the earth ignores, and art to the Heaven notorious,
Thou passes in such glory,
Which the World has envy, and even Heaven is amazed.
God save thee, O beautiful Daisy,
In the crown of JESUS thou, already, features,
For by him thou wert esteemed,
Be open, Lady, to be our patron
So as in this way
We may have a good life, and a better death. Amen.
℣With thy beauty, and grace.
℟Walk, and reign, O pure Virgin.

Prayer

We ask thee Lord of the whole World,
That Barbara, who is thy Virgin Martyr,
May achieve from thee,
And may be of worth to us,
To reach from thee in this way
To take the Sacraments beforehand,
And achieve our intent
In a happy death,
And free us from wickedness, which is notorious,
So as we may go to enjoy the eternal glory,
Do not deny us, my God, thy Succour
For Christ thy Son, and our Lord.
Amen.

The virtues of this prayer are very great; for Saint Barbara gave it to a devotee of hers, and Pope Urban sent it as a great gift to the Bishop of Cochin Dom Fr. Miguel Rangel, who took it with him to his grave, and it gave life to many people. It has particular virtue against thunder, lighting, plague, and corrupt air. A miracle is mentioned in which a lightning bolt fell over twenty, and among all the people who carried this prayer it only killed one, who did not carry it.

34 *Hymno de S.Barbara.*

HYMNO A
S. BARBARA

Deos vos ſalve, ò Virgem glo-
rioſa.
Barbara ſingular, e generoſa,
Do alto Paraiſo mais flammante,
Agradavel a Deos, Roſa vernante,
Que foſtes em toda a idade
Lyrio jucundo, flor da Caſtidade.
Deos vos ſalve, fe moſa creatura,
Galante toda, toda bella, e pura,
Que por mais eſtimada

Na

In order to free one from the infestations of demons, by the virtue of JESUS CHRIST, and by the intercession of the saints, with the proper prayer of Saint Robert, patron to defend and free us from Malefica.

	J	
N	✠	R
	J	

Qui verbum caro factum est, & habitavit in nobis, nascens ex Maria Virgine, per ineffabilem pietatem, & misericordiam suam piissimam, & per intercessionem ejusdem Beatæ Mariæ Virginis, & Angelum, Sanctorumque, omnium, & maximé Apostolorum, & Evangelistarum suorum Joannis & Matthæi, Marci, & Lucæ, ipsum quæsumus, ut dignetur nos liberare, & conservare ab omni infestation Sathanæ, & Ministrorum ejus. Qui cum Patre, & Spiritu Sancto vivit, & regnat in sæcula sæculorum. *Amen.*

Prayer of Saint Robert

℣Ora pro nobis, Sancte Roberte.
℟Ut à Dæmonio liberemos per gratiam Christi.

Oremus

Omnipotens æterne Deus, qui de pulvere elevas pauperem, ut solium gloriæ teneat, & tumidiores superbias humilitate te confundis; presta, quæsimus, ut, sicut in Sancto Robert Confessore tuo, te pro victoriis contra ducem superbiæ mirabilem prædicamus; ita ejus humilitatis exemplo, & orationis suffragio, paupertatem, & humilitatem sectantes, superbas astutias Dæmonis superemus. Per Dominum nostrum Jesum Christum Filium tuum, qui tecum, & Spiritu Sancto vivit, & regnat, per onmnia sæcula sæculorum. *Amen.*

SANCTUS, SANCTUS, SANCTUS, Dominus Deus Sabaoth, plena est omnis terra gloria tua.

Remedy for anything one may want to reach from God, of which the most miraculous Lady of the Rock is the patron

Antiphon

O Holiest Virgin of the Rock, Joachim, Anne, and Joseph, I give thee my heart, and my soul, and reach for me from thy greatly beloved Son everything which might be used for my salvation, and thy glory, honour, and her glory.

V: Pray for us, Virgin Mother of God, and Lady of the Rock.
℟So as we may be worthy of the promises of Christ.

Prayer

My Lord Jesus Christ, who with admirable providence wished that the sacred image of thy Holiest Mother of the Rock be kept free from the Saracens; and then after these were expelled it would miraculously appear, for the benefit of the faithful, who take use of its power, and offer it vows : make it so, as our hearts enflamed in devout affection, and our souls free from all enemies, we may appear purified in thy presence so as to intuitively see in Heaven the purest original of such a miraculous copy, and so as to enjoy the happiness of blessedness, where equally with thy

Eternal Father, and with the Holy Spirit thou lives, and reigns forever without end. *Amen.*

It is not just that in the end of this recipe I would not recite a great gift, which with the medicine of the blessed olive oil of our Lady of the Rock I operated in the Royal Convent of Odivelas, while I was on Mission with license from the Most Revered Father M. Doctor Fr. Joseph Cardoso D. general Abbot, and Reformer of the congregation of Saint Bernard, Almoner of His Majesty, and of his Parish, who being so good, and desiring the spiritual well-being of his subjects conceded me the license to make this Mission, and to generally confess the Nuns, where, for my consolation I greatly praised God for so much virtue, and commotion in the Missions, and I observed that I never entered the Church, be it in the morning or the afternoon without seeing the Confessionaries filled with Confessors, and the frequency of Sacraments, for surely every day there were three tables of communion, and even for the seculars, and maids, and a very laborious Choir, singing, that at times I observed three or four sung Masses, being the Revered Doctor Fr. Caetano de São Payo the Abbot, and the Most Illustrious Sister Lady Luiza de Moura the Abbess of the Monastery.

Great gift that our Lady of the Rock gave to a Nun

After I entered with the Mission, and the feverous devotion of our Lady of the Rock, and the sung Rosary, and the praying of other devotions to our Lady, and blessings of the olive oil, and with it healing the infirm, a certain Sister Maria do Carmelo, Nun of the same Monastery of Odivelas, who suffered from horrible pain from a swollen and dislocated knee, by placing the olive oil of our Lady, she was found sane and free from all harm and lesion in the morning, which was keeping her from walking, and to further confirm herself in the devotion, and faith of our Lady of the Rock, suffering from a strong flux in her chest, without being able to take a breath, and placing the olive oil as a cross over her chest, she immediately was relieved, and free from anxiety, and afflictions, of which she had a great deal. In this way does the Holiest MARY save those who seek, and serve her.

It is certain that those who come close to Mary our Holiest Lady of the Rock, do not walk away without experiencing many improvements : let us all come to this precious Apothecary, let us refer to it with living faith, let us cry at her sovereign feet, for we shall rise from them sane and safe, and be she praised day, and night, so as we may praise her in the company of her greatly beloved Son eternally in that glory. *Amen.*

End of the recipes of the invocations of the Saints.

Remedy for as many Novenas as one may wish to do of the vocations of Our Lady, and the Confessor, Martyr and Virgin Saints.

Such is done by the same method as the Novena of the Rock, above, and say all the preparation of this, and the Litany, and the Prayer of Our Lady, and for the Prayer of the vocation of the Lady, say the one you may wish to do, instead of that of the Rock, and the vocation of the Lady to whom the Novena is done. And if this is a Confessor, or Martyr Saint, say the prayer, if you cannot find the Saint in the recipes of the vocations above, instead of the name of the Saint place the name of the one you wish to make the Novena to, and in this way you may do all Novenas you may wish.

LITANY OF THE SAINTS

Kyrie eleison,
Christe eleison.
Christe audi nos.
Christe exaudi nos.

Pater de Cœlis Deus,	Miserere nobis.
Fili Redemptor mundi Deus,	Miserere nobis.
Spiritus Sancte Deus,	Miserere nobis.
Sancta Trinitas unus Deus,	Miserere nobis
Sancta MARIA,	Ora pro nobis.
Sancta Dei Genitrix.	Ora.
Sancta Virgo virginum,	Ora.
Sancte Michael,	Ora.
Sancte Gabriel,	Ora.
Sancte Raphael	Ora.
Omnes sancti Angeli, & Archengeli,	Orate pro nobis.
Omnes sancti beatorum spirituum ordines,	Orate pro nobis.
Sancte Joannes Baptista,	Ora.
Sancte JOSEPH,	Ora.
Omnes sancti Patriarchæ, & Prophetæ,	Orate pro nobis.
Sancte Peter,	Ora.
Sancte Paule,	Ora.
Sancte Andrea,	Ora.
Sancte Jacobe,	Ora.
Sancte Joannes,	Ora.
Sancte Thoma,	Ora.
Sancte Jacobe,	Ora.
Sancte Philippe,	Ora.
Sancte Bartholomæe,	Ora.
Sancte Mathæe,	Ora.
Sancte Simon,	Ora.
Sancte Thaddæe,	Ora.
Sancte Mathia,	Ora.
Sancte Barnaba,	Ora.
Sancte Luca,	Ora.
Sancte Marce,	Ora.
Omnes sancti Apostoli, & Ecangelistæ,	Orate.
Omnes sancti discipuli Domini,	Orate.
Omnes santi Innocentes,	Orate.
Sancte Stephane,	Ora.
Sancte Laurenti,	Ora.
SancteVincenti,	Ora.
Sancti Fabiane, & Sebastiane,	Orate.
Sancti Joannes, & Paule,	Orate.
Sancti Cosma, & Damiane,	Orate.
Sancti Gervasi, & Protasi,	Orate.

Omnes sancti Martyres,	Orate.
Sancte Silvester,	Ora.
Sancte Gregori,	Ora.
Sancte Ambrosi,	Ora.
Sancte Augustine,	Ora.
Sancte Hieronyme,	Ora.
Sancte Martine,	Ora.
Sancte Nicolae,	Ora.
Omnest sancti Pontifices, & Confessores,	Orate.
Omnes sancti Doctores,	Orate.
Sancte Antoni	Ora.
Sancte Benedicte,	Ora.
Sancte Bernarde,	Ora.
Sancte Dominice,	Ora.
Sancte Francisce,	Ora.
Omnes sancti Sacerdotes, & Levitæ,	Orate.
Omnes sancti Monachi, & Eremitæ	Orate.
Sancta Maria Magdalena,	Ora.
Sancta Agatha,	Ora.
Sancta Lucia,	Ora.
Sancta Agnes,	Ora.
Sancta Cæcilia,	Ora.
Sancta Catharina,	Ora.
Sancta Anastasia,	Ora.
Omnes sanctæ Virgines, & Viduæ,	Orate.
Omnes Sancti, & Sanctæ Dei,	intercedite pro nobis.
Propitius esto,	parce nobis Domine.
Propitius esto,	exaudi nos Domine.
Ab omni malo,	libera nos Domini.
Ab omni peccato,	libera.
Ab ira tua,	libera.
A subitanea, & improvisa morte,	libera.
Ab infidiis diaboi,	libera.
Ab ira, & odio, & omni maa voluntate,	libera.
A spiritu fornicationis,	libera.
A fulgure, & tempestate,	libera.
A morte perpetua,	libera.
Per mysterium sanctæ Incarnationis tuæ,	libera.
Per adventum tuum,	libera.
Per Nativitatem tuam,	libera.
Per Baptisimum, & sanctum jejunium tuum,	libera.
Per crucem, & passionem tuam,	libera.
Per mortem, & sepulturam tuam,	libera.
Per sanctam Resurrectionem tuam,	libera.
Per admirabilem Ascensionem tuam,	libera.
Per adventum Spiritus Sancti Paraclite,	libera.
In die judicii,	libera.

Peccatores, te rogamus audi nos.
Ut nobis parcas, te rog.
Ut nobis idulgeas, te rog.
Ut ad veram pœnitentiam nos perducere digneris, te rog.
Ut Ecclesiam tuam sanctam regere, & conservare digneris, te rog.
Ut dommum Apostolicum, & omnes Ecclesiasticos ordines in sancta religione conservare digneris, te rog.
Ut inimicos sanctæ Ecclesiæ humiliare digneris, te rog.
Ut Regibus, & Principidus Christianis pacem, & veram concordiam donare digneris, te rog.
Ut cuncto populo christiano pacem, & unitatem largiri digneris, te rog.
Ut nosmetipso in tuo sancto servitio confortare, & conservare digneris, te rog.
Ut mentes nostras ad cœlestia desideria erigas, te rog.
Ut omnibus benefactoribus nostris sempiterna bona retribuas, te rog.
Ut animas nostras, fratrum, propinquorum, & benefactorum nostrorum ab æterna damnatione eripias, te rog.
Ut fructus terræ dare, & conservare digneris, te rog.
Ut omnibus fidelibus defunctis requiem æternam donare digneris, te rog.
Ut nos exaudire digneris, te rog.
Fili Dei, te rog.
Agnus Dei, qui tollis peccata mundi, parce nobis, Domine.
Agnus Dei, que tollis peccata mundi, exaudi nos, Domine.
Agnus Dei, qui tollis peccata mundi, miserere nobis.
Christe audi nos.
Christe exaudi nos.
Kyrie eleison.
Christe eleison.
Kyrie eleison.
Pater noster

V: Et ne nos inducas in tentationem.
℟Sed libera nos à malo.
V: Domine exaudi orationem meam.
℟Et clamor meus ad te veniat.

Oremus

Deus, cui proprium est misereri sempre, & parcere, suscipe deprecationes nostras : ut nos, & omnes famulos tuos, quos delictorum catena constringit, miseration tuæ pietatis clemanter absolvat.

Exeudi, quæsumus Domine, supplicum preces, & consitentium tibi parce peccatis : ut pariter nobis indulgentiam tribuas benignus, & pacem.

Ineffabilem nobis, Domine, misericordiam tuam clementer ostende : ut simul nos & à peccatis omnibus exuas, & à ponis, quas pro his meremur, eripias.

Deus, qui culpa offenderis, pœnitenta placaris, preces populi tui supplicantis propitius respice, & flagella tuæ iracundiæ, quæ pro peccatis nostris meremus, averte.

Instructions for the sick and dying

Protestation of Faith, which one should do in the name of the infirm, even if this is unable to speak, so as to bring him inner joy

My Most High Lord God, Almighty, Father, Son, and Holy Spirit. I poor sinner, thy servant, confess thy great name, I confess and firmly and plainly believe in thy Holy Catholic Faith and all the articles in it, as thy Saints, and Faithful who are in Heaven, and on earth, believed and believe. I believe, Lord, and thus confess the Catholic Faith, as this is held, and believed by the Holy Mother Roman Catholic Church; and in this Most Holy, and most true Faith, I protest to live, and die: this ratification, and protestation of my Faith I do on this hour of my thought with complete soul, and heart, (*or, I cannot do this with my mouth, and as such I request that this be done in my name*) and with such deliberation, strength, and spirit I do this so as I may never, by any cause, impatience, adversity, or temptation, nor by anything which might happen to me, this confession be able to unsay, or be parted from it. And if by any chance, with the strength of this illness, with furies, I may lose my judgment due to visions, or illusions of the Devil, due to my sins, or due to my lack of faith, or by diabolical malice, or due to any other thing which might happen (and may God not allow this), if I say any blasphemy, madness, or indecent word, gestures, and impatient attitudes against God Our Lord, or against his Saints, or against my soul, I say, that from this day forth I unsay all such things, and place it as not having been said, for it never was, nor is it my intention to separate myself from my God, nor from his Holy Faith, nor from the path of the Just, and Saints of the Catholic Church, and what it teaches. And this confession, protestation, ratification, and intention with which I do this now, and in my name is done, I want it to be firm and valid forever, and this one thousand times, and even more I ratify, sign, and confirm with all my soul, heart, intention, and will, and in testimony of this truth, I take the Virgin Mother Our Lady, Mother of God, Queen of Heaven, and earth, the Angel of my Guard, the Prince of the Angels Saint Michael, the Archangels, Saint Gabriel, and Saint Raphael, with all the Angelic Spirits, and the Apostles Saint Peter, and Saint Paul, and Saint John Evangelist, all the Holy Apostles, and finally Saint John the Baptist, and Saint Ignatius Confessor, and the saint of my name, and Saint Steven with all the Martyrs and Saints in Glory, and the courtesans of Heaven my sponsors, and I plead to all, the present who see, and hear this Protestation of Faith in my name that they be witnesses of this my confession, and pray to God Our Lord that I be confirmed in it.

There should be the care that the infirm should receive the Absolutions of the Brotherhoods, and Third Orders which he is a part of, which are below, and a further one from the reigning Pontiff valid for all. Place over the infirm the following precept several times, which can be made by any person of great faith.

I, as a creature of God, made in his image, in the name of the Most High, Father, Son, and Holy Spirit, and of Jesus, Mary, and Joseph, with most living faith I order thee, O disgraced spirits, and cursed demons, that thou be immediately gone, gone to the depths of Hell, leave this creature free from all which is temptation, and thy attacks. I say once again : With most living faith in the powers, and efficiency of the most powerful Name of Jesus I order thee, demons, and infernal spirits, that thou be gone to the depths of Hell forever.

Cast holy water throughout the whole house several times, and take care to call Priests, who may aid the agonizing in dying well, and to drive away demons, as Ministers of God, for in this hour these wage a great war, and assist the dying to resist them; and should there be no Priests available this can be done by a secular, who might volunteer for this.

Supplication

O Purest Virgin Mary Mother of God, and our Mother, Mother of mercy, Lady, and Patron of sinners, I as the greatest of them ask thee, most loving Mother, have mercy on me in this so dangerous hour, aiding me, succouring me, holding me, and defending me from my enemies. *In manus tuas, Domine, commendo spiritum meum* : In thy Divine hands, my God, I commend my spirit, and my soul, and in thine Holiest Mother Mary my Lady. Blessed Angels, assist me in this my arduous departure from present life, and free me from the temptations of the infernal enemy. Holy Angel of my guard, defend me in this fearful hour, driving away with thy power the infernal squadrons, and do not abandon me in this last need, so as my soul may arrive by thy help safely to eternally enjoy its Creator. Glorious Archangel Saint Michael, Saint of my Name, Saint Peter, Saint Paul, and all the further Apostles, Lord Saint Joseph, Saint Joachim, Lady Saint Anne, and all other Saints of the Court of Heaven, be my patrons, and intercessors in this extreme necessity, and aid me with thy patronage in the Divine tribunal, defending my soul, rebating the accusations of my adversaries, and reaching for me a favourable sentence, so as I may eternally accompany thee in that Glory. *Amen.*

Always repeat the Holiest Names of Jesus, and Mary.

Saint Paul, Apostle

Office of agony

Being with the dying in agony, light a white candle, (and being this blessed with the blessing of the Brothers of the Holiest Rosary, so much the better) and placing one hand over the dying, and another on an image of the crucified Jesus Christ, having a Rosary around the neck, and another one on your right arm, always casting holy water, the priest shall say what follows, with the assistance responding:

Kyrie eleison.
Christe eleison.
Kyrie eleison.

Sancta Maria,	ora pro eo, vel ea.
Omnes Sancti Angeli, & Archageli,	orate pro eo, vel ea
Sancte Abel,	ora pro eo.
Omni Chorus Justorum,	ora pro eo.
Sancte Abraham,	ora pro eo.
Sancte Joannes Baptista,	ora pro eo.
Sancte Joseph,	ora pro eo.
Omnes Sancti Patriarchæ, & Prophetæ,	orate pro eo.
Sancte Petre,	ora pro eo.
Sancte Paule,	ora pro eo.
Sancte Andrea,	ora pro eo.
Sancte Joannes,	ora pro eo.
Omne Sancti Apostoli, & Evangelistæ,	orate pro eo.
Omnes Sancti Discipuli Domini,	orate pro eo.
Omnes Sancti Innocentes,	orate pro eo.
Sancte Stephane,	ora pro eo.
Sancte Leurenti,	ora pro eo.
Omnes Sancti Martyres,	orate pro eo.
Sancte Silvester,	ora pro eo.
Sancte Augustine,	ora pro eo.
Omnes Sancti Pontifices, & Confessores,	orate pro eo.
Sancte Benedicte,	ora pro eo.
Sancte Pater Dominice,	ora pro eo.
Sancte Pater Francisce,	ora pro eo.
Omnes Sancti Monachi, & Eremitæ,	orate pro eo.
Sancta Maria Magdalena,	ora pro eo.
Sancta Lucia,	ora pro eo.
Omnes Sanctæ Virgines, & Viduæ,	orate pro eo.
Omnes Sancti, & Sanctæ Dei,	intercedite pro eo.
Propitius esto,	perce ei, Domine.
Propitius esto,	libera eum, Domine.
Ab ira tua,	libera eum, Domine.
À periculo mortis,	libera eum, Domine.
À mala morte,	libera eum, Domine.
À pœnis Inferni,	libera eum, Domine.
Ab omni malo,	libera eum, Domine.

À potestate diaboli, libera eum, Domine.
Per Nativitatem tuam, libera eum, Domine.
Per Crucem, & Passionem tuam, libera eum, Domine.
Per gloriosam Resurrectionem tuam, libera eum, Domine.
Per admirabilem Ascensionem tuam, libera eum, Domine.
Per gratiam Spiritus Sancti Paracliti, libera eum, Domine.
In die Judicii, libera eum, Domine.
Peccatores, te rogamus audi nos.
Ut ei parcas, te rogamus audi nos.
Kyrie eleison.
Christe eleison.
Kyrie eleison.

Prayer

Christian soul, go from this world in name of God the Father ✠ Almighty, who created thee; in the name of Jesus Christ, ✠ Son of the living God, who suffered for thee; in name of the Holy Spirit, ✠ who copiously was communicated to thee. Be parted, and leave this mortal body with the favour, and Succour of the Holy Angels, and the Archangels; the Thrones, and Dominions; Cherubim, and Seraphim; the Patriarchs, and Prophets; the Saintly Apostles, and Evangelists; the Holy Martyrs, Confessors, Monks, Priests, and Hermits; Virgin Saints, and Wives of Jesus Christ; of all Saints of God, who may give thee a place of rest, and enjoyment of eternal peace in the Holy City of Celestial Zion, where thou may praise him for all centuries of centuries. *Amen.*

Prayer

Merciful God, clement God, God, who, according to the greatness of thy infinite mercy, forgives the sins of those who suffer for having committed them, and thou gives them the liberty of absolution of past guilt, and offices, place thine eyes of mercy over this thy servant (NN) propitiously hear him, and concede to him the forgiveness from all his sins, for with all his heart he asks for this by means of his humble confession. Renew, and repair, most merciful Father, the breaks, and ruins of this soul, and the sins it did, and contracted either due to its weakness, or by the cunning, and deceit of the Devil. Admit it, and incorporate it in the body of thy Triumphant Church, as a living member of it, redeemed with the precious blood of thy Son. Have compassion, Lord, of his moans, may the compassion of his sighs move thee. Succour, and aid the one who places his trust in nothing else than thy mercy, and admit him in thy friendship, and grace. By the love, which thou has for Jesus Christ thy beloved Son, who with thee lives, and reigns for all centuries of centuries. *Amen.*

I commend thee to God Almighty, my dear brother, to whom I ask to hold, and favour thee, as his creature, so as paying with death the pension of this life, thou may come to see the sovereign Artifice, who from the dust of the earth made thee. When thy soul leaves thy body, may it leave to receive the bright army of the Holy Saints, to accompany and defend, and celebrate thee; the glorious College of the Saintly Apostles favour thee, being judges and accusers of thy cause; the triumphant invincible Martyrs Succour thee; the most noble company of the illustrious Confessors receive thee in their midst, and with the soft fragrance of lilies, which they carry, symbol of the soft fragrance of their virtues, comfort thee; the Choirs of the Saintly joyful, and contented Virgins receive thee; that entire blessed company of Celestial Courtesans with open arms of true friendship offer thee entry unto the glorious bosom of the Patriarchs; may the face of thy Redeemer Jesus Christ present itself to thee soft, merciful, and appeasable, and may he give thee a seat among those who always assist in his presence. May thou never experience the horror of the eternal darkness, nor the crackling of its flames, not the penalties, which torment the condemned. May the cursed Satan surrender to thee with all his allies, and while thou passes in front of him in the company of the Angels may the miserable tremble, and retire fearful into the thick darkness of his shadowy home.

May God rise in thy favour, and his enemies, who bother him, retreat from his presence. May they disappear as smoke in the air, and as wax melts before a fire, may thy sins perish in front of the face of God, and the Just be rewarded, and be joyful by his sight. May the infernal armies be confounded and retreat, and the ministers of Satan not dare to impede thy path to Heaven. May Christ, who was crucified for thee, free thee from torment. May Christ, who gave his life for thee, free thee from the eternal death. May Christ the son of God place thee living among the meadows, and forests of Paradise, which never dry, nor wither, and as a true Shepherd recognize thee as a sheep in his flock, and absolve thee of thy sins, and seat thee at his right hand among the chosen, and predestined. May God make thee so beautiful, that thou may see thy Redeemer face to face, and that always assisting in his presence, thou may know with blessed eyes the manifest truth of his Divinity, in the company of the Courtesans of Heaven may thou enjoy the sweetness of his eternal contemplation for all centuries of centuries. *Amen.*

Prayer

Receive, Lord, the soul of this thy servant in the palace of eternal health, for she can only hope for thy mercy. *Amen.*

Free her, Lord, from all the dangers of Hell, and the snares of its penalties, and any further tribulations, which in this hour may come. *Amen.*

Free her, Lord, as thou freed Enoch, and Elias from the universal death of the world. *Amen.*

Free her, Lord, as thou freed Noah from the waters of the Deluge. *Amen.*

Free her, Lord, as thou freed Abraham from the fires of the Chaldeans. *Amen.*

Free her, Lord, as thou freed Isaac from the sacrifice, and from the hands of his father Abraham. *Amen.*

Free her, Lord, as thou freed Lot from Sodom, and its flames. *Amen.*

Free her, Lord, as thou freed Moses from the hands of Pharaoh, King of Egypt. *Amen.*
Free her, Lord, as thou freed Daniel from the lions' den. *Amen.*
Free her, Lord, as thou freed the three boys from the furnaces of Babylon, and from the hands of that wicked king. *Amen.*
Free her, Lord, as thou freed Susanna from false witness. *Amen.*
Free her, Lord, as thou freed David from the hands of King Saul, and from the Giant Goliath. *Amen.*
Free her, Lord, as thou freed Saint Peter, and Saint Paul from the prisons, and dungeons. *Amen.*
And as thou freed Saint Thecla, Virgin, and glorious Martyr, from three atrocious torments, thus free, Lord, the soul of this thy servant, and make it so as she may enjoy thee, and the celestial good with thee. *Amen.*

Prayer

My Lord Jesus Christ, Saviour of the world, we all ask thee for the soul of this thy servant, and we ask thee, and plead to thee, for thou came down from Heaven to earth for thy love of it, moved by such great mercy, do not abstain from placing him, and arranging him in the bosom and rest of the Holy Patriarchs. Recognize, Lord, this thy creature, who received its being not from strange and false gods, but from thee, who art a living and true God, without there being any other, who may deserve this name, but thee, who makes works similar to these. Bring joy, Lord, to this soul with thy sight, without remembering its past wickedness, nor the affections, nor the passions, which the impetuous, and the ardour of her disorderly appetites woke in her; for, even if there may be sin, she did not deny the Father, nor the Son, nor the Holy Spirit, but rather she believed in a Trine and single God, and had zeal in his honour, and worshipped, and faithfully revered him, as her Creator, and of all Creatures.

Prayer

We plead to thee, Lord, do not carry the memory of the crimes, and ignorance of the youth of this thy servant, but rather place thine eyes solely on thy clemency, and mercy, and remember it, so as to give her part of the inaccessible light of thy clarity. May the Heavens open to her, and the Angels reveal themselves smiling to her, and thou, Lord, admit her in thy Kingdom. May Saint Michael Archangel receive her, who deserved to be General Captain, and Prince of the Heavenly Militia. May the Saintly Angels of God come to receive her, and take her to that Holy City of the Celestial Jerusalem. May the Blessed Saint Peter, who was given charge of the Heavenly keys, give her entrance. May Saint Paul Apostle, who deserved to be the precious vase of the Lord, aid her. May Saint John the Apostle, and Evangelist, the favoured, and beloved, and validated by the Prince of glory, to whom the Celestial secrets were made manifest, aid her. May all the remaining Apostles, to whom the Lord God gave the power to condemn, and absolve, plead for her. May all the Saints, and chosen of God, who in this world suffered torments for Jesus Christ, be her patrons, so as this thy servant being free from the prison of the body, deserve to reach the Glory of Heaven by the worth of our Lord Jesus Christ, who with the Father, and with the Holy Spirit lives and reigns for all centuries of centuries. *Amen.*

Being with the dying in his last agonies, repeat the precepts, casting holy water throughout the whole house. The assistants should pray, as a choir, the Holiest Rosary, or the Most Sacred Chaplet of the Mother of God as above, or at least one Terço; and while being prayed, or before, or after, the Priest, or any other person, should calmly say, accompanying the dying with his heart, if he cannot do this with his mouth, the following:

Clamours of the last agony

Jesus, Jesus, Jesus, into thy Holiest Hands I deliver my spirit.

Jesus, Jesus, Jesus, and my Redeemer, receive my soul.

Jesus, Jesus, Jesus. Holiest Mary Mother of God, plead for this sinner, but also thy son.

Jesus, Jesus, Jesus. Mary Mother of God, Mother of mercy, defend me from the enemies, and assist me in this so risky an hour.

Jesus, Jesus, and my sweetest Jesus, it weighs with all my heart having offended thee, for being thou who thou art, entirely my lover, worthy of being loved above all things. Forgive me, my Jesus, by thy Holiest Wounds, and by thy Passion, and Death.

Jesus, Jesus, Jesus. The Divine Word was made man in the purest loins of the Holiest Mother. May the fineness of thy Incarnation, Lord, be in my worth.

Jesus, Jesus, Jesus Christ, peaceful King, defend me from all danger.

Jesus wins, ✠ Jesus reigns, ✠ Jesus rules, ✠ Jesus defends us from all evil. ✠ This is the Cross of the Divine Redeemer, ✠ flee, and be gone, enemies of the souls redeemed with the blood of Jesus Christ.

Jesus, Jesus, Jesus, I firmly believe in all which the Roman Catholic Church tells me to believe in, for thou, my God, thus has taught. I hope to be saved by thy mercy.

Jesus, Jesus, Jesus, I propose to love thee forever, and I love thee above all things. May the title of the Holy Cross be in my worth: Jesus of Nazareth King of the Jews.

Jesus, Jesus, Jesus, in thy Divine Hands I place my salvation, in thy Holiest side I hide my soul to purify it with the Divine blood.

Jesus, Jesus, Jesus, Mary, Joseph, Joachim, and Anne, I offer thee my heart, and my soul.

Jesus, Jesus, Jesus, assist me in the last agony.

Jesus, Jesus, Jesus, and my sweetest Jesus, be for me Jesus. Jesus, Mary, and Joseph, be in my worth, and defend me. Jesus, and Mary, receive my soul. Jesus, and Mary, and one thousand times Jesus, be in my worth, and aid me.

Once the Rosary, Chaplet, or Terço is done, sing the Litany of our Lady, and some person should continue the sighs with the dying until he dies; and dying, immediately pray the twelfth Station, and the Rosary, or Chaplet once again, applying the Indulgences, and buying some Bulls for the Dead, and apply these to his soul.

ABSOLUTIONS FOR THE HOUR OF DEATH

The Priest, in performing the absolution should inform the infirm to have the name of JESUS in his mouth and heart, so as in this way he may earn indulgences.

ABSOLUTION OF THE HOLY CRUSADE

The Confession having been made by the infirm, or the assistants, the Priest shall immediately say:

Misereatur tui omnipotens Deus, et dimissis peccatis tuis, perducat te ad vitam aeternam.

Indulgentiam, ✠ absolutionem, et remissionem peccatorum nostrorum, tribuat nobis omnipotens et misericors Dominus.

By the authority of God Almighty, and the Blessed Apostles, Saint Peter, and Saint Paul, and of our most Holy Father, especial conceded to thee, and committed to me, I absolve thee of all censorship of greater, or lesser excommunication, suspension, or forbiddingness *à jure, vel ab homine*, and from all other censorships, and penalties, which thou might have incurred by any cause, even if the absolution of these is reserved to the Apostolic See, which according to this is conceded to them, and I restore thee to the communion of a faithful Christian. As such I further absolve thee from all thy sins, crimes, and excesses, that thou has confessed to me, and would confess, should these come to thy memory, even if their absolution is reserved to the Apostolic See; and I offer thee plenary Indulgency, and fulfilled remission of all thy sins now, and in any other time confessed, forgotten, or not known, and the penalties, which thou would be obliged to suffer for these in Purgatory. In nomine Patris, & Filii, & Spiritus Sancti. *Amen.*

ABSOLUTION, OR PAPAL BLESSING WITH PLENARY INDULGENCE FOR THE HOUR OF DEATH, CONCEDED TO EVERY FAITHFUL CHRISTIAN BY THE PONTIFICATE OF BENEDICT XIV

The Priest should begin in the following way:

℣Pax huic domui.

℟Et omnibus habitantibus in ea.

Antiphon

Ne reminiscaris, Domine, delicta famuli tui, (vel ancillæ tuæ) neque vindictam sumas de peccatis ejus.

Kyrie eleison.
Christe eleison.
Kyrie elison.
Pater noster.
℣Salvum fac servum tuum (vel ancillam tuam)
℟Deus meus sperantem in te.
℣Domine exaudi orationem meam.
℟Et clamor eus ad te veniat.
℣Dominus vobiscum.
℟Et cum spiritus tuo.

Oremus

Clementissime Deus, Pater misericordiarum, & Deus totius consolationis, qui neminem vis perire in te credentem, atque sperantem; secundum multitudinem miserationum tuarum respice propitius famulum tuum N. (vel ancillam tuam N.) quem tibi vera fides, & spes Christiana commendat. Visita eum in salutari tuo, & per Unigeniti tui Passionem, & Mortem omnium ei delictorum suorum remissionem, & veniam clementer indulge, ut ejus anima in hora exitus sui. Te judicem propitiatum inveniat, & in sanguine ejusdem Filii tuia ab omni macula abluta transire ad vitam mereatur perpetuam. Per eumdem Christum Dominum nostrum.

The Confession having been made by the infirm, or the assistants, the Priest shall immediately say:

Misereatur tui omnipotens Deus, et dimissis peccatis tuis, perducat te ad vitam aeternam.

Indulgentiam, ✠ absolutionem, et remissionem peccatorum nostrorum, tribuat nobis omnipotens et misericors Dominus.

Dominus noster Jesus Christus, Filius Dei vivi, qui Beato Petro Apostolo dedit potestatem ligandi, atque solvendi, per suam piissimam misericordiam recipiat confessionem tuam, & restituat tibi stolam primam, quam in Baptismate recipisti : & ego facultate mihi ab Apostolica Sede tributa, indulgentiam plenariam, & remissionem omnium peccatorum tibi concede. : In nomine Patris et Filii et Spiritus Sancti.

Per Sacrosancta humanæ reparationis mysteria remittat tibi omnipotens Deus omnes præsentis, & futuræ vitæ pœnas, Paradisi portas aperiat, & ad gaudia sempiterna perducat. *Amen.*

Benedicat te Omnipotens Deus Pa✠ter, Fi✠lius, & Spiritus ✠ Sanctus. *Amen.*

In case the dying is not able to confess, if he at least repents his sins and invokes the Holiest Name of Jesus with his mouth, or his heart, this Papal Absolution will always be beneficial.

ABSOLUTION OF THE BROTHERS OF THE HOLIEST ROSARY OF THE DOMINICANS

For the confession of the infirm, or of any other creature, the prayers should say:

Misereatur tui omnipotens Deus, & dimissis peccatis tuis, perducat te ad vitam aeternam.

Indulgentiam, ✠ absolutionem, & remissionem peccatorum nostrorum, tribuat nobis omnipotens & misericors Dominus.

And in this way for all others.

Dominus noster JESUS Christi Filius Dei vivi potestatem ligandi, atque solvendi, per suam piissimam misericordiam recipiat confessionem tuam, & remittat tibi omnia peccata, quæcumque, & quomodocumque in toto vitæ decursu commisisti, de quibus corde contritus, & ore confessus es; restituens tibi stolam primam, quam in Baptismate recipisti, & per indulgentiam plenariam à Summis Pontificibus Innocentio VIII & Pio V. Confratribus sanctissimi Rosarii in articulo mortis constitutis concessam liberet te à præsentis, & futuræ vitæ pœnis, dignetur Purgatorii cruciatus remittere, portas inferni claudere, Paradisi januam aperire, teque ad gaudia sampiterna perducere, per sanctissima suæ vitæ, Passionis, & Glorificationis Mysteria sanctissimo Rosario comprehensa. Qui cum Patre, & Spiritu Sancto vivit, & regnat in sæcula sæculorum. *Amen.*

ABSOLUTION OF THE THIRD ORDER AND BROTHERS OF OUR LADY OF MOUNT CARMEL

Misereatur tui omnipotens Deus, & dimissis peccatis tuis, perducat te ad vitam aeternam.

Indulgentiam, ✠ absolutionem, & remissionem peccatorum nostrorum, tribuat nobis omnipotens et misericors Dominus.

Dominus noster JESUS Christus Dei Filius, qui omnia mirabilia tormenta pro peccatoribus subiit, ut eos ad vitam revocaverit, qui salvat omnes, & neminem vult perire, nec mortem peccatorum, sed vitam sempre inquirit : ipse nunc sua piissima misericordia te respiciat, avertat omnem iram, & indignationem, atque per indulgentissima misericordiæ suæ viscera tibi remittat universas iniquitates tuas, & quascumque pœnas ex rigore maximæ justitiæ tuæ. Ego autem ipsius Domini nostri JESU Chirsti indignus famulus, & minister ex auctoritate Sanctorum Apostolorum Petri, & Pauli, ac Sanctæ Romanæ Ecclesiæ te plenariè obsolvo ab omnibus peccatis tuis. Item ex privilegiis per Summos Pontifices concessis Fratribus, Sororibus, & Confratribus MARIÆ de monte Carmelo, aque ex licentia, potestate, & comissione mihi à meis superioribus imposita, ego in quantum possum, & debeo, declaro te consegui indulgentiam plenariam, & remissionem omnium peccatorum tuorum, si tamen hac vice è vita migraveris pro ultimo articulo mortis tuæ. In nomine Patris, ✠ & Filii, ✠ & Spiritus ✠ Sancti. *Amen.*

The infirm should invoke the Holiest name of Jesus, if not being able to do so with his mouth, at least with his heart, the Priest should say:

Ego eâdem auctoritate tibi dispenso super omni negligentia, siquam contraxisti, istum sacrum habitum deferendo, & declare, ac significo te creaturam Dei fore absolutam hic, & ante tribunal Domini nostri JESU Christi ad omnibus pœnis tibi in Purgatorio debitis propter peccata, quæ contra bonitatem Dei vivi, & veri commisisti, teque manifestè restitutam illi statui innocentiæ, qua in Baptismo per facrum Salvatoris lavacrum induta fuisti. In nomine Patris, ✠ & Filii, ✠ & Spiritus ✠ Sancti. *Amen.*

ABSOLUTION OF THE BROTHERS OF THE GIRDLE OF OUR FATHER SAINT AUGUSTINE[130]

Misereatur tui omnipotens Deus, & dimissis peccatis tuis, perducat te ad vitam aeternam.

Indulgentiam, ✠ absolutionem, & remissionem peccatorum nostrorum, tribuat nobis omnipotens & misericors Dominus.

Dominus noster JESUS Christus per suam piisimam misericordiam, & Sanctissimam Passionem te absolvat, & ego auctoritate ipsius, ac Beatorum Apostolorum Petri, & Pauli, & Sanctissimi Dimini nostri Divina Providencia Papæ (N.) & Sanctæ Romanæ Ecclesiæ ex speciali gratia tibi concessa, & mihi commista, virtute cujuscumque tuæ gratiæ, vel diplomatis, in quantum possum, & valeo, & mihi permittitur, absolvo te ab omni sententia excommunicationis maioris, vel minoris, (*and if one is a Priest one adds here the words* suspensionis, & interdicti) & à participatione cum excommunicatis, & restituo te sacrosanctis Sacramentis Ecclesiæ, communioni, & unitati fidelium.

Item eadem auctoritate, qua fungor, & quatenus mihi concessa est à Summo Pontifice Romano, cujus vices in hac patte gero, ego te absolvo plenariè à peccatis tuis specialiter confessis, pariterque oblitis cum eorum circumstantiis, concedo tibi omnes gratias, & indulgentias, quas habes, &

130 Translator's note: this refers to a particular blessed girdle of black leather used by the members of the 'Archconfraternity of the Black Leather Belt of Saint Monica, Saint Augustine and Saint Nicholas of Tolentine', one of the 'Confraternities of the Cord'.

ego in hac die concedere possum. In nomine Patris, ✠ & Filii, ✠ & Spiritus ✠ Sancti. *Amen.*

And if the penitent is close to death, add the following:

Item eodem modo, quo meliùs possum, & in quantum claves Ecclesiæ se extendunt, Apostolicam, & Pontificam benedictionem tibi impertior, ac proinde concedo tibi indulgentiam plenariam omnium pœnarum in præsenti vita, vel in Purgatorio pro peccatis tuis debitarum; & dispenso tecum super residuum pœnitentiæ, si maior tibi erat imponenda, & volo, ut omnia bona, quæ feceris, & mala, quæ perpessus fueris propter Deum, sint meritoria, velut pœnitentia imposita ad remissionem pœnæ debitæ pro tuis peccatis, pro quibus etiam satisfiat ex meritis Passionis Domini nostril JESU Christi, & omnium Sanctorum. In nomine Patris, ✠ & Filii, ✠ & Spiritus ✠ Sancti. *Amen.*

ABSOLUTION OF THE THIRD ORDER OF SAINT FRANCIS

Misereatur tui omnipotens Deus, & dimissis peccatis tuis, perducat te ad vitam aeternam.

Indulgentiam, ✠ absolutionem, & remissionem peccatorum nostrorum, tribuat nobis omnipotens & misericors Dominus.

Dominus noster JESUS Christus per merita suæ Sacratissimæ Psssionis te absolvat, & gratiam suam tibi infundat, & ego auctoritate ipsius, ac Apostolorum Petri, & Pauli, & Summorum Pontifium, mihi in hac parte commissa, & tibi concessa absolvo te ab omni vinculo excommunicationis maioris, vel minoris, siquod in curristi, & restituo te unioni, & participationi Fidelium, necnon Sanctis Sacramentis Ecclesiæ. Item eâdem auctoritate, quatenus ad præsens forum spectat, ego te absolvo ab omnibus peccatis tuis, tibi relaxo omnes pœnas Purgatorii, quas pro peccatis commissis meruisti, concedens tibi remissionem, & indulgentiam plenariam omnium peccatorum tuorum, & restituo te illi statui innocentiæ, in quo eras quando baptizatus fuisti. In nomine Patris, ✠ & Filii, ✠ & Spiritus ✠ Sancti. *Amen.*

ABSOLUTION OF THE THIRD ORDER OF SAINT DOMINIC

Misereatur tui omnipotens Deus, & dimissis peccatis tuis, perducat te ad vitam aeternam.

Indulgentiam, ✠ absolutionem, & remissionem peccatorum nostrorum, tribuat nobis omnipotens & misericors Dominus.

Dominus noster JESUS Christus Filius Dei vivi, qui Beato Petro Apostolo suo dedit potestatem ligandi, atque solvendi, per suam piissimam misericordiam te absolvat, & auctoritate ipsius, & Beatorum Petri, & Pauli Apostolorum ejus, & auctoritate Apostolica ex speciali gratia mihi commissa à Santissimo Domino nostro Sixto IV ego absolvo te à vinculo excommunicationis maioris, & minoris, suspensionis, & interdicti, si teneris, in quantum ego possum, & restituo te sanctis Sacramentis Ecclesiæ, communioni, & unitate fidelium. In nomine Patris, ✠ & Filii, ✠ & Spiritus ✠ Sancti. *Amen.*

Item eadem auctoritate mihi commissa, & tibi concessa, ut supra, ego absolvo te ab omnibus peccatis tuis, quæcumque toto decursu vitæ commisisti, de quibus corde contritus, & ore confessus es, & quorum memoriam habes, nec recordaris usque ad præsentem diem, de quibus consiteri minimè recordatus fuisti, ac puritati eidem, in quantum claves Sanctæ Matris Ecclesiæ se extendunt, remitto tibi etiam pœnas Purgatorii, quas propter culpas, & ofensas contra Deum, & proximum, & te ipsum commissas incurristi, & hoc, si de hac, qua ægrotas, infermitate decedas; si non, ex misericordia Dei salva tibi sit, donec fueris in mortis articulo constitutus. In nomine Patris, ✠ & Filii, ✠ & Spiritus ✠ Sancti. *Amen.*

ABSOLUTION OF THE BROTHERS OF THE SACRED ORDER OF THE MOST HOLY TRINITY

Misereatur tui omnipotens Deus, & dimissis peccatis tuis, perducat te ad vitam aeternam.

Indulgentiam, ✠ absolutionem, & remissionem peccatorum nostrorum, tribuat nobis omnipotens & misericors Dominus.

Authoritate Domini nostri Jesu Christi, & Sanctorum Apostolorum Petri, & Pauli, & Sedis Apostolicæ gratia concessa Confratribus Ordinis Sanctissimæ Trinitatis, declaro te consequi indulgentiam plenariam, & remissionem omnium pœnarum, quas pro peccatis tuis debebas solvere in Purgatorio; si tamen hac vice vita non migraveris, hæc eadem indulgentia tibi reservata manet pro ultimo articulo mortis tuæ. Item communico tibi Confrati orationse, Missas, suffragia, jejunia, labores, cæteraque bona opera, quæ per Dei gratiam in Ordine Sanctissimæ Trinitatis fiunt, & fient. In nomine Patris, ✠ & Filii, ✠ & Spiritus ✠ Sancti.

℟ Amen.
℣Dominus vobiscum.
℟Et cum spiritu tuo.

Oremus

A desto, Domine, supplicationibus nostris, & istam creaturam ad tuam sanctissimam imaginem factam, tua providentia ineffabili conservatam, & in tuo sancto nomine ad nostram confraternitatem spiritualium honorum participationem repectam, bene✠dicere digneris, & præsta, ut unigeniti Filii tui pretioso sanguine redempta, & ipsius meritis, & satisfactionibus adjuta, ad vitam pervenire mereatur æternam. Per eumdem Christum Dominum nostrum. *Amen.*

One should know that any Confessor, even if missing the Priestly commissaries of the Third Orders, or the Directors of the Brotherhoods, may still cast any of the above absolutions, be them Regular or Secular Confessors, and in the absence of these, any Priest; for this privilege is given to the third Orders, or their Brother, and this should be observed so as the dying may not be deprived from these plenary indulgences at the hour of their deaths.

Formula

℣Pax huic domui.

℟Et omnibus habitantibus in ea.

Antiphon

Ne reminiscaris Domine delicta famuli tui (*or your servant*) neque vindictam sumas de peccatis ejus. Kyrie eleison. Christe eleison. Kyrie eleison. Pater Noster, qui es in caelis, sanctificetur nomen tuum. Adveniat regnum tuum. Fiat voluntas tua, sicut in caelo et in terra. Panem nostrum quotidianum da nobis hodie, et dimitte nobis debita nostra sicut et nos dimittimus debitoribus nostris. Et ne nos inducas in tentationem, sed libera nos a malo. *Amen.*

℣Salvum fac servum tuum (*or your servant*).

℟Deus meus.

℣Domine exaudi orationem meam.

℟Et clamor meus ad teveniat.

℣Dominus vobiscum.

Oremus

Clementissime Deus, Pater misericordiarum, & Deus totius consolationis, qui neminem vis perire in te credentem, atque sperantem, secundum multitudinem miserationum tuarum respice propitius famulus tuum (N.) quem tibi vera sides, & spes Christiana commendant. Visita eum in salutari tuo, & per Unigeniti tui Passionem, & Mortem, omnium ei delictorum suorum remissionem, & veniam clementer indulge, ut ejus anima in hora exitus sui te judicem propitiatum inveniat, & in sanguine ejusdem Filii tui ab omni maculâ abluta, transire ad vitam mereatur perpetuam. Per eumdem Christum Dominum nostrum. *Amen.*

Then the infirm should say, or one of the Priests:

Misereatur mei omnipotens Deus, et dimittat mihi omnia peccata mea: liberet me ab omni malo, salvet et confirmet in omni opere bono, et perducat me ad vitam æternam. *Amen.*

Afterwards:

Dominus noster JESUS Christus Filius Dei vivi, qui Beato Petro Apostolo suo dedit potestatem ligandi, atque solvendi, per suam piissimam misericordiam recipiat confessionem tuam, & restituat tibi stolam primam, quam in Baptismate recepisti. Et ego facultate mihi ab Apostolica Sede tributa indulgentiam plenariam, & remissionem omnium peccatorum tibi concedo. In nomine Patris, ✠ & Filii, ✠ & Spiritus ✠ Sancti.

Per sacrosancta humanæ reparationis mysteria remittat tibi omnipotens Deus omnes præsentis, & futuræ vitæ pœnas, Paradisi portas aperiat, & ad gaudia sempiterna perducat. Amen. Benedicat te omnipotens Deus, Pater, & Filius, & Spiritus Sanctus. *Amen.*

EXTREME UNCTION AND VIATICUM

Prayer

Which the infirm should say, when he is given the Viaticum[131]

My Lord Jesus Christ, God, and true Man, Creator, and my Redeemer, I give thee one thousand graces for this great benefit, that thou concedes to me, that I may receive thee sacramented in my soul by means of the Viaticum for my transit into eternal life. May all the Saints, and Angels of Heaven give me these same graces for I am not worthy of such an incomprehensible mercy. It weighs on me, Lord, having been ungrateful of thee throughout all my life; but I hope to reach thy mercy in thy blood : may thy holiest will be fulfilled in me Lord. *Amen.*

Prayer

For when the infirm is prepared for Extreme Unction

My Lord Jesus Christ, God, and true man, Creator, and my Redeemer, who left in thy holy Church this holy Sacrament of Extreme Unction, so as with it our souls may be strengthened so as to triumphantly rise from the last battle, being victorious over the Devil, and his infernal cunnings, and so as the relics of our guilt, and bad habits of our sins may cease, and so we may achieve health in our souls, and also our bodies, if this is convenient to thee. I, Lord, fully offer myself in everything into thy divine hands. I give thee one thousand graces for this great benefit, and plead to all the creatures of Heaven, and earth, that they aid me in giving thee these graces. May thy holiest will be fulfilled in me Lord. *Amen.*

ACT OF CONTRITION

Which should be said to the infirm, or the dying, making a pause in each paragraph, so as not to distress the infirm, and so as these may understand what is being said

Most beloved crucified Jesus, for those three hours, in which thou wert in the arms of the Cross pining, and complaining to the eternal Father, for the blood, which thou shed for our souls, I ask thee, that thou remembers my soul in this most dangerous hour, and I also ask thee, that thou listens to these voices now. My God of my heart, and my Jesus, my Father, and my Redeemer, prostrated at thy divine feet, regretful of my

131 Translator's note: the name given to the Eucharist when administered to a dying person as part of the Last Rites.

faults, with my eyes on thy Wounds it weighs on me, Lord, the offences I made against thee, the thoughts I had, the words I said without fear of thy justice, and the deeds I have done without respect to thy Majesty; I was blind on the path of perdition, I madly persevered in that blindness of sin, without heeding the lights of thy aid, without heeding the rays of thy inspirations, running loose behind vice, going away from thy eyes, and separating from thee my profits; but now that I know my error, in the most heartfelt tears I wish to drown my faults, in the most sincere sighs I wish to bury my desires. I no longer wish for any other worship than thine, breaking all those idols, to whom I gave worship, into pieces : I wish for no other favour but thine, scratching from my memory those who took me from thy grace : I internally tire of all the things of the world, and I tire of myself, for I am tired very late : he only loves thee, he only seeks thee as a father this prodigal son, as the shepherd of this lost sheep, as a Lord of this disobedient slave, and as a God of this such ungrateful creature.

It weighs on me having committed offences towards thee, which art countless, crimes which have no count : I wish I had a pain, which was not only the same as the treason, which I made against thee, but so much more greater than it, as much as the distance from my sin to thy mercy. I am not content, Lord, with a penalty, which may break my heart; for let it not solely be a pain, but break my heart in so many pieces, as wert the times I offended thee, and even still not satisfy my desire : give me, my most beloved Jesus, as many hearts as wert my sins, so as I may feel at the same time the same pain in all of them, so as all may break in satisfaction of thy offence, and may all of them come together for the relief of my will. Let my life not end so soon, so as my penalty may last longer; but even still, beloved God of my heart, for my whole life is still too short for the feelings of he who committed one century of faults.

I propose, Lord, with all my heart to never offer thee again : ah Lord, who can believe in this intent with tears of blood! Who can with pieces of a soul certify this promise! I am so firm in my intent of serving thee, and worshipping thee, which it seems to me, that it is more likely for Heaven to fall over the earth, than me falling again into guilt. Remove, Lord, the penances of Purgatory, remove those of Hell, for I wish to show thee that it is not the fear of the flames which makes me abandon my faults, thou art my beloved Father, it is not the rigour of thy justice, it rather is the knowledge of thy divine essence : however my Lord, multiply the Purgatory into as many as my sins, as many Hells as are my crimes; for even in the sight of all of this I wish to love thee, and I wish to stay in the same intent of not offending thee, for being thou who thou art. Thou, as a true Medic, heal the wounds, which wert done by my looseness; thou, as a loving Father, have mercy on my disobedience; thou, as beloved shepherd, receive in thy flock this sheep lost for such a long time; thou, as a true Lord, take possession of this slave who was parted from thee for so many years : most beloved Jesus forgive my crimes by the pain of thy torments, forgive my faults by the blood of thy wounds, and may this be,

Lord, before the stone falls on this statue, before the wind blows off this leaf, before the sea capsizes this boat; for thee, Lord, all time is time; for thy divine mercy a sea of guilt is a small river; for thy mercy an eternity of sin is a brief instant.

Do not despise, Lord, my pleas; for even if I am a sinner, thou art Jesus; do not despise a contrite and humbled heart; do not turn thy back on a repented creature. If the Magdalene with tears in her eyes deserved thy forgiveness from so many faults, I also cry at thy divine feet, I also wish to wash them with my cries only to achieve thy Succour. If a crucified sinner obliged thee to such, for confessing that he had offended thee, I Lord confess, that I have offended thee more than Dismas, and more than the Magdalene, and more than all the condemned who are burning in the flames of Hell; and crucified in my pain I plead from the interior of my soul, I ask thee from the core of my heart, that thou forgive my faults by thy clemency, by thy pity, and by thy mercy. *Amen.*

Most beloved Mother of God, and patron of sinners, be all the goods, which art given by thy Son, thought thy merciful hands, humbly do I ask thee to reach for me the forgiveness of my faults, which I just now asked him with tears; allow, Lady, that I may achieve this by the pain, which thou had in the torments of his Passion, by the pain, which thou had in the martyrdom of thy loneliness. *Amen.*

MARY Mother of grace, defend me. Our Father, Hail Mary.
MARY Mother of mercy, Succour me. Our Father, Hail Mary.
MARY Mother of pity, aid me. Our Father, Hail Mary.

Pray the Clamours of the last agony.

Practices for Mass

REMEDY TO ASSIST WITH DEVOTION TO THE SACRIFICE OF MASS

The Sacrifice of Mass is the most pleasing thing to God, and the time which we take to assist it with devotion, is the most convenient to negotiate with God, and ask him for a grace both for us, as for the souls in Purgatory. It is certain that the Mother of God recommended to the Patriarch Saint Dominic, and to the Blessed Alanus de Rupe, that they recommend to all faithful Christians to pray the Rosary in the time of Mass.

One of two things, either whoever hears Mass knows how to meditate on the Mysteries and what they represent, or he does not. It is without a doubt that if he knows how to meditate, with greater advantage he shall listen to Mass, meditating on the five Sorrowful Mysteries of the Rosary, or three, or two, which is represented by the Sacrifice, and at the end of the meditation on each mystery, praying one Our Father, and ten Hail Marys. And if he doesn't know how to meditate, it is better to pray the Rosary with devotion, than being with the senses distracted in the government of the home, and the chest murmuring, or doing something even worse. I have it as a most prudent advice that every faithful Christian should pray the Rosary, which he may do so not only in devotional Mass, but also in the obligation ones.

In favour of whoever wishes to accompany the Priest in the ceremonies of Mass with the considerations, and affections of the heart, I shall declare what the Priestly vestments represent, and afterwards the main ceremonies with their brief prayers. Pick out from these delicacies the form which is most pleasing to you, and is more convenient for your spiritual wellbeing.

The entering of the Priest in the Sacristy to cover himself with the Priestly vestments represents the entry of the Son of God into this world in the Virginal Tabernacle of the purest womb of the holiest MARY, where he was dressed with our humanity to go celebrate this Sacrifice on the Calvary mount.

The Amice represents the veil, with which the face of the Lord JESUS was covered, when his enemies told him, injuring him, *Prophesy, who is it that smote thee.* The Alb represents the white vestment, with which Herod, mocking the Lord, sent him to Pilate. The Rope represents the first knot, and ropes, with which the Lord was tied, when he was arrested. In the

Maniple is represented the second knot, with which his hands were tied to the column, when he was flogged, and it is placed on the left arm, which is closer to the heart so as to signify the love with which the Lord received the cruel floggings in satisfaction of our guilt. In the Stole is represented the rope, which was cast around his neck, when he carried the Cross on his back to be crucified. In the Chasuble is represented the tunic, which the executioners stripped from the Lord JESUS, when they crucified him.

PRACTICAL METHOD OF HEARING MASS

Act of Contrition

My God, my Father, my Creator, and my supreme good, I sinned, I sinned my Lord; however, it weighs on me, God, and my love, and it weighs supremely on my whole heart having offended thee, for being thou who thou art, worthy of being loved above all things. I claim, my God, with the favour of thy grace to never again sin. I sinned, Lord, have mercy on me.

Offering

Most high God, and my Lord, I offer thee this Mass in the union of all the worth of my Lord JESUS Christ, and his Mother the Holiest Mary, by the exaltation of the holy Mother Church, peace, and agreement among the Christian Princes, extirpation of heresy, for all the temptation of the Supreme Pontiff, and apply all its fruits, and indulgences for me, and further people, and the souls in Purgatory, to whom I owe, observing the order of justice, and charity. I hope, my God, and my JESUS, and ask that this sacrifice work upon me, and in the further faithful such marvellous effects, as is proper of thy incomparable virtue. Amen.

The Priest, coming to the Altar, represents Jesus going into prayer in the Garden.

O thou divine Master, who in order to teach me to seek the remedy, and consolation in works thou entered the Garden to pray to thy eternal Father, give me, my JESUS, grace, so as I may seek thee every day in prayer; and knowing in it thy divine will, I may know how to conform all the desires of my will to it. Amen.

The bowing of the Priest while saying confession represents Jesus sweating blood, and in mortal agonies

O thou most clement JESUS, who fainted with the horrors of my ungratefulness, who with the torments of thy passion saw thyself sweating blood, and in deathly agonies, give me such a vivid knowledge of my faults, and thy finenesses, that my heart may cry contrite tears of blood. Amen.

The Priest going up to kiss the Altar Stone represents the kiss Judas gave to his Divine Master, when he offered him up.

O thou most patient JESUS, I give thee infinite grace for the example, that thou gives me to suffer the greatest treasons from my enemies : I ask thee to give me grace, so as I may imitate thy patience, and so as my mouth may not sacrilegiously touch thy sacramented body. Amen.

The Priest going from the middle of the Altar to read the Introitum, represents the arrested Christ, going to the tribunal of Annas.

O thou most wise JESUS, who to confound the greed of the sinners, thou art suffering the offences, as the wise men of the world despised thy divine wisdom, make me humble of heart, words, and deeds, so as I may imitate thee. Amen.

When the Priest returns to the middle of the Altar to say the Kyries, *this represents Christ going to the home of Caiaphas, where Peter denied him, and he was slapped.*

O thou most beloved JESUS, who by my love in the house of Caiaphas, wert denied three times by thy disciple, and hurt by a sacrilege with a cruel slap, make my faith lively, so as I may never deny thee, and give me grace to endure for thy love the greatest offences. Amen.

The Priest saying the first Dominus vobisoum *represents Christ placing his eyes on Saint Peter after he denied him.*

O thou Divine Medic, who placing his eyes on Peter, immediately cured him of his infirmities, making him aware of his errors so as to contritely weep for them, concede to me as much light, as necessary in order to know mine, and to weep for them bitterly. Amen.

The Epistle represents the accusation which was done to the Lord in the presence of Pilate.

O thou sweet JESUS, who being taken to the house of Pilates, wert falsely accused, give me patience, so as I may suffer for thy love, and with the worth of my soul suffer the false testimonies of the world. Amen.

The Priest, saying before the Gospel Munda cor meum, *represents Christ hearing in the presence of Herod false testimonies without defending himself.*

O thou beloved JESUS, who, so as to please the eternal Father, did not defend thy innocence, seeing thyself insulted in the presence of Herod, concede to me thy grace, so as I may know how to suffer the injuries of the world for thy love. Amen.

The change in the Missal, and the reading of the Gospel represents Jesus going from the house of Herod to the house of Pilate.

O thou Jesus of infinite kindness, who to satisfy the re-incidence of my faults, wished to be taken from the house of a tyrant to that of another tyrant, concede to me such a firm contrition of my sins, that I may always serve, and love thee. Amen.

The Priest uncovering the Chalice, represents Christ when he was stripped to be flogged.

O thou beloved JESUS, who in order to show me the red of thy blood, consented to being stripped with such affront : concede to me the valour, so as I may strip from all my vicious habits, and cover myself with the holy fear of never offending the again. Amen.

The Priest offering the Host, and the Chalice, represents Christ tied to the column, and offering to his eternal Father his floggings.

O thou JESUS most innocent Lamb, who with such gentleness suffered tied to a column five thousand flogs, and thou offered them to thy eternal Father for my remedy : tie me, Lord, with the prisons of charity to that column, so as not even the greatest labours in the world may part me from thee. Amen.

The Priest covering the Chalice, represents when they placed the crown of thorns over the head of the Lord Jesus.

O thou Jesus, King of Kings, who for my greed and vanity suffered in thy head a crown of thorns : concede to me with humility all further virtues, and perseverance in thy grace so as I may be crowned with thee in Heaven. Amen.

The Priest coming to the Lavabo represents when Pilate washed his hands from condemning Christ while being innocent.

O thou JESUS of immense love, who suffered the dissimulation of sinners, with which they intend to wash their guilt in the sacrilegious constitutions : concede to me tears of true contrition, so as with truth I may wash away all my sins. Amen.

When the Priest says Orate fraters, *this represents when Pilate showed the Lord to the people, saying:* Ecce homo.

O thou JESUS, my benefactor, who for the immensity with which I have despised thy benefits, suffered having been shown to the people, as an evildoer, teach me of my ungratefulness, so as I may know how to serve, and love. Amen.

The Preface represents how the Lord Jesus after being flogged, was condemned to death on the Cross.

O thou most beloved JESUS, my Redeemer, who in order to free me from the eternal death wished to die on the Cross : concede to me a spirit of continuous mortification in recognition of such a great benefit. Amen.

The Priest in the first Memento represents JESUS with the Cross on his back.

O thou JESUS, divine Isaac, who with such conformity took the Cross of my sins through the streets of Jerusalem over thy divine shoulders : concede to me grace, and light, so as with joy, and conformity I may take, in thy continuity, the Cross of my state. Amen.

The Priest continuing with the Canon, represents how the holy woman Veronica cleaned the blood from the Lord on the path of bitterness.

O thou Lord, and my God, who over thy Divine face, which is the joy of the Angels, my sins cast so many stains : concede to me the fate of washing all that blood with tears of pain, and love. Amen.

The Priest blessing the Host, and the Chalice, represents Christ laid, and nailed to the Cross.

O thou JESUS, my Divine Master, who in order to take satisfaction from my sins, thou suffered being nailed to a Cross with such hard nails, awaken my heart so as to find unity with thee crucified. Amen.

The Priest raising the Host, represents Christ rising in the height of his Cross.

O thou JESUS crucified by my love, who with pieces of heart, and tears of blood cried, and felt the faults, with which I offended thee so much, and was crucified! It weighs on me having sinned, have compassion, and mercy on me. Amen.

The Priest raising the Chalice, represents the Lord on the Cross shedding blood from his wounds.

I love thee, most precious blood of my Saviour, which from his wounds flowed as my remedy, fall over my heart, and break it with pain, so as I may achieve thy mercy. Amen.

The priest in the Memento for the dead represents the Lord praying on the Cross, and asking to his eternal Father forgiveness for his enemies.

O thou most clement JESUS, since thou had such compassion for thy enemies, seeing them dead with guilt, that thou asked thy eternal Father for their forgiveness, resurrect me from my sins, and give me the life of thy friendship so as I may imitate thee in the love of my enemies. Amen.

The Priest saying Nobis quoque peccatoribus, *represents the forgiveness, which the Lord gave to the Good Thief on the Cross.*

O thou most merciful JESUS, who with so much mercy thou received the contrition of such a great sinner, who at the last hour gave him Paradise, accept the confession of my faults in this hour, and give me contrition, so as I may deserve his, and thy company. Amen.

The Priest saying the Our Father signifies the recommendation, which the Lord did of his mother to Saint John the Evangelist.

O thou beloved Father of mercy, who does not abandon the souls, who seek thee by means of the Cross : concede to me, Lord, such fine love, that purging all my judgment, and will, I may reach to have a Mother as thy Holiest Mother. Amen.

The Priest breaking the Host, signifies the Lord Jesus dying.

O thou beloved JESUS, God, and Man, who for having given me life, and having united me with God, suffered the death blow, which separated thy soul from thy holiest body: concede to me that I may die to the vices, and that I may completely waste away from the desire of self will, so as I may live with thee eternally. Amen.

The Priest casting the particle into the Chalice, represents how the Lord descended into Limbo.

O thou most patient JESUS, and Redeemer of the world, who in order to show thy charity thou descended down to Limbo to confirm the redemption of the captive souls, come down to my soul with the effective aid of thy grace to give me the awaited freedom. Amen.

The Priest saying the Agnus Dei *represents the Lord converting the many souls in Calvary; and he repeats it three times to signify the instance of the sinner contritely asking for mercy.*

O thou most clement JESUS, who in the forgiveness, which thou asked for the sinners, taught me to always cry my faults, and to continue to ask thee for mercy : concede to me a true pain for my sins, so as I may deserve thy mercy. Amen.

The Priest communing represents how the Lord after he was dead was entombed.

O thou most merciful JESUS, who in a new stone sepulchre wished to be entombed, I give thee here my chest as a tomb, where thou shall find a marble heart : I ask thee to break this stone of its hardness so as to receive thee with the finest tenderness of love. Amen.

In the wine, with which the Chalice is purified, is represented how the Lord was embalmed in the sepulchre by Joseph, and Nicodemus.

O thou most sacred body of my beloved JESUS, what fortunate creature would I be, if I knew how to anoint thee with the oil of the most ardent charity : give me such an amount of tears of love, that I may reach thy divine feet as the loving Magdalene. Amen.

The Priest covering the Chalice, and saying the Postcommunio, signifies the resurrected Jesus.

O thou most beloved JESUS, and my Divine Master, who in order to animate me to suffer in this world with the hope of the eternal prize, resurrected from death, which was given by my sins, immortal, and glorious : concede to me to accompany thee in those sufferings, so as I may also be in thy company in eternal glory. Amen.

The Priest saying, turned towards the people, Dominus vobiscum, represents the resurrected JESUS appearing to his Holiest Mother , and to his disciples.

O thou my beloved JESUS, who, to console thy Holiest Mother, and thy disciples appeared to them after thou resurrected : concede to me the grace of serving, and loving thee in the labours of this miserable life so as to deserve thy eternal sight in Heaven. Amen.

The Priest saying the final prayers, represents the Lord in the forty days, in which he detained himself on earth with the disciples.

O JESUS moaning for the good of my soul, since thou detained thyself for forty days with thy disciples before rising up to Heaven, detain thyself inside my heart, and do not be gone from my soul, so may the fire of thy love burn my faults, vices, and all impulses, and desires from my judgment, and may my free will be melted and destroyed. Amen.

The Priest saying the last Dominus voviscum *represents the rising of the Lord to Heaven.*

O thou sweetest JESUS, who after teaching us the path to Heaven by the exercises of prayer, and mortification, rose in glory, make it so as imitating thee, I may die of missing thee. Amen.

The Priest casting the blessing to the people, represents the coming of the Holy Spirit over the Apostles.

O thou most benign JESUS, and my Redeemer, who to console the entire Church in thy absence, sent to it as a Master the Divine Holy Spirit, and so as it may detain itself in my heart in thy love thou sent it as tongues of fire, make it that my will be entirely extinguished, and my understanding be illuminated, so as I may only love thy love, and only by thy kindness have hope. Amen.

Those who wish to perform spiritual communion when the priest is communing, and other times during the day, according to the instructions of his Director, may do so in the following way.

SPIRITUAL COMMUNION

Spiritual communion consists in the feverous exercise of those virtues by which without actually receiving the most divine Sacrament of the Altar, one may participate in the many fruits of the same Sacrament. In this exercise its acts are those special Acts of Living Faith over the same Sacrament, Acts of Hope, and Charity.

First of all bless yourself, pray a Hail Mary in praise of the Mother of God, and make an examination of conscience over the faults, and defects you may have committed after your last confession, or sacramental, or spiritual communion. Once the conscience is examined, and considering the kindness of God offended by you, make with intention of soul some of the Acts of Love which are in the Novena of the Lady of the Rock above, whichever you may want.

Having done the Act of Contrition, imagine that you are in a Church in front of the Altar, that the Priest opens the Tabernacle, and shows you the sacred particle in the customary way of the Sacramental communion. Fixed in the imagination, make the following Acts of Faith and Hope.

I believe with living Faith that in the Holiest Sacrament of the Eucharist there is the body, blood, soul, and divinity of my Lord JESUS Christ as real as he is in Heaven. I hope, my God, and my JESUS, for salvation, if dignifying I receive thy holiest body, or unite myself with thee for love. As I so hope, so do I desire.

Making the communion outside of Mass, one only needs to do what follows:

Consider that the Divine JESUS, with the love and kindness of a Father, is saying to the interior of your soul: Daughter, I am the Divine Lamb, who purifies the sins of the world. Give me, daughter, thy heart, that I wish to enter into it so as to sanctify it. Hear these words, or similar, and go with your heart in the following Acts of Charity explained in these sighs.

SIGHS

1. Is it possible, that my Jesus is asking me for my heart?! I, my Jesus, who am I, and thou, who art thee!? I am the most ungrateful creature, and

thou the supreme kindness. But if such is what thou wants, come, for I love thee, and desire to love with all the love of the Seraphim.

2. Is it possible, Divine love, that thou wants to enter into my heart?! I, my beloved sacramented God, very much desire thee inside of me. For if thou desires such, come, light a flame of thy love. Come, my JESUS, that I desire to be ablaze in thy love.

3. Is it possible, my Jesus, and divine Father, that thou art asking for my heart to be thy house?! Know that my soul is sighing for thy love. Come, father of love, come cure the hunger of this soul, thy daughter, even if unworthy.

4. Is it possible, that my JESUS, son of the always Virgin MARY, wishes to enter in my heart?! This grace must be the work of the Mother of God. Come then, love of my soul. Enter, my JESUS, and be forever a transformation of my being in thee.

5. Is it possible, my JESUS, and my Glorifier, that thou wishes to enter into my heart?! For my heart, my JESUS, wishes to always be thy sustenance. Come beloved JESUS, come, my love, to glorify me with thy love, that I only love thee, and only thee do I wish to love.

In any of the sighs, if you feel your will moved, continue to repeat it, or in the Acts which the Lord may inspire you to do, since these are only presented here as examples, and one only needs to use one or two. The will being moved by any of them, it is customary to make the Act of Admiration of the divine goodness, and of confusion of your ungratefulness towards God, and the Acts of Humility in the knowledge of your vileness, and the Acts of Contrition. Make the intention to emend your life (or do this several times, picking the means of conserving this), and in particular to avoid that fault, or defect, in which you usually fall into, or of exercising that virtue, of which you have the greatest necessity. After the mentioned Acts, and with some sighs of which you feel less desire, as if you are already enjoying the divine bread of the Angels, enter into offering grace with some of the following Jaculatorias, or with some others of greater fervour.

Jaculatorias

1. Is it possible that inside my heart is that JESUS, who redeemed me?! My God, here is my soul, resolved to give thee pleasure, for I love thee. What does thou wish from me?

2. Soul of mine, where am I, that I do not die of amazement, joy, and love? Inside my heart is the same God of Heaven! I shall love this divine love forever, and I shall never leave it.

3. Soul of mine, is it possible, that the Divine Medic came to this poor house? How did I earn such a gift? Look then, love of mine, to such infirmity. Speak, speak to this heart, that I want to serve thee, and only thee forever love. Live, live JESUS, and his love lives forever in my heart. *Amen.*

Exorcisms

EFFECTIVE EXORCISM

Or Spiritual Remedies for all afflictions, of which there might be suspicion that these are caused by the Devil, or by any unknown natural cause

Precept

Which should be done with faith, confidence, and inner peace

I command by virtue of the holiest name of Jesus to the Devil, or demons, who cause me *such, or such infirmity, or affliction, or pain,* (*name it*) to move it no more, and that they desist from it, and leave my humours, which in any way they move, or have moved, in their equality, with all other operations free, so as to serve my good God. And if this affliction is moved by any humour, even if natural, or element, by virtue of the holiest name of Jesus with full faith I order them to compose themselves, and cease their disconcertment, so as in this way without this affliction and pain I may further serve, and praise, with all my heart, my God, and Lord Jesus Christ, for whose love I live, and desire health, as my Redeemer.

℣Omnis, qui invocaverit nomen Jesu.
℟Hic in tribulatione salvus erit.

Oremus

Deus, qui unigentum Filium tuum constituisti humani generis Salvatorem, & Jesum vocari jussisti : concede propitious, ut cujus sanctum nomen veneramur in terries, ejus quoque aspectu perfruamur in Cœlis. Per eumdem Jesum Christum Dominum nostrum. *Amen.*

In Vernacular

Let us pray

God, who constituted thy only-begotten Son Saviour of the world, and ordered him to be called JESUS, favourably concede to us who on earth venerate such a holy name, that we may enjoy his sight in Heaven. For this same Lord JESUS Christ, our Lord. *Amen.*

Detestation, which should be done by the infirm on whom the exorcism is performed

And thee, cursed demon, enemy of God, rebel to me, and thy Lord, apostate of me, and thy Creator, with whose authority does thou dare to vex me, and torment me, through thyself, or through thy most miserable ministers with sorceries, and maleficas, with or without thy presence among them? I, by the faith which I have in the sacred name of JESUS, powerfully order thee, that to the precept, which shall be immediately placed over thee by this Reverend Exorcising Priest, Minister of God, and of the Holy Church, thou shall suddenly, and without delay be parted from me with thy evildoings, and may these immediately be destroyed, and annihilated, and from henceforth thou shall not have any more power to molest me, or vex me, neither internally, nor externally, for I have faith, and certain hope in God, that I shall be immediately free by the virtue of the holiest name of JESUS, faith of my salvation, and convenient spiritual good.

Immediately the Exorcist should warn the infirm how important it is to have a great faith, and for this to further protect himself in it he should say:

I firmly believe, that now the Devil shall part from me, and that all his evil doings shall be destroyed by the divine virtue, as long as this my health, and freedom be useful to my salvation. Thus I hope, and thus I trust in my God.

Immediately cast holy water on the infirm saying:

Per aspersionem hujus aquæ, cum Dei adjutorio, destruantur in te omnia maleficia diabolic, & ipse diabolus manifestè exeat à te, & infundatur in te virtus Spiritus Sancti. *Amen.*

Offer him the Cross to kiss, saying:

Ecce Crucem Domini nostri JESU Christi, ✠ fugite partes adversæ : vicit Leo de tribu Juda, Radix David. Alleluia.

Precept

Præcipio tibi, quicumque es, spiritos immunde, & omnibus sociis tuis hunc Dei famulum obsidentibus, (vel possidentibus) ut per Mysteria Incarnationis, Passionis, Resurrectionis, & Ascensionis Domini nostri JESU Chirsti, per missionem Spiritus Sancti, & per Adventum ejusdem Domini nostri ad judicium, ut mihi Dei Ministro, licèt indigno, prorsus in omnibus obedias, neque hanc creaturam Dei, vel circumstantes, aut eorum bona ullo modo offendas.

Effective Exorcism

In nomine JESU Christi Nazareni, Æterni Patris Filii, qui est benedictus in sæcula sæculorum. Amen. Qui est, & qui erat, & qui venturus est : qui dilexit nos, & lavit nos in sanguine suo, quique Ecclesiæ ejus sponsæ omnimodam contulit potestatem calcandi super serpentes, &

infernales scorpiones, in eumque credentibus dedit facultatem plenissimam de hominum corporibus , cunctisque de rebus eis spectantibus dæmones coercendi, cruciandi, & expellendi; necnon omnia malefica, incantationes, fascinationes, præstigia dissipandi, destruendi, & anihilandi. Cum ego igitur ipsiusmet, JESU Christi Salvatoris nostri, & Ecclesiæ ejus legitimus, licèt indignus, sim Minister, ea auctoriate, qua per ordinem Exorcistatus, & Sacerdotii fungor, & per fidem, quam firmissimè teneo, *præcipiendo præcipio vobis* omnibus, & singulis spiritibus rebellibus, & generis sitis tam hic præsentibus, quam absentibus, seu fueritis vocati, seu invocavi, aut spontanei, aut missi, vel etiam per divinam dispensationem permissi, quòd nullatenus, neque nunc, nec in posterum accedere, seu divexare hanc valeatis creaturam in sacro Baptismate renatam.

Imponendo signanter vobis, quód, quatenus eam obsedeatis, seu possideatis, semota illicò omni vestra diabolica fraude, morborum inductione, membrorum occupatione, potentiarum oppressione, phantasmatumque illusione, in puris naturalibus dimittere debeatis hoc plasma Dei, sic, & tali pacto, quòd per auctoritatem Summi Imperatoris, vobis nunc intimatam, inhibitum omninò sit sub quocumque prætextu quamlibet illi afferre molestiam, nec in corpore, nec extra corpus, nec per visionem, nec per terrorem, neque de die, neque de nocte, nec dormiendo, nec vigilando, nec comedendo, nec orando, nec quidquid temporale, seu spirituale faciendo. Quòd si mendacissimè existimetis ligatos vos teneri vinculo alicujus præcepti, adorationis, suffumigationis, pacti, artis, & facturæ, seu per caracteres impressos in lapidibus, in laminis, in ceris, in chartis virgineis, seu per aliquod præparatum verbis, herbis, & lapidibus, seu per sacramentalia, & Sacramenta ipsa, aut in nominibus Angelorum, & magni Dei cum observatione temporum, lunationum, dierum, & horarum, & minutorum, etiam cum pacto expresso, aut tacito, etiam juramento firmato, & interposito, omnia ista, & omnia alia superstitiosa, vana, inania, & diabolica, quatenus opus sit, exprimenda.

Ego idem Dei famulus per Deum vivum, per Deum Sanctum, per Deum Omnipotentem, & Unum in essentia, & Trinum in Personis, Patrem scilicet, Filium, & Spiritum Sanctum, à quo est omnis potestas in Cœlo, & in terra, necnon per virtutem, & efficaciam Sanctissimæ Crucis, cujus imaginem hic damus, ✠ & cui omne genu flectitur, destruo, dissipo, irrita facio, & ad nihilum redigo, sic, & taliter, quòd ad nihilum valeant ultrà, nisi quòd derideantur, contemnantur, pedibusque conculcentur.

Audite ergo, rebelles, hujus præcepti virtutem, Omnipotenti Deo in me præcipienti obtemperate. Humiliamini sub potenti manu Dei, dimittite nunc, & absque ulla interposita mora in ista creatura omnem lanquorem, & omnem infirmitatem. Discedite, maledicti, in ignem æternum, qui paratus est vobis, & omnibus confociis vestris, & sicut fumus jecoris piscis combusti (dictante Raphaele Archangelo) spiritum à Sara fugavit, ita verba ista præceptiva, ac eficacissima potentissimè expelant vos, quòd non ampliùs ad hanc creaturam signo Crucis munitam accedere audeatis, sed hinc indè distante stetiss, & longè ad ea, tamquam infernus distat à nobis.

Per Jesum ✠ Christum Dominum nostrum, qui venturus est judicare vivos, & mortuos, & sæculum per ignem. *Amen.*

Another Exorcism

In nomine Sanctissimæ Trinitatis, Patris, & Filii, & Spiritus Sancti, & in virtute sanctissimi nominis JESU. Ego (N.) Minister Exorcista Sanctæ Ecclesiæ Dei per auctoritatem mihi consessam contra vos, spiritus infernales, qui hanc creaturam Dei (N.) per vestra maleficia, vel cum præsentia vestra, vel absque illa, vexatis, termino omnia maleficia, incantationes, ligationes, signaturas, facturas, tumores, infestationes, inquietudines, perturbationes, dolores, & tormenta quæcumque huic creaturæ Dei (N.) arte diabolica intulistis. Et eadem auctoritate te (N.) creaturam Dei absolvo ab omnibus maleficiis, incantationibus, ligationibus, signaturis, & facturis, & ab earum effectibus : quæ omnia extermino, & vobiscum expello, confringo, dissipo, destruo, extirpo, & erradico, ne de cætero te infestare valeant.

Absolvat te (N.) Dominus JESUS Christus ab omni vinculo facturæ, & maleficii per virtutes, & potentias spirituum malignorum tibi facto, sive sit in aere, aut plumbo, aut in argento, aut in auro, aut in aliquo filato bombycino, vel fysico, vel lineo, vel laneo, vel in ossibus hominum mortuorum, vel viventium, vel animalium terrastrium, vel volatilium, vel aqueorum. Et si est in libro, vel in charta etiam virginea, vel in aliquo ligno, vel in aliquibus verbis, vel in herbis, vel in lapidibus, vel in capillis, plumbis, lanis, vel paleis, vel in quibusvis creaturis, & si est in sepulchro Hebræorum, paganorum, hæreticorum, & Christianorum; & si est in agro, vel vinea, vel pratis, vel nemoribus, aut in montibus, vel vallibus, vel cavernis, vel in fontibus, vel extrà, & si est in Oriente, vel Occiente, vel Septemtrione, vel eridie, & si est in vestimentis, vel cincturiis, vel in trivio, aut in domo, vel in pariete, vel in thoro, aut desuper, aut desubter, in rebus domûs, vel domorum, aut in arbore, aut in fovea, aut in puteo, vel cisterna, aut in profundo, vel abysso, aut in sylva, vel spelunca solitaria, aut in deserto, vel in divisionibus marium, vel fluminum, vel in statua, vel in clausura ferrea, vel lignea, vel in conjunctura membrorum, vel consumpta per ignem, vel potatione, vel comestione, vel tactu, vel visu, vel odoratu, vel auditu, quocumque loco sit, & quomodocumque factum sit etiam ad mortem, & sub quibusvis verbis, & rebus, quorum hæc omnia terminentur, dissolvantur, & anihilentur, & eradicentur ad hac creatura Dei (N.) & tu Domine solve, & libera eam ab omnibus malis, & tentationibus dæmonum, & malignis spiritibus, & ab omni vinculo maleficii.

Lenitive Precepts

Ego (N.) ut Minister Christi, & Ecclesiæ, impero tibi, sive vobis, dæmones maledicti, in nomine JESU Christi, ut statim cesset omnis vexation, & omnis afflictio à te, vel à vobis causata in ista creatura.

Ego (N.) ut Minister JESU Christi, impero tibi, vel vobis, dæmones, ut sinatis hanc creaturam Dei posse orare, loqui, consiteri, accipere corpus Christi, & cætera spiritualia exercere absque ullo impedimento in maxillis, neque in parte aliqua sui corporis.

Ego, ut Minister Christi, præcipio tibi, five vobis, dæmones, in nomine JESU Christi, ne impediatis huic creaturæ Dei comedere, bibere, requiescere, & sua naturalia exercere.

In this, or in a similar way the Exorcist may place the precepts, which he may feel, who should be warned to predict all the deceits of the Devil, who is always on guard.

Expulsive Precept

Ego (N.) ut Minister Christi, & sanctæ Ecclesiæ Dei, auctoritate mihi conceffa à Christo Domino, in nomine Sanctissimæ Trinitatis, Patris, & Filii, & Spiritus Sancti, & in virtute sanctissimi nominis JESU impero vobis, dæmones infernales, qui maleficium intulistis huic creaturæ Dei aut cum præsentia vestra, vel absque illa, ut statim sine mora totaliter recedatis cum omnibus maleficiis vestris destructis, & ea non illi iterùm faciatis, neque redeatis. Sic volo, sic jubeo, ut Minister JESU Christi. In nomine Patris, & Filii, & Spiritus Sancti. *Amen.*

Immediately say over the infirm

Extinguatur in te (N.) omnis virtus diabolica per impositionem manuum mearum, & per invocationem omnium. Sanctorum Angelorum, Archengelorum, Patriarcharum, Prophetarum, Apostolorum, Martyrum, Confessorum, ac Virginum, & omnium simul Sanctorum in nomine Patris, ✠ & Filii, ✠ & Spiritus ✠ Sancti. *Amen.*

Precept to bind demons

Ego (N.) ut Minister Christi, & Ecclesiæ sanctæ Dei in vitute sanctissimi nominis JESU frœnum vobis pono, X dæmones maledicti, & in virtute ejusdem sanctissimi nominis JESU fortiter ligo vos, & præcipio, quòd non ascendatis superiùs ad caput creaturæ istius, nec terreatis, aut lædatis eam vigilando, dormiendo, sedendo aut stando, sed sinatis eam orare, comedere, bibere, dormire, laborare, ambulare, quiescere, & omnia alia agere, quæ spectant ad honorem Dei, & salutem animæ, & corporis ejus. In nomine Patris, ✠ & Filii, ✠ & Spiritus ✠ Sancti. *Amen.*

If the Exorcist sees that the infirm is not completely free, make some new Acts of Faith, and humbling oneself in the presence of God, praying the Chant of the *Magnificat, Benedictus*, &c. And urging the infirm to also have faith, which he should have, one may repeat the above exorcisms and precepts one and another time. And when finishing, the infirm not feeling the pain, of which he was suffering, and being free, he shall say the following:

Action of grace for the freedom of the infirm

My Lord JESUS Christ, I give thee infinite grace, for by the worth of thy holiest Passion, of thy precious blood, and of thy infinite kindness thou freed me from the Devil, and his maledictions; and thus I ask, and beg thee now for thou to preserve me, and keep me, so as the Devil, from henceforth may no longer harm me in any way; for I want to live, and die under the protection of thy holiest name.

Immediately the Exorcists shall sing the hymn Te Deum laudamus

Te Deum laudámus : te Dominum confitemur.
Te æternum Patrem omnis terra veneratur.
Tibi omnes Angeli; tibi cæli & universae potestates.
Tibi Cherubim & Seraphim incessabili voce proclamant:
Sanctus, Sanctus, Sanctus, Dominus Deus Sabaoth.
Pleni sunt cæli & terra majestatis gloriæ tuæ.
Te gloriosus Apostolorum chorus;
Te Prophetarum laudabilis numerus;
Te Martyrum candidatus laudat exercitus.
Te per orbem terrarum sancta confitetur Ecclesia:
Patrem immensæ majestatis;
Venerandum tuum verum & unicum Filium;
Sanctum quoque Paraclitum Spiritum.
Tu Rex gloriæ, Christe.
Tu Patris sempiternus es Fílius.
Tu ad liberandum suscepturus hominem, non horruisti Vírginis uterum.
Tu, devicto mortis aculeo, aperuisti credentibus regna cælorum.
Tu ad dexteram Dei sedes, in gloria Patris.
Judex crederis esse venturus.
Te ergo quæsumus, tuis famulis subveni, quos pretioso sanguine redemisti.
Æterna fac cum sanctis tuis in gloria numerari.
Salvum fac populum tuum, Domine, & benedic hæreditati tuæ.
Et rege eos, & extolle illos usque in æternum.
Per singulos dies benedícimus te.
Et laudamus nomen tuum in sæculum, & in sæculum sæculi.
Dignare, Domine, die isto sine peccato nos custodire.
Miserere nostri, Domine, miserere nostri.
Fiat misericordia tua, Domine, super nos, quemadmodum speravimus in te.
In te, Domine, speravi: non confundar in æternum.

And afterwards the following

℣Confirma hoc, Deus, quod operatus es in nobis.
℟Á Templo santo tuo, quod est in Jerusalem.
℣Sit nomen Domini benedictum.

℟Ex hos nunc, & usque in sæculum.
℣Osende nobis, Domine, misericordiam tuam.
℟Et salutare tuum da nobis.
℣Domine, exaudi orationem meam.
℟Et clamor meus ad te veniat.
℣Dominus vobiscum.
℟Et cum spiritu tuo.

Oremus

Omnipotens sempiterne Deus, qui liberare dignatus es hunc famulum tuum (N.) à vexatione Satanæ, & ministrorum ejus: mitte in eum septiformem Spiritum Sanctum Paraclitum de Cœlis.

Quæsumus, omnipotens Deus, famulum tuum (N.) respice, ut te largiente regatur in corpore, & te servante custodiatur in mente. Per Christum Dominum nostrum. *Amen.*

Immediately turning to the infirm, say, while standing

Dominus JESUS Christus apud te sit, ✠ ut te defendat : intra te sit, ✠ ut te conservet : ante te sit, ✠ ut te deducat : post te sit, ✠ ut te custodiat : ita ut dæmones non amplius possint nocere tibi nullo modo, sed totaliter à te recedant : super te sit, ✠ ut te benedicat, qui cum Patre, & Spiritu Sancto in unitate perfecta vivit, & regnat per omnia sæcula sæculorum. *Amen.*

Virtus Sanctæ Crucis, qua signo ✠ te, sit super te, circa te, ante te, post te, & in omnibus partibus tuis. Amen. Benedicat ✠ tibi Deus, & custodiat te : ostendat tibi faciem suam, & misereatur tui, convertat vultum suum ad te, & det tibi salutem, & pacem. *Amen.*

Benedictio Dei omnipotentis, Patris, ✠ & Filii, ✠ & Spiritus ✠ Sancti descendat super te, & tecum maneat sempre. *Amen.*

Cast the holy water.

And if the infirm does not have these words with him, one should write them for him on a piece of paper, putting his name in them, and after this is blessed one should recommend that these are always carried with him.

Holiest words against diabolic malediction, which should always be carried by the infirm

In nomine Pa✠tris, & Fi✠lii, & Spiritus ✠ Sancti. Amen. Hel ✠ Heloym ✠ Sother ✠ Emmanuel ✠ Sabaoth ✠ Agia ✠ Tetragrammaton ✠ Agios ✠ Otheos ✠ Ischyos ✠ Athanatos ✠ Jehova ✠ Ya ✠ Adonay ✠ Saday ✠ Homousion ✠ Messias ✠ Esereheye ✠ Increatus Pater ✠ Increatus Filius ✠ Increatus Spiritus Sanctus ✠ JESUS ✠ Christus vincit ✠ Christus regnat ✠ Christus imperat ✠ si diabolus ligavit, vel tentavit te (N.)

Suo effectu, per sua opera Christus, Filius Dei vivi, per suam misericordiam liberet te ab omnibus spiritibus immundis, qui venit de Cœlo, & incarnatus est in utero Beatissimæ Virginis MARIÆ causa humanæ salutis, & ejiciendi diabolum, & omnem malignum spiritum à te in profundum Inferni, & abyssi. Ecce Crucem ✠ Domini, fugite partes adversæ, vicit Leo de tribu Juda, Radix David.

Remedy and exorcism to expel all forms of animals, birds, beasts, and critters, which either due to sorcery, or for any other diabolical reason are harmful, which destroy crops and persecute the creatures

The Exorcist being dressed with a surplice, and a purple stole, coming before the Cross, and with holy water, as soon as these come to the infected place, he should say while blessing himself:

℣ Adjutorium nostrum in nomine Domini.
℟ Qui fecit cœlum, & terram.
V Sit nomen Domini benedictum.
℟ Ex hoc nunc, & usque in sæculum.
℣ Domine, exaudi orationem meam.
℟ Et clamor meus ad teveniat.
℣ Dominus vobisum.
℟ Et cum spiritu tuo.

Oremus

Preces nostras, quæsumus Domine, clementer exaudi, ut qui justè pro peccatis nostris affligimur, & hanc ærumnam horum animalium (N.N.) & persecutionem patimur, pro tui nominis gloria abe eadem misericorditer liberemur, & procul tuâ potentia expulsa nulli noceant; & hos agros, frutus, vineas, arbores (vel quæcumque alia loca) in tranquillitate dimittant, quatenus ex eis provenientia tuæ maiestati deserviant, & nostræ necessitati absque nocumento subveniant. Per Christum, Dominum nostrum.

Oremus

Omnipotens sempiterne Deus, omnium bonorum remunerator, tuam potentiam nobis concede in afflictionibus constitutis, ut quatenus hos pestiferos vermes, & quæcumque alia animalia in perniciem fructuum, frugum, segetum, aut vinearum huc advecta, nostris supplicationibus inclinatus ab hac regione expellas, extermines, profligas, & à nostris finibus discedere imperes; & per tuam clementiam ab hac peste, & incommodis liberati maiestati tuæ congruas referamus gratiarum actiones. Per Christum, Dominum nostrum.

Oremus

Tribulationem mostram, quæsumus omnipotens Deus, propitius respice, & fructus terræ, quos nobis misericorditer impendisti, conservare, & augere digneris, ut tibi jugiter samulemur, & in bonorum temporalium affluentia gratulemur. Per Christum, Dominum nostrum.

Conjuro vos, vermes, sive animalia (N.N.) &c quæ per maleficium diaboli noxia estis hominibus, & bonis eorum, quæ tritiea, vineas, hortos, montes, lucos, prata, & ripas fluminum, olera fructifera, olivas, & fructus terræ destruitis, & comminuitis, per JESUM Christum Dominum, & Redemptorem nostrum, ut nullo modo noceatis deinceps graminibus, frugibus, vineis, campis, &c sed procul hinc discedatis, & omnis virtus, & potestas nocendi vobis adimatur.

Expulsive precept to demons

Audite dæmones maledicti ultimum meum præceptum vobis factum, & ei illicò obedite. Ego (N.) ut Minister Christi, & Ecclesiæ in nomine Sanctissimæ Trinitatis, Patris, & Filii, & Spiritus Sancti, & in virtute sanctissimi nominis JESU impero vobis, dæmones infernales, siqui hoc malum vermium, aut horum animalium his vineis, campis, &c intulistis, vel per maleficium, aut vestram iniquam virtutem huc adduxistis, ut illicò sine more ab his agris, campis, vineis, pratis, & aquis, &c omne, quod noxium est, amoveatis, & hos vermes, vel hæc animalia discedere faciatis, quæ in primis ego extermino ad quæcumque loca, ubi nullis fructibus usui hominum necessariis nocere possint, & ibi eis pabulum assigno. Discedite ergo animalia nocentia, & vos cum omni vestra malitia, iniqua virtute, aut maleficio, o dæmones infernales; quia sic volo, sic præcipio, sic jubeo, ut Minister Christi, & Ecclesiæ. In nomine Patris, & Filii, & Spiritus Sancti, ac in virtute JESU Christi.

Immediately taking the Cross, and with it blessing the earth, the field, or vine, say:

Ecce Cru✠cem Domini, fugite partes adversæ.

℣Dominus vobiscum.

℟Et cum spiritu tuo.

Oremus

Largire, & conservare fructus terræ dignare, Domine Deus noster, ut temporalibus gaudeamus auxiliis, & spiritualibus proficiamus incrementis. Per Christum, Dominum nostrum.

Oremus

Oramus te, Domine Deus noster, ut hos agros, & vineas serenis oculis, hilarique vultu respicere digneris, tuamque super eos mitte bene✠dictionem, ut non grando surripiat, non turbo subvertat, non vis tempestatis detruncet, non æstus exurat, non animalia noxia corrodant, neque inundation pluviæ exterminet, sed fructus incolumes, uberesque usui nostro ad plenam maturitatem perducas. Per Christum, Dominum nostrum.

Having said these prayers, cast holy water in the form of a Cross to the four corners, saying:

Benedictio Dei omnipontentis, ✠ Patris, ✠ & Filii, & Spiritus ✠ Sancti descendat, & maneat super hos agros, vineas, & fructus. *Amen.*

Exorcism against thunder storms

Per signum ✠ Crucis de inimicis nostris ✠ libera nos, ✠ Deus noster, in nomine Patris, ✠ & Filii, & Spiritus ✠ Sancti. Amen. Christus Rex venit in pace. Et Deus homo factus est. Verbum caro factum est. Christus de Virgine natus est. Christus per medium illorum ibat in pace. Christus crucifixus est. Christus sepultus est. Christus resurrexit. Christus ascendit. Christus imperat. Christus regnat. Christus ab omni fulgure nos defendat. Verbum caro factum est. Christus nobiscum est. Sate.

Ecce signum ✠ sanctissimæ Crucis, fugite partes adversæ : vicit enim vos, & mundum Dominus noster JESUS Christus Filius Dei, Imperator summus, leo de tribu Juda, Radix David.

Sub tuum praesidium
confugimus,
Sancta Dei Genetrix.
Nostras deprecationes ne despicias
in necessitatibus nostris,
sed a periculis cunctis
libera nos semper,
Virgo gloriosa et benedicta.

℣Exurge Christe, adjuva nos.
℟Et libera nos propter nomen tuum.
℣Ora pro nobis sancta Dei Genitrix.
℟Ut digni efficiamur promissionibus Christi.

Oremus

Omnipotens sempiterne Deus, qui dedisti famulis tuis in Confessione veræ fidei æternæ Trinitatis gloriam agnoscere, & in potentia maiestatis adorare unitatem, quæsumus, ut ejusdem fidei firmitate ab omnibus sempre muniamur adversis.

Concede nos famulos tuos, quæsumus Domine Deus, perpetua mentis, & corporis sanitate gaudere, & gloriosa Beatæ MARIÆ sempre Virginis intercessione, à præsenti liberari tristitia, & æterna perfrui lætitia. Per Christum Dominum nostrum. *Amen.*

Antiphon

Veni sponsa Christi accipe coronam quam tibi dominus praeparavit in aeternum Alleluia Alleluia.

℣Specie tua et pulchritudine tua intende prospere procede et regna.

Intercessio nos, quæsumus Domine, Beatæ Barbaræ Virgines, & Martyris tuæ sempre adjuvet, ut non subitò moriamur, sed ante diem mortis nostræ sanctissimi corporis, & salibriter muniamur, & ad omni malo protegamur, & ad cœlestia regna perducamur. Qui cum Patre & Spiritu Sancto vivit & regnat Deus per omnia secula. *Amen.*

Afterwards say the Litany of the Saints.

Exorcism, and blessing for sick animals

℣Adjutorium nostrum in nomine Domini.
℟Qui fecit cœlum, & terram.
℣Dominus vobiscum.
℟Et cum spiritu tuo.

Oremus

Misericordiam tuam, Domine, suplices exoramus, ut hæc animalia, quæ gravi infirmitate vexantur, tua bene✠dictione sanentur; extinguatur in eis omnis diabolica potestas, nec ulterius ægrotent; esto eis vitæ defesion, & remedium sanitatis. Exorcizo, & signo ✠ vos in nomine JESU Christi Nazareni Domini nostri, & Redemptoris, & salvo vos ab omnibus infirmitatibus vestris, & doloribus, & veniat super vos sanitas perfecta. *Amen.*

Oremus

Deus, qui laboranibus hominibus etiam de mutis animalibus solatia subrogasti, supplices te rogamus, ut sine quibus non alitur humana conditio, nostris facias usibus non perire. Per Christum, Dominum nostrum.

Exorcism in benefit of marriage, for those who are bound by sorcery

In nomine Sanctissimæ, & individuæ Trinitatis, Patris, ✠ & Filii, ✠ & Spiritus ✠ Sancti conjuro vos omnes dæmones tam absentes, quam præsentes, per eum, qui vos ejecit de superno Cœlorum habitaculo, qui fertis malum contra genus humanum, & fabricastis, & conservastis malum, & maleficum huic creaturæ Dei (N.) à maléfico, *seu* maléfica procuratum, vel aliquo alio modo illi inflictum, ut ubicumque illud sit positum statim, & sine more ab illo loco amoveatis, & in virtute Dei Omnipotentis illud destruatis, & omne impedimentum illi injectum, festinater ad nihilum redigatis, ut libere, & sine difficultate matrimonio uti possit, ad honorem Dei Omnipotentis, qui illum creavit, & matrimonialiter eum conjunxit. In nomine Patris, ✠ & Filii, ✠ & Spiritus ✠ Sancti. *Amen.*

Sprinkle holy water in a Cross, and say:

Iterum, atque iterum conjuro vos, ✠ dæmones infernales, in quacumque mundi parte sitis, & habitatis, quibus data est potestas fascinandi, & maleficiendi corpus istius creaturæ Dei nostri, & ipsum impediendi ab usu legitimo matrimonii, per Patrem, ✠ & Filium, ✠ & Spiritum ✠ Sanctum, & per Jesum Christum Filium Dei potentissimi, Creatoris omnium, qui omnia ex nihilo creavit : vos constringo, & cogo, ut non habeatis potestatem conservandi, quandocumque maleficium, ligaturam, facturam, & incantationem arte diabolica, à quovis malefico, vel malefica fabricatam, & illi inflictam, & vobis præcipio, ut non obstante, quocumque pacto tacito, vel expresso, in virtute ejusdem Dei Omnipotentis omnia maleficia destruatis, & ad nihilum illa redigatis, non obstantibus quibuscumque conventionibus, & pactis inter vos, & maleficum, seu magma initis ad impediendum hunc famulum Dei (N.) ab usu legitimo matrimonii. Quod si more vestro bestiali, præceptis meis vobis in virtute Dei factis, obedire contempseritis, auctoritate, & in virtute Dei Omnipotentis, & Domini nostri Jesu Christi, præcipio Lucifero, & omnibus spiritbus, & sulphuris, vos præcipitent, ligent, & acrius, ac durius solito, vos excruciet, & omnibu pœnis vos affligant in sæcula sæculorum. *Amen.*

Extinguatur in te (N.) omnis virtus diabolica per impositionem manuum mearum, & per invocationem omnium Sanctorum Angelorum, Archangelorum, Patriarcharum, Prophetarum, Apostolorum, Martyrum, Confessorum, ac Virginum, & omnium simul Sanctorum in nomine Patris, ✠ & Filli, ✠ & Spiritus ✠ Sancti. *Amen.*

Anoint with blessed oil, and sprinkle, and bless the quarter, bed, clothes and food.

Exorcism against roundworms

Potestas Dei Pa✠tris, Sapientia Dei Fi✠lii, & virtus Spiritus ✠ Sancti liberet, & sanet te, creatura Dei, ab infirmitate lumbricorum. *Amen.*

In nomine Jesu Christi Nazareni con✠juro vos, ascarides, seu lumbricos, ut conversi in aquam recedatis à corpora isto in honorem Dei, & devotionem S. Antonii de Padua, qui oret pro nobis. *Amen.*

Per signum Sanctæ ✠ Crucis, quo signo te, efficiaris sana ab omni infirmitate, & vermes isti procul moriantur, & exeant à corpore tuo, ut in Domino gaudentes dicamus : Dum appropiant super te nucentes, ipsi infirati sunt, & ceciderunt.

℟ Si quæris miracula, mors, error, calamitas, dæmon, lepra fugiunt, ægri surgunt sani.

Cedunt mare, vincula, membra, resque perditas petunt, & accipiunt juvenes, & cani.

℣ Pereunt pericula, cessat & necessitas, narrent hi, qui sentiunt, dicant Paduani.

Cedunt mare, vincula, membra, resque perditas, petunt, & accipiunt juvenes, & cani.

Gloria Patri, & Filio, & Spiritui sancto, sicut erat in principio, & nunc, & semper & in sæcula sæculorum. *Amen.*

Cedunt mare, vincula, membra, resque perditas petunt, & accipiunt juvenes, & cani.

Antiphon

Ò lingua benedicta, quæ Dominum sempre benedixisti, & alios benedicere fecisti, nunc manifestè apparet, quanti meriti extitisti apud Deum.

℣Ora pro nobis Beate Antoni.

℟Ut digni effiamur promissionibus Christi.

Oremus

Ecclesiam tuam, Deus, Beati Antonii Confessoris tui deprecatio votiva lætificet, ut spiritualibus sempre muniatur auxiliis, & gaudiis perfrui mereatur æternis. Per Christum Dominum nostrum. *Amen.*

Holy Offices

OFFICE OF THE IMMACULATE CONCEPTION OF THE VIRGIN MARY OUR LADY CONCEIVED WITHOUT ORIGINAL SIN

MATINS

Now, my lips,
Say, and announce
The great praise
Of the Virgin Mother of God.
Be in my favour,
Sovereign virgin,
Free me from the enemy
With thy valour.

Glory be to the Father, the Son,
And to Love also,
Who is one single God,
And three persons,
Now, and forever,
And without end. *Amen.*

Hymn

God save thee Virgin,
Lady of the World,
Queen of the Heavens,
And Virgin of virgins.
Star of the morning,
God save thee full
Of divine grace,
Beautiful, and elegant.
Give privileges, Lady
In favour of the world,
For it recognizes thee,
As its defender.
God nominated thee
Already in the ab æterno
As Mother of the Word,
With which he created
Earth, sea, and Heavens,
And he chose thee
As wife of God.
God chose her,
Already from long ago
In his tabernacle
A home he gave her.
Hear, Mother of God,
My prayer,
May thy chest be touched
By my clamours.

Prayer

Holy Mary, Queen of the Heavens, Mother of our Lord JESUS Christ, Lady of the World, who doesn't abandon or despise any sinner : place, Lady, the eye of thy mercy on me, and reach for me from thy beloved Son the forgiveness of all my sins, so as I, who now venerates with devotion thy immaculate conception, may deserve to, in the other life, reach the prize of blessing by the worth of thy most blessed Son JESUS Christ our

Lord, who with the Father and the Holy Spirit lives, and reigns forever. *Amen.*

PRIME

Be in my favour,
Sovereign Virgin,
Free me from the enemy
With thy valour.
Glory be to the Father, the Son,
And to Love also,
Who is one single God,
And three people,
Now, and forever,
And without end. *Amen.*

Hymn

God save thee, Table
Adorned for God,
Sacred column
Of great firmness.
Dedicated House
Of the eternal God,
Always kept,
Virgin, from sin.
Before birth,
Thou wert, a Holy Virgin,
In the blessed womb
Of Anne conceived.
Thou art the creating
Mother
Of the living mortals:
Thou art the door of the Saints,
The lady of the Angles.
Thou art a strong squadron
Against the enemy,
Star of Jacob,
Refuge of the Christians.
The Virgin created him,
God in the Holy Spirit,
And all his works
With her he adorned them.
Hear, Mother of God,
My prayer,
May thy chest be touched
By my clamours.

Prayer

Holy Mary, Queen of the Heavens, *as above.*

TERCE

Be in my favour,
Sovereign Virgin,
Free me from the enemy
With thy valour.
Glory be to the Father, the Son,
And to Love also,
Who is one single God,
And three persons,
Now, and forever,
And without end. *Amen.*

Hymn

God save thee, Throne
Of the great Solomon,
Ark of the Covenant,
Veil of Gideon.
Clear Iris of Heaven,
Bush of vision,
Honeycomb of Samson,
Blossoming rod,
Which was chosen
To be his Mother,
And from thee was born,
The Son of God.
And thus freed us
From original sin,

Of no sin
Is there a sign in thee.
Thou who inhabits
There in those heights,
Thou has thy throne
Above the pure clouds.
Hear, Mother of God,
My prayer,
May thy chest be touched
By my clamours.

Prayer

Holy Mary, Queen of the Heavens, *as above.*

SEXT

Be in my favour,
Sovereign Virgin,
Free me from the enemy
With thy valour.
Glory be to the Father, the Son,
And to Love also,
Who is one single God,
And three persons,
Now, and forever,
And without end. *Amen.*

Hymn

God save thee, Virgin,
Temple of the Trinity,
Joy of the Angels,
Example of purity.
Who brings joy to the sad
With thy clemency,
Garden of delights,
Palm of patience.
Thou art blessed earth,
And a priest,
Thou art of chastity
Royal symbol,
City of the Most High,
Oriental Gate,
Thou art the same grace,
Singular Virgin.
As a scented lily
Among hard thorns,
Thou art as such, Lady,
Among the creatures.
Hear, Mother of God,
My prayer,
May thy chest be touched
By my clamours.

Prayer

Holy Mary, Queen of the Heavens, *as above.*

NONE

Be in my favour,
Sovereign Virgin,
Free me from the enemy
With thy valour.
Glory be to the Father, the Son,
And to Love also,
Who is one single God,
And three persons,
Now, and forever,
And without end. *Amen.*

Hymn

God save thee, City
With towers garrisoned,
With the arms of David
Well fortified.
Of supreme charity
Always ablaze,
The strength of the Dragon
Was frustrated by thee.
O powerful woman,
O undefeated Judith,

Who supported
The great David.
Healer of Egypt
Born of Rachel,
Saviour of the World
Mary gave him to us.
Thou art all beautiful,
My companion,
In thee there is no sin
Of the original one.
Hear, Mother of God,
My prayer,
May thy chest be touched
By my clamours.

Prayer

Holy Mary, Queen of the Heavens, *as above.*

VESPERS

Be in my favour,
Sovereign Virgin,
Free me from the enemy
With thy valour.
Glory be to the Father, the Son,
And to Love also,
Who is one single God,
And three persons,
Now, and forever,
And without end. *Amen.*

Hymn

God save thee, Clock,
Who running late,
Served as a sign
To the Word incarnate,
So as man may rise
To the supreme heights,
God comes down from Heaven
For the creatures.
With the clear rays
Of the Son of Justice
The Virgin is splendorous,
Making the Son envious.
Thou art a beautiful lily,
Who exhales scent
Among the thorns:
Of the serpent of wrath
Thou broke it
With thy power,
The lost blind
Thou enlightened
Thou made born
Such a fertile Son,
And as a cloud
Thou covered the world
Hear, Mother of God,
My prayer,
May thy chest be touched
By my clamours.

Prayer

Holy Mary, Queen of the Heavens, *as above.*

COMPLINE

Be in my favour,
Sovereign Virgin,
Free me from the enemy
With thy valour.
Glory be to the Father, the Son,
And to Love also,
Who is one single God,
And three persons,
Now, and forever,
And without end. *Amen.*

Hymn

God save thee, Virgin,
Immaculate Mother,
Queen of clemency,
Crowned with stars.
Thou above the Angels
Art purified,
At God's right hand
Thou art adorned with gold.
For thee, Mother of grace,
May we deserve to see
God in the heights
With all pleasure.
For thou art the hope
Of the poor lost,
And Safe haven
Of sailors.
Star of the Sea,
And certain health,
And door, who is
Open to Heaven.
It is shed oil,
Virgin, thy name,
And thy servants
Have always loved thee.
Hear, Mother of God,
My prayer,
May thy chest be touched
By my clamours.

Prayer

Holy Mary, Queen of the Heavens, *as above.*
Humbly we offer
To thee, pious Virgin,
These prayers,
So as on our guide
May thou go in front,
And in agony
Thou may give us spirit,
O Sweet Mary. *Amen.*

OFFICE OF THE GLORIOUS PATRIARCH ST. JOSEPH

MATINS

Open my lips,
Divine Lord,
My mouth shall say
Thy great praises.
Be my aid,
Almighty God,
In saving me
Be diligent.

Glory be to the Father, the Son,
And to Love also,
Who is one single God,
And three persons,
Now, and forever,
And without end. *Amen.*

Hymn

Joseph of the noble lineage
Of David generated,
And of JESUS Christ
The beloved Father.

Given as husband
To the sacred Virgin,
From Heaven destined
As her guard.

Antiphon

Thou, Saints, honoured
The Patriarchs,
For the bread of life
Thou conserved it.
Pray for us,
O blessed Joseph,
So as we may be worthy
Of the Promises of Christ. *Amen.*

Prayer

We ask thee, Lord, humbly, that we may deserve to be aided by the worth of the sacred husband of the Virgin thy Mother, so as that which our possibilities do not reach, may be conceded to us by his intercessions. God who lives, and reigns with the Father, and Holy Spirit forever. *Amen.*

PRIME

Jesus, Mary, Joseph
Be my aid,
Almighty God,
In saving me
Be diligent.
Glory be to the Father, the Son,
And to Love also,
Who is one single God,
And three persons,
Now, and forever,
And without end. *Amen.*

Hymn

Blessed, and sacred Joseph,
Who seeing expecting

Thy beloved wife,
Suspended, and disturbed.
With this care,
Thou could not come,
To give her, or deny her
Thy sacred side.
In this agony
The sacred Angel
Announced to thee
News of joy.

Antiphon

Thou, Saints, honoured
The Patriarchs, *as above.*

Prayer

We ask thee, Lord, *as above.*

TERCE

Jesus, Mary, Joseph
Be my aid,
Almighty God,
In saving me
Be diligent.
Glory be to the Father, the Son,
And to Love also,
Who is one single God,
And three persons,
Now, and forever,
And without end. *Amen.*

Hymn

Saint, who on the journey
To Bethlehem went
To pay the offer
With the expecting Virgin,
Where would be born
The Lord of the world,
Who in thy arms
Took refuge.

Antiphon

Thou, Saints, honoured
The Patriarchs, *as above.*

Prayer

We ask thee, Lord, *as above.*

SEXT

Jesus, Mary, Joseph
Be my aid,
Almighty God,
In saving me
Be diligent.
Glory be to the Father, the Son,
And to Love also,
Who is one single God,
And three persons,
Now, and forever,
And without end. *Amen.*

Hymn

When in Herod
The great wrath
Against the Innocent
Was greatly lit.
Thou being warned
By the blessed Angel,
With Christ, and the Virgin
Fled Egypt.

Antiphon

Thou, Saints, honoured
The Patriarchs, *as above.*

Prayer

We ask thee, Lord, *as above.*

NONE

Jesus, Mary, Joseph
Be my aid,
Almighty God,
In saving me
Be diligent.
Glory be to the Father, the Son,
And to Love also,
Who is one single God,
And three persons,
Now, and forever,
And without end. *Amen.*

Hymn

Dead the enemies,
From there thou left
For Galilee,
And thou also took.

The baby Jesus,
And the holy Virgin,
And in Nazareth
Thou made a home.

Antiphon

Thou, Saints, honoured
The Patriarchs, *as above.*

Prayer

We ask thee, Lord, *as above.*

VESPERS

Jesus, Mary, Joseph
Be my aid,
Almighty God,
In saving me
Be diligent.
Glory be to the Father, the Son,
And to Love also,
Who is one single God,
And three persons,
Now, and forever,
And without end. *Amen.*

Hymn

Saint, who lost
The beloved child,
And among the Doctors
Was found by thee.

Being of the age
Of twelve years;
And then thou kept him
With the greatest care.

Antiphon

Thou, Saints, honoured
The Patriarchs, *as above.*

Prayer

We ask thee, Lord, *as above.*

COMPLINE

Jesus, Mary, Joseph
Be my aid,
Almighty God,
In saving me
Be diligent.
Glory be to the Father, the Son,
And to Love also,
Who is one single God,
And three persons,
Now, and forever,
And without end. *Amen.*

Hymn

O famed Saint,
Who deserved
To die in the arms
Of the merciful Jesus.
And of the pious Virgin,
From where thou left
To enjoy the glory
For joyful ages.

Antiphon

Thou, Saints, honoured
The Patriarchs, *as above.*

Prayer

We ask thee, Lord, *as above.*

Recommendation

These prayers
With good intent
I said, O Saint Joseph,
For thy intercession.
So as thou remembers
Me up in Heaven,
And we may live together
In the glory with God
Our Lord. *Amen.*

Prayer, and offering as a slave

O Holiest Joseph, my Father, and Lord, humbling myself before thy feet with body and soul, I humbly ask thee by the love of Jesus, and Mary, that thou receives me as thy slave, even if unworthy, that I offer myself as such with all my will, renouncing any freedom, which I may have had until this day, for I no longer wish to be my own, but rather thine, as I am of Jesus, and Mary, so as in this way I may have all three in my heart, as the Trinity of the earth, which I, even if miserable, in this life with thy consideration hope, by thy intercession, to see Heaven, where I may eternally enjoy, and praise Jesus, Mary, and Joseph. *Amen.*

Various Blessings

Way of blessing water, for sprinkling

℣Adjutorium nostrum in nomine Domini.
℟Qui fecit cœlum, & terram.
℣Dominus vobiscum.
℟Et cum spiritu tuo.

Exorcism of salt

Exorcizo te, creatura salis per Deum vivum, ✠ per Deum verum, ✠ per Deum Sanctum, ✠ per Deum, que te per Eliseum Prophetam in aquam mitti jussit, ut sanaretur sterilitas aquæ, ut efficiaris sal exorcizatum in salutem credentium, & sis omnibus sumentibus te sanitas animæ, & corporis, & effugiat, atque discedat à loco, in quo aspersum fueris, omnis phantasia, & nequitia, vel versutia diabolicæ fraudis, omnisque spiritus immundus adjuratus per eum, qui venturus est judicare vivos, & mortuos, & sæculum per ignem. *Amen.*

Oremus

Immensam clementiam tuam omnipotens æterne Deus humiliter imploramus, ut hanc creaturam salis, quam in usum generis humani tribuisti, bene✠dicere, & sancti✠ficare tua pietate digneris : ut sit omnibus sumentibus salus mentis, & corporis, & quidquid ex eo tactum, vel respersum fuerit, careat omni immunditia, omnique immunditione spiritalis nequitiæ. Per Dominum nostrum Jesum Christum, Filium tuum : qui tecum vivit & regnat in unitate Spiritus Sancti Deus, per omnia sæcula sæculorum. *Amen.*

Exorcism of water

Exorcizo te, creatura aquæ, in nomine Dei Patris ✠ omnipotentis, & in nomine JESU Christi ✠ Filii ejus Domini nostri, & in virtute Spiritus Sancti, ✠ ut fias aqua exorcizata ad effugandam omnem potestatem inimici, & ipsum inimicum eradicare, & explantare valeas cum angelis suis apostaticis : per virtutem ejusdem Domini nostri JESU Christi, qui venturus est judicare vivos, & mortuos, & sæculum per ignem. *Amen.*

Oremus

Deus, qui ad salutem humani generis, maxima quæque sacramenta in aquarum substantia condidisti : adesto propitius invocationibus nostris, & elemento huic multimodis purificationibus præparato virtutem tuæ bene✠dictionis infunde, ut creatura tua mysteriis tuis serviens, ad abigendos dæmones, morbosque pellendos divinæ gratiæ sumat effectum, ut quidquid in domibus, vel in locis fidelium hæc unda respexerit, careat omni immunditia, liberetur à noxa : non illic resideat spiritus pestilens, non aura corrumpens : discedant omnes insidiæ latentis inimici; & siquid est, quod, aut incolumitati habitantium invidet, aut quieti, per invocationem sancti nominis tui expetita, ab omnibus sit impugnationibus defensa. Per Dominum nostrum Jesum Christum, Filium tuum : qui tecum vivit & regnat in unitate Spiritus Sancti Deus, per omnia sæcula sæculorum.

Cast the salt into the water three times in the form of a Cross while saying this prayer.

Comistio salis, & aquæ pariter fiat in nomine Patris, ✠ & Filii, ✠ & Spiritus ✠ Sancti. *Amen.*

℣Dominus vobiscum.

℟Et cum spiritu tuo.

Oremus

Deus invictæ virtutis Author, & insuperabilis Imperii Rex, ac semper magnificus triumphator, qui adversæ dominationis vires reprimis : qui inimici rugientes sævitiam superas : te Domini trementes, & suplices deprecamur, ac petimus, ut lanc creaturam salis, & aquæ dignanter aspicias, benignus ilustres, pietatis tuæ rore sanctifices, ut ubicumque fuerit aspersa, per invocationem sancti nominis tui omnis infestatio immundi spiritus abigatur, terrorque venenosi serpentis procul pellatur, & præsentiæ Sancti Spiritus nobis misericordiam tuam poscentibus adesse dignetur. Per Dominum nostrum Jesum Christum, Filium tuum : qui tecum vivit et regnat & unitate Spiritus Sancti Deus, per omnia sæcula sæculorum. *Amen.*

Blessing of the place, or house of the infirm

℣Adjutorium nostrum in nomine Domini.

℟Qui fecit cœlum, & terram.

℣Dominus vobiscum.

℟Et cum spiritu tuo.

Oremus

Benedic ✠ Domine Deus omnipotens locum istum, & domum istam, ut sit in eis sanitas, castitas, victoria, virtus, humilitas, bonitas, & mansuetudo, plenitudo legis, expulsio diaboli, & gratiarum actio Deo

Patri, & Filio, & Spiritui Sancto, & hæc benedictio maneat sempre super hunc locum, & super habitantes in eo, nunc, & sempre.

℟Amen.

Sprinkle the holy water in the entire house, saying.

Asperges me, Domine, hyssopo & mundabor,
Lavabis me, & super nivem dealbabor.
Miserere mei, Deus, secundum magnam misericordiam tuam.
Gloria Patri et Filio & Spiritui Sancto
Sicut erat in principio, & nunc, et semper, & in sæcula sæculorum. *Amen.*

Blessing of the bed

℣Adjutorium nostrum in nomine Domini.
℟Qui fecit cœlum, & terram.
℣Dominus vobiscum.
℟Et cum spiritu tuo.

Oremus

Benedic ✠ Domine thalamum hunc, ut recumbens in eo, in tua pace consistat, & in tua voluntate permaneat, & sanescat, & liberetur à diabolo, & ad regna Cœlorum perveniat. Per Christum, Dominum nostrum.

Sprinkle the bed with the holy water.

Blessing of a new house

Oremus

Te Deum Patrem omnipotentem suppliciter exoramus pro hac domo, & pro habitatoribus ejus, ac rebus, ut eam bene✠dicere, & sancti✠ficare, ac bonis omnibus ampliare digneris : tribue eis, Domine, de rore Cœli abundantiam, & de pinguedine terræ vitæ substantiam, & desideria voci eorum ad effectum tuæ miserationis perducas. Ad introitum ergo nostrum bene✠dicere, & sancti✠ficare digneris hanc domum, sicut benedicere dignatus es domum Abraham, & Isaac, & Jacob; & intra parietes domus istius Angeli tui lucis inhabitent, eamque, & ejus habitatores custodiant. Per Christum Dominum nostrum.

℟Amen.

Sprinkle the holy water.

Blessing of the quarter, in which the sick sleeps, and the new house, and that which is thought to be disturbed by the Devil

℣Adjutorium nostrum in nomine Domini.
℟Qui fecit cœlum, & terram.
℣Dominus vobiscum.
℟Et cum spiritu tuo.

Oremus

Omnipotens sempiterne Deus, qui Sacerdotibus tuis præ cæteris tantam gratiam contulisti, ut, quidquid in tuo nomine ab eis agitur, à te fieri credatur : quæsumus immensam clementiam tuam, ut hanc domum, quam modò visitaturi sumus, visites, & bene✠dicas, fiatque Sanctorum tuorum meritis fuga dæmonum, & Angeli pacis ingressus. Per Dominum nostrum Jesum Christum, Filium tuum : qui tecum vivit & regnat in unitate Spiritus Sancti Deus, per omnia sæcula sæculorum.

Oremus

Bene✠dic, Domine Deus Omniptens, locum istum, & hæc bene✠dictio supere eum maneat, & super habitantes in eo. Angeli tui lucis eum inhabitent, eumque & ejus habitatores custodiant, & defendant contra omnes insidias inimici : & siqua adversa, & contraria sunt ab eo in hoc loco machinata, & fabricata, auctoritate majestatis tuæ expellantur. Per Christum Dominum nostrum.

Oremus

Domine Sancte, Pater Omnipotens, Æterne Deus, per merita Sanctorum tuorum bene✠dic domum istam, sicut dignatus es benedicere domum Patrum nostrorum Abraham, Isaac, & Jacob, & aliorum Sanctorum tuorum in lege gratiæ. Per Dominum nostrum Jesum Christum, Filium tuum : qui tecum vivit & regnat in unitate Spiritus Sancti Deus, per omnia sæcula sæculorum.

Oremus

Domine Jesu Christe, qui dixisti Apostolis tuis : In quamcumque domum intraveritis, salutate eam dicentes : Pax huic domui : quæsumus, & humiliter deprecamur, ut veniat Angelus pacis super domum istam, & super omnes famulos, & famulas tuas, & exterminetur diabolus ab ea, ut quietè vivant, qui is ea habitant, & habitaturi sunt, eisque salutem, & æternam gloriam concede. Qui vivis, & regnas in sæcula sæculorum.

Oremus

Bene✠dic, Domine, domum istam, ut sit in ea sanitas, sanctitas, & pax, & plenitudo tuæ Divinæ Legis, & benedictio tua larga descendat super omnes habitantes in ea. Per Christum Dominum nostrum.

Sancti Angeli Dei descendant in hanc domum, eamque defedant, & protegant ab omnibus dæmonibus, & spiritibus malignis per pietatem Dei, & per infinita merita Domini nostri Jesu Christi, qui vivit, & regnat in sæcula sæculorum. *Amen.*

Oremus

Conserva, Domine, domum istam sempre impollutam, & à spiritibus immundis flagellantibus, & conturbantibus libera eam. Sanctificet, & bene✠dicat hoc habitaculum Sanctissima Virgo Maria, quam deprecamur, ut à domo ista repellat omnes diaboli insidias : & nunquam in posterum fiant is ea peccata, vel maleficia, sed omnia opera diaboli destruantur, &

deficiant in ea. Per Dominum nostrum Jesum Christum, Filium tuum : qui tecum vivit & regnat in unitate Spiritus Sancti Deus, per omnia sæcula sæculorum.

Oremus

Concede, misericors Deus, per tuam bonitatem, ut hæc domus sit bene✠dicta à tua sancta dextera : & ab ea dæmones fugiant confusi, nec ullo modo possint stare, nec latere, vel die, vel nocte, ut omnes habitantes in ea securi sint, & quiescant in pace, sine turbatione, strepitu, & sine aliquo nocumento diabolico; sed tua bene✠dictio sit super hanc domum, & super omnes habitantes in ea. Per Dominum nostrum Jesum Christum, Filium tuum : qui tecum vivit & regnat in unitate Spiritus Sancti Deus, per omnia sæcula sæculorum. *Amen.*

Pax, & bene✠dictio copiosa Sanctissimæ Trinitatis, Beatissimæ Virginis Mariæ, & Sancti Ubaldi descendant super domum hanc, ut habitantes in ea possint devotè orare, quiescere, vivere, & alia opera sancta sine perturbatione facere, & liberè exercere. Per Dominum nostrum Jesum Christum, Filium tuum : qui tecum vivit & regnat in unitate Spiritus Sancti Deus, per omnia sæcula sæculorum. *Amen.*

Sprinkle the holy water in all quarters.

Blessing of Crosses

℣Adjutorium nostrum in nomine Domini.
℟Qui fecit cœlum, & terram.
℣Dominus vobiscum.
℟Et cum spiritu tuo.

Oremus

Rogamus te, Domine Sancte, Pater Omnipotens, Æterne Deus, ut digneris bene✠dicere hoc signum Crucis : ut sit remedium salutare generi humano, sit soliditas Fidei profectus bonorum operum, redemptio animarum; sit solamen, & protectio, ac tutela contra sæva jacula inimicorum. Per Christum Dominum nostrum. *Amen.*

Oremus

Ben✠dic, Domine, hanc Crucem tuam, per quam eripuisti mundum à dæmonum potestate, & superasti Passione tua suggestorem peccati, qui gaudebat in prævaricatione primi hominis per ligni vetiti sumptionem, (*cast the holy water as a Cross, and say:*) santificetur hoc signum Crucis in nomine Pa✠tris, & Fi✠lii, & Spiritus ✠ Sancti, ut orantes, inclinantesque se propter te, Domine, ante istam Crucem, inveniant corporis, & animaæ sanctitatem. Qui vivis, & regnas in sæcula sæculorum. *Amen.*

Once the Blessing is finished, the Priest should worship the Cross, and devoutly kiss it, and offer it to be kissed by all other people present.

Blessing for images

℣ Adjutorium nostrum in nomine Domini.
℟ Qui fecit cœlum, & terram.
℣ Dominus vobiscum.
℟ Et cum spiritu tuo.

Oremus

Omnipotens sempiterne Deus majestatem tuam suppliciter exoramus, ut iconem hanc, in qua gloriosissimæ imagines tuæ, & Filii tui Domini nostri JESU Christi, gloriosæque Virginis MARIÆ, aliorumque Sanctorum (N. & N.) depictæ sunt, bene✠dicere, & sancti✠ficare digneris, ante quam quicumque ob devotionem se ad ipsam devote adorandam inclinaverint, salutem mentis, & corporis consequantur, & à cunctis periculis liberentur, & quidquid justè petierint, obtinere mereantur. Per aumdem Dominum nostrum Jesum Christum.

Sprinkle the holy water.

Blessing of new fruit

℣ Adjutorium nostrum in nomine Domini.
℟ Qui fecit cœlum, & terram.
℣ Dominus vobiscum.
℟ Et cum spiritu tuo.

Oremus

Bene✠dic, Domine, hos novos fructus, (N.) & præsta, ut qui ex eis in tuo sancto nomine vescerentur, corporis, & animæ salute potiantur. Per Christum, Dominum nostrum.

Sprinkle the holy water.

Blessing for bread

℣ Adjutorium nostrum in nomine Domini.
℟ Qui fecit cœlum, & terram.
℣ Dominus vobiscum.
℟ Et cum spiritu tuo.

Oremus

Domine JESU Christe, panis Angelorum, panis vivus æternæ vitæ, bene✠dicere dignare panem istum, sicut benedixisti quinque panes in deserto, ut omnes ex eo gustantes, inde corporis, & animæ percipiant sanitatem. Qui vivis, & regnas, Deus per omnia sæcula sæculorum.

Sprinkle the holy water.

Blessing of boats, and ships

℣Adjutorium nostrum in nomine Domini.
℟Qui fecit cœlum, & terram.
℣Dominus vobiscum.
℟Et cum spiritu tuo.

Oremus

Propitiare, Domine, supplicationibus nostris, & bene✠dic navem istam dextera tua sancta, & omnes, que in ea vehentur, sicut dignatus es benedicere arcam Noe ambulantem in diluvio. Porrige eis, Domine, dexteram tuam, sicut porrexiste Beat Petro ambulante supre mare, & mitte sanctum Angelum tuum de Cœlis, qui liberet, & custodiat sempre eam ab universis periculis cum omnibus, quæ in ea erunt; & famulos tuos, repulsis adversitatibus, portu sempre optabili, cursuque tranquillo tuearis, transactisque rectè, retèque perfectis negotiis omnibus, iterato tempore ad propria cum gaudio revocare digneris. Qui vivis, & regnas, Deus per omnia sæcula sæculorum.

Sprinkle the holy water.

Blessing of wine, water, or any other drink for the infirm bewitched

℣Adjutorium nostrum in nomine Domini.
℟Qui fecit cœlum, & terram.
℣Dominus vobiscum.
℟Et cum spiritu tuo.

Exorcizo te, ✠ creatura aquæ, vini, &c. per eum, qui in Cana Galileæ aquam in vinum convertir, ut nulla communicatio sit tibi cum spiritibus maledictis, sed fias potus optimus, & sanctus ad sanadas creaturas quascumque ex te bibentes, ab omnibus maleficiis, incantationibus, ligationibus, signaturis, facturis, febribus, infestationibus, perturbationibus, & ab omnibus infirmitatibus animæ, & corporis. Per ipsum Jesum Christum Dominum nostrum. *Amen.*

Oremus

Domine Deus, Pater omnipotens, statutor omnium elementorum, qui per JESUM Christum Filium tuum Dominum nostrum substantiam hanc in refocilationem sitis, & corporum salutem esse voluisti : te supplices deprecamur, ut exauditis orationibus nostris, eam tuæ pietatis aspectus sanctifices, ✠ ac benedicas, ✠ quam ego in nomine JESU benedico, ✠ & sanctifico, ✠ atque ita omnium spirituum immundorum ab hac recedat incursio, ut quicumque ex ea sumpserit, ei gratia tuæ benedictionis adveniat, & mala omnia, te propitiante, ab eo procul recedent. Per aumdem Dominum nostrum Jesum Christum.

Sprinkle the holy water.

Blessing for food, drink, or medicine for any infirm

℣Adjutorium nostrum in nomine Domini.
℟Qui fecit cœlum, & terram.
℣Dominus vobiscum.
℟Et cum spiritu tuo.

Oremus

Bene✠dic, Domine, hanc escam (*potum, seu medicinam*) benedictione sancta tua : ut sit omnibus utentibus ea salus mentis, & corporis, & contra omnes morbos, atque universas insidias inimicorum tutamen, & salutare remedium, tantamque virtutem per signaculum Sanctæ ✠ Crucis, & benedictionem recipiat, ut omnes infirmitates, & dolores sanet, spiritus malignos repellat, maleficiaque omnia dissolval. Per Christum Dominum nostrum. *Amen.*

Sprinkle the holy water.

Blessing of the vestments of Priests and Nuns

℣Adjutorium nostrum in nomine Domini.
℟Qui fecit cœlum, & terram.
℣Dominus vobiscum.
℟Et cum spiritu tuo.

Oremus

Domine JESU Christe, qui tegumen nostræ mortalitatis induere dignatus es : obsecramus immensæ largitatis tuæ abundantiam, ut hoc genus vestimentorum, quod sancti Patres ad innocentiæ, & humilitatis indicium ferre sanxerunt, ita bene✠dicere dignare : ut qui hoc usus fuerit, te induere mereatur Christum Dominum.

Sprinkle the holy water.

Blessing of paper, and holy words, which are written in this

℣Adjutorium nostrum in nomine Domini.
℟Qui fecit cœlum, & terram.
℣Dominus vobiscum.
℟Et cum spiritu tuo.

Oremus

Domine Deus Omnipotens, bonarum virtutum dator, & omnium benedictionum largus insusor, suplices te rogamus, ut manibus nostris opem tuæ bene✠dictionis infundas, & hanc chartam tantam obtineat virtutem, ut omnia, quæ in illa scribentur, ad effectum salutis æternæ perducere valeant, & omnis fallacia, & virtus diaboli exeat ad illa; & caracteres, ac litteras in ea positas ad abigendos dæmones, morbosque pellendos virtute Spiritus Sancti bene✠dicere digneris : & omnibus eis utentibus, & secum portantibus concede, ut in conspecto tuo sancti, & immaculati, atque irreprehensibiles appareant, omnesque infirmitates, & insidias diaboli latentis, per auxilium misericordiæ tuæ ab eis fugiantur. Per Christum Dominum nostrum. *Amen.*

Sprinkle the holy water.

Blessing of seeds for sowing

℣Adjutorium nostrum in nomine Domini.
℟Qui fecit cœlum, & terram.
℣Dominus vobiscum.
℟Et cum spiritu tuo.

Oremus

Omnipotens sempiterne Deus, Creator generis humani, humiliter, & devotè exoramus clementiam tuam, ut hoc semen, quod in tuo Sanctissimo Nomine saturi sumus in agris nostris, bene✠dicere, & multiplicare, atque ad maturitatem perducere digneris, ut per universum mundum laudetur dextera tua. Per Christum Dominum nostrum. *Amen.*

Sprinkle the holy water.

Blessing of the cord Saint Thomas Aquinas in order to preserve chastity[132]

℣Adjutorium nostrum in nomine Domini.
℟Qui fecit Cœlum, & terram.
℣Sit nomen Domini benedictum.
℟Ex hoc nunc, & usque in sæculum.
℣Domine exaudi orationem meam.
℟Et clamor meus ad te veniat.
℣Dominus vobiscum.
℟Et cum spiritu tuo.

Oremus

Domine JESU Christe, Fili Dei vivi, puritatis amator, & custos, obsecramus immensam clementiam tuam, ut sicut ministerio Angelorum Sanctum Thomam Aquinatem cingulo castitatis cingere, & à labe corporis, & animæ præservare fecisti : ita ad honorem, & gloriam ejus bene✠dicere, & sanctificare digneris cingula ista, ut quicumque ipsa circa renes reverenter portaverit, ac tenuerit, ab omni immunditia mentis, & corporis purificetur, atque in exitu suo per manus Sanctorum Angelorum tibi dignè præsentari mereatur. Qui cum Patre & Spiritu Sancto vivit & regnat Deus per omnia secula. *Amen.*

---

132 Translator's note: the cord of the 'Confraternity of the Cord of Saint Thomas', another of the 'Confraternities of the Cord'. This particular cords contains fifteen knots, and a devotee should pray fifteen daily Hail Marys with it.

Sprinkle the holy water.

Blessing of the Cord of Our Father Saint Francis,[133] *which is used solely by those who wish to be Brothers of the Cord, and this should be given by the Prelate, or any Priest, with authority, having around his neck a white stole, and the intended should be on his knees*

℣Adjutorium nostrum in nomine Domini.
℟Qui fecit Cœlum, & terram.
℣Sit nomen Domini benedictum.
℟Ex hoc nunc, & usque in sæculum.
℣Domine exaudi orationem meam.
℟Et clamor meus ad te veniat.
℣Dominus vobiscum.
℟Et cum spiritu tuo.

Oremus

Deus, qui ut servum redimeres, Filium tuum per manus impiorum ligari voluisti, bene✠dic quæsumus Cingulum istud, & præsta, ut famulus tuus, qui eo, velut ligamine pœnitentiali sui corporis cingitur, vunculorum ejusdem Domini nostri Jesu Christi perpetuò memor existat, & in societate, quam ingreditur, perenniter perseveret, tuisque cum effectu sempre obsequiis se alligatum esse cognoscat. Per eumdem Christum Dominum nostrum. *Amen.*

Sprinkle the holy water on the cord, and bless this with three sprinkles.

Holding the blessed rope, gird yourself and say:

Præcingat te Dominus cingulo salutis, ut contra hostes omnes munitus, acriùs pugnare, & faculiùs devicere valeas. Per Christum Domnium nostrum. *Amen.*

Following:

℣Salvum fac servum tuum.
℟Deus meus sperantem in te.
℣Esto ei Domine turris fortitudinis.
℟A facie inimici.
℣Nihil proficiat inimicus in eo.
℟Et filius iniquitatis non apponat nocere ei.
℣Domine exaudi orationem meam.
℟Et clamor meus ad te veniat.
℣Dominus vobiscum.
℟Et cum spiritu tuo.

133 Translator's note: the cord of the 'Archconfraternity of the Cord of Saint Francis', another of the 'Confraternities of the Cord'. This particular cord contains either three – for friars –, four – for Poor Clares –, or five knots – for the Secular Franciscans. The three knots represent poverty/charity, chastity and obedience, the extra knot of the Poor Clares represents enclosure, and the five knots represents the same as the friars' but adding penitence and detachment. A wearer should pray 5(+1) Our Fathers, Hail Marys and Gloria Patris daily.

Oremus

Domine Jesu Christe, qui Beato Petro Apostolo tuo significans, qua morte clarificaturus esset Deum, prædixisti, per alium in senectute ipsum fore cingendum, famulum tuum, quem cingulo nostræ Religionis præcingimus, tua quæsumus claritate præcinge, & tui nominis metu salutari constrige, ut tua ei opitulante gratia, in societatis, quam ingreditur devotione usque in finem jugiter perseveret. Qui vivis, & regnas Deus, per omnia sæcula sæculorum. *Amen.*

Take the cord down, and say:

Benedictio Dei Omnipotentis Pa✠tris, & Fi✠lii, & Spiritus ✠ Sancti descendat super te, (*vos*) & maneat simper. *Amen.*

Blessing of the Cord of Saint Joseph[134]

℣Ajutorium nostrum in nomine Domini
℟Qui fecit caelum & terram.
℣Dominus vobiscum.
℟Et cum spiritu tuo.

Oremus

Domine Jesu Christe, qui virginatis consilium & amorem lingeris atque castitatem praecipis: oramus clementiam tuam, ut hæc cingula castitatis tesseram bene✠dicere, & sancti✠ficare digneris, ut, quicumque pro castitate servanda illis præcincti fuerint, intercedente beato Joseph, sanctissimæ Genitricis tuæ sponso, gratam tibi continentiam, mandatorumque tuorum obedientiam servente, atque beniam peccatorum suorum obtineant, & santitatem mentis & corporis percipiant, vitamque consequantur æternam: Qui vivis & regnas cum Deo Patre in uniate Spiritus Sancti Deus, per omnia sæcula sæculorum. *Amen.*

Oremus

Da, quæsumus, omnipotens æterne Deus: ut purissimæ Virginis Mariæ, ejusque sponsi Joseph, integerriman virginitatem, eorum intercessionibus puritatem mentis & corporis consequamur. Per Christum Dominum nostrum. *Amen.*

Oremus

Omnipotens sempiterne Deus, qui castissimo viro Joseph purissimam Mariam semper Virginem, & puerum Jesum commisisti; te suplices

---

134 Translator's note: the cord of the 'Archconfraternity of the Cord of Saint Joseph', another of the 'Confraternities of the Cord'. This particular cord is typically made of linen or cotton; it contains seven knots representing the seven joys and seven sorrows of Saint Joseph. Used around the waist it indicates purity, chastity and humility, and by the shoulders obedience. One should pray seven Gloria Patri in honor of the seven pains and seven sorrows of Saint Joseph daily, followed by the prayer of purity:

O Keeper of the Virgin, Father Saint Joseph, to whose faithful protection was trusted Jesus Christ, innocence itself, and Mary, Virgin of Virgins, in the name of Jesus and Mary, that double deposit which was so dear to thee, I plead and beg thee that thou always conserves me free from all impurity, so as, with a pure spirit and heart, and chaste body, I may always serve faithfully Jesus, and Mary. Amen.

exoramus; ut fideles tui, qui his cingulis in honorem, & sub protectione ejusdem sancti Joseph praecincti fuerint, te largiente, & ipso intercedente, in castitate semper devote persisant. Per eumdem Dominum nostrum Jesum Christum Filium tuum: Qui tecum vivit & regnat in unitate Spíritus Sancti Deus, per omnia sæcula sæculorum. *Amen.*

Oremus

Deus, innocentiae restitutor & amator: quæsumus, ut fideles tui, qui hæc cingula adhibuerint, intercedente beato Joseph, sanctissimæ Genitricis tuæ sponso, in lumbis suis sint semper pracincti, & lucernas ardentes gestent in manibus suis; ac similes sint hominibus exspectantibus dominum suum, quando revertatur a nuptiis, ut, cum venerit & pulsaverit, confestim aperiant ei, & in æterna gaudia recipi mereantur. Qui vivis & regnas in sæcula sæculorum. *Amen.*

The priest places incense in a thurible, sprinkles the cord with holy water and says:

Asperges me, Domine, hyssopo et mundabor: lavabis me, ec super nivem dealbabor

Next he fumigates it, and finally says:

Oremus

Deus misericors, Deus clemens, cui bona cuncta placenta, sine quo nihil boni inchoatur, nihilque boni perficitur: adsint nostris humilimis precibus tuæ pietatis aures, & fideles tuos, qui in tuo santo nomine cingulo benedicto in honrorem & sub protectione sancti Joseph praecincti fuerint, a mundi impedimento, vel sæculari desiderio defende; & concede eis, ut in hoc santo proposito devoti persistere, & remissione percepta ad electorum tuorum valeant pervenire consortium. Per Dominum nostrum Jesum Christum Filium tuum; Qui tecum vivit & regnat in unitate Spiritus Sancti Deus, per omnia sæcula sæculorum. *Amen.*

Blessing of the Rings, which are usually carried in favour of the Virgin Mary, and her chastest husband Saint Joseph

℣Adjutorium nostrum in nomine Domini.
℟Qui fecit Cœlum, & terram.
℣In Conceptione tua Virgo immaculate fuisti.
℟Ora pro nobis Patrem, cuius Filium peperisti.
℣Pra pro nobis Beatissime Joseph.
℟Ut digni efficiamur promissionibus Christi.
℣Domine exaudi orationem meam.
℟Et clamor meus ad te veniat.

℣Dominus cobiscum.

℟Et cum spiritu tuo.

Oremus

Omnipotens Æterne Deus, qui unigenitum Filium tuum Jesum per piissimæ Virginis Mariæ purissimas manus fasciis ligari, & involvi, à Sanctissimo Josepho ulnis gestari, ac manibus impiorum durissimis vinculis ferreis, & funibus ligari, crudeliter constrigi, & trahi permisisti, ut nos à vinculo peccati, cruciatibus æternis clementer eriperes, bene✠dic, Domine, annulos istos, & catenulas, & vincula, quæ fideles tui in signum sacræ mancipationis gestare decernunt : & præsta, ut quicumque in memoriam fasciarum, & vinculorum dilectissimi Filii tui, ac Beatissimæ Matris ejus Mariæ, Sanctissimique Josephi devotè ea portaverint, & Sanctissimæ Virginis, ac Beatissimi Josephi Sponsi ejus perpetuò famulato, & obsequiis sese dedicaverint, in articulo mortis suæ ab omnibus peccatis obsoluti, perpetua libertate donati, cum omnibus Sanctis corona gloriæ perfrui mereantur in Cœlis. Per eumdem Christum Dominum nostrum. *Amen.*

Sprinkle the holy water.

Method of offering the already blessed rings:

Jesus, Joseph, and Mary, I offer thee my heart, and my soul.

Antiphon

Tulit Rex annulum suum de manu sua, & dedit eum in manu Joseph, vestivitque cum stola byssina, & collo torque auream circumposuit.

℣Annulo suoo subharravit eum.

℟Ut præpositum eum scirent universæ terræ.

℣Domine exaudi orationem meam.

℟Et clamor meus ad te veniat.

℣Dominus vobiscum

℟Et cum spiritu tuo.

Oremus

Omnipotens Æterne Deus, qui justo judicio disperdis superbos, & exaltas humiles, quique antiquum Patriarcham Joseph ob insignem eductum, supremum Ægypti dominum constituisti, & Regio annulo, ac torque auræ condecorasti : da, ut qui secundi Josephi castissimæ Beatissimæ Mariæ Sponsi, ac Unigeniti tui neutritii sacrum annulum, quo sibi innocentissimam, ac sempre illibatam Virginem Mariam desposavit, in terris nostra devotione colimus, ejus intercessione, & patrocinio à te in Cœlis desponsari mereamur. Per eumdem Christum Dominum nostrum. *Amen.*

When the Minister gives the ring to the recipient, he shall say:

Accipe, frater, (*vel soror*) hunc annulum in honorem, & memoriam desponsationis Beatæ Mariæ Virginis cum Sancto Joseph in signum castitatis, temperantiæ, & confraternitatis, ad laudem, & gloriam ejusdem

Genitricis Mariæ, & Sancti Joseph. In nomine Pa✠tris, & Fi✠lii, & Spiritus ✠ Sancti. *Amen.*

Santa Maria, & incomprehensibilis Dei Genitrix Virgo immaculate cum Sacratissimo Joseph, intercede pro nobis. *Amen.*

Et benediction Dei Omnipotentis Pa✠tris, & Fi✠lii, & Spiritus ✠ Sancti descendat super te, & maneat semper. *Amen.*

One should warn all devotees of the Virgin Mary our Mother, and Lady, that these should also be so especially of her Sacred Husband the Lord Saint Joseph, referring to him, as their protector, in all their needs, and spiritual, and temporal labours, asking for his blessing on your knees every day, as a Father, venerating him in some image of his, or by kissing his blessed ring, and praying an Our Father so as to have his propitious protection.

Blessing of the habits of the dead, which is the exclusive responsibility of the district Prelates

℣Adjutorium nostrum in nomine Domini.
℟Qui fecit cœlum, & terram.
℣Dominus vobiscum.
℟Et cum spiritu tuo.

Oremus

Domine Jesu Christe, seminator, & inspirator religiosi propositi, qui indumentum nostræ carnis pro salute humani genris suscipere voluisti, & in præsepio vilibus pannis involvi non horruisti : respice propitius ad preces humilitatis nostræ, & hanc religiosam vestem, & chordam B. P. N. Francisci bene✠dicere, & sancti✠ficare digneris, & concede, ut quicumque ad involvendum suum corpus in morte illas tulerit, vel petierit remissionem peccatorum per Summos Ecclesiæ tuæ Pontifices concessam assequatur. Qui vivis, & regnas in unitate cum Deo Patre, in unitate Spiritus Sancti, Deus per omni sæcula sæculorum. *Amen.*

Sprinkle the holy water.

Blessing of the Rosary

℣Adjutorium nostrum in nomine Domini.
℟Qui fecit cœlum, & terram.
℣Dominus vobiscum.
℟Et cum spiritu tuo.

Oremus

Omnipotens, & misericors Deus, qui propter eximiam charitatem tuam, qua dilexisti nos, Filium tuum unigenitum Dominum nostrum JESUM Christum de Cœlis in terram descendere, & de beatissimæ Virginis MARIÆ Dominæ nostræ utero sacratissimo, Angelo nuntiante, carnem suscipere, crucemque, ac mortem subire, & tertia die gloriosè à mortuis resurgere voluisti, ut nos eriperes de potestate diaboli : obsecramus immensam clementiam tuam, ut hæc signa Rosarii in honorem, & laudem ejusdem Genitricis Filii tuia ab Ecclesia tua fideli dicata, bene✠dicas, & sancti✠fices, eisque tantam infundas virtutem Spiritus Sancti, ut quicumque horum quodlibet secum portaverit, atque in domo sua reverenter tenuerit, & in eis ad te secundum ejusdem sanctæ societatis instituta divina contemplando mysteria devotè oraverit, salibri, & persevaranti devotione abundet, sitque consors, & particeps omnium gratiarum, privilegiorum, & indulgentiarum, quæ eidem societati per sanctam Sedem Apostolicam concessa fuerunt, ab omni hoste visibili, & invisibili sempre, & ubique in hoc sæculo liberetur, & in exitu suo ab ipsa beatíssima Virgine MARIA Dei Genitrice tibi plenus bonis operibus præsentari mereatur. Per eundem Christum Dominum nostrum. *Amen.*

Sprinkle the holy water.

Blessing of the Marian, and Seraphic Chaplet, which can be given by any Minor Priest, wearing a surplice, and a white stole, or if this is missing, of any other colour

℣Adjutorium nostrum in nomine Domini.
℟Qui fecit cœlum, & terram.
℣Dominus vobiscum.
℟Et cum spiritu tuo.

Oremus

Omnipotens, & misericors Deus, qui propter nimiam charitatem tuam, qua dilexisti nos, Filium tuum Dominum nostrum Jesum Christum pro Redemptione nostra de Cœlis in terram descedere, & Beatissimæ Virginis Mariæ utero sacratissimo, Angelo nuntiante; carnem suscipere, Crucemque, ac mortem subire, & tertia die gloriosè à mortuis resurgero voluisti, ut nos eriperes de potestate diaboli : obsecramus immensam clementiam tuam, ut hæc signa Coronæ in honorem, & laudem ejusdem Genitricis Filii tui ab Ecclesia tua fideli dicata, bene✠dicas, & sancti✠fices, eisque tantam Spiritus Sancti infundas virtutem : ut, quicumque horum quodlibet secum portaverit, vel dixerit, aut in domo reverenter tenuerit, & in eis ad te Divina contemplando Mysteria devote oraverit, salubri, & perseveranti devotione abundet, & consequatur omnes gratias, & Indulgentias, quæ eidem per Sanctam Sedem Apostolicam concessa fuerunt, ad omnique hoste maligno visibili, & invisibili sempre, ac ubique in hoc, & in futuro sæculo liberetur; & in exitu suo à Beatissima Virgine Maria Dei Genitrice, & Sancto Ubado tibi plenus bonis openibus præsentari mereatur. Per eumdem Christum Dominum nostrum. *Amen.*

Sprinkle the holy water.

The Minister when offering the Chaplet should say:

Accipe, frater (*vel soror*) Coronam annorum, & Mysterium Immaculatæ Virginis Mariæ, quibus decentre ornatos, & protectus (ornate, & protecta) securus (secura) vivas, ac recitando, vitam æternam desiderare valeas. *Amen.*

Sancta Maria, & incomprehensibilis Dei Genitrix Virgo immaculata, intercede pro nobis. *Amen.*

Et benedictio Dei Omnipotentis Pa✠tris, & Fi✠lii, & Spiritus ✠ Sancti descendat super te, & maneat sempre. *Amen.*

For anything you wish to bless

℣Adjutorium nostrum in nomine Domini.
℟Qui fecit cœlum, & terram.
℣Dominus vobiscum.
℟Et cum spiritu tuo.

Oremus

Bene✠dic, Domine, creaturam istam, (N.) ut sit remedium salutare generi humano, & præsta per invocationem tui sancti nominis, ut quicumque ea usi fuerint, corporis sanitatem, & animæ tutelam accipiant. Per Dominum nostrum Jesum Christum, Filium tuum : qui tecum vivit & regnat in unitate Spiritus Sancti Deus, per omnia sæcula sæculorum. *Amen.*

Sprinkle the holy water.

Blessing of oil, to anoint the sick and vexed

℣Adjutorium nostrum in nomine Domini.
℟Qui fecit cœlum, & terram.
℣Dominus vobiscum.
℟Et cum spiritu tuo.
℣Sit nomen Domini benedictum.
℟Ex hoc nunc, & usque in sæculum.

Exorcizo te creatura olei per Deum ✠ Patrem omnipotentem, per Filium ejus ✠ JESUM Christum, & per Spiritum ✠ Sanctum, ac per Sancta MARIAM ✠ Virginem, & omnes Angelos, ✠ & Sanctos, ut omnis virtus diaboli, omnis exercitus adversarii, omnis incursus, omnis tumor, & dolor, & phantasma Satanæ, minestrorumque ejus eradicetur, & effugiat ab his, qui ex te biberint, vel se unxerint, maleficia cuncta diabolica destruas, & consumas, & medicina optima, & sancta efficiaris, menti, & corpori sanitatem restituens, nec valeant dæmones se latitare in corporibus ipsis, sed in virtute potentissimi nominis JESU se manifestent, & obedientiam Ministris JESU Christi præstent, & exeant cum omnibus maleficiis. In nomine Patris, ✠ & Filii, ✠ & Spiritus ✠ Sancti. *Amen.*

℣Dominus vobiscum.
℟Et cum spiritu tuo.

Oremus

Omnipotens æterne Deus, qui olivas creasti, ex quibus ad universi condimentum liquorem suavissimum emanare fecisti, & in sanctis Sacramentis oleo uti jussisti, & eo infirmis ungi ordinasti, dignare hoc oleum benedicere, ✠ sanctificare, ✠ & consecrare, ✠ ut quicumque ex eo biberint, vel se unxerint, uniti sint sanctarum virtutum complemento, & ad eis eradicentur omnes facturæ, maleficia, incantationes, phantasmata, tumores, dolores, & ligationes quomodolibet contra creaturas tuas factæ, sit omnium operum Satanæ, & ministrorum ejus destructio, expulsio, & exterminatio; & sic in nomine sancto tuo hoc oleum benedico, ✠ sanctifico, ✠ & consecro, & omnibus benedictionibus Dei ✠ repleo, ac ita benedictum, sanctificatum, & consecratum creaturis à diabolo vexatis in unctionis usum, & potum trado ad extirpandum, & eradicandum omne nesas diaboli : sitque omnium operum Satanæ destructio, & exterminatio; & quisquis hoc oleo usus fuerit, non possit in eo diabolus latitare, immo se manifestare astrictus sit. Hoc etiam oleum benedico, ✠ sanctifico, ✠ & consecro ✠ ad restituendum obsessis, & febricitantibus valetudinem, ægrotantibus sanitatem, ad extinguendum venena, dolores, & tumores, ad comprimendum noxia, & ad depellendum adversa; & quisquis ex eo usus fuerit ad omni pariter languore, & infirmitate sanetur. Per eundem Christum Dominum nostrum. *Amen.*

Sprinkle the holy water.

When the Exorcist anoints the infirm on his forehead, lips, wrists, hands, and on any other vexed areas, which he may do so in a convenient and honest way, he shall say the following:

Sicut Sanctus Sanctorum unctus fuit Spiritu Domini, sie Spiritus Sanctus sit super te, creatura Dei, quam ego ungo sacrati olei liquore; & per istud sanctum oleum, & unctionem sacram libero te, & absolvo te ab operibus Satanæ, ac destruo omnia maleficia, incantationes, ligationes, signaturas, facturas, dolores, tumores tibi arte diabolica factos, ut in omni parte olei sancti, & crucis ✠ virtute munita, diabolicos impetus viriliter contemnere valeas, ac hoc medicamento sancto omnem dæmonis infestationem procul repellere possis, prout ego repello, anhilo, & destruo. In nomine Patris, ✠ & Filii, ✠ & Spiritus ✠ Sancti. *Amen.*

℟Domine exaudi orationem meam.

℣Dominus vobiscum.

℟Et cum spiritu tuo.

Oremus

Domine JESU Christe, qui es saluas, & medicina vera, à quo omnis sanitas : qui intulisti, ut languidos olei liquore tangentes ungamus : quæsumus clementiam tuam, ut hanc tuam creaturam diabolica vexatione laborantem sanare digneris, fiat que sibi hæc olei sacra perunctio morbi præsentis expulsio; & sicut oleo sancto tuo unxi eam, sic manus tua auxilietur ei. Qui cum Patre, & Spiritu Sancto vivis, & regnas in sæcula sæculorum. *Amen.*

Blessing of roses

℣Adjutorium nostrum in nomine Domini.
℟Qui fecit cœlum, & terram.
℣Dominus vobiscum.
℟Et cum spiritu tuo.

Oremus

Deus creator, & conservator generis humani, dator gratiæ spiritualis, & largitor æternæ salutis, benedictione tua sancta bene✠dic has rosas, quas pro gratiis tibi exsolvendis,cum devotione, ac veneratione Beatæ, semperque Virginis MARIÆ Rosarii, hodie tibi præsentamus, & petimus benedici, & infundi in eis per virtutem Sanctæ Cru✠cis benedictionem cœlestem, ut qui eas ad odoris suavitatem, & repellendas infirmitates humano usui tribuiste, talem signaculo Sanctæ Cru✠cis benedictionem accipiant, ut quibuscumque in infirmatibus appositæ fuerint, seu qui eas in domibus suis portaverint, ab infirmitate sanentur, discedant diaboli, contremiscant, & fugiant pavidi cum suis ministris de habitationibus illis, nec amplius tibi servientes inquietare præsumant. Per Dominum nostrum Jesum Christum, Filium tuum : qui tecum vivit et regnat in unitate Spiritus Sancti Deus, per omnia sæcula sæculorum. *Amen.*

Sprinkle the holy water.

Blessing of incense, rue, and other things for fumigation in a holy fire, and to be carried by the infirm

℣Adjutorium nostrum in nomine Domini.
℟Qui fecit cœlum, & terram.
℣Dominus vobiscum.
℟Et cum spiritu tuo.

Oremus

Bene✠dic, Domine Jesu Christe, hanc rutam, (*seu incensum, &c*) & infunde ei per tuam charitatem benedictionem tuam cœlestem : ut quicumque ex ea suffumigatus fuerit, vel secum habuerit, nullus inimicus ei nocere possit, & à quocumque loco, ubi sparsa, vel posita fuerit, recedat diabolus, & omnes spiritus maligni hunc odorem sentientes fugiant procul, & separentur ab hac creatura Dei (N.) quam redemisti pretioso sanguine tuo, & de cætero non lædatur à morsu antiqui serpentis. Per te Jesu Christe, Salvator mundi, qui vivis, & regnas Deus, per omnia sæcula sæculorum. *Amen.*

Sprinkle the holy water.

Blessing of fire, in which one should burn the signs of sorcery, which may appear

℣Adjutorium nostrum in nomine Domini.

℟Qui fecit cœlum, & terram.
℣Dominus vobiscum.
℟Et cum spiritu tuo.

Oremus

Domine Deus Omnipotens, cui assistit exercitus Angelorum cum tremore, quorum servitium spirituale, & ignem esse cognoscitur : dignare respicere, & bene✠dicere, & sancti✠ficare istam creaturam ignis, ut, eo combustis maleficii signis, intensissimè torqueantur dæmones; & omnes languores, omnesque infirmitates, atque insidiæ inimici effugiant, & separentur à plasmate tuo. Nunquam lædetur à morsu antiqui serpentis, quod pretioso sanguine Filii tui redemisti. Qui tecum vivit & regnat in unitate Spiritus Sancti Deus, per omnia sæcula sæculorum. *Amen.*

While burning the malefica say:

Sicut hæc instrumenta hæreticalia, & maleficialia creaturas Dei vexantia in tumum nunce es conversurus, & ad nihilum redacturus, sic in virtute Jesu Christi operations, & vexations diabolicæ evanescant, & cuncta maleficia, incantationes, fascinationes, ligaturæ, signaturæ, & omnia diabolica à cunctis membris hujus maleficiati eradicentur, confringantur, & annihilentur, sine tamen spirituali, nec corporali læsione eorum. Per eum, qui venturus est judicare vivos, & mortuos, & sæculum per ignem. *Amen.*

Blessing of candles from the Brotherhood of the Rosary

℣Adjutorium nostrum in nomine Domini.
℟Qui fecit cœlum, & terram.
℣Dominus vobiscum.
℟Et cum spiritu tuo.

Oremus

Domine JESU Christe lux vera, qui illuminas omnem hominem venientem in hunc mundum, effunde per intercessionem Virginis MARIÆ Matris tuæ, & per quindecim ejus Rosarii Mysteria bene✠dictionem tuam super hos cereos, & candelas, & sanctifica lumine tuæ gratiæ; & concede propitius, ut sicut hæc luminaria igne visibili accensa nocturnas depellunt tenebras, ita corda nostra invisibili igne, ac Spiritus ✠ Sancti splendore illustrata omnium vitiorum cæcitate careant, ut puro mentis oculo cernere sempre possimus quæ tibi sunt placita, & nostræ saluti utilia, quatenus post hujus sæculi caliginosa discrimina, ad lucem indeficientem pervenire mereamur. Qui vivis, & regnas Deus, per omnia sæcula sæculorum. *Amen.*

Sprinkle the holy water.

Blessing of statues of Jesus Christ our Lord, the Blessed Virgin Mary and any other saint

℣Adjutorium nostrum in nomine Domini.

℟Qui fecit cœlum, & terram.
℣Dominus vobiscum.
℟Et cum spiritu tuo.

Oremus

Omnipotens sempiterne Deus, qui Sanctorum tuorum imagines (*sive effigies*) sculpi, aut pingi non reprobas, ut quoties illas oculis corporeis intuemur, toties eorum actus, & sanctitatem ad imatandum memoriæ oculis meditemur : hanc; quæsumus, imaginem (*seu sculpturam*) in honorem, & memoriam unigeniti Filii tui Domini nostri JESU Christi, *vel* beatissimæ Virginis MARIÆ Matris Domini nostri JESU Christi, *vel* beati (N.) Apostoli tui, *vel* Martyris, aut Confessoris, aut Pontificis, aut Virginis adaptata benedicere, ✠ & sanctificare ✠ digneris, & præsta, ut quicumque coram illa unigenitum Filium tuum, *vel* beatissimam Virginem, *vel* gloriosum Apostolum, *sive* Martyrem, *sive* Confessorem, *aut* Virginem suppliciter colere, & honorare studuerit, illius meritis, & obtentu à te gratiam in præsenti, & æternam gloriam obtineat in futurum. Per eumdem Christum Dominum nostrum. *Amen.*

Sprinkle the holy water.

Various Prayers

Act of Contrition, to be sung before a Mission, during any time

O my beloved Lord
My supreme good, and my God
Forgive my heart
Fully contrite
With excessive sorrow
I cry an infinite horror
For the excessive love
I have for thee
I would rather be killed
Than to offend God
I would rather die
Than to further sin.
If in order to condemn myself
I turned my back on thee Lord
Now with great pain
I am regretful.
So as not to prevail
The entire Hell against me,
I ask thee Eternal Lord
Mercy.

Prayer for the Pope

Omnipotens sempiterne Deus, miserere famulo tuo Pontifici nostro (N.) & dirige eum secundum tuam clementiam in viam salutis æternæ : ut te donante tibi placita cupiat, & tota virtute perficiat.

Another

God, Shepherd, and Director, which thou art of all the faithful, be propitious, Lord, with thy servant (NN) which thou elected as Shepherd of thy Church : give him, sovereign Lord, we ask, and concede to him that with his word, as with his examples, all the children of the Church may take profit, and that with his flock he may arrive at that life which lasts forever. By the same Lord Jesus Christ, who lives, and reigns with thee for all centuries of centuries. *Amen.*

Prayer for Peace

Deus, à quo sancta desideria, recta consilia, & justa sunt opera : da servis tuis illam, quam mundus dare non potest, pacem : ut & corda nostra mandatis tuis dedita, & hostium sublata formidine, tempora sint tua protection tranquilla.

Prayer for Chastity

Ure igne sancti Spiritus renes nostros, & cor nostrum, Domine : ut tibi casto corpore serviamus, & mundo corde placeamus.

Prayer to request the assistance of the divine aid for any action one may undertake

Actiones nostras, quæsumus Domine, aspirando præveni, & adjuvando prosequere : ut cuncta nostra oratio, & operatio à te sempre incipiat, & per te cœpta finiatur.

Prayer for all the faithful, living and dead

Omnipotens sempiterne Deus, que vivorum dominaris, simul & mortuorum, omniumque misereris, quos tuos side, & opere futuros esse prænoscis : te suplices exoramus, ut pro quibus effundere preces decrevimus, quosque vel præsens sæculum adhuc in carne retinet, vel futurum jam exutos corpore suscepit, intercedentibus omnibus sanctis tuis, pietatis tuæ clementia omnium delictorum suorum veniam consequantur. Per Dominum nostrum Jesum Christum, Filium tuum : qui tecum vivit & regnat in unitate Spiritus Sancti Deus, per omnia sæcula sæculorum. *Amen.*

℣Domine exaudi orationem meam.
℟Et clamor meus ad te veniat.
℣Exaudiat nos omnipotens, & misericors Dominus
℟Amen.
℣Fidelium animæ per misericordiam Dei requiescan in pace.
℟Amen.

Unfailing remedy for all people who suffer from nightmares, afflictions, ghosts, and dishonest dreams

As I suffered from this ill of nightmares, and wanting to abandon the Mission after returning from the Sertões of the Cuiabá, and Goyazes for thinking myself in the ends of my life, and wanting to find a cure, the Most Reverend João de Santa Isabel, Priest of the always enlightened Order of the Carmel, told me to pray, before going to bed, on my knees in front of an image of the Holy Christ the Hymn of the Compline in order to see myself completely free from similar harm, which I have done, and because of this I have made a vow to our Lady, that in every book I offer for printing I may teach this devotion to the faithful.

Hymn

In Latin
Te lucis ante terminum
Rerum Creator poscimus,
Ut pro tua clementia
Sis præsul, & custodia.
Procul recedant somnia,
Et noctium phantasmata.
Hostemque nostrum comprime,
Ne polluantur corpora.
Præsta, Pater piisime,
Patrique compar unice,
Cum Spiritu Paraclito,
Regnans per omne sæculum. Amen

In Vernacular
Before this day ends
I plead, O Creator of souls,
That by thy clemency,
Thou may always be in my guard.
Make it so as away from me
Bad dreams, and ghosts are driven,
And that the common enemy
May not do harm to my body.
Give me, O most merciful Father,
By thy Son this grace,
And also for thy love,
All three one substance.

Holiest words against lightning, storms and thunder[135]

Christus Rex venit in pace.
Et Deus Homo factus est.
Verbum Caro factum est.
Christus de Virgine natus est.
Christus per medium illorum ibat in pace.
Christus Crucifixus est.
Christus Mortuus est.
Christus Sepultus est.
Christus Resurrexit.

135 Translator's note: this prayer is usually attributed to Saint Benedict Joseph Labre, an 18th-century Franciscan Tertiary.

Christus Ascedit.
Christus Imperat.
ChristusRegnat.
Christus ab omni fulgure nos defendat
Verbum Caro factum est.
Christus nobiscum est.

State

Our Father, Hail Mary, Creed.

For the Feast Triduum[136]

Te Deum laudamus : te Dominum confitemur.[137]
Te æternum Patrem : omnis terra veneratur.
Tibi omnes Angeli : tibi cæli, & universæ potestates.
Tibi Cherubim & Seraphim : incessabili voce proclamant:
Sanctus, Sanctus, Sanctus, Dominus Deus Sabaoth.
Pleni sunt cæli & terra majestatis gloriæ tuæ.
Te gloriosus Apostolorum chorus,
Te Prophetarum laudabilis numerus.
Te martyrum candidatus laudat exercitus.
Te per orbem terrarum sancta confitetur Ecclesia,
Patrem immensæ majestatis,
Venerandum tuum verum & unicum Fílium,
Sanctum quoque Paraclitum Spiritum.
Tu Rex gloriæ Christe.
Tu Patris sempiternus es Filius.
Tu ad liberandum suscepturus hominem: non horruisti Virginis uterum.
Tu, devicto mortis aculeo aperuisti credentibus regna cælorum.
Tu ad dexteram Dei sedes : in gloria Patris.
Judex crederis esse venturus.
Te ergo quæsumus, tuis famulis subveni : quos pretioso Sanguine redemisti.
Æterna fac cum sanctis tuis : in gloria numerari.
Salvum fac populum tuum, Domine : & benedic hæreditati tuæ.
Et rege eos, & extolle illos usque in æternum.
Per singulos dies, benedicimus te.
Et laudamus nomen tuum in sæculum : & in sæculum sæculi.
Dignare, Domine, die isto : sine peccato nos custodire.
Miserere nostri Domine : miserere nostri.

136 Translator's note: a three day religious celebration. In Catholicism the most common is the Paschal Triduum, from Maundy Thursday to Easter Sunday.
137 Translator's note: this is the Hymn 'Te Deum', also called the 'Ambrosian Hymn' or 'A Song of the Church'. It is commonly used in the Liturgy of the Hours, particularly the Matins.

Fiat misericordia tua Domine super nos : quemadmodum speravimus in te.
In te Domine speravi: non confundar in æternum.

Hymn

Tantum ergo Sacramentum[138]
Veneremur cernui:
Et antiquum documentum
Novo cedat ritui:
Præstet fides supplementum
Sensuum defectui.
Genitori, Genitoque
Laus, & jubilatio,
Salus, honour, virtus quoque
Sit & benedictio,
Procedenti ab utroque
Compar sit laudatio. *Amen.*

In Vernacular to worship the Holiest Sacrament

Such a great Sacrament
Bowing we worship:
Heed the new Sacrifice
The ancient documents,
And our living faith rise
From the senses failing:
To the Father, and the Son generated
With joy the praise we give,
Power, blessing, salvation
In them only recognized.
And to the Holy Spirit of both
In equal and perfect praise.

Antiphon

Ó sacrum convivium, in quo Christus sumitur : recolitur memoria passionis eius : mens impletur gratia : & futurae gloriæ nobis pignus datur, Alleluia.

℣Panem de cœlis præstitisti eis, Alleluia.

℟Omne delectamentum in se habentem, Alleluia.

Oratio

Deus, qui nobis sub Sacramento mirabili, passionis tuæ memoriam reliquisti : tribue quæsumus; ita nos Corporis, & Sanguinis tui sacra mysteria venerari; ut redemptionis tuæ fructum in nobis jugiter sentiamus. Qui vivis, & regnas cum Deo Patre.

138 Translator's note: this hymn is made up of the second two verses of the 'Pange Lingua', written by St. Thomas Aquinas. It is used in the Catholic service during the benediction of the Blessed Sacrament.

SEVEN PENITENTIAL PSALMS

Antiphon

Ne reminiscaris Domine delicta nostra, vel parentum nostrorum: neque vindictam sumas de peccatis nostris.

Psalm 6

Domine, ne in furore tuo arguas me : neque in ira tua corripias me.

Miserere mei, Domine, quoniam infirmus sum : sana me Domine, quoniam conturbata sunt ossa mea.

Et anima mea turbata est valde : sed tu, Domine usquequo?

Convertere, Domine, & eripe animam meam, salvum me fac propter misericordiam tuam.

Quoniam non est in morte, qui memor sit tui : in inferno autem quis confitebitur tibi?

Laboravi in gemitu meo, lavabo per singulas noctes lectum meum : lacrymis meis stratum meum rigabo.

Turbatus est à furore oculus meus : inveteravi inter omnes inimicos meos.

Discedite à me omnes, qui operamini iniquitatem : quoniam exaudivit Dominus vocem fletus mei.

Exaudivit Dominus deprecationem meam : Dominus orationem meam suscepit.

Erubescant, & conturbentur vehementer omnes inimici mei : convertantur, & erubescant valde velociter.

Gloria Patri, & Filio, & Spiritui Sancto : Sicut erat in principio, & nunc, & semper, & in sæcula sæculorum. *Amen.*

Psalm 31

Beati, quorum remissæ sunt iniquitates; & quorum tecta sunt peccata.

Beatus vir, cui non imputavit Dominus peccatum ; nec est in spiritu eius dolus.

Quoniam tacui, inveteraverunt ossa mea : dum clamarem tota die.

Quoniam die ac nocte gravata est super me manus tua : conversus sum in ærumna mea, dum configitur spina.

Delictum meum cognitum tibi feci; & iniustitiam meam non abscondi.

Dixi: Confitebor adversum me iniustitiam meam Domino: & tu remisisti impietatem peccati mei.

Pro hac orabit ad te omnis sanctus : in tempore opportuno.

Verumtamen in diluvio aquarum multarum : ad eum non approximabunt.

Tu es refugium meum, à tribulatione quæ circumdedit me : exsultatio mea, erue me à circumdantibus me.

Intellectum tibi dabo, & instruam te in via hac, qua gradieris, firmabo super te oculos meos.

Nolite fieri sicut equus & mulus, quibus non est intellectus.

In camo & fræno maxillas eorum constringe, qui non approximant ad te.

Multa flagella peccatoris : sperantem autem in Domino misericordia circumdabit.

Lætamini in Domino, & exsultate, iusti, & gloriamini, omnes recti corde.

Gloria Patri, & Filio, & Spiritui Sancto : Sicut erat in principio, & nunc, & semper, & in sæcula sæculorum. *Amen.*

Psalm 37

Domine, ne in furore tuo arguas me, neque in ira tua corripias me.

Quoniam sagittæ tuæ infixæ sunt mihi : & confirmasti super me manum tuam.

Non est sanitas in carne mea, à facie iræ tuæ : non est pax ossibus meis à facie peccatorum meorum.

Quoniam iniquitates meæ supergressæ sunt caput meum, & sicut onus grave gravatæ sunt super me.

Putruerunt, & corruptæ sunt cicatrices meæ à facie insipientiæ meæ.

Miser factus sum, & curvatus sum usque in finem : tota die contristatus ingrediebar.

Quoniam lumbi mei impleti sunt illusionibus : & non est sanitas in carne mea.

Afflictus sum, & humiliatus sum nimis : rugiebam à gemitu cordis mei.

Domine, ante te omne desiderium meum, & gemitus meus a te non est absconditus.

Cor meum conturbatum est, dereliquit me virtus mea, & lumen oculorum meorum, & ipsum non est mecum.

Amici mei, & proximi mei adversum me appropinquaverunt, & steterunt.

Et qui juxta me erant, de longe steterunt, & vim faciebant qui quærebant animam meam.

Et, qui inquirebant mala mihi, locuti sunt vanitates :& dolos tota die meditabantur.

Ego autem tamquam surdus non audiebam : & sicut mutus non aperiens os suum.

Et factus sum sicut homo non audiens : & non habens in ore suo redargutiones.

Quoniam in te, Domine, speravi : tu exaudies me, Domine Deus meus.

Quia dixi: Nequando supergaudeant mihi inimici mei : & dum commoventur pedes mei, super me magna locuti sunt.

Quoniam ego in flagella paratus sum, & dolor meus in conspectu meo semper.

Quoniam iniquitatem meam annuntiabo : & cogitabo pro peccato meo.

Inimici autem mei vivunt, & confirmati sunt super me : & multiplicati sunt, qui oderunt me inique.

Qui retribuunt mala pro bonis detrahebant mihi : quoniam sequebar bonitatem.

Ne derelinquas me, Domine, Deus meus : ne discesseris à me.

Intende in adiutorium meum, Domine Deus salutis meæ.

Gloria Patri, & Filio, & Spiritui Sancto : Sicut erat in principio, & nunc, & semper, & in sæcula sæculorum. *Amen.*

Psalm 50

Miserere mei, Deus, secundum magnam misericordiam tuam.

Et secundum multitudinem miserationum tuarum dele iniquitatem meam.

Amplius lava me ab iniquitate mea, & à peccato meo munda me.

Quoniam iniquitatem meam ego cognosco, & peccatum meum contra me est semper.

Tibi, soli peccavi, & malum coram te feci : ut justificeris in sermonibus tuis, & vincas cum judicaris.

Ecce enim in iniquitatibus conceptus sum : & in peccatis concepit me mater mea.

Ecce enim veritatem dilexisti : incerta, & occulta sapientiae tuæ manifestasti mihi.

Asperges me hyssopo, & mundabor : lavabis me, & super nivem dealbabor.

Auditui meo dabis gaudium, & lætitiam : & exultabunt ossa humiliata.

Averte faciem tuam à peccatis meis, & omnes iniquitates meas dele.

Cor mundum crea in me, Deus : & spiritum rectum innova in visceribus meis.

Ne projicias me à facie tua, & spiritum sanctum tuum ne auferas à me.

Redde mihi lætitiam salutaris tui : & spiritu principali confirma me.

Docebo iniquos vias tuas, & impii ad te convertentur.

Libera me de sanguinibus, Deus, Deus salutis meæ, & exultabit lingua mea justitiam tuam.

Domine, labia mea aperies, & os meum annuntiabit laudem tuam.

Quoniam si voluisses sacrificium, dedissem utique : holocaustis non delectaberis.

Sacrificium Deo spiritus contribulatus : cor contritum, & humiliatum Deus, non despicies.

Benignè fac, Domine, in bona voluntate tua Sion : ut ædificentur muri Jerusalem.

Tunc acceptabis sacrificium justitiae, & oblationes, & holocausta : tunc imponent super altare tuum vitulos.

Gloria Patri, & Filio, & Spiritui Sancto : Sicut erat in principio, & nunc, & semper, & in sæcula sæculorum. *Amen.*

Psalm 101

Domine, exaudi orationem meam, & clamor meus ad te veniat.
Non avertas faciem tuam à me : in quacumque die tribulor, inclina ad me aurem tuam.
In quacumque die invocavero te, velociter exaudi me.
Quia defecerunt sicut fumus dies mei, & ossa mea sicut cremium aruerunt.
Percussus sum ut fœnum, & aruit cor meum : quia oblitus sum comedere panem meum.
À voce gemitus mei : adhaesit os meum carni meæ.
Similis factus sum pelicano solitudinis : factus sum sicut nicticorax in domicilio.
Vigilavi, & factus sum sicut passer solitarius in tecto.
Tota die exprobrabant mihi inimici mei, & qui laudabant me, adversum me iurabant.
Quia cinerem tamquam panem manducabam, & potum meum cum fletu miscebam.
À facie iræ, & indignationis tuæ : quia elevans allisisti me.
Dies mei sicut umbra declinaverunt : & ego sicut fenum arui.
Tu autem, Domine, in æternum permanes, & memoriale tuum in generationem, & generationem.
Tu exsurgens misereberis Sion : quia tempus miserendi ejus, quia venit tempus.
Quoniam placuerunt servis tuis lapides eius : & terræ ejus miserebuntur.
Et timebunt gentes nomen tuum, Domine, & omnes Reges terræ gloriam tuam.
Quia ædificavit Dominus Sion, & videbitur in gloria sua.
Respexit in orationem humilium : & non sprevit precem eorum.
Scribantur hæc in generatione altera: & populus, qui creabitur, laudabit Dominum.
Quia prospexit de excelso sancto suo : Dominus de Cœlo in terram aspexit.
Ut audiret gemitus compeditorum : ut solveret filios interemptorum.
Ut annuntient in Sion nomen Domini : & laudem ejus in Jerusalem.
In conveniendo populos in unum, & Reges, ut serviant Domino.
Respondit ei in via virtutis suæ : Paucitatem dierum meorum nuntia mihi.
Ne revoces me in dimidio dierum meorum : in generationem, & generationem anni tui.
Initio tu, Domine, terram fundasti : & opera manuum tuarum sunt Cœli.
Ipsi peribunt, tu autem permanes :& omnes sicut vestimentum veterascent.
Et sicut opertorium mutabis eos, & mutabuntur : tu autem idem ipse es, & anni tui non deficient.
Filii servorum tuorum habitabunt : & semen eorum in sæculum dirigetur.

Gloria Patri, & Filio, & Spiritui Sancto : Sicut erat in principio, & nunc, & semper, & in sæcula sæculorum. *Amen.*

Psalm 129

De Profundis clamavi, ad te Domine : Domine, exaudi vocem meam.
Fiant aures tuæ intendentes : in vocem deprecationis meæ.
Si iniquitates observaveris, Domine : Domine, quis sustinebit?
Quia apud te propitiatio est : & propter legem tuam sustinui te, Domine.
Sustinuit anima mea in verbo ejus : speravit anima mea in Domino.
À custodia matutina usque ad noctem:, speret Israel in Domino.
Quia apud Dominum misericordia, & copiosa apud eum redemptio.
Et ipse redimet Israel ex omnibus iniquitatibus eius.
Gloria Patri, & Filio, & Spiritui Sancto : Sicut erat in principio, & nunc, & semper, & in sæcula sæculorum. *Amen.*

Psalm 142

Domine, exaudi orationem meam, auribus percipe obsecrationem meam in veritate tua : exaudi me in tua justitia.
Et non intres in judicium cum servo tuo : quia non justificabitur in conspectu tuo omnis vivens.
Quia persecutus est inimicus animam meam : humiliavit in terra vitam meam.
Collocavit me in obscuris, sicut mortuos sæculi, & anxiatus est super me spiritus meus, in me turbatum est cor meum.
Memor fui dierum antiquorum, meditatus sum in omnibus operibus tuis : in factis manuum tuarum meditabar.
Expandi manus meas ad te : anima mea sicut terra sine aqua tibi.
Velociter exaudi me, Domine : defecit spiritus meus.
Non avertas faciem tuam à me : & similis ero descendentibus in lacum.
Auditam fac mihi mane misericordiam tuam, quia in te speravi.
Notam fac mihi viam, in qua ambulem; quia ad te levavi animam meam.
Eripe me de inimicis meis Domine, ad te confugi : doce me facere voluntatem tuam, quia Deus meus es tu.
Spiritus tuus bonus deducet me in terram rectam : propter nomen tuum, Domine, vivificabis me, in æquitate tua.
Educes de tribulatione animam meam, & in misericordia tua disperdes inimicos meos.
Et perdes omnes qui tribulant animam meam : quoniam ego servus tuus sum.
Gloria Patri, & Filio, & Spiritui Sancto : Sicut erat in principio, & nunc, & semper, & in sæcula sæculorum. *Amen.*

Antiphon

Ne reminiscaris, Domine delicta nostra, vel parentum nostrorum, neque vindictam summas de peccatis nostris.
Kyrie eleison.
Pater noster.

℣Et ne nos inducas in tentationem, sed libera nos a malo.

℟Amen.

℣Salvos fac servos tuos.

℟Deus meus, sperantes in te.

℣Dominus vobiscum, vel Domine exaudi, repetitur finita Oratione, postquam fuerit responsum, Amen.

Oremus

Deus cui proprium est misereri sempre, & parcere, suscipe deprecationem nostram, ut quos delictorum catena constringit, miseratio tuæ pietatis clementer absolvat. Per Christum Dominum nostrum. *Amen.*

Prayer for sin

Exaudi quæsumus Domine supplicum preces, & consitentium tibi parce peccatis, ut pariter nobis indulgentiam tribuas benignus, & pacem. Per Christum Dominum nostrum. *Amen.*

Apostle's Creed

Credo in Deum Patrem omnipotentem, Creatorem Cæli & terræ. Et in Jesum Christum Filium ejus unicum Dominum nostrum, qui conceptus est de Spiritu Sancto, natus ex Maria Virgine, passus sub Pontio Pilato, crucifixus, mortuus, & sepultus : descendit ad inferos : tertia die resurrexit a mortuis. Ascendit ad Cælos, sedet ad dexteram Dei Patris omnipotentis : inde venturus est judicare vivos & mortuos. Credo in Spiritum Sanctum, Sanctam Ecclesiam Catholicam, Sanctorum communionem, remissionem peccatorum, carnis resurrectionem, vitam aeternam. *Amen.*

Athanasian Creed

Quicumque vult salvus esse, ante omnia opus est, ut teneat catholicam Fidem.

Quam nisi quisque integram, inviolatamque servaverit : absque dubio in æternum peribit.

Fides autem Catholica hæc est, ut unum Deum in Trinitate, & Trinitatem in unitate veneremur.

Neque confundentes personas; neque substantiam separantes.

Alia est enim persona Patris, alia Filii, alia Spiritus Sancti.

Sed Patris, & Fili, & Spiritus Sancti una est divinitas, æqualis gloria, coæterna majestas.

Qualis Pater, talis Filius, talis Spiritus Sanctus.
Increatus Pater, increatus Filius, increatus Spiritus Sanctus.
Immensus Pater, immensus Filius, immensus Spiritus Sanctus.
Æternus Pater, æternus Filius, æternus Spiritus Sanctus.
Et tamen non tres æterni, sed unus æternus.
Sicut non tres increati, nec tres immensi sed unus increatus & unus immensus.
Similiter omnipotens Pater, omnipotens Filius, omnipotens Spiritus Sanctus.
Et tamen non tres omnipotentes; sed unus omnipotens.
Ita Deus Pater, Deus Filius, Deus Spiritus Sanctus.
Et tamen non tres Dij : sed unus est Deus.
Ita Dominus Pater, Dominus Filius, Dominus Spiritus Sanctus.
Et tamen non tres Domini : sed unus est Dominus.
Quia, sicut singillatim unamquamque personam Deum, ac Dominum confiteri Christiana veritate compellimur : ita tres Deus, aut Dominos dicere, Catholica Religione prohibemur.
Pater â nullo est factus, nec creatus nec genitus.
Filius â Patre solo est : non factus, nec creatus, sed genitus.
Spiritus Sanctus à Patre, & Filio : non factus, nec creatus, nec genitus : sed procedens.
Unus ergo Pater, non tres Patres. Unus Filius, non tres Filii. Unus Spiritus Sanctus, non tres Spiritus Sancti.
Et in hac Trinitate nihil prius, aut posterius : nihil maius aut minus : sed totæ tres Personæ coæternæ sibi sunt, & coæquales.
Ita ut per omnia, sicut jam supra dictum est, & unitas in Trinitate, & Trinitas in unitate veneranda sit.
Qui vult ergo salvus esse, ita de Trinitate sentiat.
Sed necessarium est ad æternam salutem, ut Incarnationem quoque Domini nostri Jesu Christi fideliter credat.
Est ergo fides recta ut credamus, & confiteamur quia Dominus noster Jesus Christus Dei Filius, Deus,& homo est.
Deus est ex substantia Patris ante sæcula genitus & homo est ex substantia Matris in sæculo natus.
Perfectus Deus, perfectus Homo : ex anima rationali & humana carne subsistens.
Æqualis Patri secundum divinitatem : minor Patre secundum humanitatem.
Qui licet Deus sit, & homo, non duo tamen, sed unus est Christus.
Unus autem non conversione divinitatis in carnem, sed assumptione humanitatis in Deum.
Unus omnino non confusione substantiæ, sed unitate personæ.
Nam sicut anima rationalis, & caro unus est homo : ita Deus & Homo unus est Christus.
Qui passus est pro salute nostra, descendit ad inferos : tertia die resurrexit à mortuis.

Ascendit ad Cælos, sedet ad dexteram Dei Patris omnipotentis : inde venturus est judicare vivos, & mortuos.

Ad cujus adventum omnes homines resurgere habent cum corporibus suis.

Et reddituri sunt de factis propriis rationem.

Et qui bona egerunt, ibunt in vitam æternam : qui veró mala, in ignem æternum.

Hæc est Fides Catholica quam nisi quisque fideliter, firmiterque crediderit, salvus esse non poterit.

Gloris Patris, & Filio, & Spiritu Sanct : Sicut erat in principio, & nunc, & semper, & in secula sæculorum. Amen

Ad maiorem Dei gloriam, & Virginis MARIÆ.

Annexe

The thirty principles of the Jacobeia, composed by the Augustinian Francisco da Anunciação, originally written for his *Reflexoens Sobre o Juizo Decizivo.* The current version was collected by Friar António Pereira da Silva and published in *A Questão do Siligismo em Portugal no Século XVIII.*[139]

1st Serve God with an uncovered face.

2nd Have total subjection and blind obedience to the director.

3rd In men filled with politics and more political than spiritual one does not find one for enterprises in the service of God, for cause of contradiction; for one walks better alone than with such company.

4th Do not be without prayer, no matter how busy you may be, and, should it be necessary, cut time from study, which the prelate and the religious man are not invited to when placed in their observance.

5th Let prayer be in the choir or at church or where one has companions; in the cell it is contingent and risky.

6th Offer with full sincerity your conscience to your director, or to whom he orders you to in the time when this is customary

7th Cut away any impediment so as to go to the Jacobeia immediately after lunch and the same should be done at dinner, should this not be prevented by obedience.

8th Let the practices in the Jacobeia always be spiritual and pull these to the spirit when they start to degenerate; the same should be done outside of it in other conversations, whenever it is possible, according to prudence.

9th Do not let yourself be taken by affection or natural inclination. Immediately cut at the source all affections of the heart and particular dealings originating from this.

10th The tepid are more difficult to convert to God than manifest sinners.

11th Seek to do everything under the advice of someone else, even that which seems right.

12th Remove yourself from familiarity with the prelates; have them supreme obedience and no familiarity.

13th Do not care about what happens in the house.

---

139 Silva, *A Questão do Sigilismo em Portugal no Século XVIII*, 81-84.

14th Be exact in your dress.

15th Do not despise anyone, nor even virtually.

16th Do not be relaxed in anything in the costume and exercises of the Jacobeia; and always be zealous in this.

17th Do not season doctrine and its precepts; know that the more harsh and effective you are, the more you attract others, for these are married to reason and God agrees; and, in seasoning, all is lost.

18th Take note of the special things found in spiritual books.

19th Before working, hold your action, carefully checking what you should do; and then may your hand not tremble nor your work falter.

20th Flee from scholarliness of spirit and of any other matters.

21st Remove yourself from all dealings with women, even spiritual, without urgent cause.

22nd Remove yourself as much as you can, without scandal, from every person who does not deal with the spirit, without despise, but only so as you will not grow cold.

23rd Know that in going on vacation, in the form of a vacation, there is never a just cause.

24th Do not visit relatives without an urgent cause.

25th Abstain completely from card games.

26th Should you fall into greater guilt, give God a greater satisfaction, for your ungratefulness is greater, given your special vocation, so as this may continue with aid in order of perseverance.

27th Don't care as much in doing as in undoing.

28th Always follow the opposite of nature, when there is no sin in this.

29th Do not use exemptions and privileges, should you have them, to miss the acts of the community, fasting, choirs, etc, without good cause.

30th Union and coalition with whom may aid us in the service of God, and to have familiar dealings with these, that to this we call Jacobeia.

Bibliography

PRIMARY SOURCES

Erhassison, Antonio Deça (Fr.), *Compendio de Devoções Utilissimas Para Todo o Fiel Christão, que se Quizer Aproveitar Deste Riquissimo Thesouro, No Qual se Contém as Principais Devoções de N.Senhora, e das Almas, Varios Exercicios Para Passar o Dia santamente, Para Ouvir Missa, Confissão e Communhão, Via-Sacra, Oração Mental, e Outras Varias Devoções e Orações Enriquecidas Com Muitas Graças, e Indulgencias, e Sua Declaração, Tudo Para Utilidade das Almas*, Lisbon: Officina de Miguel Manescal da Costa 1758.

Sequeira, Angelo de, *Botica Preciosa e Thesouro Precioso da Lapa. Em que Como em Botica, e Thesouro se Acha Todos os Remedios Para o Corpo, Para a Alma, e Para a Vida. E Huma Receita das Vocações dos Santos para Remedio de todas as Enfermidades, e Varios Remedios, e Milagres da N. Senhora da Lapa, e Muitas Novenas, Devoçoens, e Avisos Importntes Para os Pays de Familia Ensinarem a Doutrina Christã a Seus Filhos, e Criados*, Lisbon: Officina de Miguel Rodrigues 1754.

Sequeira, Angelo de, *Exercicios Devotos, Com que os Padres da Igreja da N.S. da Lapa das Confissões da Cidade do Porto Costumaõ Louvas a Rainha do Ceo, e da Terra. Varias Novenas da Lapa, e Mais Santos q̃ estaõ Collocados na Mesma Igreja, Extrahidos do Livrinho Pedra Iman : o que Tudo se Pode Exercitar, e Praticar nas Muitas Igrejas de N.S. da Lapa, e Onde Ella Estiver Collocada, e em Todos o Tempo, Lugar, e Casa, que o Devoto Quizer Chegar a Deas, e a N.S. e nos Conventos das Religiosas, e Mais Igrejas*, Porto: Officina de Francisco Mendes Lima 1759.

Sequeira, Angelo de, *Livro do Vinde, e Vede, e do Sermam do Dai do Juizo Universal Em Que se Chama a Todos os Viventes Para Vierem, e Verem Humas Leves Sombras do Ultimo Dia o Mais Tremendo, e Rigoroso do Mundo*, Lisbon: Officina de Antonio Vicente da Silva 1758.

Sequeira, Angelo de, *Penitente Arrependido, e Fiel Companheiro, Para se Instruir Huma Alma Devota, e Arrependida a Fazer Huma Boa Confissaõ Commua, e Geral, Sem Pejo, Nem Medo do Confessor. E Varios Solliloqios Para Antes, e Depois da Sagrada Communhaõ. Com Devoçoens Uteis a Todo o Christão, e Duas Visões do Ceo, e Inferno*, Lisbon: Officina de Antonio Vicente da Silva 1757.

Sequeira, Angelo de, *Pedra Iman da Novena da Milagrosissima Senhora da Lapa, que se venera nos Seminarios do Rio de Janeiro, e Campo dos Guaitacazes, e mais Igrejas, Capellas, e Altares nos Bispados de S. Paulo, e Rio de Janeiro, e mais partes do Brasil, e Portugal*, Porto: Officina Episcopal do Capitão Manoel Pedroso Coimbra 1753.

SECONDARY SOURCES

Anon., *A Manual of Devout Prayers, and Other Christian Devotions; Fitted for all Persons and Occasions*, n.p.: n.p. 1725.

Arquivo Português de Lendas; CEAO - Centro de Estudos Ataíde Oliveira, http://www.lendarium.org/.

Azevedo, Manoel (friar), *Correçam de Abusos, Introdusidos Contra o Verdadeyro Methodo da Medicina, & Farol Medicinal Para Medicos, Cirurgiões, & Boticarios. II.Parte. Em Tres Tratados. O Primeyro da Fascinaçam, Olhado, ou Quebranto, & que he Infirmidade Mortal, Naõ Só Para os Meninos, Mas Tambem Para os de Mayor Idade, cõ Todos os Sinaes Para Se Conhecer, & os Mais Experimentados, & Selectos Remedios Para se Curar. O Segundo da Mais Breve, e Experimentada Curaçaõ das Bexigas, & Sarampaõ. O Terceyro de Quanto Proveyto Sejam os Pós Purgativos do Ouro Preparado, Cujas Excellencias, & Qualidades Se Veraõ Com as Grandes Experiencias, Que Por Muytos, & Diversos Medicos se Fizeraõ Com os Ditos Pós*, Lisbon: Officina de Manoel, & Joseph Lopes Ferreyra 1705.

Castro, Zélia Osório de, 'Jacobeia,' em Azevedo, Carlos Moreira (dir.), *Dicionário da História Religiosa de Portugal*, vol. 3, Lisboa: Círculo de Leitores 2001, 5-7.

Catholic Church, *The Divine Office for the Use of the Laity: Containing All the Offices From Advent to Easter*, Manchester: T. Haydock 1806.

CEAO – Centro de Estudos Ataíde Oliveira, http://www.ceao.info/.

Challoner, Richard (Bish.), *The Garden of the Soul; A Manual of Spiritual Exercises and Instructions For Christians, Who, Living in the World, Aspire to Devotion: With an Explanation of the Mass*, New York: D. &J. Sadlier & Co. 1871.

Coelho, Cesário, *Venerável Irmandade de Nossa Senhora da Lapa: Factos da Sua História*, Porto: Imprensa Socia 1973.

Costa, Elisa Maria Lopes da, 'A Jacobeia: Achegas para a História de um Movimento de Reforma Espiritual no Portugal Setecentista,' *Arquipélago: História*, 2:XIV-XV (2010-2011) 31-48.

Espírito Santo, Moisé, *Origens Orientais da Religião Popular Portuguesa – Seguido de: Ensaio Sobe Toponímia Antiga*, Lisbon: Assírio & Alvim 1988.

Ferreira-Alves, Joaquim Jaime B., 'Nótulas Setecentistas: O Padre Ângelo de Sequeira em Vila Real,' *Estudos Transmontanos e Durienses* 8 (1999) 83-91.

Jana, Isilda, *Histórias à Lareira*, Abrantes: Palha de Abrantes 1997.

Lamego, Alberto, *A Terra Goytacá: Á Luz de Documentos Inéditos*, 4 vol., Paris/Brussels: L'Edition d'Art, 1913-1914.

Leitão, José, *Bibliotheca Valenciana*, London: Hadean Press 2017.

Leite, Antonio, *Historia da Appariçam e Milages da Virgem da Lapa*, Coimbra: Impressão de Diogo Gomez de Loureiro 1639.

Marcocci, Giuseppe & Paiva, José Pedro, *História da Inquisição Portuguesa (1536-1821)*, Lisbon: A Esfera dos Livros 2016.

Mello, Francisco Manoel de (Dom), *Tratado da Sciencia Cabala: ou Noticia da Arte Cabalistica*, Ocidental Lisbon: Officina de Bernardo da Costa de Carvalho, 1724.

Moncada, L. Cabral de, *Mística e Racionalismo em Portugal no Século XVIII: Uma Página de História e Política*, Coimbra: Casa do Castelo, Editora 1952.

Moraes, Rubens Borba de, *Bibliografia Brasileira do Período Colonial: Catálogo Comentado das Obras dos Autores Nascidos no Brasil e Publicados Antes de 1808*, São Paulo: Instituto de Estudos Brasileiros 1969.

N.a., *Juizo Decisivo que a Real Meza Censoria com o Pleno Concurso de Todos os Seus Deputados e Assistancia do Procurador da Coroa Estabeleceo de Uniforme Acordo Nas Repetidas Sessões, Que Nella se Tiveram Em Execução do Decreto de 18 de Janeiro de 1769 Em que Sua Magestade Mandou Ver, e Consultar o Livro Intitulado Theses, Maximas, Exercisios, e Observacias Espirituaes da Jacobea*, Lisbon: Regia Officina Typografica 1769.

Neto, Diósnio Machado, 'O "Atalaia da Fé" Contra as Máculas do Século: O Missionário Músico Ângelo Siqueira,' *OPUS: Revista Eletrônica da Associação Nacional de Pesquisa e Pós-graduação em Música* 11 (2005) 63-97.

Paiva, José Pedro, 'A Igreja e o Poder. Da Reforma Pombalina até 1820,' em Azevedo, Carlos M. (dir.), *História Religiosa de Portugal*, vol. 1: 'Humanismos e Reformas', Lisbon: CEHR-UCP, Círculo de Leitores 2000, 135-185.

Paiva, José Pedro, *Baluartes da Fé e da Disciplina: O Enlace Entre a Inquisição e os Bispos em Portugal (1536-1750)*, Coimbra: Imprensa da Universidade de Coimbra 2011.

Paiva, José Pedro, *Os Bispos de Portugal e do Império (1495-177)*, Coimbra: Imprensa da Universidade de Coimbra 2006.

Pereyra, Bernardo, *Anacephaleosis Medico-Theologica, Magica, Juridica, Moral, e Politica na qual em recompiladas Dissertaçoẽs; e Divizoẽs, se mostra a infalível certeza de haver qualidades maléficas, se apontaõ os sinais por onde possaõ conhecerse; e se descreve a cura assim em geral, como em particular, de que se devem valer nos achaques procedidos das ditas qualidades maleficas, e Demoniacas, chamadas vulgarmente Feitiços, Obra necessária para os Medicos, e muito precisa para os exorcistas, pelas advertências, que inclue para obviar os inumeráveis absurdos, que se cometem tanto na applicaçaõ dos remedios mágicos, e naturais, como na dos Divinos, e Ecclesiasticos, e especialmente nos Exorcismos. Que se mostra naõ devem, nem podem prohibirse absolutamente pelos Ordinarios, antes tem estes obrigação de mandar Exorcizar. Ajuntamse Varias Digressoens Medico Theologicas, Politicas, e Practicas; fallase sobre o uso do leyte nas febres podres, da Kina Kina, dos banhos, dos soros, e sobe o uso das sangrias dos braços; e escrevemse outros documentos utilíssimos para o bom acerto de curar principalmente febres, em cujo Methodo ha muitos abuzos com os tais remedios, de que ou se naõ valem os Medicos por tímidos, ou de que naõ cessaõ por temerários, Esvese huã Digressão Medico Botanica das virtues da herva Veronica*, Coimbra: Officina de Francisco de Oliveyra 1734.

Queirós, Maria Helena, 'Jacobeia e redes clientelares: Fr. Luís de Santa Teresa e Fr. João da Cruz (O.C.D.): (Auto)retrato de dois irmãos em Braga (1730-1735),' *História: Revista da FLUP*, IV:2 (2012) 79-96.

Ribeiro, António Vitor, *O Auto dos Místicos: Mística, Religião Popular e Inquisição*, Lisboa: Chiado Editora 2015.

Rubert, Arlindo, 'O Missionário do Brasil: Padre Ângelo de Sequeira (1707-1776),' *Revista do Instituto Histórico e Geográfico Brasileiro* 320 (1978) 136-161.

Santa Maria, Agostinho de, *Santuario Mariano: E Historia da Imagẽs Milagrosas de Nossa Senhora, e das Milagrosamente Apparecidas, em Graça dos Prègadores, & dos Devotos da Mesma Senhora*, 10 vol., Lisbon: Officina de Antonio Pedrozo Galrão 1707-1723.

Silva, António Pereira (Fr.), *A Questão do Sigilismo em Portugal no Século XVIII: História e Política nos Reinados de D. João e D. José I*, Braga: Tipografia Editorial Franciscana 1964.

Silva, Innocencio Francisco da, *Diccionario Bibliographico Portuguez*, 23 vol., Lisbon: Imprensa Nacional 1858-1923.

V.a., *Literatura Portuguesa de Tradição Oral*, n.p.: Projecto Vercial – Universidade de Trás-os-Montes e Alto Douro, 2003.

Vasconcellos, Antonio de, *Tratado do Anjo da Guarda*, 2 vol., Évora: University of Évora 1621-1622.

Index

O

P

Q

R

S

T

PUBLISHED BY AVALONIA
WWW.AVALONIABOOKS.COM

www.ingramcontent.com/pod-product-compliance
Lightning Source LLC
LaVergne TN
LVHW050951080826
845145LV00005B/1474

* 9 7 8 1 9 1 0 1 9 1 1 9 4 *